East West Mimesis

East West Mimesis

Auerbach in Turkey

Kader Konuk

Stanford University Press

Stanford, California

Stanford University Press
Stanford, California

This book has been published with the assistance of the Office of the Vice
President for Research, the College of Literature, Science, and the Arts, the
Department of Comparative Literature, and the German Department at the
University of Michigan.

Portions of Chapter 4 were originally published in *Ethnic Europe: Mobility,
Identity, and Conflict in a Globalized World*, edited by Roland Hsu, © 2010, the
Board of Trustees of the Leland Stanford Junior University. Reprinted by
permission of Stanford University Press.

Printed in the United States of America on acid-free, archival-quality paper

Library of Congress Cataloging-in-Publication Data

Konuk, Kader.
    East West mimesis : Auerbach in Turkey / Kader Konuk.
        p. cm.
    Includes bibliographical references and index.
    ISBN 978-0-8047-6974-7 (cloth : alk. paper)
        1. Auerbach, Erich, 1892–1957. 2. Literary historians—Turkey—Istanbul.
    3. Philologists—Turkey—Istanbul. 4. Jewish refugees—Turkey—Istanbul.
    5. Humanism—Turkey—History—20th century. 6. Turkey—Intellectual
    life—20th century. 7. Europe—Intellectual life—Turkish influences.
    8. Turkey—Civilization—Western influences. I. Title.
    PN75.A9K66   2010
    809—dc22
    [B]   2009048662

Typeset by Westchester Book Group in Adobe Garamond regular, 11/13.5

For Vanessa and Sefa

Contents

Illustrations

Acknowledgments

I WISH TO EXTEND MY THANKS to the following institutions, which supported my work with generous grants and fellowships: the National Endowment for the Humanities, the Wissenschaftskolleg zu Berlin (Institute for Advanced Study), the Zentrum für Literatur- und Kulturforschung (Center for Literary and Cultural Research) Berlin, the Deutscher Akademischer Austauschdienst (German Academic Exchange Service), and the Literaturarchiv (Literary Archive) Marbach. In particular, I thank the University of Michigan for ongoing support through the German Department, the Department of Comparative Literature, the Center for Middle Eastern and North African Studies, the Rackham Graduate School for Graduate Studies, the Office of the Vice President for Research, and the College of Literature, Science, and the Arts. I am grateful to successive chairs of the German and Comparative Literature departments—Fred Amrine, Tobin Siebers, Geoff Eley, Helmut Puff, Julia Hell, and Yopie Prins—who have, without fail, supported this project from its inception. This book has benefited from the generous support, advice, and enthusiasm of my colleagues at the University of Michigan, who at various stages have read and critiqued the manuscript. In particular, I thank Vanessa Agnew, Kathryn Babayan, Carol Bardenstein, Kerstin Barndt, Sara Blair, Catherine Brown, Kathleen Canning, Rita Chin, Alina Clej, Fatma Müge Göçek, Gottfried Hagen, Michael Kennedy, Vassilios Lambropoulos, Lydia Liu, Tomoko Masuzawa, Christi Merrill, Joshua Miller, Johannes von Moltke, Damani Partridge, David Porter, Jim Porter, Robin Queen, Anton Shammas, Scott Spector, George Steinmetz, Ruth Tsoffar, Silke-Maria Weineck, and Patricia Yaeger.

Archivists in Germany and Turkey acceded to my numerous requests, providing me with access to files, letters, photographs, newspapers, and lectures that helped me tell the story of Turkish exile. Peter Grupp at the Politisches Archiv des Auswärtigen Amts (Political Archive of the Foreign Office) and Christoph König at the Literaturarchiv Marbach were immensely helpful. I am also grateful to archivists at the Bundesarchiv (Federal Archive) in Berlin, the newspaper archive of the Staatsbibliothek Berlin, the archive of the Akademie der Wissenschaften (Academy of Sciences) in Berlin, and, in particular, the İstanbul Üniversitesi Arşivi (Istanbul University Archive). Without the libraries at the University of Michigan and the Zentrum für Literatur- und Kulturforschung Berlin this book could not have been written. I owe particular thanks to librarian Beau Case, who was always attentive to my needs and interests, and to Feyza Sayman, who helped me access the precious early Turkish translations of Dante's *Commedia*. In Berlin, I thank librarians Ruth Hübner, Halina Lemke, and Jana Lubasch for their patience and resourcefulness during the past years.

At Stanford University Press, I owe special thanks to senior editor Norris Pope for his enthusiasm and care during the review process, and to editorial assistant Sarah Crane Newman for the attention she paid in giving the manuscript its final shape. I am grateful to Stanford University Press's two readers, one of them being Nina Berman, whose careful and detailed reading allowed me to improve the historical argument I make in this book. I am also indebted to Katie Trumpener and an anonymous reader for another press. I benefited immensely from the breadth and depth of their knowledge and am grateful for their instructive recommendations on revising the manuscript. Helen Tartar, in particular, stands out as a model of generosity and graciousness.

I have been inspired and encouraged by a wider community of scholars across the disciplines and am gratified by the enthusiasm they showed in the subject of this book. In particular, I thank Leslie Adelson, Süheyla Artemel, Marc Baer, Rıfat Bali, Karlheinz Barck, Seyla Benhabib, Nina Berman, Cevat Çapan, Oğuz Cebeci, Silvia Cresti, Ned Curthoys, Güzin Dino, Gisela Ecker, Marty Elsky, Amir Eshel, Herrmann Fuchs, Cathy Gelbin, Saime Göksu, Galit Hasan-Rokem, Roland Hsu, Aslı Iğsız, Djelal Kadir, Georges Khalil, Wolfgang Klein, Erol Köroğlu, Rita Koryan, Jonathan Lamb, Wolf Lepenies, Harry Liebersohn, Suzanne Marchand, Reinhart Meyer-Kalkus, Aamir Mufti, Angelika Neuwirth, Jane Newman, Esra Özyürek, Jeffrey

Peck, Helmut Peitsch, Charles Sabatos, Hinrich Seeba, Samah Selim, Helmut Smith, Alexander Stephan, Robert Stockhammer, Eleonora Stoppino, Shaden Tageldin, Franziska Thun, Edward Timms, Maria Todorova, Paolo Tortonese, Martin Treml, Martin Vialon, Daniel Weidner, Sigrid Weigel, and Zafer Yenal.

I owe special thanks to research assistants Sultan Açıkgüloğlu, Sarah Affenzeller, Adam Brown, Susan Buettner, Joshua Hawkins, Kathryn Sederberg, Shannon Winston, and, above all, Seth Howes and Başak Çandar, who assisted me with great resourcefulness in collecting and digitizing material in libraries and archives. The Turkish-German Studies Group at the University of Michigan provided a welcome and lively forum for discussing ideas related to this book. Students in my graduate seminars on Auerbach and on Postcolonial Studies asked probing questions that helped me better formulate some of my ideas; my undergraduate courses on German Ethnicities and Modernism likewise provided a helpful context—I thank all the students, and, in particular, doctoral candidates Nick Block, Efrat Bloom, Gen Creedon, Adile Esen, Ela Gezen, Spencer Hawkins, Solveig Heinz, Amr Kamal, Michael Rinaldo, Corine Tachtiris, Patrick Tonks, Simon Walsh, and Orian Zakai for their stimulating engagement with issues of exile, migration, and transnationalism.

Translations from Turkish into English are mine; translations from German into English are generally Vanessa Agnew's. I am especially thankful to Victoria Holbrook, who carefully translated two of Auerbach's lectures (see appendix) that hitherto have been available only in Turkish. I am, beyond words, indebted to Vanessa Agnew, who edited my work numerous times. Without her care, patience, and eloquence this book would not be what it is now. I also owe thanks to editors Mary Hashman, Ellen Lohman, Ellen McCarthy, Carol Sickman-Garner, and Louise Goldberg for working on the manuscript. John Donohue at Westchester Book Services coordinated the copyediting. Staff members at the University of Michigan, the Wissenschaftskolleg zu Berlin, the Zentrum für Literatur- und Kulturforschung, and the National Endowment for the Humanities assisted me in numerous ways. Cynthia Avery, Marya Ayyash, Christine Hofmann, Wolfgang Kreher, Jutta Müller, Sonia Schmerl, Jim Turner, Peggy Westrick, and, above all, Sheri Sytsema-Geiger dealt patiently and resourcefully with funding questions, visas, and the logistics of transnational scholarship.

The support and patience of my friends has sustained me over the years. My thanks go especially to Sabine Boomers, Robert Debusman,

Marina Gnotzig, Karein Goertz, Renate Härle, Katie Jones, Diana Perpich, Teresa Pinheiro, Carol and Pete Sickman-Garner, Ayşe Tekin, and Inga and Till Tomann. My father, Veysel Konuk, who died without seeing the completion of this book, and my mother, Sakine Konuk, raised me in the spirit of Alevi humanism. Only on finishing this book did I realize what must have spurred my interest in the origins of humanist thought in Turkey. It is, I now know, because, as a child of migrants growing up in Germany, I puzzled over my first piece of Turkish literature—a poem by Yunus Emre on a plaque in our living room.

My uncle Mahmut Oluklu, who was trained as a teacher in the humanist village institutes, and my aunt Elife I thank for their unconditional love. My dear sisters Özlem, Belkıs, Lale, and Leylâ, and my cousins Selim Oluklu and Zehra Keskin, all share a rare capacity to laugh, dance, and spin stories about the poignancy and beauty of life. I thank them for encouraging me each step of the way. My Agnew family, too, has spoiled me richly—Jonno, Dave, Rose, Emma, Viv, and Michelle. Nancy graciously cleared her desk for me, filled the fridge, and shared her family's past; Neville's curiosity and warmth spurred me on; and Patricia is a paragon of enthusiasm and creativity.

Above all, I am grateful to the most generous and talented of all, Vanessa. With her gift of being true to herself at all times, she never fails to inspire me. Writing this book has not only been contingent on her love, loyalty, editing skills, and endless cups of tea; it is the result of our intellectual companionship. My precious, infinitely curious daughter, Sefa, I thank for having arrived in our lives with a dimple on her cheek. Both turned my life around.

East West Mimesis

Introduction

LEAVING BEHIND THE LIFE he cared about, Erich Auerbach arrived in Istanbul late in the summer of 1936. No one remembers whether he came by ship or by train, but had he taken the northerly route, he would have come on the Orient Express, passing through Austria, Hungary, Romania, and Bulgaria. Already, there were Nazi uniforms on station platforms in Munich, as well as other, more heartening sights—peasants beginning their harvest, the Jewish quarter in Budapest, and the medieval architecture of Bucharest. During the three-day journey eastward, the Prussian scholar might have wondered at what point Europe ceased to be Europe and the familiar no longer spelled home. Yet, even at the end of the line, where minarets punctured the sky, it would have been difficult to locate Europe's boundary. In Istanbul, the Orient Express ran parallel to the old walls of Constantinople and came to a stop in the Sirkeci terminal—a rather modern building designed by one of his own countrymen. For passengers arriving from the West, the station represented the city at its best: it was located on the shores of Byzantine Constantinople, where many of the guides and station's clerks spoke French or German.

But perhaps Auerbach sailed via Italy and Greece, the cradle of classical Europe. With his monograph on Dante, the precursor of Renaissance humanism, in his baggage, he would have likely embarked in Genoa, crossed the Mediterranean, and put in at Piraeus, near Athens. This was the route connecting Goethe's land of lemon blossoms to the country that had long been referred to as "the sick man of Europe." While these

1

were the dominant Western tropes characterizing classical Europe and the Orient, republican Turks saw the connection between the West and the East in different terms. After all, this was the sea route that in Byzantine times had linked Rome to Constantinople. Referring to intellectual émigrés from fascist Europe, the Turkish minister of education liked to invoke the Byzantine scholars who had taken this route to escape the Ottomans after their conquest of Constantinople in 1453. With them went the Greek, Roman, and Byzantine manuscripts that, it is still often said, contributed to the spread of classical education in Western Europe.[1] Metaphorically speaking, this learning was now coming back with the arrival of scholars like Auerbach. As we will see, the Turkish minister would say that their escape from Europe catalyzed the Turkish Renaissance in the twentieth century: European scholars would revive classical education in the city once hailed as the greatest center of learning in the world.

Paul Signac (1863–1935), *Istanbul, Hagia Sophia*. Watercolor. Private collection. Photo: Visual Arts Library. By permission of Art Resource, New York.

There was a splendid view for sea passengers anchoring in the mouth of the Golden Horn. In Galata, between old Constantinople and the city's Genoese quarter, one could take in the culturally and religiously diverse topography of the city. Looking north were the old Christian and Jewish quarters of Pera, with the Galata tower crowning the city's seven hundred-year-old Genoese district, home to numerous churches and synagogues. Close by was also a thirteenth-century Dominican church, where Angelo Giuseppe Roncalli (later Pope John XXIII) would provide Auerbach with access to a rich library.[2] On arrival, Auerbach was probably welcomed by a Turkish university administrator or a German scholar who accompanied him to one of the Pera hotels overlooking the Bosporus and the many Ottoman palaces and mosques near the Golden Horn. Were he lucky, his hotel room would have had a view of the Hagia Sophia, the fifteen-hundred-year-old domed Byzantine cathedral, which had been converted into a mosque after the Ottoman conquest. Just a year before Auerbach's arrival, the Hagia Sophia had been transformed again, this time into a museum that opened its doors to everyone, irrespective of faith. This transformation was indicative of Turkey's latest move toward secularization, but it also signified Turkey's desire to claim the region's classical history as its own.

Of course, Auerbach was no accidental tourist, no ordinary traveler here to enjoy Istanbul's sights and to reflect upon its recent metamorphosis from the Ottoman Empire to the Turkish Republic. He was a professor of Romance philology and probably would have never left Germany of his own accord. But in October of the previous year, 1935, a university administrator at Marburg University had summoned him to a meeting that he and his wife, Marie, had been dreading for some time. Auerbach knew exactly what was coming. Under the recently introduced Nuremberg laws, he was designated a "full Jew," a category that authorized Nazis to ostracize and disenfranchise him as "non-Aryan." The administrator asked Auerbach to confirm that he fell into this category. According to a decree from the German ministry of education, this was reason enough for Marburg University to terminate Auerbach's employment. For two years, he had hoped he would be spared this moment because of the exceptional status granted to Jews, like himself, who were veterans of World War I. But the following day, the dreaded letter was delivered, sealing his dismissal as the director of the Romance Seminar.[3] Reluctantly, Auerbach now came to accept that the family's only recourse was to leave Germany: if Marie, his teenage son Clemens, and he were to escape further discrimination and dehumanization—indeed, if they were to preserve their lives—they would have to go into exile.

This book follows the plight of humanist scholars like Auerbach who escaped Nazi persecution by seeking exile in a Muslim-dominated society. As we will find, the exile's itinerary represents a larger set of historical forces, forces that, on the one hand, expelled them from fascist Germany and, on the other, functionalized them for a program of cultural renewal in Turkey. From 1933 on, for the scholars dismissed from German universities (among them Leo Spitzer, Alexander Rüstow, Ernst von Aster, and Hans Reichenbach), Turkey provided a haven where tertiary and governmental institutions offered to hire philologists, philosophers, historians, architects, natural scientists, economists, and musicians in order to support the country's modernization reforms. Istanbul University alone employed forty German scholars from various disciplines to promote the secularization and modernization of higher education. Auerbach joined this cohort in 1936 as the chair of the nation's leading faculty for Western languages and literatures. His tenure in Istanbul lasted eleven years, during which time Turkey implemented significant political, cultural, and educational changes. Coincidentally, these years also witnessed the wartime destruction of Europe.

East West Mimesis asks how a German-Jewish philologist, deemed "un-German" by the Nazis, experienced exile in a predominantly Muslim society. Could a Jew possibly find a home in such a place? There were, of course, historical precedents for this kind of hospitality: the Ottoman Empire of the late fifteenth century had provided a refuge for Sephardic Jews escaping persecution in the Iberian Peninsula. It seems unsurprising, then, that republican Turkey, founded in 1923, drew on this tradition and once again opened its doors to persecuted Jews from Europe. By the same token, we need to remember that the late Ottoman Empire took a hostile stance toward its own ethnic and religious minorities, with more than a million Armenians persecuted, deported, and killed under Ottoman rule during World War I.[4] The ethno-religious nationalism among Ottoman Turks during the early twentieth century also impacted the status of the Greek-Orthodox population in republican Turkey. In 1924, this resulted in the forced exchange of populations between Turkey and Greece: Turkey deported its Greek-Orthodox residents in exchange for Muslims living in Greece.

Parallel to this upsurge of ethno-religious nationalism was, paradoxically, the secularization of political and educational structures. And
it was under the umbrella of secularization and modernization that German scholars, many of them Jewish, were hired. Initially, appointees
signed contracts in which they agreed to learn Turkish within three years
so they would be able to teach and publish in the language. It soon became clear, however, that the émigrés could not acquire proficiency so
quickly—most of them continued to teach and publish in German and
French.[5] We would expect that this Turkish language requirement was
part of a broader program of integration. Yet, as I show in chapter 3, the
émigrés were not, in fact, required to assimilate into Turkish society. Instead, they became part of a European intellectual elite: this was a migrant community that was not meant to disavow difference but rather to
preserve its distinguishing feature—its Europeanness. In exchange for
protection from Nazism, German scholars were meant to help implement Turkey's broad-ranging Westernization reforms. Provocatively, the
book suggests that modern Turkish identity was not autochthonous: it
was, in some measure, forged with the help of the émigré, that is to say,
with the help of privileged outsiders within Turkish society. Émigrés
took on special significance when Turkey decided to reclaim the region's
classical heritage and re-create modern culture in the image of ancient
Europe. Investigating the émigrés' role in wartime Turkey will help us
understand the relationship between philology, cultural heritage, and
Turkey's modernization reforms.

East West Mimesis addresses another anomaly highlighted by the
Turkish reforms: despite the forced population exchange between Greece
and Turkey in 1924 and an ongoing antipathy between the two nations,
leading Turkish intellectuals and government officials were soon promoting Greco-Roman learning as a basis for promoting modern Turkish
literature. In this process, Turkey's Ottoman, Persian, and Arabic heritage was not entirely overwritten, but it was now rivaled by the Greco-
Roman classics; and where students might once have studied Ottoman
poetry, their syllabi soon included works by Plato, Sophocles, and Homer.
How, then, are we to explain the anomaly between Turkey's new relationship to the Greco-Roman heritage and the deportation of its Greek
subjects? How can we explain its paradoxical relationship not only to its
ethnic minorities but also to its own past? We might say that Turkey intended to "purify" the body politic and create unity among its remaining

citizens. But the new heritage politics served an additional function—namely, forging a path to the West and establishing a set of cultural commonalities between Western Europe's ancient heritage and modern Turkey.

Westernization and Mimesis

The Turkish government under Mustafa Kemal Atatürk identified a need for change and was willing to embrace radical cultural and political reform. It was confronted with the problem of how to implement rapid change and where to look for inspiration. Turkish reformers, among them the ministers of education Reşit Galip (1932–1933) and Hasan Ali Yücel (1939–1946), sought earlier models and asked themselves how they could adopt such models without seeming overly derivative. Like the Ottoman Porte, the republican government would seek answers to these questions by looking to the West—to Western legislation, architecture, technology, science, literature, art, clothing styles, and material culture generally. Republican Turks decided to widen the scope of Ottoman Westernization reforms that had marked the cultural, economic, political, and military transformation of the Ottoman Empire during the previous two hundred years. These earlier Westernization reforms arguably were a response to the defeat of the Ottomans at Vienna in 1683, a turning point that denoted the end of the empire's expansion. Alternatively, the Ottoman reforms have been interpreted as part of a longer trajectory of economic and political changes that affected the Ottoman Empire and Western Europe simultaneously.[6]

The first of these reforms began in 1718 and was retrospectively coined *Lale Devri*, the Tulip Era, signifying the mutually dependent relationship between Western Europe and the Ottoman Empire. The tulip bulb, which paradoxically had been imported into Western Europe via Ottoman Constantinople in the sixteenth century, first caused an economic craze in Western Europe before it became synonymous with Ottoman efforts to adopt aspects of Western culture. Sultan Ahmed III set off this tulip vogue with a lasting impact on Ottoman art and garden design and an interest in foreign goods among members of the Ottoman elite.[7] In 1730, a revolt against Ahmed III put a sudden end to what came to be regarded as the decadent Lale Devri. The reforms of the nineteenth century, in contrast, were less elitist. Established at a time when the empire faced the loss of a number of Mediterranean provinces, most importantly Greece, Algiers, and Egypt, the new modernization efforts encompassed a broader spectrum of Ottoman society. The civilian clothing reform of 1829, which replaced the turban with the fez, robes with frock-coats, capes, and trousers, and slippers with black leather boots, indicated the Ottoman equation of Westernization with modernization.[8] A decade later, a number of decrees called *tanzimat* initiated the fundamental reorganization of Ottoman society, specifically targeting the empire's military, administrative, and educational structures. From a cultural point of view, the nineteenth century may be thought of as a Francophile age. The appropriation of French culture left lasting traces in Ottoman intellectual life as Persian and Arabic influences slowly gave way to French ones. As one would expect, French literature played a particularly important role during this period of cultural reorientation, marking the beginning of the Ottoman newspaper, novel, and short story in the second half of the nineteenth century.

The Ottoman Empire was not the only political entity with a predominantly Muslim population to undergo Westernization reforms during the nineteenth century. Khedive Ismail, for example, announced during his reign in Egypt (1863–1879) that his country was "no longer part of Africa. It is part of Europe."[9] This statement would seem to imply that there was a general trend toward Westernization. The differences between Egypt and the Ottoman Empire, however, centered on the question of sovereignty. Egypt stood under quasi-colonial Anglo-French control in the nineteenth century and had political reasons for claiming that it belonged to Europe. The Ottoman Empire, on the other hand, was a sovereign empire. It continued to lose its provinces, including Egypt, to Western Europe, Russia, and the Balkans, but it essentially made an autonomous decision to undertake modernization. To see late Ottomans and early republican Turks primarily as a people under the hegemonic influence of Western European powers would thus be too narrow, if not misleading. Rather than adopting a postcolonial studies approach and reiterating Edward Said's generalizing claim that the Orient per se was subject to Western imperialist interests, I am interested in a more nuanced, historically specific study of East West relationships, one that highlights Ottomans and Turks as agents, not victims, of Westernization.[10]

Cemal Nadir, *Hicret!* (Exodus!), December 1, 1928. Reprinted from Sabine Küper-Büsch and Nigar Rona, *Die Nase des Sultans: Karikaturen aus der Türkei / Padişahın Burnu: Türkiye'den Karikatürler* (Istanbul: Dağyeli Publishers, Bilgi University Press, 2008), 17. Source: Dağyeli Press.

Like his Ottoman predecessors, Atatürk believed that modernization necessitated Westernization. However, the founder of the new republic broadened the reach of earlier reforms and made an additional strategic step: he called on Turkish citizens to identify as Europeans, even while seeking political independence from Western European countries like France. In consequence, the reforms of the 1920s and 1930s signified a consistent change in the political, educational, legal, and cultural basis of the republic, with secularization being its main guiding principle. The reforms meant that there would be no more fez wearing, the Ottoman script was erased, religious schools were outlawed, the caliphate and religious courts were abolished, the alphabet was Latinized, and the Islamic calendar was replaced with the Gregorian one.[11] Women gained the right to vote, entered public life, enrolled as students at universities, and themselves became associated with the spirit of progress and modernity.[12]

This book focuses on an important aspect of this watershed moment, namely, the educational reform of 1933, which secularized education, and the humanist reforms of 1939, which instituted a highly influential translation bureau dedicated to translating and publishing scores of Western classics into modern Turkish.[13] The translation bureau (*tercüme bürosu*) was novel in its scope and ambition but had, like other aspects of Turkey's reforms, precedents in Ottoman times. Like the first translation chamber (*terceme odası*) that had been established in the early nineteenth century under Mahmud II, the translation bureau of the 1930s intended to accelerate sociopolitical changes.[14] However, the significant role given to translating Western classics, among them numerous Greek and Roman works, was completely unprecedented. Hasan Ali Yücel, the minister of education who established the translation bureau, saw in the translation project a way of emphasizing commonalities, not differences, between East and West.[15] Chapter 2 discusses these reforms, which inaugurated a broad translation project and helped secularize education but also staged Western plays, concerts, and operas.

Yet for all this, republican Turkey would be continually plagued by the problem of cultural appropriation. Like any other reform movement, the reform movement in Turkey was suspected of having thrown the baby out with the bathwater and rejected its own generative potential. This fear was felt by Turks, who were concerned about severing themselves from their Ottoman achievements; it was also a charge taken up in the West, where Turks were only too readily dismissed as derivative. This book is about one particular episode in Turkey's process of national renewal and about its worries over copying Western models. If the subject of this book is a historically specific one, it also contains lessons to be learned for the present, when building nations along Western lines is at the top of many foreign policy agendas. Historically, Turkey would address this problem by parsing the definition of mimesis. The Westernization reforms constituted a kind of cultural mimesis because they tried to generate, rather than simply copy, European culture.[16] In this air of change, republican Turks tried to dissociate themselves from the *züppe*, the Europeanized dandy, and from the *kukla*, Europe's marionette—both prominent figures in late Ottoman literature. In place of the insufficiently Westernized Ottoman would stride a modern Turk, someone who could cut a jaunty figure in Europe itself.

East West Mimesis explains how Auerbach could find European culture at home in Istanbul, even while the humanist tradition was being banished from Europe. Paradoxically, Auerbach's own deracination in Europe was, as Katie Trumpener and others suggest, to some extent mirrored in his host country, which tried to substitute the Ottoman past for a new national culture.[17] At the very moment when Europe was being systematically destroyed, Auerbach, while in Istanbul, tried to pinpoint the nature and origins of Western European culture. Confronted by wholesale destruction, the writer and scholar has perhaps two open avenues—to attempt to explain the annihilation or try to salvage what is being lost. Auerbach chose the latter. Which texts, he asked himself, made up the core of Europe's literary traditions, and how did their narrative styles evolve? What was the relationship between representing reality (or what he called mimesis) and the way in which we think about the past? Between 1942 and April 1945, Auerbach answered these questions with his magnum opus, *Mimesis: Dargestellte Wirklichkeit in der abendländischen Literatur* (*Mimesis: The Representation of Reality in Western Literature*), a work that would later be foundational for the discipline of comparative literature, particularly in the United States.

Auerbach's book spans the history of Western European literature from Homer and the Hebrew Bible via Dante to Proust and Woolf. Perhaps most importantly, Auerbach argued that "the way in which we view human life and society is the same whether we are concerned with things of the past or things of the present. A change in our manner of viewing history will of necessity soon be transferred to our manner of viewing current conditions."[18] It was an idea of elegant simplicity: history is the product of narration. More than this, our understanding of the present derives from the way we think about what came before. This insight influenced, and continues to influence, a range of fields, including literary theory, history, comparative literature, and cultural history. The pathbreaking book promoted its author into one of the most significant critics of his time. He came to be known for his "characteristic wide horizon, encyclopedic knowledge and artistic sensibility," as his fellow émigré Leo Spitzer would put it.[19] In the postwar period, *Mimesis* also paved the way for his career at Pennsylvania State University, then Princeton, and finally Yale.

We can use Auerbach as a guide to understanding Turkey's humanist reforms and the way in which nation building was approached through changes to literature and philology. I make this claim not merely because of Auerbach's pivotal role in the humanities. Rather, the motivation for focusing on Auerbach is a methodological one. His seminal work provides the key concepts we need for understanding the very context in which he produced the book—most importantly, the idea of Europe, concepts of history, and the function of mimesis within processes of cultural and political reform. We can, in other words, use *Mimesis*, and the critical concepts it exemplifies, as a lens for analyzing the context within which the work arose. In this sense, my book provides more than the *Entstehungsgeschichte* of *Mimesis*, a history of its origins. It represents instead an attempt to read cultural history with literary critical tools and, as such, provides a methodological model that could be applied to other cultural and political contexts. In using the concept of mimesis, I distinguish between mimesis as a textual practice used for representing reality and mimesis as a form of cultural practice deployed in the Westernization of Turkey as a whole. This bifurcated approach helps us understand the decisive role played by literature, philology, and curricula in the process of nation building. It further shows that concepts of history and practices of representation are neither incidental to polities nor inseparable from each other: Turkey's mimetic appropriation of Western culture was, simultaneously, a realist and historical project.

Westernizing Turkey meant establishing secular education and changing the Turkish habitus; it also meant generating new ideas about the past. *East West Mimesis* focuses on the impact of the humanist movement on the invention of a new Turkish past as distinct from the Ottoman one. Nineteenth- and early twentieth-century Ottoman intellectuals had already reflected upon the changing concept of history and the nature of literature in the course of the Westernization reforms. For example, Ahmet Hamdi Tanpınar, one of Turkey's most important modern authors, reflected on the crisis of realism, history, and literature in his literary and intellectual history of the late Ottoman Empire. The intellectual life in early republican times, he wrote, was also affected by this crisis.[20] The modern turn meant that writers in the 1920s and 1930s were charged with employing greater realism and with showing modern life as it really was.[21] Re-creating the Western habitus not only generated a new sense of reality but, as I have already suggested, also altered the notion of the nation's past. With the new boundaries of the Turkish Republic and the decision to appropriate Western culture in ways that surpassed the earlier Ottoman reforms, the sense of history and cultural legacy were radically altered.

The ways in which the ruins of Asia Minor were viewed is one case in point. It was only during the late nineteenth century that Ottomans began to show an archeological interest in the pre-Islamic Phoenician and Hellenistic past. The Imperial Museum that was founded in Istanbul in 1869 signified a "step in the self-incorporation of the Ottoman Empire into a European-dominated modernity."[22] Abdul Hamid II (r. 1876–1909) is reported to have said: "Look at these stupid foreigners! I pacify them with broken stones."[23] Whether or not this is true, we see that the archeological remains of ancient Europe assumed a prominent place in the national imagination during early republican times.[24] Ruined columns and statuary, which, like the Pergamon altar, had been presented as gifts or sold to European sovereigns during Ottoman times, could now be claimed as the remnants of an exemplary ancient past, a past that was shared by the middle classes in London, Berlin, Paris, Rome, or Athens, as well as by the peasantry in Anatolia. Atatürk's Turkey was entering the modern age by appropriating Europe's classical heritage.

Exile and the Trope of Detachment

This book tackles two basic questions: it asks how being in Istanbul shaped the writing of *Mimesis*, and how *Mimesis* helps us understand Istanbul. More generally, it inquires into the condition of exile and the status of the outsider in processes of cultural and political change. Many scholars have taken Auerbach as their subject and focused on the first question, asking whether he could have written *Mimesis* anywhere other than in Istanbul or some place equally remote. The assumption has long been that *Mimesis*, like much exilic work, was the product of intellectual isolation—a corollary to the artist secluded in his garret. It is unsurprising that the notion of lonely exile has stuck. After all, early twentieth-century Turkey is associated with a bygone age: we think of old manuscripts and Ottoman scholars in fretted libraries, not the tickertape world of New York and London or the celluloid glitz of Los Angeles. *East West Mimesis* addresses this stereotype, overturning the idea that, during the 1930s and 1940s, Istanbul was hermetically sealed off from Western culture. Yet rethinking the context for Auerbach's scholarship implies more than just questioning the image we have inherited of him. The resulting contextualization of Auerbach's work, and of Istanbul itself, allows us to question one of the important premises of exile studies, namely, that exile is synonymous with isolation and that isolation is, in and of itself, intellectually and artistically productive. For many contemporary critics, exile still represents a state of critical detachment and superior insight that is supposed to arise when intellectuals are expelled from their homes and forced to take up residence elsewhere.

It concerns me, however, that this line of thought too readily reduces exile to a mere metaphor for uprootedness: disconnected from his or her social and political context, the exile is coupled with possibilities for cultural transfer and transnational exchange. Too easily does the exilic condition acquire almost utopian possibilities: the exile is suddenly unencumbered by indigenous tradition, emerging instead as the new mediator between systems, a perspicuous commentator on both the endogenous and exogenous. I argue that this view of exile distorts the historical record. This view diminishes the existential plight of those who were expelled during the war, even as it elevates the individual case to a general paradigm. Against this view of exile qua detachment, I propose a condition of multiple attachments. The task of the book is, then, to investigate these new attachments and tease out their implications both for the individual and for the respective societies at large. Rather than salvaging the positive in the exilic condition, I ask what it meant to go into exile and what arose therefrom. Moreover, what larger significance did exile have for its agent—Germany—and for its beneficiaries—Turkey and the United States? As we will find, the answers to these questions are less straightforward than we tend to assume.

Over the last decade, Emily Apter, Jane Newman, Selim Deringil, and Seth Lerer began to question Auerbach's isolation in exile. Apter, for instance, notes that Auerbach's "jaundiced depiction of his loneliness in the wilderness" probably presented a "distorted picture" of exilic life in Istanbul.[25] I think she is right. We ought to revise this perception of Auerbach—the legendary figure who was supposed to have written his greatest work cut off from the very sources and cultural context that lay at its heart. More than this, together with Angelika Bammer, Sophia McClennen, Anton Kaes, Caren Kaplan, and Alexander Stephan, I call for a new approach to the study of exile, one that recognizes both the historicity of exile and the exile's material existence.[26] The payoff in adopting this approach is a more differentiated portrait of the individual as well as of the status of exile within large-scale historical processes.

In critiquing the equation of exile with isolation, I enter a disciplinary debate about the task of comparative literature as distinct from national literature. In the United States at least, comparative literature is influenced by the history of exile, and to this day, exile remains a significant topic within the field. My intervention is, however, in keeping with recent self-scrutiny among comparatists. Challenged by violent conflicts between the three monotheistic religions, globalization, and new forms of imperialism, the discipline is now attempting to redefine its purpose.[27] By investigating secular scholarship as the outgrowth of an exchange between German émigrés and Turkish reformers, I hope to stimulate the interdisciplinary, transnational debate about exile and secularism within the humanities.

In making my case for a contextualized understanding of *Mimesis*, I take on a number of critics. Abdul JanMohamed, for one, insists that

Auerbach's place of exile was irrelevant to *Mimesis*. The book, he says, "could have been written in any other part of the non-Occidental world without significant difference."[28] Azade Seyhan similarly argues that Auerbach's work exhibits not "even the faintest trace of the exilic experience."[29] Yet, as I show, the evidence for such claims is rather thin. Indeed, they boil down to a remark made by Auerbach himself about the inadequacy of Istanbul's libraries. As I show in chapter 5, this oft-cited remark has been promoted to a generalized condition of insufficiency: at the periphery of the Western world we find not plenitude but lack, not familiarity or even difference but absence. We can trace the genealogy of this view to the critic Harry Levin and, most importantly, to Edward Said. In *The World, the Text, and the Critic*, Said regards Auerbach's dislocation and distance from Europe as the enabling condition for the writing of *Mimesis*. According to Said, for a scholar like Auerbach who was trained in medieval and renaissance Roman literatures, Istanbul

represents the terrible Turk, as well as Islam, the scourge of Christendom, the great Oriental apostasy incarnate. Throughout the classical period of European culture Turkey was the Orient, Islam its most redoubtable and aggressive representative. This was not all, though. The Orient and Islam also stood for the ultimate alienation from and opposition to Europe, the European tradition of Christian Latinity, as well as to the putative authority of ecclesia, humanistic learning, and cultural community. For centuries Turkey and Islam hung over Europe like a gigantic composite monster, seeming to threaten Europe with destruction. To have been an exile in Istanbul at the time of fascism in Europe was a deeply resonating and intense form of exile from Europe.[30]

Said conflates Auerbach's view of modern Turkey with an oversimplified Orientalist discourse rooted in the European Middle Ages and the Renaissance.[31] My interest is in disambiguating this Orientalist discourse from Auerbach's exposure to the cultural politics at Istanbul University and in highlighting his role as the spokesman for the humanist idea in a rapidly Westernizing country. Said's view of Auerbach's exile is problematic because it suggests that there was a continuous, homogeneous Orientalist discourse prevailing in Western Europe from the Middle Ages onward and that this prevented the philologist from comprehending the particular situation in which he found himself. Said did not acknowledge that the rapprochement between modern Turkey and Western Europe was the result of age-long contact and exchange between Ottomans and Europeans.

The "executive value of exile," to use Said's term, lies not simply in Auerbach's alienation from his habitual cultural environment but in the particular cultural, historical, and intellectual environment of modern Turkey, an environment that offered a new home for the humanist tradition.[32] In other words, Auerbach's work was not only "steeped in the reality of Europe," as Said argues; it was also rooted in the reality of Istanbul. As if to anticipate Said's charge, Auerbach wrote that his work was "quite consciously a book that a particular person, in a particular situation, wrote at the beginning of the 1940s."[33] Our first task, then, is to investigate this particular person—the German-Jewish Dante scholar from Marburg University who chaired the faculty for Western languages and literatures at Istanbul University for more than a decade. The other, perhaps more important, task of this book is to explore the particularity of exile in Istanbul, a city that had been the center of Ottoman imperialism for half a millennium and now played a critical role in revivifying Turkish culture through humanism. As I show, the relationship between the philologist and this context is precisely what allowed Auerbach to realize his scholarly project. This correlation, in turn, constitutes the structure of *East West Mimesis*.

Said's notion of 1930s Istanbul as a place of "Oriental, non-Occidental exile and homelessness"—a place that was enabling in its very threateningness and remoteness—is a notion that remains pervasive in comparatist scholarship.[34] Exile has been transformed into a theoretical factum and construed as a condition for generating new forms of critical consciousness in the humanities. JanMohamed, for example, draws on the trope of exile for his concept of the border intellectual.[35] Aamir Mufti elaborates on this in his work on secular criticism in a postcolonial framework where he explores the "ethical possibilities" of minority existence.[36] Both of these scholars cleave to Said and see the space on the edge as potentially productive. I, on the other hand, am less interested in tracing the significance of Auerbach to Said. Rather, I investigate how ideas about exile and isolation are connected to the trope of detachment in literary and literary critical discourses of the early twentieth century. Hence, I show how the trope of detachment, central to the aesthetics of modernism, came to assume a different meaning after the onset of mass emigration in 1933.

This book conclusively shows that Auerbach did not see Turkey as the antithesis of European humanism. In fact, Auerbach referred to Istanbul as a "fundamentally Hellenistic city," a city in which the Arab, Armenian, Jewish, and Turkish elements "meld[ed] or coexist[ed] in a single entity."[37] By "Hellenistic," Auerbach clearly meant Western, even if the valence of the term has changed over time. In its five hundred pages, *Mimesis* makes virtually no mention of Turkey: only the epilogue refers explicitly to 1940s Istanbul, and the references to other places in Turkey are merely incidental. But rather than insisting on Turkey as a missing subject within *Mimesis*, as other critics have been inclined to do, we can think about what this omission meant. I would argue that Turkey was neither a blind spot nor an oversight on Auerbach's part. Chapter 5 suggests that Turkey works *ex negativo* in the author's circumscription of the Judeo-Christian world: it is via this lacuna that the Judeo-Christian world first emerges as a bounded one. In other words, through its exclusions, *Mimesis* exemplifies how the West came to think of itself as different and separate from what is now called the Middle East. This chapter also traces the links between the scholarship Auerbach produced while in Istanbul and the location of his exile. Included among my finds are a number of lectures that Auerbach gave to large public audiences. In dealing with this material, my aim is not to reduce Auerbach's exilic scholarship merely to its Turkish context. I use it instead to show how he connected with his new surroundings and how he responded to some of the challenges posed by a rapidly modernizing society.[38]

It is, of course, difficult to quantify the relationship between location and creativity and to prove the influence of Istanbul on Auerbach's thought. Yet simply disavowing such a connection on evidentiary grounds implies that we subscribe to the notion of the romantic genius, whose creativity either is divinely inspired or springs from barren ground. Personally, I have no truck with such a view, but nor would Auerbach have seen himself in such terms. He may have been something of an elitist, but with his interest in historiography, the representation of reality, the role of the vernacular, and humanism as the basis for European culture, Auerbach was not alone while in Istanbul. To the contrary, we will find that these were the very questions preoccupying the Turkish reformers, intellectuals, and students who were in contact with Auerbach at the time. Thus, rather than emphasizing dislocation and difference as catalytic for exilic scholarship, it is the exilic place that concerns us here. This differentiated picture makes it clear that Auerbach did not stumble into an intellectual and political void when he migrated to Turkey: in some sense, he found himself at home in exile. For a certain class of educated Turks in the 1930s and 1940s, Turkey not only *was* Europe, it housed the origins of Europe. This, as we will see, provoked émigrés in Istanbul and Ankara to reflect on the idea of Europe and the challenges posed by Turkey's Westernization project.

Reading in the Archives

To date, our knowledge about German-Jewish life in Turkey has been rather sketchy, due in no small part to the paucity of archival research on the topic and the difficulty in gaining access to Turkish archives. But for anyone willing to make the trip now, and with knowledge of German, Turkish, and French, there is information to be found in the documents of the German consulate in Istanbul, the German embassy in Ankara, the Foreign Office in Berlin, and the Nazi Ministry for Education, which are archived in the Politisches Archiv des Auswärtigen Amts and the Bundesarchiv in Berlin. Other sources are held in the Literaturarchiv Marbach, the newspaper archive of the Staatsbibliothek Berlin, and the archive of the Akademie der Wissenschaften in Berlin. Research trips to these various institutions unearthed letters, memoirs, newspaper articles, journals, lectures, declassified consular reports, and governmental correspondence that all demonstrate the extent to which Auerbach was, in fact, integrated into a larger émigré community in Istanbul. Turkish sources, above all at the Istanbul University archive, helped complete the picture by shedding light on the nature of the humanist reform movement, the political and social status of Jews in Turkey, and the cultural topography of Istanbul during this period.

How one reads archival sources depends of course on one's disciplinary training. As both a literary critic and a student of cultural history, I am interested in applying literary critical tools to sources not typically associated with literature. However, rather than using archival sources to compile historical facts and attempt an objective view of the past, this book identifies some of the central devices and figures that structure the rhetoric used in these sources. Through the process of interpretation, this book illuminates intersections between the politics and poetics of the modern Turkish nation in its early stages. Among the productive outcomes of this approach is the capacity to discern the tropes of assimilation, imitation, and mimicry that inform a broad range of contemporaneous Turkish as well as German discourses.[39] What emerges is a thick description of the social and political milieu that informed the encounter between exiled philologists and Turkish humanists. Whether we define this as either cultural studies or cultural history is a question of choice. Decisive, however, is that the literary, social, political, and historical are regarded as intertwined areas of inquiry in this interdisciplinary study.

My overarching approach, then, is not simply to read Turkey into *Mimesis* but to read *Mimesis* against Turkey and render Auerbach's work productive for our understanding of Turkey and East West relations generally. In establishing this relationship between the author's work and its context, I once again draw on Auerbach's own approach. While in Istanbul, Auerbach worked on the concept of the *figura*—a rhetorical device that establishes links between two otherwise unconnected events or persons. The sacrifice of Isaac discussed in the opening chapter of *Mimesis*, for instance, becomes meaningful because it prefigures another event—the sacrifice of Christ. According to Auerbach's reading, the first event is both preserved and fully realized in the latter, and the two historically unrelated events now come to signify each other.[40] Using the concept of the figura, I make a connection between Auerbach's *Mimesis* and the history of Istanbul. The two poles of my figura are, first, the series of Westernization reforms and, second, Auerbach's magnum opus. By reading Auerbach's work against the Turkish Westernization reforms, we gain insights into the spatial and temporal conditions governing education, scholarship, translations, and literary production at the time. We also come to see mimesis not merely as a literary technique but also as a broad cultural strategy informing many aspects of Turkish life.

By invoking the figura as a form of historical parenthesis, I also highlight the differences between the two mimetic projects laid out above—first, mimesis as a cultural mode at work in the Westernization reforms; second, Auerbach's mimesis as a literary mode for representing reality. Both forms of mimesis work to establish the relationship between the present and the past. The cultural mode—imitating European humanism—introduces a new historical legacy to Turkey, namely, the legacy of the ancient Greek and Roman worlds. The literary mode in turn shapes—as Auerbach argues—our concept of history itself. Investigating Auerbach in Turkey thus allows me to show that the national and the humanist movements were intertwined at this crucial point in Turkey's long identification with the West. I argue that the Westernization reforms, in fact, prefigure the essentially Eurocentric scope of *Mimesis*.

There is something admittedly risky about arguing for a figural relationship between Turkey's Westernization reforms and a work like *Mimesis*. It is worth remembering, however, that the new Turkey was anxious to disassociate itself from the legacy of the Ottoman Empire. The Westernization reforms of the preceding two centuries were regarded as having been either too superficial or too inconsistent, and modern Turks were keen to make a new start. As in *Mimesis* itself, the latest reforms relegated Islam and the Ottoman Empire to the periphery. If secularization liberalized education in ways unimaginable under the Ottomans, it nonetheless instituted Europhilia as the new religion. Europhilia—by which I mean a preference for Western literature, clothing, and other aspects of cultural and political life—became the norm that reinforced the reformers' division of Turkish citizens into two factions—progressive Westerners and conservative Muslims.

Before considering Auerbach's role as the representative of the humanist tradition, we need to inquire about the politics of humanism and ask who Auerbach was prior to exile. Auerbach's origins—the "philologist's heritage," as he referred to it—were naturally formative for his thinking. Indeed, we might ask whether it would have been sufficient to trace *Mimesis* to Auerbach's intellectual development during the Weimar Republic. In what follows, we will find that Auerbach reflected on and wrote about representation, memory, history, and even exile long before he faced exile himself. Explaining Auerbach's later scholarship merely by referencing his philological training in the Weimar Republic does not, in my view, shed much light on the subject. In summary, rather than following a deterministic, biographical model, this book situates *Mimesis* within its intellectual and geocultural context and maps out how the meaning of humanism, history, and mimesis was shaped by the transnational encounter between Turkish and exiled German scholars.

Chapter 1 traces the origins of Auerbach's "philologist heritage," comparing his humanist worldview with that of his contemporaries Walter Benjamin and Victor Klemperer. Here, I situate Auerbach's pre-exilic work within debates concerning the philosophy of history and inquire into the fate of humanism during the Nazi era. The schism between bourgeois and socialist humanism at the international humanist conference in Paris in 1935 is of particular relevance, for it helps us understand how humanism served as a capacious umbrella for various cultural, political, educational, and scholarly approaches. Chapter 2 focuses on the particularities of Turkish humanism as a way of renewing Turkish culture. It shows that Turkish reformers in the 1930s drew on the Renaissance model to develop a system of education based on Western classical learning. The chapter asks how Turkish identity was constructed via the outsider. Émigrés like Auerbach, Leo Spitzer, and others played an important role in educating students in philology and providing them with a humanist worldview. Exiled philologists, philosophers, historians, and librarians overhauled disciplinary practices, introduced new academic writing styles, and set up research libraries. The chapter explains why Turkish intellectuals demanded, for example, that Ottoman literature ought to be approached via Shakespeare. In investigating the challenges of re-creating modern culture in the image of ancient Europe, this chapter concludes that Turkey's humanist reform of 1939 was tantamount to a kind of classical humanism with socialist leanings.

In analyzing tropes of authenticity and inauthenticity, chapter 3 argues that anxieties regarding appropriation and assimilation impacted the status of Turkish and German Jews in different ways. Three tropes— the mimic, the *dönme*, and the eternal guest—are shown to have informed notions of Jewishness, Turkishness, and Europeanness during the nationalization and modernization period. By tracing these tropes in a range of sources, including university lectures, newspapers, university contracts, letters, and German consular reports, the chapter discloses how and why Jewish émigrés were granted privileged status in Turkey, even while Turkish Jews were being subjected to discrimination. Against the view that exile in 1930s Istanbul represented "an active impingement of European selfhood," I argue here that Auerbach's Europeanness and in fact his Jewishness were the very reasons why he was hired to help modernize Istanbul University in the first place.[41]

In chapter 4, we find that Auerbach's exile was dictated by the same force he sought to flee—National Socialism. The chapter thus traces the émigrés' path through the topography of German Istanbul, where consular officials impeded intellectual work and Nazis spied in university lecture halls. Hitherto undiscovered documents in the German consular archive, unpublished letters by Spitzer and Auerbach, university correspondence, and Istanbul's first philological journals reveal the difficulties that arose when Nazis intervened in the émigrés' academic and personal affairs. By examining the hiring and departmental policies at Istanbul University, we find that Turkish university administrators in fact cooperated with Nazis. Chapter 4 goes on to investigate the battle over teaching German literature at Istanbul University: this culture war began with a crisis between Spitzer and the German consulate, continued with Auerbach trying to prevent the hiring of Nazi Germanist Hennig Brinkmann, and ended with Turkey's declaration against Nazi Germany in 1944. Auerbach would respond to the culture war by giving voice to a vision of "international philology." Like émigré comparatist René Wellek in the United States after the war, Auerbach cast himself as a kind of international ambassador with the aim of encouraging productive collaboration among the Istanbul faculty. Having witnessed the havoc wrought by extreme nationalism, he now directed his academic agenda toward transcending the nation as the main organizing principle of Western European philology.

Having left Germany as a Dante-scholar, Auerbach became a comparatist in Turkish exile—partly because he wanted to rescue a world destroyed by the Nazis and partly because his role in Turkey was that of a Europeanist. But, ironically, the idea of Europe that he developed in *Mimesis* came at the cost of denying the very cultural site in which he found himself while in exile. Chapter 5 thus challenges three conventional explanations concerning the originality of Auerbach's authorship, namely, the unavailability of books, the poor state of scholarship and intellectual dialogue, and, finally, detachment as a precondition for critical thinking. We find that the catalyst for *Mimesis* was a vibrant intellectual circle that included prominent cultural historians like Alexander Rüstow and the tremendous weight that humanist scholarship already carried in Istanbul. *East West Mimesis* concludes, then, that Auerbach drew on the modernist trope of detachment when staging himself as an isolated intellectual in exile. Finally, this chapter focuses on a hitherto unknown lecture Auerbach delivered on Dante—one of the principal figures of exile in the Western world—whose *Commedia* had been banned in the Ottoman Empire because of its offensive portrayal of Mohammed in the inferno. In discussing the 1939 lecture, the chapter situates Auerbach in relationship to the new intellectual avenues that opened with Dante's translation into Turkish. It addresses the strange fact that, notwithstanding Turkey's new progressive and secular atmosphere, Auerbach downplayed the affiliations between the Judaic, Christian, and Islamic worlds.

In the 1930s, Turks saw Auerbach not as a Jewish outcast but as a European who could help reintroduce the humanist heritage of old Constantinople. Yet in the 1990s, perceptions would shift: in the wake of the quincentennial commemoration of the Sephardic Jews' exile to the Ottoman Empire, Turkish scholars "rediscovered" the émigrés of the 1930s as "Jews" and depicted them as figures of modernity in Turkish historiography. If we look for Auerbach's place in Turkey today, we find that his minority position as a Jew is woven into the narrative about Westernization. In the epilogue, I argue that the hiring of German Jewish scholars is presented as proof of Turkey's capacity to surpass its Western model: Europe failed its Jewish citizens, yet Turkey displayed humanity toward the persecuted. However, it should be clear that such narratives paper over Turkish anti-Semitism and the country's atrocities against Greeks, Armenians, and Kurds. *East West Mimesis* attributes such revisionism to Turkey's ongoing need to prove itself sufficiently European to warrant membership in the European Union. And it answers this need with a more critical account of the past and a more hopeful view for the future.

1

Humanism Goes East

THE SON OF BOURGEOIS German-Jewish parents, Erich Auerbach was born in 1892 in Berlin, imperial Germany's glittering capital.
The neighborhood where the family lived, Berlin-Charlottenburg, was a
prosperous part of the city and home to many middle-class Jewish residents, including the great thinker and writer Walter Benjamin, born in
the same year. Between 1895 and 1910, Charlottenburg's Jewish population more than quadrupled, reaching some 22,500 inhabitants. This
growth in population warranted the building of a new place of worship
and, two houses from the Auerbach residence on Fasanenstraße, there
appeared a large synagogue consecrated by the rabbi Leo Baeck (1873–
1956) in 1912.[1] The fact that there was a synagogue practically next door
and a growing number of Jewish Germans in the neighborhood did not,
of course, mean that Auerbach was raised in a religious household.
Rather, the family's lifestyle was similar to that of most assimilated Jewish Germans in Berlin. The young Auerbach was enrolled in a French
school founded by the late seventeenth-century Protestant emigrants
from France, the Huguenots. This Französisches Gymnasium provided a
comprehensive humanist education and prided itself on having educated
prominent writers like Adelbert von Chamisso (1781–1838) and Heinrich
von Kleist (1777–1811). Around the turn of the century, the Romance
philologist Victor Klemperer (1881–1960) and the writer Kurt Tucholsky
(1890–1935) were enrolled in the same school. Here the young Auerbach
learned French and acquired a firm grounding in classical Roman and
Greek texts. He would take a number of intellectual detours before

Penelope Painter (fifth century BCE), *The Nurse Euriklea Washing Ulysses' Feet after His Return*. Attic red-figured skphos (440 BCE) from Chiusi. Museo Archeologico, Chiusi, Italy. Photo: Erich Lessing. By permission of Art Resource, New York.

dedicating his life fully to philology, but the influence of his early school-
ing is clear.

As a young man, Auerbach first studied law, a decision that might
have been influenced by the professional restrictions imposed on Jews during the Wilhelminian era (1871–1918).[2] Although he eventually abandoned
this career path for a degree in Romance languages and literatures, for
most of his life he would insist on the validity of the law, even when doing
so flew in the face of all common sense. It could not be said that the young
Auerbach subscribed to any of the political and religious enthusiasms that
gripped his contemporaries: we can think of him neither as a revolutionary
Marxist, pacifist, nor Zionist but instead as a conformist. With the outbreak of World War I, he committed himself to the cause of the German
Empire, volunteered as an infantryman, and fought in northern France.[3]
After four brutal years of warfare, he was among the millions of veterans to
be awarded a second-grade military medal. With a scar on his foot left by
a severe injury, Auerbach returned from the front to his native Berlin.[4]

Almost thirty years later, shortly after the subsequent world war,
Auerbach published his groundbreaking work, *Mimesis: The Representation of Reality in Western Literature*, which famously opens with the image
of Odysseus's long-anticipated and oft-deferred homecoming. The chapter, "Odysseus' Scar," opens with a scene in which the long-lost warrior,
disguised as a stranger, is welcomed as a guest into his own home. When
his old nurse, Euryclea, washes his feet in a gesture of hospitality, she recognizes Odysseus through a scar he acquired in his youth. At the very
moment of recognition the scene is interrupted and the story of the hero's
scar unfolds. Auerbach analyzes this scene in conjunction with another
famous scene of crisis and disclosure in ancient texts—the biblical story of
Abraham's interrupted sacrifice of Isaac. By distinguishing the Homeric
from the biblical style, Auerbach shows how narrative styles are connected
to evolving concepts of history and reality, and this insight has become
the hallmark of his scholarship. Needless to say, there is more that could
be made here of Auerbach's choice of textual excerpts—something that
David Damrosch, Djelal Kadir, Vassilis Lambropoulos, Seth Lerer, and
James Porter have shown in their discussions of this opening.[5] But suffice
it to say that Auerbach's use of Odysseus's scar is indicative of his own
method: he treats the scar like a fragment representing a greater reality,
while the textual fragment of the *Odyssey* is, in turn, shown to be emblem-
atic of the Homeric style generally. It is thus not incidental that the motifs

of this first chapter characterize elements of Auerbach's own life—rupture, sacrifice, exile, hospitality, and new beginnings.

We need only look to Auerbach's return from the battlegrounds of World War I to find one such new beginning and the decision to pursue a calling in philology. The veteran was now determined to write a dissertation in Romanistik, the discipline of Romance languages and literatures, where he specialized in the early French and Italian Renaissance. Romanistik allowed German scholars of his generation to avoid what he called "the spirit of their own nation." By studying this field, Auerbach wrote, "there was little danger that they would be carried away by a patriotic involvement with their own national character."[6] This might have explained the initial appeal of the discipline.[7] Certainly, Romance scholarship in Weimar Germany opened up a broader view of culture than Germanistik, the discipline devoted to the study of German languages and literatures, but Romanistik also likely appealed to Auerbach because it was strongly influenced by German historicism. By emphasizing the classical and Christian civilizations as the common ground between German and Romance cultures, Romanistik offered him a "historical perspective embracing Europe as a whole."[8]

Auerbach first deepened this historical perspective, which would remain central to all his scholarship, when he began translating the work of the Italian philosopher Giambattista Vico (1668–1744) into German. Vico had gone unrecognized among his contemporaries because of his stance against Cartesian philosophy and the idea of progress. Auerbach, however, showed Vico's significance to nineteenth-century Romanticism.[9] By translating a selection from *Scienza Nuova* (*New Science*, 1725) Auerbach reintroduced Vico, who imagined history to evolve in cyclical stages, to a modern German audience in the early 1920s. Notwithstanding the religious dimension of Vico's views—Auerbach disparagingly referred to his "tedious Catholicism"—Vico's notion of history laid the ground for a secular vision of culture and history.[10] Auerbach's Vico translation also revived what seems like a most modern idea, namely, that narration is the foundation of history. Vico's theory of historical knowledge is based on the assumption that it is possible to understand the past because we are in fact the ones who generate history's narrative.[11] The Italian philosopher claimed specifically that the "entire development of human history, as made by men, is potentially contained in the human mind, and may therefore, by a process of research and re-evocation, be understood by men."[12]

The task of the historian is thus to re-create a mental map of the past.[13] For Auerbach, whose purpose was "always to write history," this approach provided the critical bridge between his own interests in philology and history.[14]

The conflagrations of the early twentieth century triggered a renewed discussion about the philosophy of history. The mass destruction seemed to prompt scholars to question earlier assumptions about progress and change. Auerbach's interests thus overlapped with those of other scholars of his generation—in particular, Walter Benjamin (1892–1940), who likewise came from a bourgeois and assimilated German-Jewish family in Berlin-Charlottenburg. By the time Auerbach returned from the battlefield, Benjamin had already studied Germanistik and developed close relationships with intellectuals like Ernst Bloch (1885–1977) and Gershom Scholem (1897–1982). While there were clear political differences between Auerbach and Benjamin, they shared the same sociocultural background and intellectual passions, and it comes as no surprise that their paths should have crossed at the end of World War I. The two men probably first met at the Preußische Staatsbibliothek Berlin (Prussian State Library), where Auerbach worked as a librarian from 1923 until 1929 while writing his *Habilitationsschrift* (professorial thesis) on Dante Alighieri. At the time, Benjamin was researching the origins of German tragic drama and worked regularly at the library. We know this because of a letter Benjamin wrote to Scholem, telling of his important discoveries about French baroque literature in the state library and his indebtedness to the librarian. In all likelihood, the librarian was none other than Auerbach.[15]

The relationship between Benjamin and Auerbach—both prominent intellectuals of the twentieth century—was not only pragmatic.[16] Karlheinz Barck and Carlo Ginzburg suggest that the two thinkers exchanged their ideas because of their common interest in questions like the changing relationship between fate and character during the course of history.[17] Theirs is a reasonable assumption, but I would emphasize that both scholars also asked how innovative works like the *Commedia*, *Scienza Nuova*, or, in Benjamin's case, bourgeois drama set the parameters for modern literature and for a new understanding of history. Given these shared interests, it is unsurprising that Benjamin and Auerbach were both preoccupied with Marcel Proust; they were among the first German scholars to recognize the significance of the French modernist's work.[18] Benjamin's 1929 essay on Proust, for instance, was concerned with the links between the subjective nature of memory and a broader philosophy of history. Here, Benjamin specifically addressed the problem of experience, remembrance, and forgetting.[19] It is, however, a little-known fact that Auerbach had applied himself to the problem of subjectivity and memory four years earlier. In his own 1925 article on Proust's *Recherche*, Auerbach analyzed the relationship between memory and reality, drawing on Dante to establish the particularity of Proust's narrative and the act of remembrance.[20] Through this work on Vico and Proust, Auerbach came to distinguish between different concepts of reality, that is, between *inneres Leben* (inner reality) and *irdischer Verlauf* (earthly course), or what he later called *irdische Wirklichkeit* (earthly reality). In his Proust essay, Auerbach interpreted the French masterpiece as a form of memory work. The narrator, he said, substitutes "empirical chronology" for the "secret and often neglected nexus between events which the biographer of the soul, who gazes back and inside, perceives as real."[21] Key to his approach in *Mimesis* would be this distinction—the subject's personal experience of reality versus a spatially and temporally bounded reality.

It seems significant that Auerbach attended to such questions as early as the 1920s. It means that long before he fled National Socialism and went into exile, long before he was deprived of the world that had shaped him, intellectuals like himself and Benjamin were already reflecting on the challenges posed by recalling and representing past experience. This thematization of memory was not, as one might suppose, first triggered by anti-Semitic persecution during the Nazi period: it was part of a wider interwar discourse concerning the representation of reality in modernity. Only later did memory work come to assume the significance that it has today, namely, a basis for diasporic identities that, to some considerable extent, define themselves in terms of what they lost. It was, in other words, when an entire generation of German Jewish scholars, artists, and writers was eradicated in Nazi Germany that remembering became the appointed task of the modern exile.

For Auerbach, the idea of detaching oneself from "earthly reality" (or "earthly course," as he variously called it) was central to his thinking. Specifically, he wondered whether divorcing oneself from one's environment afforded one greater perspicuity. It was a question he took up in a number of pre-exilic studies. In the preface to his translation of *Scienza Nuova*, for example, he characterized Vico as an unacknowledged "stranger in his native town," someone who lived detached from his surroundings.[22] He also admired Vico as a scholar who was able to think beyond the limits of his own time and hence anticipate nineteenth-century Romanticism and historicism. Auerbach believed that Vico's own *äußeres Schicksal* (manifest fate) was so unimportant to him that he could develop his ideas untrammeled by the spirit of his time and place.[23] The idea of an entirely solitary existence gripped Auerbach, who was by now working on Dante. In *Dante: Dichter der irdischen Welt* (*Dante: Poet of the Secular World*), published in 1929, Auerbach analyzed the *Commedia*, where Dante envisions an infernal journey accompanied by the classical Roman poet Virgil. Auerbach interpreted the *Commedia* as the author's attempt to recuperate a world that had been lost as the result of exile.[24] He suggested that Dante's exile from Florence in 1302 sharpened his poetic talents and motivated him to write the *Commedia*. Not yet foreseeing that he would soon have to go into exile himself, Auerbach stressed that Dante's exilic work constituted the founding moment for national

Domenico Peterlini, *Dante in Exile*, circa 1860. Photo: Alfredo Dagli Orti. Galleria Palatina, Palazzo Pitti, Florence, Italy. By permission of Bildarchiv Preussischer Kulturbesitz / Art Resource, New York.

literatures, not only in Italy but in Western Europe generally. In taking on this project, Auerbach seems to have unwittingly chosen a model for his own exile.

Both Auerbach's early work and *Mimesis* link mental disassociation to a certain psychological disposition and to the experience of sociopolitical rupture and spatial dislocation. The dream state, for example, signifies a condition of mental detachment from the world around one. This is how he saw Vico, as someone so "fanatically" immersed in his pursuit of truth that he "went through his earthly life as if it were a dream."[25] The same image occurs in Auerbach's later review of Proust's *Recherche*, but this time with a negative connotation: the narrator is so disconnected from his surroundings that he is said to have become a prisoner of his own subjectivity.[26] With regard to Dante, Auerbach also attended to the way in which experience is represented and remembered. He argued that the fourteenth-century exile transports his listeners to a new world "so permeated by the memory of the real that the memory itself seems real." Life, in contrast, becomes, in Auerbach's reading of the *Commedia*, a mere fragment and a dream.[27] This fragment is seen as the distillation of earthly reality, a metonym in which the part encapsulates the whole. Once detached from the whole, the fragment signifies all that is missing, and, like a dream, it intensifies human experience.

Mimesis uses the concept of the fragment as an *Ausgangspunkt*, a point of departure, for reflecting on the history of Western European literature. Arguably, this was in keeping with the modernist concern with fragmentation and detachment. In *Mimesis*, we find this reflected in Auerbach's analysis of key authors like Homer, Dante, Proust, and Woolf. I will take up this point again in chapter 5, where I examine the relationship between Auerbach's methodology and the task of the modern philologist. We will find that Auerbach invoked the modernist trope of detachment when he presented himself as an isolated intellectual in exile. Contrary to Auerbach's self-staging in the epilogue to *Mimesis* (and the assertions of many contemporary scholars), I argue that the "earthly reality" of Auerbach's Istanbul exile from 1936 to 1947 did in fact influence his work. While he might have idealized Dante as a writer who rose above his material circumstances to produce some of the most powerful literature ever written, Auerbach tended to mythologize his own experience. He portrayed himself as intellectually isolated when there were useful libraries and bookstores available to him. Indeed, Istanbul offered other visceral reminders of the times in which he lived—Nazi spies who tried to curtail his activities, cutthroat politics at Istanbul University, rising anti-Semitism in Turkey, and, of course, devastating reports from home. We will find that Auerbach was actually quite earthbound: he took quiet comfort from the circle of German émigrés who swapped books, read one another's manuscripts, and exchanged ideas.

Subito Movimento di Cose: Sudden Change of Circumstances

Auerbach had but a few years to gain experience in his chosen field before the political conditions governing German universities drastically changed and he was forced to leave the country. With the publication of his professorial thesis on Dante, Auerbach was appointed professor of Romanistik at Marburg University and soon became chair of the Romance department, or *Seminar*, as it is called in German. His friend Walter Benjamin was less fortunate: he could not find a position when Frankfurt University failed his professorial thesis on German tragic drama.[28] Unable to secure a footing in the academy, Benjamin turned his hand to freelance writing, an insecure livelihood in the best of times. Hitler's rise to power in January 1933 prompted Benjamin to take refuge in Paris. A few months later, many of Auerbach's and Benjamin's German-Jewish and Marxist peers lost their tenured academic positions when a law regarding the *Wiederherstellung des Berufsbeamtentums*, the so-called restitution of tenured civil service, was passed by the Nazi government.[29] With this law, the National Socialists established legal grounds for forcing into retirement those professors who were either opponents of Nazism or of "non-Aryan blood." As a result, numerous so-called non-Aryan scholars were forced to emigrate immediately, many of them with the help of Jewish organizations that facilitated their hiring at universities abroad. In 1933, philosophers Theodor W. Adorno (1903–1969) and Ernst Cassirer (1874–1945) first sought exile in the United Kingdom; Romance scholar Leo Spitzer (1887–1960) and physicist/philosopher Hans Reichenbach (1891–1953) in Turkey; historian Alex Bein (1903–1988) in Palestine; philosopher Max Horkheimer (1895–1973) in Switzerland; and Romance scholar Leonardo Olschki (1885–1961) in Italy.[30] As a result of this exodus, émigré communities sprang up in places like London, Los Angeles, New York, Paris, and Istanbul.

"I am Prussian of the Jewish denomination living in Berlin-Charlottenburg," Auerbach had declared in 1921, the year in which he completed his doctoral dissertation at the University of Greifswald.[31] The extent to which Auerbach's "Jewish denomination" mattered to his way of life and to his scholarship after 1933 is a question that has been addressed by scholars including Gert Mattenklott, James Porter, and Martin Treml.[32] Even if Auerbach had once chosen to define his Jewish background in such neutral terms, the Nazi legislation now redefined people like himself as "full Jews," "non-Aryans," and "un-German." With the drastic racialization of Jewishness, Auerbach grasped right away that he was being denied the "right to be German," as he put it in a letter to a former mentor.[33] Thanks to the exceptional status granted to World War I veterans, Auerbach was spared immediate dismissal from Marburg University. During the ensuing years, however, his authority at the university would be systematically undermined. In the end, he was prohibited from teaching and examining altogether, a task he passed on to his assistant, Werner Krauss (1900–1976), a promising young Romance scholar who later joined the resistance.[34] In a climate in which scholars such as himself were regularly banned from teaching and publishing, Auerbach came to realize that a career in Germany was untenable. His protective status as a war veteran lost its validity in 1935. By then, it was clear that he would have to face emigration like most of his "un-German" contemporaries.

At the end of that summer, Auerbach went to Italy, meaning perhaps to test the waters of exile. In any event, the trip allowed him to circumvent Nazi censorship and revive his contacts with scholars and friends abroad. Most crucially, his former colleague, Leo Spitzer, traveled from Istanbul to Bologna to talk with him in person about an opportunity that had opened up in Turkey. It seems surprising that Spitzer extended a hand to Auerbach. In early 1933, Spitzer had been disgusted to hear that Auerbach tried to distance himself from the "distress caused by Jew-baiting, [and] . . . even celebrated" it. To date, there is no indication that Auerbach really welcomed the surge of anti-Semitism after Hitler's election—it seems that the allegations were the result of mean-spirited academic gossip. But Spitzer was convinced by what he had heard and complained to the philosopher Karl Löwith (1897–1973) in April 1933 that it had taken Auerbach a while to acknowledge that he "shared the same boat as us." Spitzer went on to say that he himself was not a "convinced Jew" and that he "owe[d] the best to the Christian influence," yet there ought to be "something called 'a feeling of atavistic solidarity' in times of distress."[35]

We do not know whether or when Spitzer changed his mind about Auerbach, but in 1935 he performed just such an act of atavistic solidarity, and this probably saved his colleague's life. Having spent two years at Istanbul University, Spitzer enjoyed the prospect of a professorship at Johns Hopkins University. In his place, he suggested that Auerbach might now chair Istanbul University's faculty for Western languages and literatures. The university had recently been restructured as a modern, secular university and, as Turkey's most prestigious institution of higher learning and leading promoter of humanism, it was actively recruiting European scholars to help implement wide-ranging Westernization reforms. Spitzer had found a temporary home in Istanbul; he had also enjoyed the company of more than forty other German émigrés, who had all been hired by the university in the fall of 1933. Since Spitzer now planned to move to the United States, a door was opening, and he discussed with Auerbach what it would take for him to leave Germany and reestablish himself in a foreign country. At the same time, Spitzer also tried to help Löwith get a position in philosophy at Istanbul University. He invited Löwith for a lecture in December 1935, but the latter had to leave with no realistic prospect of employment in Istanbul.[36] Later, the philosopher managed to get positions in Japan and the United States. Auerbach, who had no prospects at the time, was naturally grateful for Spitzer's suggestion and understood it as "a mark of his friendship."[37] He had once before succeeded Spitzer when the latter left Marburg University in 1930 for a position at the University of Cologne. This time, Auerbach had reservations about succeeding Spitzer in Istanbul, but he was also aware that time was running out. There was not long to deliberate. Soon after Auerbach met Spitzer in Bologna, the Nuremberg laws were passed in an effort to further racialize Jewish Germans and preserve the so-called purity of German blood. The law defined Jewishness in terms of bloodlines and, without exception, officially banned the employment of Jews in public institutions.

The increasingly anti-Semitic climate in Germany meant that there was stiff competition in the foreign labor market, and this included, of course, competition for Spitzer's professorship at Istanbul University. At least three other Romance philologists vied for the position—the modern philologist Victor Klemperer and the medievalists Ernst Robert Curtius

(1886–1956) and Hans Rheinfelder (1898–1971). At the time, Klemperer was desperately applying to foreign organizations that assisted scholars in emigrating. Among them were the Notgemeinschaft deutscher Wissenschaftler im Ausland (Aid Organization for German Academics Abroad) in Zurich, the Emergency Committee in Aid of German Scholars in New York, and the Academic Assistance Council in London. The Zurich-based Notgemeinschaft showed tremendous resourcefulness and managed to place numerous German scholars in Turkey.[38] Klemperer knew that his days as a professor at Dresden University were numbered and he inquired about Spitzer's position at Istanbul University in May 1935, only to learn that he was competing against Curtius. He learned this from his close friend, physicist Harry Dember, who had taken up a position at Istanbul University two years earlier. Klemperer hoped that Curtius, who was not Jewish, was not serious about emigrating.[39] Later he found out that Auerbach, who like himself needed to leave sooner rather than later, had entered the race for the position.

While Klemperer weighed the prospect of exile in Turkey versus South America or Palestine, he recalled his friend's reassurances about Turkey. Istanbul might be located at Europe's "outer edge," Dember had said, but the city was, "still, in Europe."[40] Klemperer was not entirely persuaded.[41] This was primarily a question not of culture or language but of geography. Foreseeing that countries at Europe's periphery might not provide the security he yearned for, Klemperer would have preferred Lima over Istanbul.[42] These reservations notwithstanding, he did all he could to be hired in Turkey. The remote possibility of Turkish exile prompted Klemperer to reflect on the meaning of Europe in his diary entries for 1935. Based on these early reflections, Klemperer published an essay, "Café Europe," after the war, in which he proposed a concept of Europe based on a certain mindset or *Geist* that was rooted in the culture of ancient Jerusalem, Athens, and Rome. Klemperer's notion of Europe abandoned geography as a delineating factor, substituting a common humanist legacy for geography. In 1935, Klemperer predicted the end of humanist Europe at the hands of the Nazis. For him, it was now avowedly Germany that did not belong to Europe: "Deutschland ist doch gewiß kein Europa mehr."[43] Exposed to the realities of daily life under the Nazis, Klemperer had little patience with émigré friends in Lima when they complained that they missed home. "I envy them, and they feel exiled," he wrote.[44] The idea that one could miss Europe seemed bizarre to the humanist, who was convinced both of the need to leave Germany without delay and of the fact that "Europe had ceased to be Europe."[45] If the European Geist was to survive, Klemperer believed that it was going to have to be elsewhere.

Regrettably, neither Istanbul nor Lima nor Jerusalem offered to take Klemperer in. Technically categorized a Jew, the baptized Christian was stuck in Germany, probably clinging to a legal loophole, where he spent the next decade writing the now famous diary that documented the Nazis' systematic dehumanization of his own people. Curtius, who briefly was targeted by Nazis, also remained in Germany, albeit under entirely different circumstances. Curtius ceased to show any further interest in moving to Turkey and managed to retain his professorship at the University of Bonn.[46] Here he wrote his major work, *Europäische Literatur und lateinisches Mittelalter* (*European Literature and the Latin Middle Ages*), published in 1948. To this day, his stance vis-à-vis Nazism has never been adequately clarified. At worst, the decision to continue working in Germany seems opportunistic and politically suspect; at best, it seems like an act of "inner emigration." This term has come to denote the act of deliberately withdrawing from social and political life in the face of overwhelming opposition. Inner emigration, however, is in fact not a useful way of thinking about the scholarly work produced during the Nazi era because it blurs the boundaries between complicity, conformism, and resistance.[47] Yet, whatever stance we take on the matter, inner emigration was not an option for Auerbach, whose concerns were far more a matter of life and death. He thought that chairing a department at Istanbul University might offer a way out and even be financially advantageous, but, for reasons that differed from Klemperer's, he had reservations of his own. He had heard Spitzer's and others' stories about Turkey, and, quite simply, he did not like the idea of living there: "This world"—by which he presumably meant Turkey—might be "quite good for a guest performance, but certainly not for long-term work."[48] From the outset, Istanbul was envisioned only as a way station, and one wonders what living there for eleven years meant to Auerbach's work. The task of this book, then, is to uncover the relationship between what Auerbach fleetingly called "this world," that is, the secular Turkish Republic that underwent radical Westernization reforms in the 1930s, and the work he produced once he joined his fellow émigrés in Turkish exile.

Accepting that exile was inevitable coincided not only with Auerbach's Italian journey in September 1935 but also with reading an excerpt from Benjamin's childhood memoirs. The previous year, Auerbach had tried to contact Benjamin via an address in Denmark, most likely Bertolt Brecht's.[49] He had heard of a job opening for a professor of German literature in São Paolo and wanted to help Benjamin escape his increasingly desperate situation in Paris. For reasons unknown, the letter never reached Benjamin. When Erich and his wife Marie Auerbach later came across Benjamin's memoirs in a Zurich newspaper, Auerbach wrote directly to the author in Paris emphasizing that the excerpt conjured up "memories of a home that vanished so long ago."[50] The vignettes, which center on turn-of-the-century Berlin, vividly captured the Auerbachs' own childhood experiences. In a second letter to Benjamin, dated Italy, early October 1935, Auerbach lamented the impossibility of Benjamin's memoirs being published in toto under the present conditions. Poignantly, he recognized that the number of German readers likely to value Benjamin's work was ever diminishing at the hands of the Nazis.[51] The question of readership continued to trouble Auerbach in later years when it came to his own exilic work. It would be the task of another exiled intellectual to find a readership for Benjamin, who died in 1940 while trying to escape the Nazi invasion of France. Theodor W. Adorno arranged and posthumously published Benjamin's now famous memoirs in 1950 under the title *Berliner Kindheit um neunzehnhundert* (*Berlin Childhood around 1900*).[52]

In many ways, Auerbach's Italian journey constituted one of the turning points in his life. It was in Italy that he resumed his correspondence with Benjamin, acknowledging the irrecoverable loss of the world they once shared. In fact, it was Florence, the city that had exiled Dante in 1302, whence Auerbach wrote to Benjamin. While staying in the Villa La Limonaia, built on the grounds of a fourteenth-century castle and surrounded by Tuscan forest, Auerbach reflected on the politics at home and faced the certainty of impending exile. In his letter, he tried to describe the conditions at Marburg University, where he had been trying to work since Hitler seized power:

I live there among honorable people who are not of our stock, who have completely different presuppositions—and they all think as I do. That is nice, but it leads to foolishness: it gives one to believe that there is something on which one could build—while the opinion of individuals, even if there are many of them, doesn't matter at all. This trip has freed me from this error for the first time.[53]

Writing from the grounds of a fourteenth-century castle in Dante's hometown foreshadows the ways in which Auerbach's own exile would soon gain meaning. For the humanist Auerbach, Italy occupied a seminal place in Europe's cultural and literary history. As I pointed out earlier, Auerbach's study of Dante demonstrated the relevance of exile and memory to the emergence of something new, namely, national literature. He argued that for Dante, "political disaster was the *subito movimento di cose*, the sudden outward change, which invariably produces a grave crisis."[54] Dante overcame this crisis, he said, by experimenting with new linguistic and narrative forms and thereby finding a truly "European voice."[55] In the most concrete terms, Auerbach already seems to have known how to tackle exile in a productive way. Years before the disaster of 1933, he argued with regard to the *Commedia* that the "mental confusion [*Verirrung*] which is the point of departure [*Ausgangspunkt*] of the poem" precedes the year 1300, when Dante was still living in Florence and the "catastrophe was still to come"; "this date, and what follows—exile, vain hopes, poverty, proud withdrawal—has no connection with his mental confusion; they are his deserved and appropriate earthly fate, they belong to him like the dignity of a high office. You will suffer and be unhappy, say Brunetto and Cacciaguida; but remember only to be proud and to preserve your standing; its rightness will be made manifest."[56] The frame that Auerbach drew here for Dante's exilic work anticipates the way in which his own exile manifested itself in his scholarship: departing from an Ausgangspunkt, he found his own European voice in the writing of *Mimesis*.

Perhaps it was during his Italian journey that Auerbach conceived of writing something unique in exile that, like the *Commedia*, would both signify the fulfillment of the old world and set the stage for a new beginning. From Italy, he wrote to the Dante specialist Karl Vossler (1872–1949) that his project on realism would have to "wait for a while; there may still be more to get out of it."[57] We do not know for certain whether Auerbach was referring here to the concept of figura and its historical manifestations.[58] But irrespective of whether his figura idea was born before or after he went into exile, it is clear that the plan for such a study came to fruition once he settled in Istanbul and Angelo Giuseppe Roncalli granted him access to the library of a Dominican church.[59] It was while in Turkish exile that Auerbach recognized the specific view of history that informs Dante's *Commedia*, namely, that a figural interpretation of past and present events had dominated during the Middle Ages.[60]

On returning from Italy to Marburg in mid-October 1935, Auerbach received the fateful letter from the university. His dismissal from Marburg

University was sealed, and he now hoped beyond anything that he would be hired in Istanbul. For this, he had the support not only of Spitzer but also of an Italian scholar whose work on Vico's philosophy of history Auerbach had translated in the late 1920s. The scholar in question was Benedetto Croce (1866–1952), a historicist and humanist who had influenced and supported Auerbach early in his career. Besides Croce, the fellow Dante enthusiast Vossler also recommended Auerbach for the vacancy in Istanbul.[61] Still, the Marburg professor had to wait until August 1936 before learning he would be made chair of the faculty for Western languages and literatures. This was the summer in which the Berlin Olympic Games provided a brief *Judenschonzeit*, a period during which the international community was lulled into thinking that Germany's Jews were being treated humanely. Klemperer quite clearly foresaw that this time would end after a few short months.[62] Understandably, he was all the more dismayed to learn during this summer that Spitzer had insisted that the professorship be offered to a scholar who spoke fluent French. Unlike Auerbach, who went to Geneva in 1936 to refresh his French, Klemperer complained that he never had this opportunity.[63] And, having missed out on the foreign appointment, he now had to submit to life under the Nazi regime: he turned in the keys to his office and returned his books to the university library.

Contrary to what Klemperer seemed to believe, Auerbach's French skills were not the reason Istanbul University hired him. Neither Curtius nor Klemperer, but rather the medievalist Hans Rheinfelder, professor of Romance philology at Munich University, came close to being employed in Istanbul. But, in its final report, the search committee evaluated Auerbach's and Rheinfelder's portfolios, and Spitzer, who chaired the committee, backed Auerbach, making a persuasive case to the dean and the university president. The two other members of the committee were the philosopher Hans Reichenbach and the economist Alexander Rüstow—with whom Auerbach would become, as we will see, engaged in an ongoing conversation about the genesis of European culture. As to be expected, the committee supported Auerbach because of his tremendous erudition, recognition in the field, experience, and maturity. Illuminating in this report is, however, the way in which the committee members presented Auerbach as someone essential to the modernization of the university. The report reads: "M. Auerbach a particuilèrement travaillé sur l'histoire littérature de la France et de l'Italie, qu'il met en rapport avec les plus grand courants de civilisation (Antiquité, Christianisme, Laïcisation modern) et il sait voir la civilisation occidentale du dehors, en critique"[*sic*].[64]

The search committee highlighted Auerbach's ability to teach European literary history from antiquity onward, encompassing the age of Christianity and modern secularism. This would be valuable when it came to secularizing the tertiary system. The report also emphasized that Auerbach approached Western culture from a critical point of view. In making this point, the search committee promoted the European scholar's distanced approach to Western culture as conducive to the interests of the university. The search committee's report offers proof that the émigrés well understood the university's concerns about Westernizing the education system. At the time, the university administration was hesitant to hire any scholar who might prioritize the interests of the scholar's own country of origin. In fact, when the dean presented the committee's recommendation to the university president, Cemil Bilsel, the dean argued that the committee recommended Auerbach over Rheinfelder because of Auerbach's Jewishness, but the Marburg professor was also, objectively speaking, the better choice.

Since the faculty for Western languages and literatures was essential to Turkey's nation-building process, the minister of culture himself was involved in the search. When Bilsel communicated the committee's report to the ministry of culture, he argued that hiring Rheinfelder would likely please the German government; on the other hand, there was a risk that Rheinfelder might spread German propaganda in Istanbul. In a follow-up letter of June 1936, Bilsel further supported Auerbach's case by referring to the advice given by the Turkish ambassador to Germany. The ambassador was convinced that it would behoove Turkey to hire a professor whose ties to Germany had been effectively severed. He believed that hiring the "superior Jew" over Rheinfelder would not necessarily prompt the intervention of German officials.[65] In the following weeks, the ministry of culture followed the advice of the university chancellor, dean, and ambassador to Germany and offered Spitzer's position to Auerbach.

The Istanbul University archive holds documents that reveal the reasons for choosing Auerbach over a pool of other outstanding German scholars seeking refuge from Nazi Germany. In summary, we can say that what spoke in favor of Auerbach were not only his wide-ranging literary interests but his critical view of Western Europe and his status as an outcast from German society. To date, contemporary Auerbach scholars have been unaware of the fact that there were important political reasons for Auerbach's appointment, interpreting the story in essentially biographical terms. Yet, it was precisely because Auerbach could not be functionalized by the German propaganda machine that he proved so desirable to the Turkish dean, university chancellor, and minister of culture. In other words, the idea of detachment that Auerbach detected in Dante, Vico, and Proust now, coincidentally, became a powerful tool for leveraging his own exile.

In some measure, Auerbach actually fulfilled his promise as a secular scholar. His response to the systematic Aryanization of German society was neither to retreat into religion nor to lobby for Zionism. The philologist led a largely secular existence—we can even say that in exile he became an agnostic scholar, interested in the cultural work of Christianity and Judaism alike.[66] The influence of Islam on Europe, on the other hand, remained a blind spot in his work. If Auerbach turned to the Hebrew Bible in exile, it was neither for theological reasons nor, I think, to provide succor. The Bible was useful as a source work for compiling a secular history of European literature. Vico, the advocate of humanist education in a Cartesian age, had provided Auerbach with the critical tools for his own outlook on history. Equipped with a broad understanding of Western European culture, a historical perspective, and a humanist vision, Auerbach was well prepared to approach the concept of Europe from a secular point of view.

Humanism's Exile

The humanist perspective that we associate with Auerbach's work dates to the fourteenth century when Greco-Roman culture began to be seen as the wellspring of European learning. I am referring here to the period known as Renaissance humanism, with its rediscovery and revival of classical Greco-Roman literature and the other arts. Its advocates called for the comprehensive reform of culture and the transformation of an apparently "dark" and ignorant age into a new order.[67] Klemperer dated the birth hour of Renaissance humanism to a letter by Francis Petrarch (1304–1374) in 1350 concerning the ascent of a mountain near Avignon.[68] Inspired by a mountain ascent in Livy's *History of Rome*, Petrarch said he decided to climb a mountain himself to "see what so great an elevation had to offer."[69] Having arrived at the summit, Petrarch opened a copy of

Augustine's *Confessions*, which he claimed to have carried with him. In it, he found a passage that he understood as a call to direct his "inward eye" at himself. Klemperer's attribution to Petrarch is enlightening because it stresses a characteristic feature of humanism—critical scrutiny and self-inquiry.[70] Above all, we see how Petrarch forged a rapprochement between classical learning and Christian thought: he took a crucial step when he coupled himself to Augustine while simultaneously reenacting Livy's account of a mountain ascent in antiquity.[71]

The return to the Latin classics and their imitation in the present defines the initial move of humanism, as exemplified in Petrarch. According to Auerbach, early humanists "sought out the manuscripts of those classics, imitated their style, and adopted their conception of literature, based on classical rhetoric."[72] Klemperer referred to the humanist of the fourteenth century as a "skilled laborer of remembering."[73] Subsequently, scholars also rediscovered Greek literature—to a great extent via the Byzantine scholars who left Constantinople after its Ottoman conquest in 1453.[74] This ongoing interest in the literature of antiquity was related, as Auerbach explained, to the idea of the Latin *humanitas*, meaning "'humanity,' 'human civilization,' [and] 'education worthy of the human idea.'"[75] It was this pedagogical notion of humanitas that inspired the rediscovery, translation, and imitation of Greco-Roman manuscripts.[76] If humanitas shaped the transfiguration of the European Middle Ages, it was not before the nineteenth century that German scholars established the term *humanism* to identify a certain trajectory of culture, history, and learning. Auerbach's own humanist perspective was consequently one that honored the early humanists of the fourteenth century and, at the same time, looked to the nineteenth-century tradition of philology and historicism.

To this day, humanism serves as a capacious umbrella for various cultural, political, educational, and scholarly approaches. Such approaches range from the classicism and vernacular humanism of the Renaissance to the historicist humanism of the eighteenth and nineteenth centuries. But we can also think of the schism between bourgeois and socialist forms of humanism in the first half of the twentieth century and Edward Said's revival of humanism's secular impetus at the century's end. Among all these competing definitions, what is relevant for us here are the fate of humanism during the Nazi regime and the role played by humanism in the modernization and secularization of Turkey.

This brings us to the question of Nazi Germany's position on humanism. Having survived the war, Klemperer gave a lecture in 1953 in the German Democratic Republic, hoping to shed light on the matter. In his lecture, Klemperer laid out the formation of European culture through humanism, the renunciation of the humanist perspective by the Nazis, and humanism's new role under socialism. He argued that a humanist European culture that traced its origins to the Greeks and Romans was of little interest to the Nazis, who believed that humanism tampered with what they thought of as the Germanic spirit.[77] In short, Nazi ideology had no place for the humanist tradition because humanism postulated a European culture that was not exclusively Germanic in origin. The Nazis were indeed antihumanists, but it would be false to follow Klemperer in constructing a direct link between Hitler's rise to power and the decline of humanism in the early twentieth century. Klemperer's 1953 lecture needs, at least to a certain degree, to be understood within its Cold War context. The philologist noted that a "Humanist Red Army" might now promote socialism. He went so far as to connect the collapse of European culture not only to the progression from capitalism and imperialism to fascism but also to the doctrine of the *Herrenmensch* (master race) prevalent in the "old" humanist thinking. In its place, Klemperer envisioned a more inclusive "new" form of socialist humanism.[78] Instead of only educating the elite, this new humanism, he explained, was committed to educating every citizen and raising the level of literacy for the ultimate advancement of civilization as a whole.

Suzanne Marchand's work gives us a more nuanced understanding of why classical humanism lost ground in early twentieth-century Germany. In contradistinction to Klemperer, Marchand reminds us that humanism was already in decline prior to 1933: by as early as 1914, humanism was under siege from two sides in the German Empire.[79] On the one hand, the German nationalist faction claimed "allegiance to classical models to be treasonous and/or unhelpful in an era of national emergency." The Orientalist faction, on the other hand, "claimed the ability to uncover and publicize a deeper, richer, history of cultural development than that offered by the classicists."[80] In Marchand's view, classical humanists had failed to establish a new, more encompassing, system of universal norms and values that would accommodate Orientalistik, the discipline dedicated to studying the languages and literatures of the Orient. Such a reorientation of humanism, according to Marchand, might have offered an alternative trajectory for explaining the emergence of civilization.[81] Humanism's decline, then, was due to two factors: first, the resistance to change and second, the widespread Germanophilia and Aryanization of culture in Nazi Germany.

By the time Auerbach was dismissed from Marburg University in 1935, classical humanism had lost much of its cache and most humanists had gone into exile. But interest in humanism was certainly rekindled in the struggle against fascism.[82] This became clear at a large, international congress in Paris in June 1935, a congress that stood under the banner of humanism and antifascism. With the support of many exiled German writers, including Anna Seghers (1900–1983) and Bertolt Brecht (1898–1956), and under the presidency of André Malraux (1901–1976) and André Gide (1869–1951), the international congress attracted worldwide attention. Approximately three thousand seats were reserved at the conference site for the five-day event. The seats quickly sold out and hundreds stood on the street to listen to the discussions via loudspeakers.[83] The conference also had wide international reach. Writers from a number of foreign countries participated in panels organized around topics like cultural legacy, nation and culture, the individual, humanism, and the writer's role in society. Prominent writers including Max Brod, Maxim Gorki, Heinrich and Klaus Mann, Lion Feuchtwanger, Boris Pasternak, Robert Musil, E. M. Forster, and Aldous Huxley were among the invitees. The main purpose of the congress was to discuss the means of defending "culture," which writers saw as being threatened and destroyed by the spread of fascism.[84] Key words like *culture* and *humanism* were not narrowly defined but left open to discussion. At the opening address, André Gide made an attempt to define *culture* in terms of the sum of the cultural particularities of each country. This he claimed as "our common good, it belongs to all of us, it is international."[85]

Although the writers at the Paris conference were unequivocal in their stance against fascism, not all participants were supporters of socialism. The question of what constituted humanist culture and its capacity to unite such politically diverse writers thus turned out to be crucial for the future of the movement. Polemical statements regarding the role of humanism vis-à-vis fascism were common in this highly politicized atmosphere. Maxim Gorki (1868–1936), most notably, drew a distinction between proletarian humanism—the humanism of Marx and Lenin—and bourgeois humanism.[86] Klaus Mann (1906–1949) took a similar position,

Gea Augsbourg (1902–1974), Conference on humanism in Paris, 1935. Front cover of *La Bête Noire*, no. 4, 1935. 1: André Gide, 2: André Malraux, 3: Jean Richard Bloch, 4: Vaillant-Couturier, 5: Eugène Dabit, 6: Heinrich Mann, 7: Nizan, 8: Kisch, 9: Waldo Franck, 10: Gérome, 11: Henri Clerc, 12: Jean Cassou, 13: Ehrembourg, 14: Julien Benda, 15: Rappoport, 17: Jean Lurçat, 19: Forster, 20: Pasternak, 21: Aldous Huxley, 22: Luc Durtain, 23: Kolsoff, 25: Gold, 26: Vildrac, 27: Dujardin, 28: Babel, 29: Plisnier, 30: Madeleine Paz, 31: Jean Guehenno, 32: Aragon, 33: H. Poulaille. (Figures 16, 18, and 24 unidentified by Augsbourg.) Source: Special Collections and Visual Resources, Getty Research Institute.

claiming that "socialist humanism is the complex and absolute antithesis to fascism."[87] Bifurcating socialist and bourgeois writers, Paul Nizan (1905–1940) likewise argued that only socialist humanists recognized the significance of the "concrete conditions of human life."[88] Although such views survived in Klemperer's postwar distinction between the old and new humanism, there was no consensus about discrediting one form over the other.[89] Rather, the conference organizers tried to build a bridge between both understandings of humanism. Regarded as the common cultural legacy of socialist as well as bourgeois writers, their aim was to defend the humanist tradition against the threat of its antithesis, fascism.

If we simply follow the distinction made in Paris, we would have to say that the form of humanism, which Auerbach took into Istanbul exile, was a bourgeois one. But as I show, such a distinction would do Auerbach an injustice. At first reading, the famous opening of *Mimesis*—"Readers of the *Odyssey* will remember"—seems exemplary of the kind of elitism that Klemperer and Gorki detected in "old," that is to say, bourgeois humanism.[90] Who, after all, could count themselves among the privileged readers of Homer and, better yet, recall it at the author's bidding? Yet, reducing Auerbach's work to this charge overlooks the fact that he achieved in exile something quite unprecedented. He might not have addressed the highly politicized debate of Paris 1935 and its implications for valuing literature in a time of crisis. He was, however, especially interested in the relationship between social rupture and literary representation. His work on nineteenth-century French literature, for example, shows how characters of the "lower" orders became the subject of serious literary representation. To be sure, his work had little to do with the literary realism that, in the aftermath of Paris 1935, Georg Lukács and others labeled the true manifestation of Marxist aesthetics: maybe this explains why *Mimesis* was never published in the German Democratic Republic. Unlike these committed Marxists, Auerbach was not primarily interested in the representation of class and the everyday. His interest in realism centered on the concept of mimesis as an aesthetic mode that shapes the way we think about the past. When he distinguished between Homer and the Hebrew Bible in the first chapter of *Mimesis*, it was not to analyze the respective treatment of daily life. Instead, he was concerned with how the relationship between past and present events was influenced by the blending of the Homeric and biblical styles in the Christian era. Auerbach's history of Western European literature was hence anchored in more than just classical antiquity and Christian thought. While in Turkish exile, Auerbach added a third foundation stone to Western European culture, namely, Judaism.

Here we come to one of the central issues addressed by this book, namely, that Auerbach's secular Judeo-Christian humanism evolved in the encounter with the humanist reforms in Turkey. The humanism that was promoted in 1930s and 1940s Turkey was, in the first instance, a brand of humanism that adapted the Greco-Roman model for the needs of a secular, national culture. While Auerbach was chairing the faculty for Western languages and literatures at Istanbul University, the ministry for education introduced a humanist reform that put into practice what some participants had aspired to at the 1935 conference in Paris—a classical, secular humanism that tried to implement some socialist ideals. It is the task of the following chapter to map out the contact zones of Auerbach's humanism and the humanist reforms of Hasan Ali Yücel, the minister of education. Yücel's reforms brought literacy and other forms of learning to Anatolian villagers while at the same time emulating the classical model on behalf of a secular, bourgeois urban elite.

This brings me to ask whether the meeting points between Auerbach's and Yücel's humanist visions were merely incidental. *East West Mimesis* answers this quite conclusively: it shows that, in the 1930s, the Turkish and Western European worlds were more closely imbricated and more acutely aware of one another's cultural politics than we tend to think. The Paris congress was dominated by writers from France, Germany, and the Soviet Union, but it also reached beyond these countries. There were invitees from Portugal, Bulgaria, Scandinavia, China, and—important for our purposes—Turkey. The writer and diplomat Yakup Kadri (1889–1974), also known as Yakup Kadri Karaosmanoğlu, was specifically invited to talk about humanism at the congress. Whether Yakup Kadri actually participated is not clear, but this is also not really the point. Wolfgang Klein, who in the 1980s recovered and edited the congress protocol, confirms that at some point during the planning of the conference, Yakup Kadri was slated to preside over a panel on humanism.[91] Surviving in the protocol is a reference to a message sent by a group of Turkish writers who demonstrated their commitment to the cause of the congress. Their message was delivered to the panel on "Nation and Culture."[92] Yakup Kadri's selection is easily explained: he, together with the author Yahya Kemal (also known as Yahya Kemal Beyatlı, 1884–1958), was one of the country's leading humanist intellectuals.[93]

Overlapping Histories

What Auerbach knew about the significance of humanism in Turkey we do not know for certain. During their meeting in Italy, Spitzer probably informed him about the restructuring of the humanities along humanist and secular lines. Auerbach, in turn, would have likely expressed his concerns about the conditions for non-Muslims in Turkey. Needless to say, having already been victim to anti-Semitism, this was a pressing concern for all prospective émigrés. But even before Auerbach met Spitzer in Italy in 1935, there were ready opportunities for Auerbach to gather information about the relationship between Muslims and non-Muslims in Turkey. Since the Ottoman Empire had been Germany's ally in World War I and Auerbach was a soldier at the time, Ottomans were not unknown players in the political and military scene. For both empires, the outcome of World War I meant the end of imperialism. Unlike Germany, the Ottoman Empire was occupied and partitioned by French, British, and Italian forces. While the German Empire evolved into the Weimar Republic without further military confrontations, it took another war, the War of Independence (1919–1922), to establish the Turkish Republic in 1923.

Besides this general knowledge about the transformation of the Ottoman Empire into the Turkish Republic, Auerbach was likely to have had some insight into the treatment of non-Muslim minorities in the Ottoman Empire. A murder was committed on March 15, 1921, in his very own neighborhood, an incident that made front-page headlines in Berlin newspapers. The target of the murder was Talat Paşa, the former Ottoman interior minister, who had sought refuge in Berlin after the occupation of the Ottoman Empire. The murder was committed in broad daylight at Steinplatz in Berlin-Charlottenburg—at the corner of Hardenbergstraße and Fasanenstraße, where Auerbach was then living. The incident attracted considerable local and international attention because the murderer was an Armenian student motivated by revenge: Talat Paşa was the prime mover behind what is now widely acknowledged as the Armenian genocide.[94]

Berlin newspapers were sympathetic to Talat Paşa as a loyal ally of the Germans during the previous war. However, they also acknowledged that he was murdered in retaliation for the *Armeniergreuel*, atrocities against Armenians. This suggests that, regardless of where Germans stood in the political spectrum, they were not entirely oblivious to Turkey's treatment of minorities and, specifically, its treatment of Armenians. For writers like Franz Werfel, this prompted the writing of a novel about the suffering of Armenians, *Die vierzig Tage des Musa Dagh* (*The Forty Days of Musa Dagh*), first published in 1933.[95] There is no indication as to whether Auerbach read Werfel's novel. Yet its very existence suggests that Western Europeans were somehow aware of the changing relationship between the Muslim majority and ethno-religious minorities during the transition to a Turkish nation-state. Margaret Anderson proves this point by showing the extent to which Germans—politicians, scholars, and journalists on the left, as well as German-speaking Zionists and liberals—knew about Ottoman atrocities against Armenians, even though they downplayed them in the press.[96]

We tend to think of places as being geographically, even culturally, discrete. Yet the topography of Berlin-Charlottenburg was, even then, marked by events unfolding more than a thousand miles to the southeast. We need only look to the example of another family living in this tony Berlin neighborhood. The Auerbachs' son Clemens (1923–2004) was born

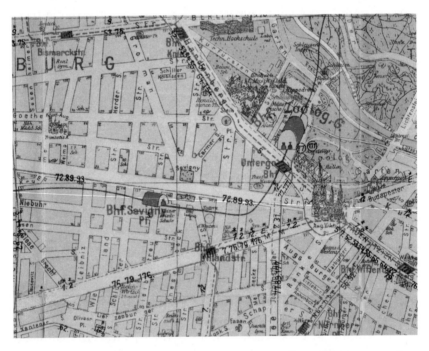

Berlin-Charlottenburg, 1921, detail of a 1921 Berlin map by Pharus. By permission of Verlag Pharus-Plan.

the same year as one Isaak Behar, the son of Ottoman Jews who had left Istanbul in 1915. Like many others, the Behars headed for Berlin, where they joined a community of approximately 150 Sephardic families.[97] In the 1920s, Behar senior worked for his brother in a carpet store called Cohen & Behar Orientteppiche on Kantstraße. This is where the family of five also lived, right around the corner from the apartment shared by the newly married Auerbach, his wife Marie, and his parents.[98] Perhaps the young Clemens and Isaak played together, or maybe the families only glimpsed one another on the street. It is history's tragic irony that the Behars, who had tried to find a better and safer life in Weimar Germany, themselves became the victims of the Holocaust. The Auerbachs managed to leave Germany and find refuge in the very city where the Behars had once lived. The Sephardic family, on the other hand, was destroyed by the Nazis. In 1938, they witnessed the burning of the synagogue on Fasanenstraße, and in 1942, Isaak Behar's parents and two sisters were deported and murdered in Riga. Isaak was the only member of his family to survive the war in hiding. More than half a century later, he preserved the story of his survival in *Versprich mir, daß Du am Leben bleibst* (*Promise Me You'll Stay Alive*).

2

Turkish Humanism

THERE WAS A TIME when Istanbul University was thought of as Germany's biggest institution of higher learning abroad.[1] When Auerbach arrived at Istanbul University, he met indeed scores of German scholars—sharing both a similar cultural background and the flight from Nazism.[2] At the faculty for Western languages and literatures, Auerbach took over from Spitzer a number of younger scholars, among them Traugott Fuchs, Spitzer's former assistant in Cologne, who described his arrival in Istanbul as "a Renaissance-like joy of a return to the conditions that existed in certain highly intellectual circles in pre-Nazi Germany."[3] There were also Spitzer's former assistant and lover Rosemarie Burkart and lecturers Heinz Anstock and Eva Buck.[4] Among the well-known scholars hired by the university were the ancient historian Clemens Bosch, who was then working on a book on Hellenistic history; the economist Alexander Rüstow, who planned to write a historical critique of civilization; and Ernst von Aster, who specialized in the history of philosophy and concepts of space and time.[5] Among Auerbach's other inspiring new colleagues was also the physicist and philosopher Hans Reichenbach, a former colleague of Albert Einstein in Berlin, who had served on the search committee for Auerbach's position and chaired the department of philosophy at Istanbul University. Like von Aster, Reichenbach had published on the philosophy of space and time before emigrating and now applied himself to the foundations and structure of knowledge. During his tenure in Istanbul, Reichenbach gave lectures and seminars in which he discussed the ideas for his book, one of them being the rejection of phenomenalist positivism in defense of realism.[6]

How productive this intellectual, interdisciplinary environment must have been for someone like Auerbach, whose own interests lay in the genesis of realism and the concept of history in Western European literature. By the time Auerbach arrived, German émigrés had already formed a stimulating academic community working on some of the fundamental questions of their time. Much of this community lived in Bebek, a district on the European shores of the Bosporus where the university had secured accommodation for its new German employees and their families. Since Robert College, an American-sponsored private school, had been established in Bebek in the nineteenth century, the neighborhood was also home to a number of Americans and other Europeans associated with the college. Émigrés ran into each other not only at the university and in Bebek but also in Pera, where most of the major European consulates, cultural centers, and foreign-language bookstores were located. A few months after Auerbach's arrival in Istanbul, his wife Marie and son Clemens followed him into exile. With them came their furniture and sixty-odd cases of books, and the family moved into a house in Bebek. This district of Istanbul was one of the prettiest places to live, with elegant wooden houses stacked on the hills above the harbor. While this picturesque setting was surely no compensation for the life these exiles had left behind, their memoirs emphasize their sense of a "common Western cultural heritage" and shared experience.[7] What created a common ground for these scholars, who, after all, came from a range of disciplines, was the experience of being cast into a new place and the need to deal with the bureaucratic mess of passports, visas, and permits. They shared, too, a common linguistic, often humanist background, intellectual interests, the need for mutual support, and, above all, a deep concern for what was happening in Europe. That this promoted a feeling of interconnectedness and the basis for intellectual exchange seems only natural.

Having settled into the émigré community, the newcomers could not overlook Istanbul's rich cultural history dating back to the ancient Greeks. The daily trek from Bebek to the university turned up the relics of Istanbul's Greek, Roman, Byzantine, and Ottoman pasts. The route took them along the Bosporus, adorned with dilapidated Ottoman palaces,

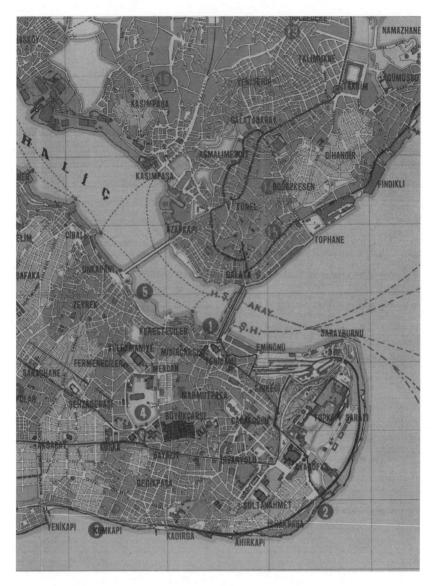

The Golden Horn with Pera in the north and old Constantinople in the south, 1934.
Istanbul University is marked with 4. Excerpt from supplementary map in Osman Nuri
Ergin, *İstanbul Şehri Rehberi* (Istanbul: Türk Anonim Şirketi, 1934). Source: University
of Michigan map library.

Margaret Bourke-White, Entrance of the University of Istanbul, circa 1940. Photo:
Margaret Bourke-White/Time & Life Pictures. By permission of Getty Images.

and a number of smaller synagogues, mosques, and churches. From there,
they crossed the bustling Galata Bridge. On his first day in Istanbul, the
law professor Ernst Hirsch, for one, paused on the bridge to get a sense of
bearings:

Looking at the people's heads, I was struck by the multiplicity and variation of skull
shapes and physiognomies. Measured against this living reality, National Socialist
race theory was turned into a farce. Here, in the betwixt and between of human
types jostling along the "Köprü," it was not only the Ottoman Empire that lived on
as a multi-ethnic state. There appeared facial characteristics straight out of antiquity,
characteristics that bore a bewildering resemblance to depictions of Babylonian, Hittite, even Egyptian, Hellenic, and Roman sculptures. The many-thousand-year human history of Asia Minor passed before my eyes.[8]

Auerbach, like Hirsch, was also tempted to make a connection between
Istanbul's ruins, history, and present inhabitants. The route from his Bebek
home to the university took him via the old walls of Byzantine Constantinople, past the Ottoman Porte, the Hippodrome, the Roman cisterns,

the Blue Mosque, and the Ottoman cemeteries. Soon after moving into the house in Bebek, Auerbach wrote to Benjamin with his own impressions of the city: Istanbul, he wrote in January 1937, is

a wonderfully situated, but also unpleasant and rough city consisting of two different parts: the old Stambool, of Greek and Turkish origin, which still preserves much of the patina of its historic landscape, and the "new" Pera, a caricature and completion of the European colonization of the 19th century, now in complete collapse. There are the remains of dreadful luxury shops; Jews, Greeks, Armenians, all languages, a grotesque social life, and the palaces of the former European embassies that are now consulates. All along the Bosporus one also sees the decayed, or decaying, museum-quality nineteenth-century palaces of sultans and pashas in a half-oriental, half-rococo style.[9]

Auerbach's letter to Benjamin touches on many of the questions that interest me about the eleven years the philologist spent in Istanbul. We find here questions about origins, imitation, assimilation, and mimicry; authentic versus inauthentic representations of Europe; Turkey's refashioning as a Western nation; the fault lines between Western Europe and Turkey; and, even, the status of non-Muslims in the modern nation. The letter specifically invites us to think about the correlation between Turkey's national renewal and its disavowal of the Ottoman historical legacy. And it allows us to glimpse the dynamics and paradoxes entailed in the Westernization process of 1930s Turkey. Turkish cultural politics aimed to create a modern, national culture in the image of Renaissance Europe. In examining this fundamental shift, we will find that the hiring decisions at Istanbul University, as we have already seen in Auerbach's case, were not accidental; they were part of the government's concerted effort to secularize and modernize university education. In dealing with this constellation of issues, this chapter also examines the role of the Turkish humanist movement in mapping a new cultural heritage onto Turkey's national territory.

The Turkish humanist movement introduced classical Western education in order to create a common frame of reference for Turkey and the West. Its proponents believed that Western classical literature was capable of affecting a "Turkish renaissance." The ensuing *hümanist kültür reformları*, the humanist culture reforms, officially announced by the minister of education in 1939, culminated in the translation of hundreds of Western classics; the staging of Western plays, concerts, and operas;

the compiling of dictionaries; a new journal on translation; and the training of teachers in classical and modern Western languages and literatures. Although Turkish humanism—primarily a pedagogical and cultural movement—developed an effective cultural grammar for translating the Western habitus, it ended in the postwar period.[10] As we will see, strong anti-Greek sentiments and anticommunist allegations against the main architect of the reform, Yücel, brought the reforms to an abrupt halt. Nonetheless, the achievements of the humanist reforms are still of vital importance today: among them are the national library, the standardization of the vernacular language, the translation project, and the country's ongoing—if contested—commitment to secular culture and education.

In light of the humanist culture reforms that governed the university curricula during Auerbach's time in Istanbul, it would be misleading to characterize Auerbach as having been cleaved from European traditions of learning. As I pointed out in the introduction, this view was promulgated by Edward Said, who thought that Auerbach saw the Orient and Islam as "fundamentally alienated from and in opposition to Europe, the European tradition of Christian Latinity, as well as to the putative authority of ecclesia, humanistic learning, and cultural community."[11] Said's image of Auerbach estranged in an Oriental world might well have served Said's own rhetorical purposes as an intellectual in exile, but my research shows something different.[12]

In fact, Auerbach found humanism at home in Istanbul at the very moment it was being banished from Europe. This chapter argues that the entire concept of modernity in 1930s Turkey was based on European learning—specifically on the humanistic tradition. This insight radically upsets existing views. In making this claim, I do not mean to downplay the significance of the Orientalist stereotyping of Turkey in the Western European imagination: work by Srinivas Aravamudan, Meyda Yeğenoğlu, and Reina Lewis, for instance, creates a powerful testimony to the kinds of racial and sexual discourses that shaped Western thinking about the Ottoman Empire and modern Turkey. I wish to emphasize, however, that Turkish experiences informed Auerbach's view of Istanbul in more complex and powerful ways than have been hitherto acknowledged.

Of course I am not the first to take Said to task, nor the first to interrogate the exile experience.[13] Emily Apter, for one, casts doubt on Auerbach's "self-portrait as a lonely European scholar" and points, as I do, to the "sizable professional, artistic, and political European community that was well established in Istanbul . . . by the time he arrived in Turkey."[14] Indeed, when Auerbach arrived in Istanbul in the fall of 1936, the German émigré community already comprised a vibrant, multidisciplinary network of scholars. But my argument here extends beyond the community of émigrés living in the seaside neighborhood of Bebek; it also links Auerbach's Turkish exile to the humanist reforms themselves. Whereas Auerbach scholars tend to characterize Istanbul as radically different from the West, Auerbach's personal correspondence and the broader, transnational context of Turkish–German relations tell another story. In 1938, Auerbach himself described Istanbul as a city with a *geschichtlich gewachsenen Schönheit, die unsereinem am meisten Freude macht*, a "historically evolved beauty that gives the likes of us the greatest joy." In his letter to Benjamin a year earlier, Auerbach had emphasized the cosmopolitan nature of Istanbul in rather negative terms. Here, however, we see how the émigré began to view the city's heterogeneous character in a different light, linking it to the classical heritage of Western Europe:

It is not only the hills on the banks [of the Bosporus] with their mostly decrepit palaces, not only the mosques, minarets, mosaics, miniatures, manuscripts, and Koran verses; but also the indescribable variety of people with their [different] ways of life and dress, the fish and vegetables that one gets to eat, the coffee and the cigarettes, the residue of Islamic piety and perfection of form. Istanbul is, after all, still a fundamentally Hellenistic city, for the Arab, Armenian, Jewish, and now the dominant Turkish element, too, all meld or coexist in an entity that is likely held together by the old Hellenistic kind of cosmopolitanism.[15]

Auerbach's letter supports David Lawton's view that, when the humanist went to Istanbul, he went to an unfamiliar culture but, at the same time, went home.[16] Auerbach's impression of a Hellenistic, cosmopolitan Istanbul might have allowed him to find his own place in exile. Above all, however, his humanist outlook corresponded to a certain degree with the interests of Turkish reformers, who were trying to link modern Turkey to the classical heritage of Western Europe. Thus, contrary to what we have been told about the fundamental cleft between East and West, humanistic learning constituted, in fact, the intellectual basis for the humanities at Istanbul University. And, as we will see, this was a project that Auerbach, along with other German émigrés and

Turkish reformers, helped bring into being. To gain a new understanding of Auerbach and the humanist reforms, I first turn to Istanbul University and its reformist policies, and then to an examination of the broader Turkish national agenda.

Secular Humanism and the Europeanization of Istanbul University

Shortly before the official end of the Ottoman Empire, Ziya Gökalp (1876–1924), the single most important architect of Turkish nationalism, proposed homogenizing and nationalizing education and culture. Unlike Auerbach, who would praise the vestiges of cosmopolitanism that remained two decades later, Gökalp thought that cosmopolitan culture was an impediment to the nation's potential.[17] The radical nationalist argued that Renaissance humanism and secularism were essential for building a bridge between "the downfall of the religious community" and the "formation of the national soul."[18] Defining the Renaissance as the return to ancient Greek and Roman texts, Gökalp pointed out that this turn away from the religious doctrine of the Middle Ages fostered the emergence of secular cultures and the process of *millileşme*, nationalization.[19]

Gökalp criticized the traditional Istanbul bookstores specializing in Arabic, Persian, European, and Ottoman books, for he associated them specifically with a kind of cosmopolitanism he despised. The division of the Ottoman education system into religious, foreign, and *tanzimat* schools (the product of Ottoman reform measures during the nineteenth century) also indicated to Gökalp national deficiencies rather than a lively cosmopolitan culture. The sociologist was particularly critical of the tanzimat schools because of their amateurish appropriation and imitation of European pedagogical practices. In 1916, only a few years after he was awarded the first chair of sociology at the leading Ottoman university, Darülfünun, Gökalp proposed unifying the education system in order to overcome what he thought were the dilettantish Europeanization measures of previous decades.[20] Gökalp's vision for a new Turkey highlights a number of essential issues that prefigure the reforms introduced after the founding of the Republic. First, Gökalp accepted a certain construction of temporality in which tradition was interpreted as backward and modernity equated with progress. Second, mapped onto this construction of temporality was the geocultural ascription of Western Europe as advanced and the Ottoman Empire as backward. Third, a new society was to evolve through a rigorous process of nationalization.[21] Fourth, certain religious beliefs and practices were thought detrimental to the development of the nation, while secularism promised the advent of modernity. Modernization, in turn, involved the purification of ethnic and cultural origins. Finally, cultural mimesis was going to ensure the metamorphosis of the Ottoman Empire into a new Turkey. The transformation was, however, potentially precarious, and Gökalp warned that one "must reject everything that looks as if it were mere imitation" so that "social evolution can follow its normal course."[22]

It was this question of how to strike the delicate balance between conscious appropriation and indiscriminate imitation that most concerned late Ottomans and early Turkish republicans. Since Gökalp recognized the significance of literature to nation-building processes in Europe, he also reflected on the role it could play in the emergence of a new Turkish consciousness.[23] Turkish literature, he proposed, needed to follow the German model since their national awakening, like Turkey's, was a belated one. Gökalp assumed that Germans went through an initial phase of imitating the French but later came to realize that the less "French" German literature was, the more it could become saturated with Germanness.[24] As a result, Germans had to abandon everything French in order to find their *milli zevk*, their national taste and style.[25] Following this rationale, Gökalp proposed that all borrowings from Persian and French be excised from Turkish language and literature. Only then, he suggested, would Turks be left with what was innately theirs.[26]

There were political reasons for measuring the development of Turkish national consciousness against that of the Germans. Competing with France and Austria-Hungary, Germans tried to influence Ottoman educational policies in the early twentieth century in the hopes of extending their commercial relations in the Middle East.[27] The Orientalist Ernst Jäckh, who supplied the Foreign Office in Berlin with information, wrote in 1911 that Ottoman educational institutions and philanthropic ventures were among the most important channels through which Germany might gain commercial influence.[28] A few years later, German scholars were dispatched to Istanbul to direct some twenty new institutes, one of which was the short-lived Institute for German Languages and Literatures.[29] As part of this venture during World War I, efforts were made to ensure that

German would become the main foreign language in the Ottoman Empire; expatriates also tried to institute German research methods at the preeminent Ottoman university. İsmet Hakkı Baltacıoğlu, professor of pedagogy and later president of Darülfünun (1923–1933), criticized the *yeni ve ecnebi bir kuvvet*, the new and foreign force that seemed to be infiltrating the institution of higher learning. Acknowledging that the scholars dispatched from Germany might have tried to achieve too much too quickly, he thought that Darülfünun was steadily sliding "toward an abyss." Instead of finding a lasting solution for Darülfünun, he thought that too much effort had been made to *Alman kalmak, Alman görünmek ve Almanca çalışmak*, to remain German, look German, and work in the German language.[30] Indeed, the German Foreign Office itself reported Ottoman anxieties about the *Ägyptisierung der Türkei*, Egyptification of Turkey—the fear that Germans would take over the Ottoman Empire in the same way the French and the British had seized control of Egypt.[31] Such anxieties encumbered the reform plans for Darülfünun. As a matter of fact, during the academic year 1916–1917, the Ottoman faculty warned that the university was in danger of becoming "too German."[32] In the face of these concerns, the plan to institute German as the medium of instruction seemed unlikely to succeed.

For Ziya Gökalp, the architect of Turkish nationalism, Germans were crucial for the future of the university, but, like Baltacıoğlu, he was not interested in mere performance and imitation. His aim was not to adopt German culture per se but rather to follow the German example in creating a unique national consciousness and style. Such projects experienced a setback when, at the end of World War I, the Ottoman Empire was occupied and German-Ottoman relations were put on ice. With the founding of the Turkish Republic in 1923, however, the country renewed its interest in Germany. German humanism and philology, as we will see, were invoked for the reinvention of Turkish culture during the new republican period. Gökalp made a critical statement regarding the state of education. In his influential essay "Toward Western Civilization" (1923), he noted, "One portion of our nation is living in an ancient [age], another in a medieval [one], and a third in a modern [one]." "How," he went on to ask, "can we be a real nation without unifying this three-fold education?"[33] His question provides crucial insights into the catalyst for the ensuing reforms.[34] One could say that Gökalp tried to rouse the slumbering national community so that it would, so to speak, awaken in modern times. This was not unlike the efforts that had been made by European nationalists during the nineteenth century, something that Benedict Anderson analyzes in *Imagined Communities*.[35] In attempting to rouse the nation, Gökalp identified the unifying potential of modern education: it would both allow the nation to be conceived as a single entity and create a sense of synchronicity with the West. Thus, the nation might achieve some parity with Western Europe.

During the first decade of the republic, reformers attempted to unify Turkey's citizens and promote their sense of affinity with their Western neighbors—measures that came, needless to say, at the expense of the country's ethnic and religious diversity. Switching from the Islamic to the Western calendar in 1926 marked a further shift from the Ottoman to the European time frame, fostering a sense of connectedness with events unfolding elsewhere.[36] Two years later, the alphabet was Latinized, and in the 1930s the education system was thoroughly overhauled. As part of this process, the government invited several foreign education reformers, including, in 1924, John Dewey. The influential American philosopher and psychologist saw education as a fundamental means of promoting social progress and emphasized the interdependence of "humanistic and naturalistic studies."[37] Yet Dewey's suggestions for educational reform in Turkey did not quite meet the reformers' expectations.[38] Looking for an alternative, the Turkish government finally hired the Swiss educator Albert Malche in 1932.

The main target of the education reforms was Darülfünun, which, from its very beginnings in 1863, had been a contested site for competing religious and enlightened forces.[39] During Ottoman times, Darülfünun had already been subject to several shakeups—including one carried out in cooperation with scholars enlisted from the German Empire. Such changes notwithstanding, Darülfünun was harshly criticized during republican times. The Turkish minister of education, Reşit Galip, criticized the university for its belated response to the new governmental interventions concerning economics, law, language, and historiography. Galip insisted that the university, too, cohere with the process of reform.[40] Malche followed his lead, suggesting that all university students be trained in one of the three principal Western European languages. Since very few scholarly books had been published in Turkey since the Latinization of the alphabet, Malche argued that students ought to study French, German, or English in order to keep abreast of international scholarship.[41] Turkish reformers agreed with the Swiss advisor and gave the study of Western languages priority over Arabic, Persian, and Ottoman.

The year 1933 was thus constructed as a kind of zero hour for modern tertiary education in Turkey.[42] The ministry of education decided to curtail Darülfünun's autonomy and refound the institution as Istanbul University, to dismiss two-thirds of its Turkish faculty, and to hire European professors and Turks trained in Europe.[43] Initially, Malche had suggested hiring European scholars from a number of different countries in the hope of avoiding the cultural and political dominance of a single European nation.[44] As it happened, however, plans for reforming the education system in the 1930s coincided with the National Socialists' rise to power and, hence, with the exclusion of German-Jewish and antifascist academics from German universities. The Turkish government seemed to realize quickly that the expulsion of scholars from Nazi Germany could become its own gain. The doors for an intellectual exchange between Turkey and Germany were thus reopened—albeit under different political circumstances: Albert Malche and the natural scientist Philipp Schwartz founded an organization to assist the emigration of academics from Germany to Turkey. The *Notgemeinschaft deutscher Wissenschaftler im Ausland* (Aid Organization for German Academics Abroad) proposed the names of more than forty German émigrés, who were immediately hired by Istanbul University; many others were employed by other universities, state-run institutes, museums, and other institutions across the country. In addition to the names I have already mentioned, among the more famous of these émigrés were composers, architects, and scholars like Ernst Reuter, Fritz Neumark, Bruno Taut, Carl Ebert, and Eduard Zuckmayer. It is estimated that through these channels alone, at least eight hundred German professionals and their families could look upon Turkey as their salvation.[45]

These German émigrés did not pose a threat to Turkey's desire for intellectual and political autonomy. The fact that they had been excluded from German universities on racial and political grounds meant that they were in a vulnerable, if not compromised, position. This in itself made it unlikely that Germans would take control of Turkey's education system. Given that the émigrés were, as one would expect, vehemently opposed to National Socialism, Turkish reformers were not as concerned as Malche had been about hiring so many scholars from a single European nation.

Reporting on the Turkish reforms, the European media were also interested in the question of which foreign influence would prevail in Turkey. The Swiss journalist and travel writer Annemarie Schwarzenbach, for example, took an express interest in Malche's activities in Turkey. In 1933, she reported for the *Neue Zürcher Zeitung* that Malche was helping Turks create a university that would educate the new Turkish elite.[46] Pointing out that Malche had had no difficulty placing a significant number of German academics at Turkish universities, she presumed that the influence of the French had diminished. Schwarzenbach went on to report that, despite the growing influence of German academics, Turkey maintained that the university was devoted to serving the sciences rather than any explicitly national interests.[47] Indeed, prior experience had shown that there were costs involved in allowing German scholars to play a leading role in the Turkish education system. Turkish politicians recalled, for instance, that during the Weimar Republic, bilateral cultural and commercial interests had been funneled through the modernization of higher education in Turkey.[48] At the time, the collaboration between Germany and the Ottoman Empire had elicited concern about the extent to which Germans were taking control. Now, however, the hiring of German scholars did not involve the German ministry of education, and the new state of affairs post-1933 seemed to suit the Turkish interest in maintaining a Westernized, but independent, system of education.[49]

In 1933, both parties—the Turkish government and representatives of the émigré scholars—attached special meaning to the emigration of intellectuals to Turkey. Philipp Schwartz, the representative of the *Notgemeinschaft*, wrote that Atatürk's vision of the rebirth of the Turkish people could now—because of a "groteske Verirrung der Geschichte" (a grotesque aberrance of history)—be realized. Schwartz was convinced that the scholars who witnessed the destruction of their world would ultimately gain recognition thanks to their mission in Turkey.[50] Reşit Galip, the minister of education, interpreted the intellectual émigrés from Europe from another point of view, construing their arrival as a compensation for the Byzantine scholars who had fled Constantinople after its surrender to the Ottomans in 1453.[51] He emphasized that the conquest of

Constantinople and the flight of Byzantine scholars to Rome had provided an important impetus for the Italian Renaissance. His hope was that something similar would, in turn, be achieved in modern Turkey through the "return" of European scholars.[52] This was a fancy piece of reasoning on his part. Nevertheless, while humanist scholarship was being destroyed by the National Socialist apparatus and many of its most respected scholars were fleeing Europe, Galip welcomed the possibility for the rebirth of European culture in Turkey. Switching from the Arabic to the Latin script and closing Darülfünun allowed Turkey to sever itself from its own Ottoman heritage and set the stage for a new beginning. Galip hoped that, in hiring the European scholars, Europe's heritage could be returned to its birthplace. Classical learning, so the rationale went, would be reborn in the very city it had once deserted.

Numerous Turkish reformers envisioned the transition from the Ottoman Empire to a Westernized, secular Turkey by drawing on the Renaissance model and by attempting to integrate humanism into the Turkish pedagogical system. While reformers disagreed about exactly how to institute humanism in Turkey, they shared a common definition of Turkish humanism as a movement that newly envisioned Turkish culture through a system of education based on Western classical learning. The nationalist Ziya Gökalp, from whom we heard earlier, for example, was not completely enamored with humanism, but he did see it as a useful means of promoting a Turkish national consciousness and wished to see a similar movement shape literature and fine art.[53]

Other intellectuals of the early republican period, including Nurullah Ataç, raised more complex questions regarding the relationship between nationalism, humanism, and Europeanization. Ataç suggested that training students in contemporary Western languages would only change Turkish society superficially and generate a sense of longing for the Western world.[54] For a society to change so that it could *represent* rather than *resemble* the West, he concluded that education in Latin and Greek had to begin at a young age.[55] Similarly, the poetry of Hafız and Fuzuli, the leading Persian and Ottoman poets of the fourteenth and the sixteenth century, respectively, needed to be approached via Shakespeare.[56] While some humanists like Ataç tried to preserve the value of Ottoman literature, the general tenor during the years of Westernization was to consider Ottoman culture as thoroughly outmoded.

Ramiz Gökçe, *Ayine* (To the Religious Service), December 8, 1922. The Ottoman retreats into a history book (*Tarih-i Osmani*). Reprinted from Sabine Küper-Büsch and Nigar Rona, *Die Nase des Sultans: Karikaturen aus der Türkei / Padişahın Burnu: Türkiye'den Karikatürler* (Istanbul: Dağyeli Publishers, Bilgi University Press, 2008), 16. Source: Dağyeli Press.

Decoupling the new Turkey from its Ottoman heritage, while simultaneously furthering the country's rapprochement with Europe, created a source of tension among citizens of the new nation. The secularization culminated, as Sam Kaplan shows, in a campaign against Muslim clerics, who were blamed for perpetuating illiteracy, material backwardness, and superstitions among the "common people." As Kaplan further shows, Kemalists, the republican statesmen and policy makers, closed hundreds of theological seminaries and dismissed Muslim clerics from educational and cultural institutions. This secular turn "entailed the dissolution of otherworldly political goals and the rejection of the absoluteness of authority in religion."[57] That the identification with the intellectual heritage of ancient Europe and the secularization of knowledge—seen as a necessary step toward modernity—would provoke criticism is to be expected.[58] The leading reformers believed that secular humanist scholarship would help transcend the old educational system and provide Turks with the tools they needed in order to "know, and even discover," themselves.[59]

Turkish reformers were not alone in imagining a future for Turkey that was predicated on classical learning. In his 1932 report, Malche himself had recommended humanist scholarship, philology, and a comparative method as the basis for *hakikî bir edebî kültür*, a genuine literary culture.[60] Malche envisioned a faculty for literature that would include a professorship in French literature, general linguistics, and comparative literature, with an emphasis on the history of ideas. Before long, the ideal scholar was found to realize this plan and head the faculty for Western languages and literatures: the Austrian Romance linguist Leo Spitzer, expelled from the University of Cologne on anti-Semitic grounds, would lead the new Istanbul faculty in the desired direction. In his report, Malche had stressed the significance of the humanities for the "refinement of the intellect" and advised the university to hire a linguist capable of establishing the philological disciplines.[61] With Spitzer, Istanbul University secured a true philologist whose interests ranged from linguistics and literature to the history of ideas. Although his tenure in Istanbul was brief, Spitzer was the scholar who indeed introduced comparative methods to the study of language and literature.

After three years at Istanbul University, Spitzer decided to accept an offer at Johns Hopkins University. This, as we know, provided the main chance for Auerbach to emigrate, when Spitzer suggested him as his successor in Istanbul. This is to say that the hiring of scholars such as Spitzer and Auerbach was no mere coincidence. These were precisely the kinds of academics that Malche and Galip had had in mind for the task of establishing philology in Turkey. Auerbach was offered the position in Istanbul because the authorities were convinced that his banishment from Germany could benefit Turkish political autonomy. While undergoing Westernization, the Turkish government had no interest in making their country politically dependent on Western Europe. In their report to the dean, Spitzer, Rüstow, and Reichenbach thus highlighted Auerbach's detached, critical view of Occidental cultures, while the university administration spoke in favor of Auerbach precisely because he would be unlikely to toe the Nazi line.[62] To put it bluntly, Auerbach's expulsion as a Jew worked in the interest of Turkey's cultural and educational politics: Auerbach could teach Western European literatures from the classical to the modern age while preserving the country's cultural autonomy.

In a speech that opened the academic year 1936–1937, Auerbach was officially welcomed by Cemil Bilsel, the president of Istanbul University, and was introduced to the academic community as a scholar of the same caliber as the much-respected Spitzer. If Auerbach had not yet realized the larger significance of his appointment to the country as a whole, this would hit home the moment the university president stepped up to the podium: the president launched his speech by stressing the responsibility of the university vis-à-vis the Turkish public. Bilsel gave the speech in Turkish, but we can safely assume that an assistant or student would have translated it into French for Auerbach and other émigrés. French, after all, was still the de facto lingua franca of Turkish academia in the 1930s. Bilsel asserted that the role of the university was central to the progress of Turkish modernity, and the onus of building the Turkish nation lay with the individual intellectual. Bilsel went on to emphasize the difficult task faced by the faculty for Western languages and literatures, which instructed forty-five hundred students from a range of disciplines in French, German, and English. Mastery of a Western language, the president stressed, was the key component in a modern tertiary education and would pave the way for training future intellectuals who could promote the country's interests.[63]

Auerbach did indeed step up to the plate. We can say that, as mediators of European knowledge, intellectuals like Spitzer and Auerbach created a blueprint for humanist scholarship in Turkey. In so doing, they generated mutual intelligibility and rendered humanist scholarship suitable for the secularization of the humanities. In the first instance, this involved reconfiguring disciplinary practices so as to promote the Europeanization of scholarship: specifically, it meant adapting and introducing the teaching of classical and Western European languages and literatures and thinking critically about the practice of translation; it also meant introducing new didactic methods, academic writing styles, analytic tools, research libraries, and other academic practices.[64] Helpful as a way of assessing such processes of cultural appropriation and adaptation is Lydia Liu's study of Chinese modernity, which shows what was at stake for literature and literary criticism in China during the same period. Liu's insights into literary practices as agents of nation building also helps us to see the role of Turkish philological faculties during the 1930s and 1940s. Liu's approach allows us to gauge the significance of translated knowledge, canon formation, literary criticism, and the humanities for the formation of national identities across the globe.[65]

The Turkish ministry of education implemented several other projects to inaugurate the beginning of modern education. One of them was the opening of the faculty for language, history, and geography at Ankara University (Ankara Dil ve Tarih-Coğrafya Fakültesi) in 1936, whose mandate was to train students in both modern and ancient languages such as Sumerian, Hittite, and classical Greek. The faculty was thus conceived as one of the principal centers for investigating Turkey's relationship to the ancient world.[66] Architecturally, the faculty was also meant to serve as a symbol for modernity and renewal. Bruno Taut, who had fled the Nazis early on, was hired in 1936 to direct the architectural bureau for the ministry of education. He designed the plans for the new building, which Taut himself understood as the "Center of the new Turkish culture."[67]

Historical Legacies

Re-creating Turkey in the image of Europe came with its contradictions. Perhaps the most glaring inconsistency concerns the spread of philhellenic humanism in the 1930s and the forced population exchange between Greece and Turkey in 1924. It seems paradoxical that Orthodox Greeks were compelled to leave Turkey when the government was simultaneously aiming to root the new Turkish culture in that of ancient Greece.[68] To be sure, the humanist project, which stressed the ancient Greek impact on Europe, was difficult to reconcile with anti-Greek sentiments then current in Turkey.[69] Yet it was ancient—not modern—Greece that humanist reformers had in their sights. Since the geographies of ancient Greece, the Byzantine Empire, and modern Turkey overlapped, the archeological findings of the late nineteenth and early twentieth centuries strengthened a sense of interconnectedness. A number of Turkish humanists went so far as to support an ethnic/racial relationship with the ancient cultures of Anatolia, including the Hittites. This allowed them to justify Turkish humanism in terms of "reclaiming what once belonged to us."[70] In order to forge a synthesis between the history of the Turkish people and that of Anatolia, Mustafa Kemal Atatürk also coined the term *yurt tarihi*, the history of the homeland.[71] This is how Anatolia came to be construed as "Turkish since antiquity."[72]

It was in this atmosphere that students during the 1930s and 1940s developed a consciousness for ancient European history as part of their own history. Güzin Dino, one of Auerbach's most remarkable students and assistants in Istanbul, recalls émigrés introducing students to the history of Constantinople and the Byzantine Empire.[73] Auerbach himself regarded Istanbul as "essentially Hellenistic," as I have noted earlier, and he saw in the Aegean city of Bursa "the marvelously Bithynic Brussa." For him, the location and character of Bursa conjured up "an Islamic Perugia."[74]

For many Turkish scholars of the period, in contrast, Anatolian history came to signify more than a historical legacy that was used to promote the country's Westernization. In chapter 3, I show that Atatürk's efforts to cleave modern Turkish history to the Anatolian past resulted in highly speculative historical accounts linking the origin of Turks to Indo-Europeans. In the postwar period, Alexander Rüstow's son Dankwart reflected on the effects of Westernization in the Near East, criticizing the "pseudo-scientific theories" like Turkey's sun language theory. "This tendency," Dankwart Rüstow wrote, "to interpret heterogenetic change as orthogenetic change provided a set of psychological compensations designed to ease the painful process of Westernization. At the same time, the glorification of the pre-Islamic Turkish past under Atatürk and of the Pehlevi period in Reza's Iran represents a common romantic technique of building up loyalty to a distant (and often mythical) past so as to break the grip of the immediate cultural heritage—and thus speed the process of change."[75] It is not clear whether German émigrés, while in Turkey, objected publicly to Turkey's conjectural and ideologically inflected history writing. In their private correspondence, however, we find that they certainly opposed the way these views were spread. The founder of the Orient Institute in Istanbul, Hellmut Ritter, for instance, wrote a letter expressing his disapproval regarding the rewriting of Turkish history:[76]

Why is it not possible to grasp that there should be a science [methodological approach] that does not conclude that the Turks descended from the Hittites and that it is not unpatriotic to disagree with this? Theology metamorphoses into nationology [nationalism]; instead of religious heretics there are political ones—that is the whole difference from before. Fixed march routes in any case. The fact that deepest religious connection and greatest intellectual freedom can coexist in one people, that one can be a modern people and yet protect historical monuments and tolerate sectarianism yet let the peasants keep their traditional clothing: none of this goes together in an Oriental's head.[77]

Ritter was quite candid about the nature of Turkish scholarship during the height of hard-line nationalism. To the Orientalist scholar, who spent decades preserving, translating, and interpreting Ottoman scripts, such unsubstantiated claims about Turkish origins were simply incomprehensible. Auerbach cohered with this view. Although he trained students in the humanist tradition, he did not support Turkey's attempt to reinvent itself by severing its own cultural and historical roots. Soon after his arrival in Istanbul, he gave voice to this view in a letter to Benjamin:

> Struggling against the European democracies, on the one hand, and the old Mohammedan–pan-Islamic sultan's regime, on the other, Kemal Atatürk had to force through every change he made; the result is a fanatically antitraditional nationalism: rejection of all existing Mohammedan cultural heritage, the assumption of a mythical relation to a primal Turkish identity, technological modernization in the European sense. . . . Result: nationalism in the extreme accompanied by the simultaneous destruction of the historical national character.[78]

Concerns about Turkey's modernization process are also evident from another of Auerbach's letters. Writing to his former assistant Freya von Hobohm in Marburg in 1938, Auerbach said that Turkey's negative relationship to its own cultural tradition was "für unsereinen traurig" (sad for people like us), even "gespenstisch" (eery), when compared with Germany.[79] To be sure, Auerbach understood why eradicating the Ottoman cultural tradition may have seemed necessary for the modernization of the republic. Nonetheless, he continued to be critical of Turkey for renouncing its Ottoman legacy and culture. He hoped for a "gradual reaction" against these developments once the "most urgent modernization measures" had been completed.[80] During his tenure in Istanbul, Auerbach saw that Turkish students were trained in Latin, Greek, and Western European languages but were no longer required to study Ottoman, Arabic, and Persian texts. Political decisions such as these, he wrote later in his essay "Philologie der Weltliteratur" (1952), contributed to the loss of historical consciousness and the standardization of culture.[81] Further contributing to the standardization of culture were Turkey's switch from the Arabic to the Roman alphabet and the establishment of the Institute for the Turkish Language, an institute that promoted the "purification" of the Turkish language by replacing Arabic and Persian words with Turkish ones. This form of language politics was typical of fascist countries at the time, among them Italy, where Mussolini suppressed the use of French in bilingual regions and replaced French-sounding place names with Italian ones. Spain under Franco and Germany under Hitler, as Auerbach was keenly aware, had also resorted to "purifying" the language.[82] Seen in this light, Auerbach's position vis-à-vis Turkish reform politics is perhaps to be expected:

Needless to say, everything is badly modernized and barbarized, and increasingly so. The government—on the whole really very clever and skillful—can do nothing but accelerate the process of modernization. It has to organize the impoverished country, which is unused to working, to instruct it in modern and practical methods so that it can live and defend itself; and like everywhere else, this takes place in the name of a purist nationalism that destroys living tradition; this rests partly on utterly mythical primordial imaginings, partly on modern-rational thought. Piety is opposed, Islamic culture regarded as Arabic infiltration; they want to be seen as at once modern and purely Turkish, and it has gone so far that the language has been totally destroyed by getting rid of the old orthography and Arabic borrowings and replacing them partly with "Turkish" neologisms, partly with European appropriations: no young person can read the older literature any more—and there reigns an intellectual directionlessness that is extremely dangerous.[83]

Such thoroughgoing changes attracted Auerbach's ire in 1938, but they also fed homegrown anxieties. Some reformers warned against the perils of plain imitation, something they saw as resulting in a kind of hypocrisy. It would be preferable, they seemed to think, if Turks were not only to imitate but actually to become European. Anxieties about this mimetic appropriation of European culture were ubiquitous. The humanist Nurullah Ataç, for instance, approached the issue philologically by studying changes in the use of the verb *taklit etmek*. He argued that in the past, the verb had had two distinct meanings: used with the dative case (*bir kimseye taklit etmek*), it meant "to imitate," while used with the accusative case (*bir kimseyi taklit etmek*), it meant "to mock." In the course of the Europeanization reforms, he pointed out that *taklit etmek* had not only ceased to be used with the dative case; it had also lost the meaning "to mock."[84] Ataç's philological exercise gives us an indication that after the establishment of the Turkish Republic, imitating the European was disassociated from subversive mockery.

Ataç was one of the most influential critics of his time. He wrote for leading newspapers and journals and rendered some fifty volumes of Greek, Latin, and French literature into Turkish. He also became one of Auerbach's colleagues when he was hired in 1937 by the faculty for Western languages and literatures to teach French. As an important advocate for the adaptation of humanist scholarship in Turkey, he was aware of the public's unease about Turkish culture losing its sense of specificity. Pointing out that European Orientalists who specialized in Arabic were nonetheless rooted in European culture, he suggested that it would be possible to train Turks as Occidentalists with expertise in Greek and Latin. This, he hoped, would promote a strong identification with European culture in Turkish society.[85]

Taking up a call by the parliamentarian and poet Yahya Kemal for a specifically Turkish historical consciousness, humanists like Ataç, Celâleddin Ezine, and Orhan Burian formulated different ideas about integrating humanism into the nationalist project.[86] Reflecting on the nationalization of the humanist tradition in France and Germany, Celâleddin Ezine argued that nations needed to supplement humanism with something of their own culture, if they were not to become mere mimics of ancient Greece and Rome.[87] Ezine made several suggestions for redressing this problem: these involved, first, establishing rules for Turkish grammar and syntax, second, compiling a comprehensive Turkish dictionary and a Turkish encyclopedia, third, founding a Turkish academy and an institution for experimental phonetics to improve spoken Turkish, fourth, transliterating classical Ottoman poetry and folk literature into the new script, and fifth, translating world classics into Turkish.[88] Many of his ideas found favor with other intellectuals. Ahmet Hamdi Tanpınar, professor of Turkish literature and parliamentarian, for instance, similarly called for literary criticism and translations of Western literature as a means of Westernizing the country.[89]

Both İsmet İnönü, the second president of the republic who succeeded Atatürk after his death in 1938, and the new minister of education, Hasan Ali Yücel, made a remarkable effort to support the kind of translation project advocated by these humanists. "Cultures that do not go through an intense age of translation," Yücel warned, "are deemed to dry up like unblessed earth and remain barren."[90] Consequently, Yücel launched the *hümanist kültür reformları* (humanist culture reforms) in 1939, which marked the beginning of a new phase in the country's cultural history. These reforms extended to the establishment of a state conservatory and series of village institutes—the *köy enstitüleri*—which tried to cultivate an intellectual elite in Anatolia rather than just in the traditional urban centers.[91]

After Yücel took over, a *milli kütüphane* (national library) and translation bureau were established; the bureau coordinated and supervised the translation of hundreds of Western classics published by the ministry of education. Sabahattin Eyüboğlu, a Sorbonne graduate who taught with Spitzer and Auerbach in the Romance Seminar in Istanbul in the mid-1930s, became the director of this translation bureau. The bureau launched a series titled *Dünya Edebiyatından Tercümeler*, Translations from World Literature. That this series had symbolic value for the new government's reform process is evident in the preface to the series, which was signed by Atatürk's successor. İnönü emphasized here that these "masterworks that were brought forth by nations since the ancient Greeks" were to now have their place within Turkish national culture.[92] In the same vein, Yücel emphasized the place of the ancient Greeks in Turkey's cultural vision and suggested that the humanist spirit could be cultivated only by making its richest intellectual component, literature, one's own. Not only would world literature extend to its readers the possibility of enriching and renewing the intellect; the nation with the richest national library and most vibrant literature would, he claimed, occupy a higher level of civilization.[93]

French literature was prioritized over other literatures in the world translation series, resulting in fully one third of the series. One in six translations was a work of German literature, one in nine was Russian, and only one in twelve was English. The most translated authors were Plato, then Molière, Balzac, Shakespeare, Dostoevsky, Goethe, Tolstoy, and finally Chekhov.[94] The translation bureau's concept of world literature, even if the series included the *Epic of Gilgamesh* and some translations of Chinese literature and philosophy, was clearly the product of French-German Europhilia. The first German work to be translated in the world literature series was Goethe's *Faust*, with most of his oeuvre following in later years, including Eckermann's conversations with Goethe about the meaning of world literature, while the first French work to be translated was Molière's *Le Misanthrope*. Well-known humanists took over other French works. Ataç, for example, translated Stendhal, Yakup Kadri Karaosmanoğlu delivered Proust's *À la Recherche du temps perdu* in Turkish, and Sabahattin Eyüboğlu, the director of the translation bureau, rendered Alfred de Musset's Romantic poetry into Turkish.[95]

Between 1940 and 1950, the ministry published 676 translated literary works of which seventy-six (that is, approximately 11 percent) were classical Greek.[96] Ataç and the young humanists Azra Erhat and Suat Sinanoğlu translated several works by Sophocles. Yücel regarded these translations from Greek as indispensable for the renewal of Turkish culture. In his preface to the translations, the minister of education explicitly rejected *taasupçu fikirler*, bigotry, against Greeks that would only impede Turkish progress. He warned that otherwise the reforms would end up "plodding along at the speed of an oxcart in the age of air travel."[97] At the opening of the state conservatory in 1941, we see Yücel once again putting his finger on something that seemed unlikely at the time—the possibility that Western literature and music would ever be thoroughly integrated into Turkish cultural life. Yücel announced that "An author may not be one of us and a composer may belong to another nation. Yet we are the ones who understand those words and sounds and bring life to them. For this reason, the plays that the state conservatory performs and the operas it stages are ours, Turkish, and national."[98] The education minister's statement suggests that it was the commitment to producing a first-rate performance rather than the notion of authentic culture that rendered a cultural artifact Turkish. We can conclude from this that using the Western European canon as a catalyst for the modernization of Turkish culture generated new ways of envisioning national identity by means that were not necessarily essentializing. Not everyone, however, was quite so willing to uphold the distinction between ancient and modern Greece.

While the playwright Celâleddin Ezine generally supported the reforms, he was cautious not to deprecate Turkey's native potential. His interest was in fostering the Turkish language as a basis for humanism. Whether Turkish humanism was ultimately going to follow classical Ottoman poetry, Turkish folk literature, or Western literature depended, in his view, on the efforts that were made to extend the range of vocabulary in the Turkish language.[99] Other scholars discussed the implications of humanism not in terms of language, literature, and culture, but in terms of history. Orhan Burian, English professor and translator of Shakespeare, suggested that, in order for humanism to be adopted in Turkey, the individual had to be defined in two ways—"as a *Turk* within history and as a *human* vis-à-vis the past and the future."[100] The statement exemplifies how republican Turks rooted the nation in a racialized past even while conceiving of themselves as a modern, radically new national community. For Burian, who regarded Atatürk as the embodiment of "Asya'nın Renaissance'ı" (Asia's renaissance),[101] the identification with the humanist tradition did not mean that Turkey ought to return to fifteenth-century Italy or sixteenth-century England. In his view, the Turkish revolution had been successful in "İslamlığın dogma'larını kökünden söküp atmıştır" (uprooting the dogmas of Islam), while humanism allowed subjects to understand themselves anew.[102] This thought, which lay behind the moment of refoundation, also necessitated the rewriting of Turkish history.[103]

Recapitulating the main ideas related to the modernization of Turkey's most important university, we can say that the reforms were part of a national agenda that linked its success to its capacity for overcoming cultural differences between East and West. The modernization reforms promoted sameness with Western Europe but simultaneously maintained a notion of national particularity. I propose that we think about Turkey's one-sided rapprochement with Europe as enacting a kind of cultural mimesis.[104] The concept of cultural mimesis also underscores chapter 3, which shows that reformers shared the dual aim of transforming Turks into Europeans while skirting the charge of mere imitation. This, I argue, was one of the main objectives involved in forming the modern national subject.

Transnational Mediations

The mechanisms underlying Turkey's accelerated, albeit guarded, appropriation of European culture were transparent to Auerbach, who recognized that the modernization reforms were predicated on an inherent essentialism. Reflecting on his own role in the process, Auerbach soberly noted the university's preference for European émigrés over local academics. The fact that émigrés did not engage in foreign propaganda, he wrote to Benjamin, made it possible for the reformers to imagine Turkey "triumphing over a hated but admired Europe by using its own weapons" (*das verhaßte und bewunderte Europa mit den eigenen Waffen zu schlagen*).[105] As Auerbach pointed out, Turkish reformers saw émigré scholars as people without a nation, people who could be cajoled into implementing Turkey's national agenda. In the transnational encounter between Germany and Turkey, émigrés seemed to need to be denationalized, that is, disassociated from a specific national affiliation, before they could represent the quintessence of Europeanness.

Caught in this contradictory position, Auerbach had a difficult task. Cemil Bilsel, the president of Istanbul University, assigned him the task of training Turkish students in the humanist tradition, in the hope that this would ultimately impact geopolitical and cultural relations between Western Europe and Turkey. Coming from a country that denied him the right to exercise his own profession, this mandate did not necessarily pose a conflict for Auerbach. Rather, he felt ambivalent because Turkish modernity was informed by deeply held racial beliefs and an all-pervasive anti-Semitism, and, as I show in chapter 3, he himself felt the sting of this anti-Semitism.

We should note that the Turkish government has helped individual victims of fascism, but it cannot categorically be defined as pro-Jewish during this period. Tellingly, it never granted general asylum to victims of Nazi persecution. We need only look to the case of Klemperer trapped in Germany and to the untold others who shared a much worse plight in the concentration camps. Instead, Turkish officials weighed each individual application against the person's desirability and the applicant's potential contribution to the modernization of the country.[106] In other words, German academics were not rescued on a humanitarian basis; they were hired primarily because of their promise as facilitators and promoters of Europeanness in the host country.

Emily Apter paints a positive picture when she writes that the transnational exchange in 1930s Istanbul paved the way for the German philological tradition to create a new understanding of comparative literature. In her article on Spitzer, Apter refers to this important moment in the disciplinary history of comparative literature as the "translational transnationalism of humanism."[107] If we, however, understand transnationalism as the outcome of an exchange between individuals and communities, independent of the interests of nation-states, then we must reconsider the Turkish case. The humanism that evolved out of the Turkish-German intellectual exchange of the 1930s and 1940s served primarily national, not transnational interests. In fact, the Notgemeinschaft negotiated the hiring of scholars directly with representatives of the Turkish nation-state—with the result that its agenda could not be readily subverted. And, contrary to what tends to be assumed nowadays, the individual was less independent actor than instrumentalized pawn in these large-scale political processes. To be sure, national boundaries were transgressed and comparative ways of thinking encouraged; yet we ought not forget that the lasting outcome of the transnational encounter was the intensification, not dilution, of Turkish nationalism and Europhilia.

It was for good reason that Auerbach was nicknamed "the Europeanist" by his émigré colleague, psychologist Wilhelm Peters.[108] Preserving the foundations of a humanist Europe served the interests of émigrés and Turks alike. For Auerbach, it meant an ethical commitment to a Europe being destroyed by the Nazis; for the Turks, it was a way to reinvent and model themselves as European. While the Nazis undermined the very basis of humanism,[109] Turkish humanists were aware of their role in maintaining the idea of a humanist Europe at its Turkish periphery. The writer Ahmet Hamdi Tanpınar, for instance, argued that, while other countries suffered devastating experiences during the war, Turkey was able to preserve its peace and even make constructive progress.[110] A few days after the surrender of the Germans to the Allies in May 1945, Tanpınar reported in a newspaper column:

Germany wanted to be Rome; but it turned itself into Carthage. . . . Today's Europe emerged on the grounds of Rome's destruction. This is why a second Rome cannot emerge. . . . Valéry wrote in one of his works: "We have finally learned to recognize that civilizations are as mortal as human beings." The roots of civilization were never before shaken as much as in this war. There were days when we were afraid that the roof and the foundation of civilization were going collapse. We should never have to go through this again.[111]

Having observed the outcome of the war from a safe distance, Tanpınar believed in the value of the humanist project in Turkey. It seems ironic, then, that, during the transition from the single-party regime to a democratic multiparty system in 1946, Turkey's humanist project ground to a halt.[112] While the brand of humanism inspired by Spitzer, and later Auerbach, sowed the seeds for a critical practice in comparative literature in the United States after World War II,[113] humanism in Turkey—with an impact that extended far beyond the curricula in literature departments—had already seen its heyday by the end of the war.

The minister of education, Yücel, who spearheaded the humanist reforms, came under increasing criticism during the postwar period. The system of village institutes, which he had introduced for the training of primary school teachers and promoting a rural intellectual elite, was branded a communist breeding ground.[114] Yücel himself was accused of passing off communism as humanism and criticized for protecting the writer Sabahattin Ali, who, in 1944, had been charged with being a communist traitor by the notorious nationalist Nihal Atsız.[115] Conservatives blamed Yücel for using the cultural reforms, including the translation project, to create a Greco-Roman basis for Turkish culture.[116] In response to this smear campaign, Yücel mounted a lawsuit on the grounds of slander—probably the single most important lawsuit of the late 1940s. Yücel eventually won, but he retired from his official duties in 1947 and many of his projects were discontinued, among them the teaching of Latin in lyceums and the highly fruitful translating work.[117] As a final gesture toward ensuring academic freedom, Yücel had enough foresight to grant universities autonomy from the government. This independence and intellectual freedom would last another three decades.[118]

Without Yücel's backing, Turkey's translation project fell by the wayside. Between 1940 and 1950, as many as seventy-six Greek classics had been translated into Turkish; during the following decade, there was a sum total of three books.[119] It is likely that the anti-Greek pogroms of the 1950s played a role in this. But there were also those who would have wished for the translation initiative to continue. Tanpınar, for one, regretted the end of the translation project because significant works of philosophy, sociology, history, and the arts had not yet been made available to Turkish readers. The existing translations of Goethe, Balzac, Stendahl, Dostoevsky, Tolstoy, Dickens, Molière, and Racine also did not meet Tanpınar's standards. In general, he criticized the many stops and starts that had characterized Ottoman intellectual life since the tanzimat reforms of the nineteenth century.[120]

During the postwar period, humanists like Tanpınar, Ataç, and Yücel lost the kind of influence that they once enjoyed. If there had ever been a window of opportunity for the democratization of cultural politics, this was now effectively closed by autocratic leaders, anticommunist campaigns, attempts to subvert secular education, and a series of military coups.[121] Even so, the humanist reforms had left their mark. We see this in the efforts of Sabahattin Eyüboğlu, who presided over Yücel's translation bureau in Ankara. Together with the classical philologist Azra Erhat and the prominent writer Halikarnas Balıkçısı, Eyüboğlu developed the notion of a specifically Anatolian brand of humanism.[122] Spitzer's student Azra Erhat, who at a very young age was hired as Georg Rohde's translator and assistant at the department for classical philology in Ankara, took on the gargantuan task of translating Homer's *Iliad* and *Odyssey* into Turkish and became one of the leading humanists in the country. She would later say that studying with Spitzer and acquiring philological skills represented a "turning point" in her life: this training impacted all her subsequent work.[123]

Erhat and others promoted a form of Anatolian humanism as the basis for Turkish culture. This constituted an important break with the official prewar rhetoric, which held that Turks were ethnically related to the ancient cultures of Anatolia. Thanks to the work of scholars like Erhat, this genealogical link was now broken. The brand of humanism promulgated by Erhat, Eyüboğlu, and Halikarnas Balıkçısı did not rest on a fictitious blood lineage but on the idea that it was possible to revive and inherit Anatolia's ancient cultures. These widely read scholars, translators, and writers promoted the idea that Turkish culture could spring from the ruins of ancient cultures. This also implied a new kind of geocultural relationship between Greeks and Turks.[124]

Although the circle around Erhat generally promoted friendly relations with Greece, there are also contravening examples. Eyüboğlu, for one, anchored Turkey's cultural origins in ancient Troy and contributed to the widespread view of modern Greeks and Turks as uneasy neighbors. In 1962, Eyüboğlu opened his essay "Iliad and Anatolia" with a quote from the Renaissance scholar Montaigne. According to Montaigne, the Ottoman conqueror of Constantinople, Sultan Mehmed II, had written to Pope Pius II expressing astonishment over Italian opposition to his victory. After all, both the Italians and Ottomans were descended from the Trojans (or so Mehmed II supposed) and, by conquering Constantinople, he meant only to take revenge on the Greeks for their killing of Hector.[125] There is indeed historical evidence that Mehmed II, having visited the site of ancient Troy, regarded the Trojans and the Ottomans as fellow Asiatics. Kritovoulos, the fifteenth-century Byzantine Greek scholar in the service of the Ottoman court, reported that the sultan cast himself as the Asiatic avenger in 1463. In his account, Kritovoulos wrote that Mehmed II looked at the ruins and the traces of the ancient city and inquired about the tombs of Achilles and Ajax. After having "congratulated and praised them, their memory and their deeds, and on having a person like the poet Homer to extol them," Mehmed II is reported to have said:

God has reserved for me, through so long a period of years, the right to avenge this city and its inhabitants. For I have subdued their enemies and have plundered their cities and have made them the spoils of the Mysians. It was the Greeks and Macedonians and Thessalians and Peloponnesians who ravaged this place in the past, and whose descendants have now through my efforts paid the just penalty, after a long period of years, for their injustice to us Asiatics at that time and so often in subsequent times.[126]

Eyüboğlu goes on to suggest that Atatürk said something similar on winning the final battle of the Greco-Turkish war in 1922. Atatürk allegedly claimed that he had finally avenged the Trojans against the Greeks.[127] In Eyüboğlu, we thus find a troubling species of humanism that attempted to reanimate mythical stories for present ends. The apparently harmless reference to the past—Turkish culture's Trojan origins—becomes more sinister when we consider how it resonated with the animosities between the Turks and Greeks in Eyüboğlu's own time.[128]

In this chapter, I have shown that humanist worldviews, however problematic, were preserved as the core of European culture in Turkey while simultaneously under siege by fascism in Europe. The humanist reforms enacted a form of cultural mimesis through which Turkey tried to become the flagship of Western European civilization.[129] The aim of the reforms, as we have seen, was not merely to copy essential ingredients of European culture but to generate a Turkish renaissance in the European model—a crucial distinction intellectuals and reformers made at the time. According to the Kemalist view, tanzimat reformers of the nineteenth century had chosen an eclectic approach to Westernization, failing to realize that the transformation of society had to be all-encompassing if it was to succeed. Twentieth-century republican reformers, in contrast, not only introduced secularism and revised the education system; they also altered the cultural practices of everyday life. The humanist critic Tanpınar once put his finger on the crux of Turkey's difficulties in this transitional phase. Quoting Dante, Tanpınar reminded his readers: "In order to represent an object, you first have to be that object."[130]

The mimetic appropriation of a Western European habitus together with a humanist worldview was tantamount to the realist reform of Turkish society, a transformation that spread from the urban centers to the rest of the country. By realist reform, I mean a process that fundamentally altered the way in which Turks perceived, and continue to perceive, reality. This was the result of a reciprocal, historically contingent process.[131] Auerbach's insight is helpful here; he argued that representing reality was linked to perceptions of the past. When Turks tried to mimetically reproduce Europe's humanist ideals, along with other European cultural practices, their views of both the present and the past changed in consort. This culminated, most importantly, in the country's new conceptualization of space and time—a new calendar and altered geopolitical relations. By claiming the remnants of Asia Minor's ancient civilizations as the country's own, the reforms generated a new sense of history, belonging, and identity.

How are we to evaluate this transformation? There is a dilemma that arises from a mimetic process that equates modernity with a certain vision of Europe.[132] Because of this, modernization still implies Westernization, just as it has since late Ottoman times. Constructing temporality along the axis of a progressive, secular, and modern Turkey (in contradistinction to a deficient, underdeveloped, and traditional Ottoman Empire) created obstacles that could not be overcome. Although humanists like Ataç raised awareness about the difference between representing and resembling Europe, there was no closing the gap between origin and copy or resolving the binary between modern and traditional. From a Western European point of view, Turkish modernity was, at best, a Platonic copy, not the result of a mimetic process in the Aristotelian sense. As a result, Turkish history, like all non-European histories, has simply become a variation on Europe's master narrative.[133] Although this narrative is, in itself, the product of a reciprocal exchange between Western Europe and its periphery, it has also become the normalized view of history. We can say, then, that in introducing the idea of modernity and national unity, Turkish reformers generated a set of problematic cross-identifications, and it is to this that we shall next turn.

3

Mimicry in Modern Turkey
The Place of German and Turkish Jews

COMMENTING ON INTERNATIONAL TENSIONS after the war that was supposed to end all wars, Albert Einstein mused about how Europe now perceived him: "By an application of the theory of relativity to the taste of readers, to-day in Germany I am called a German man of science and in England I am represented as a Swiss Jew. If I come to be regarded as a *bête noire*," he went on, "the descriptions will be reversed, and I shall become a Swiss Jew for the Germans and a German man of science for the English!"[1] With his usual concision, Einstein pointed out the interchangeability of Jewish, Swiss, and German affiliations at a time of rising anti-Semitism and shifting European relations. But the physicist's 1919 statement in the London *Times* would prove sadly prescient, for within two decades he would indeed become a German bête noire and be forced to leave Europe, ultimately becoming an American citizen. We can think of Einstein's comment as an epigraph for this chapter, which explains how the very scholars who were labeled un-German and degenerate by the Nazis came to be construed as "European men of science" by the Turkish reformers. To go one step further, I suggest here that Turkey's Europeanization necessitated the instrumentalization, but simultaneous disavowal, of the émigrés' Jewishness.

Émigrés to Turkey in the 1930s often said that Turkey was "unscathed by the Western plague"—a country untouched by either fascism or anti-Semitism.[2] This positive rhetoric has been handed down to us in the present, and many people, ranging across the entire confessional and political spectrum, view Turkey as the savior of hundreds of Germany's exiled scholars and their families. Taking a critical look at the status of Turkish and German

Jews between 1933 and 1945, we find, however, that the émigrés' place of exile was by no means immune to the kinds of bigotry, racism, and anti-Semitism that benighted Western Europe at the time. This chapter shows that the Turkish government did not explicitly pursue fascist and expansionist goals; even so, racialist and anti-Semitic views were widespread, and there was considerable public debate about the loyalty of Jewish Turks to the new nation.

Turkey, as we know from the previous chapter, did not commit itself to saving Jews from rising anti-Semitism in Europe—not even to saving all Jewish scholars who were willing to continue their work in the interest of its modernization project. In fact, Turkey's desultory attitude toward imperiled Jews is evident from another letter written by Einstein in September 1933. Communicating with the prime minister, İsmet İnönü, Einstein made the unusual offer of forty highly skilled and experienced "professors and doctors from Germany" who would be willing to work in Turkey "for a year without any remuneration in any of your institutions, according to the orders of your government." Although the offer came from a person as eminent as Einstein and implied no financial burden on the Turkish government, it was firmly declined.[3] As honorary president of the Union des Sociétés OSE, a Paris-based Jewish organization, Einstein tried to act as a mediator between his needy colleagues and the Turkish government.[4] İnönü declined Einstein's offer, implying that it contravened Turkish aims:

Although I agree that your proposal is very attractive, I have to inform you that I see no possibility to make this suggestion compatible with the laws and regulations of our country. As you surely know, distinguished Professor, we have already engaged under contract more than forty professors and physicians who have the same qualities and the same capacities, and most of whom are under the same political conditions as those who are the object of your letter. These professors and doctors have agreed to work here in conformity with the current laws and regulations. At present, we are trying to finalize a delicate mechanism, namely an organization comprising members who are very different by their origins, cultures, and languages. This is why at present, under the circumstances in which we are, it will unfortunately not be possible for us to hire a greater number of these gentlemen.[5]

The prime minister's rejection seems inexplicable when we consider that Turkish institutions continued to hire German émigrés, most of Jewish background, through other channels. But unlike the Zürich-based Notgemeinschaft, the Union des Sociétés stood specifically for the protection of Jews, something that the organization's letterhead made clear.[6] We can only speculate about his motives, but perhaps the prime minister did not want to set a precedent by hiring German scholars at the instigation of a patently Jewish organization. To be sure, Jews occupied a rather ambiguous place within the young Turkish Republic. In 1923, the republican government instituted what we can think of as a dual assimilatory policy: it required citizens—regardless of ethnic or religious background—to conform to a unified Turkish culture and language. At the same time, it implemented an equally assimilatory Westernization project that was designed to achieve cultural recognition from the heart of Europe: national powers like France, Germany, and Britain were supposed to confer legitimacy on the incipient Turkish state.

In examining the official rhetoric surrounding Turkey's minority populations and its relations with foreign states, we find that the period of Turkish renewal between 1923 and 1946, that is, between the foundation of the republic and the end of the humanist reform, was characterized by three dominant tropes—the eternal guest, *dönme*, and mimic. This chapter explores how these rhetorical tropes were used in interconnected ways to characterize Jewishness, Turkishness, and Europeanness. The cultural resonances of these tropes echo to this day: the notion of the eternal guest, as historian Rıfat Bali points out, evokes the migration of Sephardic Jews to the Ottoman Empire at the end of the fifteenth century. The term *dönme*, in turn, refers to Ottoman citizens who converted from Judaism to Islam in the seventeenth century. Since then the dönme has been associated with falseness and betrayal. The mimic was an anti-Semitic trope used by the Nazis, but, as we will see, the epithet was also used in late Ottoman and modern Turkish discourses of Westernization. Notwithstanding its Nazi associations, the mimic remains a powerful trope for signifying the failed process of Europeanization in present-day Turkey. By charting a genealogy of these tropes, I think we can learn something about the high price of Turkish modernity: we discover what was concealed, suppressed, and appropriated. By extension, we also learn something about the discursive continuities between Turkish modernity and the global postmodern.

Creating New Historical and Racialist Narratives: The Dönme and the Mimic

In the 1990s, Turkish civic leaders organized a series of public events to commemorate something long past—the arrival of Sephardic Jews in the Ottoman Empire after their expulsion from Spain and Portugal at the end of the fifteenth century. At the quincentennial commemoration, parallels were drawn between the Sephardic Jews, who had introduced the Ottomans to new technologies like book printing, and the German Jews, who in 1933 pioneered new methods in a wide variety of disciplines.[7] The tendency to draw such links points to the current fad for historical analogy, a fad that sees the past as a fecund repository for lessons in the present. Such lessons were not, in fact, drawn in the 1930s. The Turkish authorities then in charge of hiring émigré scholars refrained from making this specific comparison, drawing no conscious links between the flight of the Jews to the Ottoman Empire and the flight of Jews from Nazi Germany to modern Turkey.

As I pointed out in chapter 2, the Turkish minister of education, Reşit Galip, did, however, invoke an alternative historical analogy, one that emphasized both comings and goings and a different set of historical figures. He construed the arrival of academic émigrés from Europe in 1933 as a compensation for the Byzantine scholars who had fled Constantinople after its surrender to the Ottomans in 1453. In contrast to the rhetoric surrounding the quincentennial celebrations in the 1990s, rhetoric that highlighted the shared Jewishness of exiles separated by five hundred years of history, it did not seem to matter in 1933 that a significant number of the imported scholars were German-Jewish. Indeed, as I show here, the scholars were greeted as Europeans and not as Jews.

Of course, one ought not conclude from this that Turkey was free of racism and anti-Semitism during the 1930s. To give one example, the year 1934 saw thousands of Jewish Turks fleeing anti-Semitic attacks in Thrace. And, although generally frowned upon by the Turkish government, anti-Semitic propaganda was disseminated by journals like *Milli İnkilap* (National Revolution) and by writers like Nihal Atsız, who promoted Turanism, a racialist movement that called for the unification of the Turkic people.[8] Anti-Semitic rhetoric also circulated within the Turkish academy. We see this in a lecture delivered at Istanbul University in 1936 by prominent historian Şemseddin Günaltay. The lecture exemplifies the ways in which terms like *mimic* and *dönme* were used to categorize the modern European Turk. I will argue that these tropes point to profound anxieties about the stability of Turkishness as a marker of "racial" identity.

Günaltay's lecture titled "The Homeland of the Turks and the Question of Their Race" specified the supposed racial origins of Turks. Contesting the thesis put forth by Western Orientalists that Turks and Mongolians belong to the selfsame "yellow race," Günaltay disavowed the "yellowness" of Turks and reclassified them as "white." According to the historian, the original homeland of the Turks was not Mongolia—as generally assumed—but Turkistan, which he referred to as the "cradle of the Neolithic age."[9] Going even further, Günaltay construed a racial relationship between the ancient Sumerians and modern Turks.[10] While Günaltay's thesis seems improbable to us today—unsupported by either historical or scientific evidence—it is important to remember that this was not just the singular opinion of a conjectural racialist historian. Such views were in fact quite common. What lent real weight to Günaltay's claims, however, was his position as both a highly visible member of the Turkish parliament and a renowned scholar who would later preside over the Türk Tarih Kurumu (Institute for Turkish History). The newly founded institute would set about creating a new historical narrative for Westernized Turkey.[11] And it was claims like Günaltay's that undergirded the *millî tarih tezi*, "national history thesis," promulgated by the institute.[12]

Günaltay's "Homeland of the Turks and the Question of Their Race" can, in other words, be seen as indicative of the kinds of racial anxieties circulating in Turkey in the decade preceding the outbreak of World War II. These anxieties were manifest in anti-Semitic tropes that underscored the lecture's rhetoric. Günaltay seized on Reşidüddin, the thirteenth-century Jewish-born Persian historian, whom he criticized for equating Turks with Mongols. Turks did *not* originate in Mongolian Central and East Asia, Günaltay countered; this was, apparently, corroborated by Ottoman as well as European Orientalist scholars.[13] Günaltay proposed that, rather than being of the "yellow race," Turks were of the "Alpine type." In order to make his point and discredit the earlier historian, Günaltay reminded his audience of Reşidüddin's Jewish heritage and invoked the figure of the Jewish imposter. He suggested that Reşidüddin's thesis about the relationship between Turks and Mongolians was nothing more than an act of *mehareti kalemiyet*, "skillful writing" (i.e., fabrication). This, he said, casting aspersions about the thirteenth-century Persian, was just the kind of writing that came easily to a dönme—or "crypto-Jew."[14]

Günaltay's use of the word *dönme* warrants some explanation. The root of the noun is *dönmek*, the verb "to turn." But *dönme* also means "to convert," and it is this sense of the word that is of particular interest to us here. Historically, the term was applied to a community in Saloniki that converted from Judaism to Islam, following the example of Sabbatai Sevi, a messianic rabbi who was forced to renounce Judaism in 1666.[15] The nature of this conversion remains ambivalent to this day, since dönme developed a form of religious practice that combined elements of both Islam and Judaism. The polydenominational character of their beliefs has meant that dönme have been difficult to classify, a fact that has always been exploitable for political ends. In 1924, when Turkey and Greece agreed to exchange their respective Muslim and Christian populations, dönme were deemed Muslim and consequently deported from Greece to Turkey. In Turkey, on the other hand, dönme were not necessarily welcomed as Muslims, and their status within the new republic remained controversial.[16] In the intervening period, the dönme often came to be thought of as people who pretended to be Muslim yet secretly practiced Judaism.[17] Even today, dönme continue to be thought of like the proverbial Trojan horse—a danger posed by something that is not what it seems to be. Thus we find that the trope often crops up in political discourse where it is used to imply conspiracy and betrayal.[18]

Günaltay's revision of the place of Turks within a racial hierarchy illustrates how notions of Turkishness, Jewishness, and Europeanness were linked in modern Turkey. It was by branding Reşidüddin a deceitful Jew that Günaltay raised the possibility of constructing Turks as both white and European. Who knows what lay behind Günaltay's insistence on Turkish whiteness and Europeanness, and his scapegoating of dönme as untrustworthy crypto-Jews? But if we see Günaltay as symptomatic of broader currents within Turkish thought, then his comments seem to illustrate the profound racial and cultural anxieties aroused by Turkey's rapid process of secularization and Westernization.[19] Günaltay explicitly discouraged his audience from subscribing to Reşidüddin's ideas; his audience was instructed instead to follow the guidelines of the new Türk Tarih Kurumu, Institute of Turkish History. Following the institute's guidelines would, he assured them, contribute to a "high Turkish culture," as he called it, and prevent Turks from indulging in base imitation.[20] In making this claim, Günaltay addressed two occult fears. The first, as I have said, was the kind of fear posed by deception and lack of authenticity. Günaltay's other fear concerned the question of imitation: Turks were cautioned about those who pretended to be like them; at the same time, they themselves were to avoid pretending to be something they were not. Conversion, he seemed to imply, was as bad as superficial imitation.

Thinking about imitation and authenticity in modern Turkey brings to mind Homi Bhabha's useful insights into the politics of appropriation. Bhabha developed mimicry as a theoretical term to characterize power relations in British India. Mimicry, he argues, is one of the most effective strategies for establishing colonial power. And crucial here is the inherent ambivalence of mimicry, since it produces an identity that is *"almost the same, but not quite."*[21] The difference between the Anglicized colonial and the English colonizer was, according to Bhabha, a difference that could be exploited in order to maintain British control over the colony. Indeed, such difference might explain the continued influence of British culture in postcolonial India. Without equating colonial strategies in British India with Turkey's self-imposed appropriation of Western European culture, there are nonetheless instructive parallels to be drawn. Bhabha's insights help us understand the anxieties that were triggered by the Europeanization of Turkey, for his notion of mimicry highlights the difference between representation and repetition. Translated into the Turkish context, Bhabha's notion of mimicry demonstrates the difference between the European, who stands for Europe, and the Europeanized Turk, who is thought merely capable of aping the foreign.

As I have suggested, these anxieties appear in Günaltay's lecture when the historian specifically cautions his audience about superficial imitation and the dangers of slavishly copying Europe. Nor was Günaltay the only one to express such sentiments; other Turkish reformists, too, warned against the kind of superficial reproduction that could only give rise to hypocrisy.[22] To sum up, we can distinguish two distinct tropes in Günaltay's lecture: first, the figure of the dönme as Trojan horse—someone who tries to subvert the national community by infiltrating it under a false guise—and second, the mimic, who is too superficially Europeanized to effectively transform Turkish society. Such rhetoric was in keeping with the general tenor of public discourse in Turkey at the time. What lent provocation to the lecture, however, was the fact that, in 1936, Günaltay was speaking not only to a homegrown audience of Turkish scholars and students: among his listeners were also the German-Jewish scholars recently hired at Istanbul University. These émigrés were the very scholars who had been stigmatized at home for subverting German culture. Paradoxically, they were now deemed useful for overcoming the opposition between Orient and Occident and thought capable of helping the Turks become more than just mimics of the West. The relationship among notions of Jewishness, Europeanness, and Turkishness was rendered more convoluted by virtue of the fact that German émigrés were hailed as exemplary Europeans in Turkey. Creating a "high Turkish culture" was to be accomplished via the European scholar, who was in many cases a German-Jewish émigré.

The German-Jewish Émigré as the Exemplary European

At this juncture, it would be worth reviewing the contradictory attitudes toward Turkey's religious and ethnic minorities. In the initial years of their academic appointments, German Jews were not officially identified as Jews. At the same time, Turkey's indigenous Jews were subject to ongoing public scrutiny of their republican sympathies. In the 1920s, Turkish citizenship had indeed been extended to everyone irrespective of religious affiliation, but in social and cultural terms Jews and Armenians were never fully acknowledged as Turks. In the case of Greeks, it was agreed that more than one million Orthodox Greeks should be deported from Turkey to Greece in exchange for the nearly half a million Muslims living in Greece. Kurds, Arabs, Azeris, Laz, and numerous other predominantly Muslim communities were consequently subordinated and homogenized under the ethnic category "Turk." The remaining Armenian and Jewish communities—seen as resistant to assimilation—were subjected to wide-ranging "Turkification" measures of the early Republic.

An assimilationist campaign was begun in 1928 in an effort to force Turkish Jews to forgo Ladino for Turkish.[23] This was intended to establish the secular basis for Turkish citizenship and so achieve a kind of isomorphism among culture, nation, and geography. Indeed, some leading members of the Turkish-Jewish community like Moiz Kohen, who took the Turkish name Munis Tekinalp, subscribed to this assimilationist platform.[24] Yet these assimilationist strategies notwithstanding, truly inhabiting Turkishness seems to have been ultimately reserved for Muslim citizens alone.[25] Put another way, we can say that the boundaries of the ethnic Turk came to be drawn along strictly religious lines.[26] I would generally agree with Marc Baer, who points out that minorities were "purified from the body politic" during the 1920s and 1930s and that "extraneous elements" came to be seen as "parasites."[27] This did not, however, apply to the hundreds of Jewish Germans and their families who migrated to Turkey in the 1930s. When German Jews were hired for the Europeanization reforms, they were not seen as parasites. To the contrary, they were regarded as facilitators of progress and a means of bridging the gap between Western Europe and Turkey.

This more nuanced view takes us one step closer to understanding why German-Jewish scholars were greeted in Turkey not as Jews—or Germans, for that matter—but as Europeans. Of course I do not mean to imply that Turkey ought to have explicitly acknowledged the émigrés' Jewishness. Letters, memoirs, and archival sources show that conditions in Turkey made it possible for Jewish émigrés to continue identifying as German scholars, something they had been effectively denied by the Nazis, who categorized and persecuted them precisely as Jews. As Spitzer put it in one of his letters, the tight-knit German academic community in Istanbul provided the context for pursuing a somewhat "German life."[28] It is, then, perhaps unsurprising that Turks tended to see the émigrés as representatives of Europe. We find this expressed in many guises. Erol Güney, a newspaper correspondent who studied philosophy at Istanbul University with Reichenbach, said of the Diderot specialist Herbert Dieckmann that "he personified for me the perfect type of European intellectual, not a German, a French, a British, but a 'real' European, much before Europe started on its long and difficult period toward unity."[29] We see this, too, in the case of the Orientalist scholar Hellmut Ritter, who had been dismissed as a homosexual from Hamburg University in 1926 and made a home in Istanbul that same year. Fruitless efforts to secure another professorship in Germany brought Ritter to write: "The Turks are utterly uninterested in my past, what I stand for here—whether one wants to acknowledge this in Germany or not, regardless whether I do or don't—in the eyes of the Turks I don't stand for the German Orientalist tradition, but rather that of Europe."[30]

My point, then, is not to criticize the Turkish authorities for having "failed" to publicly acknowledge the fact that many of the émigrés had been vilified as Jewish, communist, or homosexual in their home countries. Rather, I want to shed light on Turkish immigration policy at this time and explain why the exiles' shared Europeanness was so strongly emphasized over the reasons that had led to their persecution in the first place. We recall that Galip, the minister of education, did not draw explicit comparisons between two historical moments of exodus, namely, the flight of the Sephardic Jews in the fifteenth century and the German Jews of his own day. It would have been logical to compare the two events, given the rich contribution made by the Sephardic Jews to intellectual and cultural life in the Ottoman Empire.[31] Galip and other Turkish officials did not explain why this resonance went unremarked. We can, however, indulge in some conjectural history and speculate why it is that past analogies are mobilized at some historical moments and not at others. My suggestion is that it did not then suit the Turkish authorities to stress the scholars' Jewishness. Drawing attention to this fact would have meant informing the Turkish public that Jewish Germans had been forced to leave their homes because they had been denied full rights as German citizens. At a time when Turkey was preoccupied with its own questions about assimilation and religious minorities, highlighting the general failure of mimetic and assimilationist projects must have seemed like a topic that was too hot to handle.[32]

For their part, the Nazis continued to construe Jews as Orientals and mimics—something a 1935 report to the Foreign Office in Berlin makes clear: "Due to their racial characteristics these people [Jewish emigrants] can adapt to the Turkish mentality particularly well and learn the country's language very quickly."[33] In this statement, racialist stereotyping goes hand in hand with notions of deceitful assimilation and mimicry. The Turkish ministry of education does not seem to have taken a clear stance against the Nazi pronouncements about Jews. As I have explained, however, it would not have been strictly within its own interests to do so. Until 1933, many, if not most, Germans of Jewish faith or background had defined themselves first and foremost as assimilated Germans. That their assimilation collapsed—or was, rather, so rapidly and effectively quashed by the Nazis—must have raised a specter for the Turks. Indeed, doubts about the viability of assimilation extended not only to Turkey's religious minorities, but to Turkey as a whole. We must remember that Turkish officials were principally concerned with assimilating Turkey's citizens to a unified language and culture. At the same time, the country itself looked to Western Europe for its model. To question assimilation, then, was to question whether appropriating and disseminating European knowledge would ever effectively transform Turks into Europeans. It would have meant asking whether Turks, like Jews, were bound to remain Orientals in the eyes of Western European Christians. And finally, it would have meant acknowledging that it was not up to the Turks themselves to determine whether they were European: the act of adjudication lay in the power of Western Europeans.[34]

Auerbach as the Eternal Guest

So far we have concentrated primarily on the firsthand accounts of émigrés and their Turkish hosts, but we learn something, too, from foreign travelers to Turkey. Swiss travel writer and journalist Annemarie Schwarzenbach, passing through Istanbul in 1933, made trenchant observations about the status of Europeans:

The Europeans are fearful in this country. None of them is at home; passing years don't change this. They are given weighty tasks; they accomplish them without the success of satisfying them. . . . They have pretty houses, tennis courts, a club, good horses. They also own this and that and live in a country that believes in the future and the benefits of reason, civilization, and progress, things that are so undervalued in Europe. The country is governed by a group of intellectually superior men, by honest democrats, who know no other goal than enfranchising their people as quickly as possible. And the Europeans who are appointed to assist in accomplishing this task may well believe that they will soon be superfluous. No one doubts the country or the people. But everyone has doubts about his own task. That is the fear.[35]

From Schwarzenbach we also learn something about the transitory character of the exile condition—something that Bertolt Brecht captured in his poem about the duration of exile: "Schlage keinen Nagel an die Wand, wirf den Rock auf den Stuhl" (Do not pound a nail in the wall, throw your coat on the chair). The émigrés in Turkey faced a kind of planned redundancy and could not readily settle, since their own superfluity was built into the Westernization reforms. Once the Westernization process was deemed complete, the country would have no further need for their services.[36] Thus, although they were regarded as necessary instructors in Western-style architecture, literature, music, and the natural sciences, their university contracts were initially limited to between three and five years. Someone like Leo Spitzer could emigrate to the United States with the prospect of spending the rest of his life there, but the German scholars who remained in Turkey could neither be sure of their employment prospects nor predict the outcome of the Westernization reforms. Most of them never became immigrants but remained émigrés.

The precariousness of life in Turkey helps explain Auerbach's attitude to his host country. After two years in Istanbul, he summed up the tribulations of living in the foreign port: *Die Reaktionäre misstrauen uns als Ausländer, die Fascisten als Emigranten, die Antisfascisten als Deutschen, und Antisemitismus gibt es auch* ("The conservatives distrust us as foreigners, the fascists as emigrants, the antifascists as Germans, and anti-Semitism exists, too").[37] Auerbach's typology provides some indication as to the complex sociopolitical climate that prevailed at the time. In the first instance, he refers to conservative, reform-leery Turks; second, to the organized network of Istanbul Nazis who tried to limit the activities of the German émigrés; and, third, to the antifascist émigrés. Anti-Semitism, so his letter implies, crisscrossed all three of these circles. The challenge for Auerbach and other Jewish scholars stemmed, in other words, from their confrontation with various politically motivated groups in Turkey, each of which competed vigorously over the direction of the reforms. If the Turkish ministry of education had an investment in the émigrés as scholars devoid of national agenda, other groups in Turkey did not perceive them in quite such politically neutral terms. Istanbul University is a case in point. In order to ensure—as if this would have been necessary—that Auerbach abstain from German propagandizing, his employment contract, dated 1936, stipulated the following terms: *Monsieur Auerbach s'engage à s'abstenir de toute activité politique, économique et commerciale et ainsi que toute activité ayant pour but de faire la propagande d'un gouvernement étranger. Il ne peut accepter aucune fonction dans des institutions ou établissements étrangers* ("Mr. Auerbach commits himself to abstaining from political, economical, and commercial activities and hence from activities serving the propaganda of a foreign government. He is not allowed to accept any other position in foreign institutions or establishments").[38]

In other words, privileges in the host country were contingent on the émigrés' agreeing to suspend any national agenda of their own. Caught between a country that no longer wanted them and a country that wanted them only conditionally and for an indeterminate, but potentially limited, period of time, we can think of them as perpetual guests. Auerbach and his colleagues may not have been officially compared with the Sephardic Jews discussed earlier, but their status in Turkey was a comparable one. Rıfat Bali argues in this regard that Sephardic Jews were perceived as guests whose loyalty to Turkey was constantly under suspicion. The notion of the Jew as guest is, Bali argues, reaffirmed in the declarations of gratitude and indebtedness that contemporary Jews express to the Turks even half a millennium after their original flight from the Iberian Peninsula.[39] This is not the place to compare notions of Jewishness in Europe and the Ottoman Empire, but it is worth considering that the Ottoman-Turkish notion of the "eternal guest" parallels that of the Jewish "eternal wanderer" in Christian thought,[40] while the dönme is akin to the figure of the mimic in European discourses.

Considerable scholarly attention has been devoted to the figure of the wandering Jew. Galit Hasan-Rokem and Alan Dundes, for example, see this trope as having always been a "pivotal reflection of Jewish-Christian relationships."[41] Rather than interpreting the wandering Jew as part of Christian legend, Edward Timms examines the trope within a specifically German context and shows its transformations from a first appearance around 1600 to its appropriation by the Nazis in the early twentieth

Margaret Bourke-White, Flock of sheep grazing among Hebrew tombstones in one of the world's oldest cemeteries near "The Field of Arrow," founded by Jews in exile from sixteenth-century Spain, overlooking "Sky Water of Europe," an old sultan's picnic grounds outside Istanbul, circa 1940. Photo: Margaret Bourke-White/Time & Life Pictures. By permission of Getty Images.

century.[42] Elizabeth Grosz, again, regards the Jew as a trope of "alterity, occupying the position of *perennial other* for millennia."[43] There is room for further research into the construction of Jewishness in the Ottoman period. Such a study would likely provide insights into the nature of Jewish-Muslim relationships and map the transition from Jews as *millet* (nation) during Ottoman times to their reclassification as a minority community based on a shared religion in the twenty-first century.[44] Thanks to Rıfat Bali's and Avigdor Levy's work, however, we can assume that the "lingering sense of Jewish insecurity and feeling of 'apartness'"[45] stemmed, at least in some measure, from the social status of Sephardic Jews as guests residing in a Muslim world.

We find evidence of this in the Turkish policies toward Jewish refugees from 1933 on. Before the outbreak of the war, Turkey was regarded as a transit country for Europe's Jews; several thousand refugees migrated to Palestine via Turkey, giving Istanbul the character of something of a waiting room.[46] Yet it is a little-appreciated fact that Jewish refugees were not generally welcome to stay.[47] This became clear when, in response to the Jewish flight from Nazi Germany in early 1939, Prime Minister Refik Saydam declared emphatically that Turkey was not going to provide refuge to Jews. He conceded that there were Jews among the people brought in to serve the country's national and administrative needs. Provision was made for their families to enter Turkey so that these people could, as he put it, "work with comfortable minds." However, he stipulated that these family members could not seek employment.[48] This shift in Turkish policy vis-à-vis Jewish émigrés also meant that Turkish consulates in Germany started to require proof of Aryan descent as a precondition for granting an entry visa to Turkey.[49] The fact that many of the German migrants to Turkey were Jewish was by now part of the public consciousness.

The newspaper *Yeni Sabah* reported in the summer of 1939 that German Jews in Turkey were being stripped of their citizenship by the German authorities.[50] While closing Turkish borders to other German Jews by demanding certificates of Aryan descent, Turkish authorities now granted citizenship to some few émigrés already employed at universities or government institutions. Hence, the migration of greater numbers of Jews to Turkey was impeded, but for earlier émigrés who had become stateless there was hope for improving their condition. Becoming a Turkish citizen meant, however, that professors were no longer eligible for the higher salary reserved for foreign professors. For scholars like Hirsch, the prospect of living in safety outweighed any financial loss.[51] There are contradictory reports about the number of émigrés who applied for Turkish citizenship and the relative success of their applications. According to German consular records, Auerbach was the only Jewish émigré not to apply for Turkish citizenship in Istanbul in 1939.[52] Joining the others would have given him a chance to solve his legal predicament, but, for some unknown reason, he instead risked statelessness. Maybe he thought that his application would not be successful; perhaps he trusted that the Turkish government would grant protection to upper-level employees at governmental and educational institutions. For other Jewish refugees desperately trying to escape fascism, there was no such choice or protection: Turkish citizenship was simply not an option.[53]

Contrary to what we might expect, acquiring Turkish citizenship did not seem to significantly impact the émigrés' social status. With or without Turkish citizenship, émigrés were equally regarded as privileged guests.[54] Being a guest has its undoubted advantages—including special treatment and elevated social status—but it also has its obligations and restrictions. Under the pressure of showing loyalty to the host country, émigrés tended to withhold substantive critique. They did not, for instance, expose any of the difficulties they faced at the university, nor were they vocal about their dealings with Turkish authorities. Indeed, Auerbach rarely commented on Turkey in public, and the country occupies only a marginal place in his published work. That he harbored a secret criticism is, however, evident from his private correspondence with friends and colleagues in Western Europe. Today, this correspondence provides us with insights into Auerbach's views on Turkish modernization and his own role in this process. It is here, in the private letters, that we find him critically assessing the country's reform measures, its nationalist politics, and its anti-Semitism.[55]

His 1938 letter to his former assistant Freya Hobohm, for example, expresses concern about Turkey's attempt to reinvent itself as a European nation by cutting itself off from its own roots.[56] Auerbach understood the logic behind abandoning the Ottoman cultural tradition in order to secularize the republic. By the same token, he remained critical of Turkey's official policy of renouncing its Ottoman heritage.[57] Such political decisions, Auerbach wrote to Walter Benjamin in 1936 (and reiterated in a 1952 essay, "Philologie der Weltliteratur" [Philology of World Literature]), contributed to the loss of historical consciousness and the standardization of culture.[58] While he may have felt safe expressing such views to friends and colleagues in Germany, Auerbach never said as much to his Turkish audiences—a point to which I will return in a subsequent chapter. In fact, it is clear that Auerbach felt censored. In a letter to another former assistant, Martin Hellweg, discussing the progress of Turkish educational reform, Auerbach was explicit about the fact that he could not publicly express what he held to be true: "was ich für die Wahrheit halte, könnte ich nicht öffentlich äußern."[59]

An excerpt from Auerbach's 1946 letter to Werner Krauss, his former colleague in Marburg, shows exactly what was expected of intellectual émigrés in Turkey. Auerbach explained why the postwar position he was offered at Berlin's Humboldt University was unsuitable, and he reflected on how working in Turkey had affected his political stance:

> I am, after all, a typical liberal. If anything, the very situation which the circumstances offered to me has but strengthened this inclination. Here I am enjoying the great liberty of *ne pas conclure*. More than in any other situation, it was possible for me to remain free of any commitment. It is exactly this attitude of somebody who does not belong to any place, and who is essentially a stranger without the possibility of being assimilated, which is desired and expected from me.[60]

The letter illuminates more than just the reasons for Auerbach's reluctance to commit to Humboldt University, then located in Soviet-occupied East Berlin; it tells us something about his standing in modern Turkey. And, coming from an assimilated German Jew expelled from his native country, his words seem rather poignant. Instead of seeking, or being called upon, to assimilate, he understood his prescribed task in avowedly unassimilationist terms. He felt that it was necessary to conserve and embody his European identity so he could be a role model for the upcoming generation of Turkish students and scholars. Moreover, he understood that Turks wanted him to remain what I have referred to as the eternal guest. This, in itself, made cultural assimilation undesirable, if not impossible. Without speculating about Auerbach's private motivations and inner thoughts, I wish to emphasize exactly how narrow was the range of choices then at his disposal. It was the very impossibility to assimilate in Turkey that ensured Auerbach's safety and social status during the war. His comfortable and stimulating life in Bebek was contingent on his continued commitment to transmitting European scholarship. The deal that Auerbach implicitly struck with Turkey was, in other words, dependent upon preserving—not transcending—difference. Accepting this deal was what allowed Auerbach to survive the Holocaust.

After the end of the war, Auerbach was once again offered Turkish citizenship. The offer by Turkish authorities had nothing to do with Auerbach's relationship to the place in which he now lived; in fact, Auerbach is known not to have spoken much Turkish. Writing to Werner Krauss, Auerbach conceded that Turkish citizenship would allow him to travel, but he thought that accepting such an offer would be dishonorable if one planned to leave the country.[61] To be sure, Auerbach's legal status would have been at least temporarily clarified by his becoming a Turkish citizen. Nonetheless, he again decided to take a risk and await the possibility of emigrating once more. It is in this light that we understand Auerbach's words in a letter to Martin Hellweg: *Türken sind wir nicht geworden, nicht einmal rechtlich, jetzt sind wir wieder passlose Deutsche, alles ist provisorisch* ("We did not become Turks, not even legally; now we are Germans without passports again, and everything is provisional").[62] Declining Turkish citizenship and hence the possibility of a lifelong commitment to Turkey, Auerbach finally took leave from Istanbul University in 1947. Without the security of an academic position, but with *Mimesis* among his papers—it had been published in Bern the previous year—Erich Auerbach and his wife Marie moved to the United States. Family reasons—his son was a graduate student at Harvard—and the hope of better working conditions at an internationally acclaimed institution undoubtedly played a role in this decision. Yet the vulnerable status of Jews in Turkey, especially between 1939 and 1943, also likely impacted his decision to leave. The following overview highlights the changes in Turkish attitudes toward European and Turkish Jews and discusses the political, cultural, and academic conditions during Auerbach's tenure in Turkey.

The Inassimilable Turkish Jew

The Turkish government enabled German-Jewish intellectuals to live and work under respectable conditions at Turkish institutions, yet, as we know, it applied a contradictory policy to other Jews fleeing the Holocaust after 1939. Among those trying to escape deportation were thousands of Jews who were still, or had once been, citizens of the Ottoman Empire and the new Turkey. Now trapped in Nazi-occupied territories, many tried to find ways of escaping to Turkey or using Turkey as a transit point. Thanks to the intervention of Turkish ambassadors and consuls like Selâhattin Ülkümen on the island of Rhodes or Behiç Erkin and Necdet Kent in France, an unknown number of Jews managed to escape deportation or were released from concentration camps because they could prove their Ottoman or Turkish citizenship. Behiç Erkin's grandson, Emir Kıvırcık, asserts that in France alone some twenty thousand Jews were thereby rescued from deportation.[63] Such claims seem exaggerated, and the numbers still need to be verified by a comparative analysis of archival sources. The records I found in German archives indicate that there were, in toto, some five thousand Turkish Jews living in occupied territories. It is not clear how many of these were saved.[64]

In fact, Corinna Guttstadt argues that between 1938 and 1945, Turkey intended exactly the opposite: rather than meaning to save people, it deliberately deprived "several thousand of its Jewish nationals living abroad of their citizenship."[65] While this may be true, files in the Berlin political archive show that a number of Turkish ambassadors and consuls in Nazi-controlled territories did attempt to protect not all but at least some of their citizens. Nazis at the 1942 Wannsee Conference had decided behind closed doors that all European Jews, including those in Turkey, were to be subject to the "final solution." Turkish authorities would later argue that Turkey did not differentiate between Jewish Turks and non-Jewish Turks and, on these grounds, tried to get some of their Jewish citizens out of France and other countries controlled by the Germans.[66]

Yet this stance did not cohere, as Guttstadt demonstrates, with internal Turkish policies at the time, nor can it be said that Turkish authorities exhausted all avenues for saving their own nationals. Indeed, the government's dealings with the Nazis sometimes seem to have been rather too cozy. In 1943, the Turkish embassy in Berlin negotiated with the Nazi Foreign Office over the timing of the transfer of Turkish Jews to Turkey. At this meeting, the Turkish representative said that his government wanted to "avoid the mass immigration of Jews, particularly of those Jews who had correct Turkish papers but have not had any contact with Turkey for decades."[67] It seems clear from this that the Turkish authorities in Germany and those in the Nazi-occupied territories were interested neither in protecting all their citizens[68] nor in treating Jewish and Muslim Turks equally.

In 1942, anti-Semitism in Turkey reached a critical level. *Struma*, a ship carrying almost eight hundred Jewish refugees from Romania, arrived near the Istanbul coast and waited for ten weeks for permission to proceed to Palestine. The ship was denied access to the Mediterranean by the British, who refused to issue visas, while the Turks allowed only a few refugees to disembark in Istanbul. Eventually, the Turks towed the crippled ship through the Bosporus to the Black Sea, where it was set adrift and later attacked by the Soviets. All but one of the passengers were killed.[69] After the tragedy and in defense of Turkey's decision, Prime Minister Saydam declared that "Turkey can not be a homeland for those who are unwanted elsewhere." This statement effectively stemmed immigration to Palestine via Turkey.[70] In addition, he dismissed Jewish journalists employed at the Turkish news agency L'Agence Anatolie.[71] It should be noted that Saydam's statement was made after the fate of the European Jewry had already been decided at the Wannsee Conference. Turkey's refusal to help Jewish refugees that same winter can be interpreted as preempting Turkey's own anti-Jewish legislation.[72]

Faced with economic difficulties in 1942, the Turkish government introduced a capital tax that discriminated between Muslims, non-Muslims (*gayrimüslim*), dönme, and foreigners (*ecnebi*). The new tax applied mostly to non-Muslim minorities, and, as a result of the regulations introduced to "Turkify" the economy, Turkish Jews lost a significant amount of property.[73] More than fourteen hundred non-Muslims, who were unable to pay the required tax, were forced to work in a labor camp in Aşkale, near Erzurum.[74] Unlike Turkish Jews, German Jews were not treated as non-Muslims. Rather, they were classified as foreigners under the tax regulation and were hence subject to a lower tax rate than "regular" non-Muslims. [75] The debate over whether dönme ought to be considered Jews or Muslims was revived in the increasingly anti-Semitic atmosphere of the early 1940s. It was decided that dönme should pay double the taxes paid by Muslims, but not as much as Jews.[76] We can conclude from this that, however they may have been thought of before, by the middle of the war Turkish Jews were clearly set apart as an inassimilable ethno-religious community. The popular anti-Semitic mobilization during this time can be seen in leading national newspapers that published cartoons depicting Jews as big-nosed, shameless profiteers.[77]

There were widespread doubts about the loyalty of Turkish Jews to the republic. As part of the debate surrounding the new capital tax, leading journalist Nadir Nadi wrote that if non-Muslims wanted to prove they were Turks, they must either sacrifice their wealth for the good of the nation or leave the country.[78] Similar reasoning underscored statements made in a university lecture given by a Turkish army major in 1943. He blamed Turkish Jews for ignoring "the commands of the nation who had given them refuge [450 years earlier!]. We are not Germans to crush them beneath our feet," he went on. "But the faith in our Government tells us that slowly but surely we will reach our end. Then, only then, will this country be ours."[79]

This exceedingly low tolerance for Jews in Turkey was also apparent to Helmuth James von Moltke, the founder of the Kreisau resistance group against Hitler who visited the country in 1943 in order to prepare a peace plan with the Allies.[80] On his two brief visits to Istanbul, Moltke met members of the émigré community, including the economist Alexander Rüstow, who had a close collegial relationship with Auerbach, and the agriculturist Hans Wilbrandt. Moltke provided Rüstow and Wilbrandt with a detailed memo about the situation in Germany and the uprising in the Warsaw Ghetto. The two émigrés functioned as mediators between Moltke and the U.S. secret service.[81] It is not clear whether Auerbach and other émigrés were aware of Moltke's plan. What is interesting for our purposes, however, is that Moltke perceived Istanbul as a racially segregated city. In a letter to his wife, Freya von Moltke, in July 1943, Helmuth James von Moltke wrote:

Everyone is highly conscious of race. Zita, Leverkühn's employee, is Greek. She does not speak to Turks. The Jews are complete outcasts here; they are addressed with the familiar Thou and no one shakes hands with them or offers them a chair, even if they are rolling in money and are thoroughly Europeanized. Levantines are children of mixed marriages with Italians or Greeks. Also, the child of a German and a Greek mother is Levantine, and is socially subordinate to Turks. It is all very strange.[82]

Moltke's impressions of everyday life in Istanbul inadvertently point to the anomaly that is at the heart of this chapter: Turkish Jews were ostracized, notwithstanding their Western European roots and habitus, even while German Jews helped Europeanize the nation. What linked both German and Turkish Jews was, however, the constant reminder of their precarious circumstances.

In the last two years of the war, matters started improving. When Auerbach reviewed his own situation during this time in a letter to Martin Hellweg after the war, he wrote: "Against all odds, we were well; the new regime did not penetrate the Bosporus; that really says it all. We lived in our apartment and didn't suffer anything worse than minor troubles and fear: until the end of 1942 things looked really bad, but then the cloud slowly lifted."[83] Indeed, after the labor camps for non-Muslim minorities were closed and the unpaid capital tax debts were dissolved in 1943, anti-Semitism diminished in intensity.[84] During the single-party regime, president İsmet İnönü had managed to keep Turkey out of the war—World War I had been a lesson in defeat. In his study of Turkish foreign policy during World War II, Selim Deringil argues that Turkey pursued a policy of "active neutrality" because leaders knew too well the military and economic weaknesses of their country.[85] Turkey waited until 1944, when Germany's defeat was obvious, to stop delivering the all-important chromite to Germany, and, at long last, it severed diplomatic relationships with the Nazis.[86] This also meant that the government, after years of severe restrictions against Jewish refugees, allowed the Jewish Agency to facilitate the transit of 6,800 refugees to Palestine. Many of these were children from Romania who arrived in Istanbul by ship, where they were transferred to trains.[87] In February 1945, Turkey finally declared war on Germany.

The Mock European

In late Ottoman discourses that negotiated notions of authenticity and inauthenticity, the figures of the *züppe* and the *kukla*, the Europeanized dandy and the puppet, were popular tropes delimiting socially acceptable levels of Westernization. The years of Auerbach's exile in Turkey were, on the other hand, informed by transnational cross-identifications and deep concerns about Turkey's Europeanness. Figures of Jewishness like the disloyal dönme and the eternal guest shaped Turkish ideas about home, belonging, and the national character. For their part, the Nazis created an image of Jews as inauthentic mimics and used this as one of the grounds for their expulsion and extermination. Turks, on the other hand, used the trope of the mimic as a corrective in the Europeanization debates of modern Turkey. *Taklitçilik*, mimicry, once a word that meant both to "imitate" and "ridicule," stopped having a subversive connotation during the course of the Europeanization reforms.[88] Not only was imitation disassociated from subversive mockery, but a distinction was introduced between the Turkish mimic and the genuinely European Turk.

4

Germany on the Bosporus
Nazi Conspiracies and Émigré Politics

ON FEBRUARY 1, 1933, just two days after Hitler seized power, Istanbul's only German-language daily, *Türkische Post* (Turkish Post), was already declaring its colors. The paper flashed the headline "Deutsch als Weltsprache" (German as world language), and, taking a page from the Nazis' own expansionist rhetoric, it set out the benefits of spreading German abroad. Familiarity with German, the lead article claimed, would promote German interests among Russian, Turkish, Arabic, and Spanish speakers, and it would enable citizens of these respective countries to cultivate valuable ties with Germany.[1] It is unsurprising that the newspaper was ready to promote the study of German in Turkey so soon after Hitler's rise to power. Such ideas caught on quickly with members of the large expatriate German community in Turkey, that is, with Germans who had settled in Turkey before 1933. For a man like Auerbach, who would consider himself lucky to escape the Nazis, such developments were worrisome, for they showed that the Nazi shadow could intrude even here, more than a thousand miles from Berlin. The image of the Nazi shadow extending so far to the east is, however, no mere metaphor. While in Istanbul, Auerbach and his fellow exiles would come under the control of Nazi agents. These agents did not have the authority to expropriate, imprison, or kill the exiles, yet the agents were a daily irritant—a perpetual reminder of the precariousness of life on the Bosporus. Moreover, they tried to curtail the influence of the German-Jewish émigrés and to minimize their role in modernizing Turkish society.

Earlier chapters showed that Auerbach did not stumble into an intellectual and political void when he migrated to Turkey: awaiting him there was a mix of humanist and nationalist thought. In this chapter, we find that Auerbach's time in exile was further shaped by the very forces he sought to flee—German fascism. The city was alive with the competing intellectual and political agendas of Turkish nationalists on the one hand and German fascists on the other. What the exiled intellectual made of this tense climate—what he took on or turned down—makes up the subject of this chapter. We will trace his path through the landscape of German Istanbul, where Nazis spied in the halls of the university and German sympathizers plotted behind closed doors. Hitherto undiscovered documents in the German consular archive and unpublished letters by Spitzer and Auerbach reveal the complex relationships and conflicts that arose from Nazi efforts to meddle in the émigrés' academic and personal lives.

National Socialism in Istanbul

Before we turn to Auerbach and the other German émigrés, it would be worth taking a brief look at the status of expatriate Germans in the Turkish metropolis. Since the mid-nineteenth century, more than a thousand German and Austrian citizens had lived in Istanbul, where they founded numerous cultural and religious organizations.[2] This expatriate German community, known as the *Deutsche Kolonie* (German colony), socialized in organizations like the Protestant Parish Istanbul (founded in 1843), the Teutonia Club (1847), the Society of German Women in Constantinople (1856), the German Hospital (1877), and the German School Istanbul (1868).[3] The founding of the Turkish Republic in 1923 saw a number of additional institutes, including the Archeological Institute Istanbul and a branch of the well-respected German Orient Institute (1929). The number and diversity of these cultural and educational venues suggest that the German community was organized around various shared forms of social, political, cultural, and religious life. It further suggests that there was a ready-made institutional framework for the cultivation of German cultural and intellectual life even prior to the advent of Nazism and the influx of new émigrés. In 1933, Nazi party officials would take advantage of this and open their first office under the auspices of the Teutonia Club. Soon many other cultural organizations likewise came under the control of the party. If the expatriate community seriously opposed such Nazi infiltration, it is not evident from the historical record. Certainly there were isolated individuals who voiced their objections. Yet the community as a whole seems to have been swayed by political developments in Germany.

The spread of Nazism, anticommunism, and anti-Semitism during the 1930s meant that a significant portion of Istanbul's German-speaking community was hostile, rather than welcoming, to the recent émigrés.[4] Those Germans with openly Nazi sympathies gravitated toward the German consulate, the Teutonia Club, the German School Istanbul, and the bookstore Kalis—all places that explicitly barred Jews and opponents of the Nazi government.[5] As part of the so-called *Gleichschaltung* (bringing into line), the Nazi party branch in Istanbul brought many of the German organizations under its control.[6] As in Nazi Germany, young Germans in Istanbul were organized in the Hitler Jugend (Hitler Youth) and the Bund Deutscher Mädchen (League of German Girls). *Türkische Post* became the official mouthpiece of the Nazi party in Turkey,[7] stipulating the role that expatriate Germans might play in disseminating Nazi beliefs.[8] And, in no time at all, it published excerpts from Hitler's *Mein Kampf* and introduced topics like "racial hygiene" to Istanbul's German readers.[9] *Türkische Post* also documented, in painstaking detail, the growing number of Nazi supporters in Turkey.[10] As early as 1935, German consul Toepke bragged that more than a quarter of the city's German residents had enrolled in the Nazi party: of the 950 citizens of the German Reich in Istanbul, as many as 225 had become official party members.[11]

The newly constituted Reichsministerium für Wissenschaft, Erziehung und Bildung (imperial ministry of science and education) continued Weimar Germany's earlier efforts to establish close ties with Turkish tertiary institutions. Turkish authorities were aware of the fact that the scholars sent by the German ministry were representatives of the Nazi government; they might have further assumed—quite correctly as it turns out—that these scholars wanted to make Turkey dependent on fascist Germany. Yet, although Turkish authorities were wary of Germany's political aspirations, they did not put a stay on relations with Nazi Germany until 1944. It is difficult to explain why Turkey may have pursued this contradictory political agenda. Perhaps the authorities wanted to hedge their bets; perhaps it was the result of competing forces within the ministry of education. For now we can say only this: even while the Turkish ministry pursued an anti-Nazi agenda by hiring émigré scholars, in some cases it simultaneously acted in complicity with the German ministry of science and education by importing Nazi scholars.

Run-ins between émigrés and Nazis in Istanbul and Ankara were thus inevitable. After the first wave of emigration in the summer of 1933, the Foreign Office in Berlin requested that the German embassy in Turkey establish formal contact and set up meetings with the émigrés. By inviting representatives of the émigré organization Notgemeinschaft to the German embassy, the ambassador hoped to persuade them to toe the party line and better attend to German economic, cultural, and political interests. The Notgemeinschaft was, of course, not quite so easily won over: two representatives, Philipp Schwartz and Rudolf Nissen, managed to prevent the swastika flag from being flown at the meeting.[12] This Pyrrhic victory notwithstanding, it was clear that the ambassador meant business, and the émigrés could not entirely ignore that fact.[13] They were, after all, in a position of considerable social and political vulnerability. They had been plunged into an unfamiliar environment by fate rather than design, they were isolated from friends and family, and many lacked the resources necessary for setting up life in a new place—familiar possessions, linguistic skills, bicultural fluency, a secure livelihood, and even, in later years, legal residency status and the liberty to move around. These problems were, to some extent, exacerbated by virtue of the fact that the émigrés were intellectuals. Their work lives and to some extent their personal lives, too, revolved around their capacity to express themselves and have their work published and understood. This dependence on the German language, German research materials, and a German audience meant they could not readily afford to ignore the expatriate community. The more Nazism spread its ghastly pall over the German community in Turkey, the more cautious and complicated the encounters between the émigrés and the German establishment would become.

It was an open secret that German consular and embassy officials, as well members of the Nazi party, closely monitored the émigrés' activities. There must have been spies and informants everywhere, for the German consulate and embassy provided the Foreign Office in Berlin with lengthy annual reports documenting the cultural and political activities of Germans, particularly émigrés, in Turkey. These reports were not only descriptive; they were also prescriptive, demonstrating a long-range vision for the German community abroad. Reports recommended instituting a Turkish-German book exchange and organizing German film screenings, theater performances, and concerts.[14] Significantly for our story, these reports also suggested ways of countering the influence of émigrés at the universities. Vice Consul Saucken's 1935 report, for example, illustrates the nature of the émigrés' predicament: the consul pointed out that émigré scholars could not impart German knowledge in the German language and simultaneously agitate against Germany. Indeed, they could not easily relinquish the very cultural resources and research material upon which their scholarship depended. This insight explains why only a handful of scholars, including the pathologist Schwartz, boycotted the purchase of German equipment needed for updating Turkish universities.[15]

Most émigrés were not as daring as Schwartz; they tried to avoid open confrontation so as not to attract attention from the embassy and consulate. Whether this strategy was expedient remains an open question, yet it was certainly understandable. And, of course, it met the Nazis' interests. In 1935, the consulate reported to the Foreign Office in Berlin that, with few exceptions, most of Istanbul's forty-six émigré scholars were not involved in anti-German activities and could thus be considered "loyal." There are, of course, many ways of interpreting this loyalty. For German consul Toepke, its meaning was clear: it was because the professors represented the high standard of German science and scholarship in Turkey that they possessed indisputable "cultural value" for Nazi Germany.[16]

The Spitzer Affair

Leo Spitzer knew his own standing in Istanbul and was quite aware of his value to the German consul. Perhaps because he relied on his influential position, he was among the few émigrés to risk an open stance against the Nazis and protest instances of anti-Semitism. In 1935, he went so far as to complain directly to Vice Consul Saucken about Ambassador Keller's "shameful" and "embarrassing" behavior toward exiled Jewish violinist Licco Amar. Amar had been concertmaster of the Berlin Philharmonic and played with Paul Hindemith in the Amar-Hindemith String Quartet.[17] While in Turkey, Amar became professor of music at the conservatory in Ankara; he played in a chamber orchestra with eminent Orientalist Hellmut Ritter, himself closely connected to the émigré community. Amar was, in other words, a musician of some note, well known to fellow émigrés and respected in the community at large. This no doubt contributed to Spitzer's sense of outrage when he witnessed the ambassador neglecting to shake Amar's hand after a performance he had given with Ritter. Presuming that the ambassador had deliberately refused to thank the violinist because he was a Jew, Spitzer wrote an enraged letter to the vice consul in December 1935:

A year ago, you spoke to me in such an open and sensitive manner about the emigrant problem that perhaps I may be allowed to voice my feelings about the recent shameful event at the Amar concert held at the German School. What an embarrassing and contradictory impression it must make on the numerous Germans and foreigners who love German music and hardly ever get to hear such outstanding offerings performed by Germans—that the official representatives of the German Reich listened to a concert by a Jewish artist and deigned to shake not his hand, but only his fellow performers, whom he himself raised to these artistic heights. Is the virus transmitted by the ear less dangerous than that of the handshake? Does one want to reverse the fact that an unwanted violinist produces Beethovenian sounds? And is the "be embraced, ye millions" supposed to be replaced by internal border lines? It is said that our times are no longer those of Beethoven; they are those of the conqueror and *real* politician. But whom can one conquer by such *real* political means? Neither of the two German groups can be satisfied by this half measure, this listening and not-wanting-to-have-listened, this attending and discriminating—and especially not the Turkish witnesses of such tragicomedy. *Beethoven* makes the right kind of propaganda: he wins *hearts*. I have a hard time understanding people who, in tolerating such cultural contrariety, bring it to the surface and lead it ad absurdum. Are they not torn apart by the lie they are complicit in, and why do they enter a stage where every one of their movements is warped by a distorting mirror? It's a bitter thought for the German that here he can only listen to German music undisturbed at Robert College, the Casa d'Italia, or the Fransız Tiyatrosu. This is what I wanted to say; forgive my openness.[18]

This hitherto unpublished letter, in which Spitzer expresses his outrage over the blatant anti-Semitism and hypocrisy of German officials, implies that it was only in American, Italian, and French cultural and educational venues that émigrés could perform and enjoy "German culture" undisturbed. Whether he meant this literally or ironically is not entirely clear, but this ambiguity in itself points to the interesting rhetorical devices that Spitzer uses in the letter. It is, for example, the figure of the Turk, who, as a witness to the ambassador's ambivalence about listening to German music played by a Jew, ultimately exposes the Nazis' bigotry of the situation. By way of alternative, Spitzer invokes the ideal of German universalism through the reference to Beethoven's Ninth Symphony, op. 125—a universalism that was being systematically destroyed by National Socialism.

With the quote *"Seid umschlungen, Millionen"* (Be embraced, ye millions) from Schiller's poem *An die Freude* (Ode to Joy), which Beethoven set into music in the final choral movement of the symphony, Spitzer conjured up the image of an ideal past. Here Germans could be at once undivided and all inclusive, particular, yet universal.[19] Spitzer's letter is also underscored by a kind of musical Orientalism—a sonic corollary of the Turkish observer to whom I referred earlier. For Spitzer, it is Beethoven's appropriation of Turkish musical idioms that functions as the ultimate signifier of German universalism: the "Turkish" march ushers in the appeal to universal brotherhood that comes with the joyful finale. It is, Spitzer suggests, this all-embracing spirit that has now come under threat. The Nazis, of course, idealized Beethoven for antithetical reasons—for them, Beethoven evidenced the very superiority of the Germans and Schiller's notion that universal brotherhood was reserved for only certain kinds of Germans.[20] In 1935, Schiller's vision had been sacrificed to this narrower interpretation: the very idea of inclusiveness had lost all practical meaning in German establishments controlled by the Nazis. The unifying motif could only survive elsewhere. It was preserved and fostered at cultural institutes in Istanbul that were beyond the Nazis' reach. We can think of this "elsewhere," then, as that liminal place where certain forms of cultural heritage, knowledge, and habitus managed to survive Nazi aggression. This is precisely the kind of elsewhere where Klemperer hoped the humanist mindset or Geist could survive.[21]

The letter is interesting in other ways, too. It shows, namely, that the relationship between German authorities and the émigré community was still quite ambivalent in the mid-1930s. This is even more evident in Spitzer's apology to the consul and vice consul in a letter dated a few days after the one quoted above. In this subsequent letter, Spitzer apologized for having jumped to his own conclusions about what transpired after the concert and seemed to try to regain Saucken's trust. He confirmed that the vice consul and his home institution, the foreign language school at Istanbul University, had always maintained a cordial, mutually satisfactory relationship, and he even implied that they had shared cultural interests.[22] One might assume that Spitzer penned his apology in mortal fear of Nazi reprisals: he had, after all, charged the vice consul with bigotry and philistinism. Yet he wrote these letters at a time when he was actively planning his departure from Turkey and preparing to take up a position at Johns Hopkins University. No doubt this conferred a degree of security and allowed him to speak his mind. By the same token, Spitzer's cautious apology calls for explanation. We can surmise that Spitzer was alternatively hotheaded in his attack of the vice consul, then remorseful by the cool light of day. There is, however, another, less psychological, reason for Spitzer's series of letters: Spitzer would have understood the importance of maintaining a cordial relationship with the authorities at the German consulate if he meant to secure his position for Auerbach attempting to flee Germany.

A few weeks before the Amar performance, in November 1935, Spitzer had informed the consul that there were plans to replace him with a French professor at Istanbul University. Spitzer pointed out to consul Toepke that such a choice would be unfortunate for both cultural and scholarly reasons.[23] He did not, indeed could not, specify that the position ought to be reserved for a needier German Jewish scholar. However, in his conversations with the German consulate, Spitzer made the case that a German rather than a French professor ought to be employed at Istanbul University. The German consulate files and the Auerbach dossier in the Istanbul University archive do not indicate that Turkish university administrators consulted the German consul in deciding for Auerbach. However, it is clear that Spitzer wanted to secure the German consul's support. Once again, we find both parties debating the future of German scholarship in Turkey and, if only for strategic reasons, working on the pretense of mutual cultural interests.[24]

This delicate state of affairs was not to last. Before long came the consulate's aggrieved response to Spitzer's outburst over the ambassador's mistreatment of musician Licco Amar. Consul Toepke characterized the letter as *"flegelhaft"* (impudent) in its expression of hatred for the consular officials and was doubly offended because Spitzer had made copies of his letter for distribution to the German community.[25] Istanbul's émigrés must have been agog, but, if we imagine that either they or the musician in question was openly grateful for Spitzer's act of resistance, we would be mistaken. Ritter and Amar themselves intervened in an effort to smooth the waters. Motivated perhaps by some indebtedness to the consul, Ritter claimed that Amar had left the concert room before the ambassador had had a chance to approach him. Amar had, he suggested, wanted to avoid a potentially awkward situation and quietly removed himself. Amar then appeared in person at the consulate to clarify the "embarrassing" misunderstanding, whereupon he accused Spitzer of "mean spiritedness" and "stupidity." As a consequence of these counter-allegations, Spitzer was threatened with prosecution for slander—something he could ill afford—and forced to write an apology to the ambassador; he was also made to clarify the "misunderstandings" on behalf of all the recipients of his original letter.[26] We can imagine that the whole affair must have made Spitzer think twice about sticking his neck out in the future.

We are unlikely ever to know what really happened at the concert: whose hands were shaken and whose were not. Nor do we know what gave rise to the competing versions of the story. But ultimately, this is of little significance. What is important is what this episode tells us about the complex, mutually dependent relationships between the émigrés and German consulate officials in the mid-1930s—a relationship that lost any degree of ambiguity only a few years later. The correspondence preserved in the consulate files is also significant because it provides us with some insights into the émigrés' alignments with various ideologically positioned groups in Turkey. In chapter 2, it was their affiliations with Turkish nationalist reformers; here we see their complex relationships with Nazis. The handshake refused or the hand never proffered shows us, finally, that Beethoven can be played both ways. While the Nazis saw themselves as the political heirs to a longstanding idea of cultural Germanness, it was the Jewish exile Spitzer who drew on a similar rhetoric of German cultural universalism in order to make his own case. Highlighting this shared rhetoric is not meant to impute fascist sympathies to Spitzer any more than it is meant to portray the Nazis as more humane. It shows instead that, in the mid-1930s, both parties were still interested in maintaining a degree of mutual cooperation and the notion of a common cultural interest. It further shows that universalism makes for strange bedfellows: the discourse can be mobilized at opposite ends of the political spectrum, sometimes for quite sinister purposes.

In order to further German interests, the German consular officials were interested in establishing a German department at Istanbul University but were confronted with an unusual departmental structure for the teaching of Western languages and literatures. Responsible for this was Spitzer, who, during the three years spent reforming Istanbul University, laid the foundation for the department of Romance philology. Under his directorship, the Romance department offered a broad range of courses that included everything from the history of French syntax, medieval theatre, and nineteenth-century realism to translation, classicism, and romanticism. Also on the curriculum were courses on Cervantes, Calderon, and the Latin language. But students might have been surprised to find that they could also take courses atypical of a Romance department, courses on, for example, Greek grammar and German philology.[27] Keeping in mind that Spitzer was trained in linguistics, it is interesting to note that he also taught literature classes in Istanbul. Among his offerings were courses on seventeenth-century French theater, French as an academic language, and literary and linguistic analysis of the new French novel.[28]

As I have suggested already, two things stand out as being peculiar in the curriculum during the Spitzer years—first, the teaching of the Greek language and, second, the addition of German to the Romance discipline. Adding Greek to the Romance department might have been an understandable disciplinary liberty. After all, it conformed to the Turkish interest in humanism and it would have helped realize Albert Malche's specific vision for Turkish modernity. The absence of a German department until as late as 1943 can, however, be explained in different terms. As we will find later in the chapter, the émigrés resisted establishing an independent department that would promote German as a national philology. As Germans they were interested in the teaching of things German, but this did not mean they necessarily wanted to see German elevated to an autonomous discipline. Instead, Traugott Fuchs, originally trained as a Romance scholar, offered seminars on German language and literature under the auspices of the Romance department.[29] This odd affiliation of German with Romance philology can also be explained when we recall that Spitzer (and later Auerbach) had been appointed to professorial chairs not of Romance, per se, but of Western languages and literatures. Such a disciplinary orientation offered the comparative-minded scholars Spitzer and Auerbach the opportunity to use the Romance discipline as a launching pad for pioneering an all-encompassing form of Western European philology. Indeed, experimenting with the conventional bounds of their discipline would become a passion that henceforth shaped their work.

This combination of interdisciplinary opportunities and Turkish humanist visions turned the department into what we would now think of as a Europhile comparative literature program. We can see this in the kinds of courses taught by Auerbach's colleagues during his first year in Istanbul: Sabahattin Eyüboğlu, the only Turkish lecturer, offered a course on the seventeenth-century French epistolary novel, while another colleague, Rosemarie Burkart, taught old French, the interpretation of Spanish texts, and a survey course on Spanish lyrics. Dieckmann—whether it was Lise-lotte or her husband, Herbert, is not clear—offered courses on Latin syntax, Latin historiography, Plautus's Bacchides, and sixteenth-century Italian literature. Eva Buck was responsible for the teaching of English, with seminars on old English, Shakespeare's tragedies, and the Renaissance. Fuchs, the nominal Germanist in the department, covered German literary history, linguistic and literary analysis, and the history of the German language.[30]

The students at the faculty for Western languages and literatures benefited from this grab-bag curriculum in many ways—but we do not know whether they would have also wanted to retain elements of the old Ottoman education. For today's scholars in the West, the odd mix of courses and disciplinary perspectives seems to have borne fruit. Emily Apter, for one, identifies Istanbul and the condition of exile as having generated no less than a new foundation for the discipline of comparative literature in the United States. Focusing on the Istanbul University journal *Romanoloji Semineri Dergisi* (*Journal of the Romance Studies Seminar*), first published in 1937, she points to Spitzer's work and his comparatist spirit as the very wellspring of the discipline. This multilingual journal, she says, "offers a glimpse into the way in which European humanism Atatürk-style . . . played a key role in transforming German-based philology into a global discipline that came to be known as comparative literature when it assumed its institutional foothold in the humanities departments in the United States."[31] Apter is right to emphasize the significance of this journal. *Romanoloji Semineri Dergisi* creates a testament to the highly innovative, interdisciplinary scholarship of the period. Publishing the work of both émigré and Turkish scholars, it shows how the convergence of Oriental and Occidental worlds, even if Europhile, could be productive for intellectual production in modern Turkey.

Rosemarie Burkart, who had followed Spitzer to Istanbul as his lover and colleague, played an important role here. When Spitzer left to take up his position at Johns Hopkins, she remained in Istanbul. Whatever the state of their personal relationship, she remained a disciple of his method, helped train students in his philological technique—the "explication de texte"—and published in the inaugural issue of *Romanoloji Semineri Dergisi*. This was the first journal Auerbach edited in Turkey, assisted by Eyüboğlu, the young advocate of humanism, who later worked closely with the minister of education, Hasan Ali Yücel. The journal is almost entirely forgotten now, remembered only, I would think, by a few historians of the discipline. But the journal is worthy of note not only for its articles in a range of languages about topics that go far beyond the discipline of Romance philology. We find, for instance, articles like Hans Marchand's investigation into the English pronoun "one" and Eyüboğlu's essay on Turkish folk riddles. Such contributions have a certain quaint interest.

The kind of innovative work to which I want to draw attention is, however, exemplified by Burkart's "Truchement: Histoire d'un mot Oriental en Français," an article that traces the origin of the old French word *truchement* back to the Crusades. It is in contributions such as this that we find the spark of something methodologically new for comparative literature, something that is significant for those who are interested in the historical turning points of the discipline. For this reason, it is worth dwelling on the article for a moment. Focusing on the semantics of interpretation and translation, Burkart elaborated on the etymological links between the official Ottoman word *dragoman*, the contemporary Turkish word for translator *tercüman*, and the French *truchement*. As Burkart shows, the word *truchement* has a rich set of associations, derived from the Arabic *tarğuman* or possibly the Assyrian *targumanu*. *Truchement* first appeared in the twelfth century and came to mean "oral translator"—a word to be distinguished from the later *interprète*, professional translator. *Truchement*, continues Burkart, "désignait une institution nécessaire au temps des grands voyages et découvertes, et que son exotisme même favorisait l'emploi métaphorique chez les précieux du XIIe jusqu'au XVIIe siècle."[32] The word, it seems, appeared in an age when the Oriental and Occidental worlds first came into closer contact with one another, hence its association with communication across linguistic boundaries. Over time, so wrote Burkart, the word was decoupled from its original meaning and came to retain only a metaphorical one.

In tracing this etymology, Burkart invited her readers to engage with the historical and political circumstances under which different words come into circulation and undergo changes. Of particular interest to her were concepts of translating, interpreting, and mediating.[33] Her own work as a translator of cultural and linguistic phenomena paved the way for further work that brought the so-called Oriental and Occidental worlds into greater proximity and opened up new forms of dialogue. Following the same vision, Eyüboğlu complemented his analysis of Turkish folk riddles with insights into French poetry, arguing for a similarity between the two genres. While Eyüboğlu's article is more suggestive and less historically grounded than Burkart's, we can still recognize in it the comparatist spirit that is characteristic of the scholarship produced under Spitzer and Auerbach in Turkey.

The journal was inspired by Spitzer's effort to achieve a rapprochement among linguistics, literary history, and the study of an individual style—something that is also captured well by Azra Erhat (Ahat) in the introduction to her article "Üslup Ilminde Yeni bir Usul" (A New Method in Stylistic Studies). We can see the imprint of Spitzer's three-year sojourn in Istanbul in almost all of the work published in this issue, which Auerbach came to edit because of Spitzer's departure. Despite her youth, Erhat stood out as a very promising young scholar in Spitzer's seminar. As we have heard in chapter 2, it was she, together with her colleague Eyüboğlu and the writer Halikarnas Balıkçısı, who would coin the term *Anadolu hümanizmi* (Anatolian Humanism) and become one of Turkey's leading intellectuals. In her introduction to the journal, surely one of her first publications, she described the "yeni filoloğ" (new philologist) as someone with expertise in both linguistics *and* literature. Following Spitzer's critique of traditional German linguistics, she insisted that *yeni filoloğ ayaklı kütüphane olmakla iktifa etmemelidir* ("the new philologist ought not to be content with being a walking library"). Instead, she called for the reinstatement of feeling and human understanding in the study of language and literature.[34]

While the journal issue may be seen as important to the development of comparative literature in the United States and the literary departments in Turkey, it is crucial to remember two things. First, the faculty for Western languages and literatures at Istanbul University established Europhilia at its core, which means that Ottoman and Turkish literature could survive Turkey's reification of national culture only if it were read through the lens of philology or if an argument could be made for commonalities with Western European literature. Introducing humanist scholarship hence meant narrowing and diminishing the significance of the Ottoman literary heritage in an effort to secularize education and culture. Second, German philology had a highly contested and ambivalent status in Istanbul during the 1930s and 1940s. There were numerous parties trying to exert control over the teaching of German language and literature: included among these were the German consulate, any number of Turkish authorities, the German ministry of science and education, and, of course, the émigré scholars themselves. The battle over culture that had started with Spitzer was taken up by Auerbach and would last until almost the end of the war.

The Auerbach Affair

An excerpt from a 1938 letter shows that Auerbach was concerned about Nazi activities in Turkey and, in particular, about the kinds of control they might come to exert in the future. "It is clear that 'they' will expel us from here when they have the power," he wrote; "then there will be no shortage of enemies here either. Of course, we basically have lots; they're just keeping quiet right now."[35] Such statements show that Auerbach read the writing on the wall. In contrast to the passionate and outspoken Spitzer, however, Auerbach tried to stay out of politics as much as possible. This said, not very much is known about Auerbach's political activities in Istanbul. In a farewell letter to Erich and Marie Auerbach before their departure to the United States in 1947, Ritter would reflect on, even excuse, Auerbach's political reserve:

You have not allowed yourself to grow bitter; you have taken it and borne it with an equanimity that demands admiration. Is it a wise life philosophy, or temperament? Maybe it is both at once which allow you to overcome many things more lightly than others. With a light hand, so it often seemed to us, you cast aside and away from yourself crushing burdens that almost pressed the life out of others. You did not surrender yourself. You did not allow yourself to be overwhelmed! You must have possessed the magic power to reduce things and make some demons harmless by driving them back, like the fisherman in the 1001 nights, into the bottle from whence they had come, unseemingly, to puff themselves up into monsters who weigh upon the soul. Or did it only seem so to us? Enough. At all times you crossed our paths with a rare serenity of the soul, which never seemed to abandon you, and perhaps it was this very magic, of the serenity of the soul, which drew us to you again even if we felt alienated by an all-too-placid hand.[36]

Much as Auerbach may have wished to keep himself out of the fray, this was not always possible. Neither his purported serenity nor his insistence on the letter of the law could prevent him from running afoul of the Istanbul Nazis.[37] His involvement with the German Excursion Club, the *Deutscher Ausflugsverein* (DAV), provides a case in point and illustrates the ways in which the émigrés' cultural activities were kept in check by the long arm of the Nazi party.

The DAV, one of the many institutions that made up the fabric of German expatriate life, had been founded in Istanbul as early as 1885, with the aim of promoting outdoor activities among its members. By the 1930s, however, the club was competing for members with the Nazi *Deutsche Arbeitsfront*, the German Labor Front. Concerned about membership numbers, the head of the Istanbul Nazi Party kept scrupulous tabs on the DAV, recording that, in 1937, 78 of its 119 members were German émigrés; Switzerland, Austria, Hungary, Turkey, and other nations were also represented among its members.[38] The remainder were certified Nazis, most of whom—at the instigation of the Nazi Party and the German consul—had recently infiltrated the club in order to overthrow its board. Auerbach was, at this time, the vice president of the club and was thus directly confronted with a problem. Consular records show that the club's board initially adopted an accommodationist policy, perhaps in the hope that this would deflect further interest by the party: the board accepted the new Nazi members on the condition that the *Sonnwendfeier*, the solstice celebrations central to Nazi symbolism, be excluded from the club's activities. The board also stipulated that national insignia, be it Turkish, German, or Swiss, be banned from the club.[39] However, this compromise did not last very long. At the general meeting of the club a year later, in March 1939, the board was dismissed and taken over entirely by Nazis.

I focus on this case because in it we can catch a glimpse of the Auerbach we know least: namely, Auerbach the member of the larger German community in Istanbul. The archive of the German consulate contains a letter by Auerbach to another club member. Dating from the time of the board coup, the letter discusses the previous general meeting and deals with a specific issue that warrants our attention. The letter shows, namely, that Auerbach insisted that there was nothing political about the new Nazi leadership of the club: the club was purely cultural. To stress this point, he sent a copy of his letter to the consulate.[40] As one can imagine, the consulate was unimpressed by this attempt to finesse the situation: consular officials knew as well as anyone about the political leanings of club members, and Auerbach seems to have lost some of his credibility. In the margin of Auerbach's letter, some consular official scribbled dismissively: "Weak attempt at twisting the story."[41]

Istanbul, den 14. April 1939.

Herrn

Oskar K r e n n ,

H i e r

Ihre Zeilen vom 7. d.M. sind in meinem Besitz und muss ich leider fest-
stellen, daß Sie wohl irrig beraten worden sind oder bezw. daß Ihre
neuerliche Annahme unrichtig ist, denn Sie waren bei Ihrer damaligen
Fragestellung durchaus von richtigen Voraussetzungen ausgegangen. Ich
kann Ihnen nur bestätigen, dass ebenso wie jeder Deutsche – so auch jeder
Ausländer – der dem "D.A.V." angehört, ordentliches Mitglied desselben ist;
allerdings würde ich dabei bei jedem Nichtdeutschen – sei es nun ein
deutschstämmiger Schweizer, oder ein anderer Ausländer – soviel Taktgefühl
als selbstverständlich voraussetzen, dass er sich als Gast fühlt und auch
als solcher zu benehmen weiss. Diese Auslegung geht auch aus meinen Zeilen vom 31.3. klar hervor. Grund und Zweck Ihrer Anfrage bleibt mir
aber deshalb noch immer vollkommen unverständlich und wahrscheinlich auch
Ihnen selbst, sonst hätten Sie nicht einen Ausweg durch eine Spiegel-
fechterei gesucht. Eine Entschuldigung Ihrerseits bei Herrn Preusser wäre
bestimmt mehr am Platze gewesen, denn für ihn war Ihre Frage bestimmt
am unangenehmsten, da er in seiner Rücktritts-Erklärung vergessen hatte,
ausdrücklich den Grund hierfür anzugeben.

Bei dieser Gelegenheit darf ich Sie noch auf eine andere irrige Auffassung
Ihrerseits aufmerksam machen. Sie haben sich an anderer Stelle dahingehend
geäussert, dass zwischen dem Schweizer-Club und dem "D.A.V." doch ein
wesentlicher Unterschied bestehe, da dieser ja eine politische Vereinigung
sei. Lassen Sie sich bitte von massgebender Stelle belehren, was eine
politische Vereinigung überhaupt ist und nehmen Sie zur Kenntnis, daß
der "D.A.V." weder mit Politik oder dergleichen je etwas zu tun hatte,
noch zu tun hat und auch nie haben wird.

Nachdem Sie es für nötig erachtet haben, mein wegen Ihres persönlichen
eigentümlichen Benehmens auch an Sie rein persönlich gerichtetes Schreiben
so aufzufassen, als ob dies gegen Sie als Schweizer gerichtet gewesen
wäre und daher glaubten, mit der Angelegenheit noch andere Stellen be –
fassen zu müssen, gebe ich zur Richtigstellung der Sache je eine Durch –
schrift dieser Zeilen an das hiesige Deutsche Generalkonsulat und an
Herrn Hänni, als dem nichtdeutschen Beisitzer unseres Deutschen Ausflugs-
Vereins.

Auerbach's letter to the German consulate, Istanbul, 1939. By permission of Politisches
Archiv Berlin.

Like other archival documents in the file box, the letter shows that Auerbach wanted to shy away from confrontation yet remained a suspicious figure for the Nazis.[42] Try as one might to avoid politics on the brink of the war, encounters with the Nazis were inevitable. With their visa and passport issues, the émigrés encountered representatives of the Nazi government at the embassy and the consulate; they also ran into them in their places of work and recreation. The problem was compounded when, in 1938, the Nazi Party in Istanbul shifted its headquarters to the German consulate. This made life even harder for those émigrés who were trying to keep a low profile. Turkish authorities made things yet more difficult by requiring Germans in 1939 to show proof of their racial origin in order to qualify for a visa. Needless to say, anyone who wanted a visa first had to run the gauntlet at the German consulate when they went to submit their application.[43]

Auerbach was constantly reminded of the tight net that the Nazis had thrown over the city. As a former professor at Marburg University, he was technically entitled to a pension, and, despite having fled the country, he tried to claim these benefits anyway.[44] The outcome of his application relied on the goodwill of the consul who reported to the German ministry of science and education. Consul Seiler seems to have been disposed toward his case and reported to Berlin in 1941 that Professor Auerbach "stayed away from any political activity."[45] Auerbach was told that, unless his conduct gave some particular cause for concern, he would receive the benefits that were due to him from Marburg University. This case illustrates why Auerbach and others may have tried to present themselves as apolitical, or at least inoffensive, to their Nazi handlers in Turkey.

Correspondence between the German consulate and the Foreign Office in Berlin makes it clear that the Nazis continued to be troubled by the émigrés' high social and political standing: if they could, the German authorities would redirect the situation to serve their own interests. The wicked ingenuity of this plan is evident from statements made by the German ambassador to Turkey, who argued that the only really effective way to "culturally infiltrate the country" was by propagating and disseminating the German language—in the same way that the French had been able to influence Turkish affairs.[46] Having used the émigrés to lay this groundwork, the Nazis aimed eventually to replace them with Nazi scholars at Turkish universities.[47] In this, they had some degree of success.

As we know from the previous chapter, the status of German Jews changed in Turkey between 1933 and 1945. Viewed by Turkish authorities initially as a people whose usefulness lay in their apparent lack of strong national or religious affiliations, they came increasingly under suspicion and threat on both fronts: rising anti-Semitism in Turkey and repeated attempts by Nazi authorities to undermine the émigrés' influence at Turkish universities all impacted negatively on their status. Nazis infiltrated university life at an institutional level but also in more banal ways. A German reading room was opened near the university dormitories. The reading room—funded by the Deutscher Buchverein (German Book Club), Verein für das Deutschtum im Ausland (Association for Germanness Abroad), and Verein der Asienkämpfer (Association of Asia Fighters)—made available German newspapers and magazines that attracted both German and Turkish readers.[48] When, in 1938, the director, a German teacher named Stumvoll, took it upon himself to adorn the room with a lamp in the shape of a swastika, the Turkish media sniffed a good story. The newspaper *Haber* called on the Turkish public to denounce Nazi propaganda in Turkey.[49] The fact that Stumvoll was employed by a Turkish lyceum only added fuel to the fire. After his interrogation by the Turkish police, he stopped offering some of the incendiary German newspapers and made a few other concessions to public pressure. Cutting off the edges of the lamp to make it look more like a cross,[50] he must have reasoned that Christian imagery might be tolerated even if Nazi symbols were not. The press was not placated by this gesture, however, and journalists reiterated their demands that the reading room be closed.

If the director of the reading room acted on his own initiative and without prior consultation with the German authorities, there are other instances in which the Nazi ministry of science and education itself infiltrated the university. The pharmaceutical chemist Kurt Bodendorf, for example, acted as an informer, making regular reports to the consulate about the activities of the émigré community.[51] Bodendorf reported early on that Auerbach moved in émigré circles but otherwise tried to avoid direct contact with Germans.[52] Despite the presence of informers like Bodendorf, the consulate did not find it easy to "drive a Nazi wedge" into the professorial faculty.[53] The émigrés tended to stick together and, on the whole, were suspicious of the kind of politics that had driven them into exile in the first place. The fact that Auerbach was in charge of the German curriculum at Turkey's top university was thus a point of contention. As we will see in the following section, the Nazis would make concerted efforts to undermine the émigré philologists. It would be the Nazi medievalist Hennig Brinkmann who spearheaded that effort.

The Brinkmann Affair: Germanistik at Istanbul

The Nazis found an ally in Yunus Nadi, the owner of the country's most influential newspaper, *Cumhuriyet*. By 1937, Nadi was already publishing articles that chastised the German scholars for their inadequate teaching and poor command of Turkish.[54] Other, politically more moderate, criticism was voiced by Turkish educators themselves. In a 1939 report to the ministry of education in Ankara, the Turkish faculty raised questions about the faculty for Western languages and literatures, now chaired by Auerbach, and criticized what was being taught there.[55] While Turkish professors debated the role of German scholars in shaping Turkish universities, the German ministry of science and education dispatched a senior civil servant named Herbert Scurla to Turkey and charged him with strengthening Germany's foothold abroad. Scurla made a fact-finding trip in 1939, which he followed up with a ministry report titled "The Activities of German Academics at Turkish Research Institutions."[56] Scurla's report stressed the necessity of "weakening the position of the emigrants at the university," because they exerted an "extraordinary influence" on Turkish academic life.[57] Scurla proposed instead that the ministry lay a firmer basis for Nazi cultural-political activities in Turkey and cultivate a Turkish hiring policy that was sympathetic to Nazi ideology. This would not be quite as easy as he might have hoped, for Scurla received a rather cool reception from the Turkish ministers and university chancellors he met while traveling in Turkey.

Realizing that little was to be gained through these official Turkish channels, Scurla resorted to threatening émigrés with expatriation if they did not fall into line. Istanbul University's faculty for Western languages and literatures was the object of particular scrutiny because of its role in training future teachers of German, English, and French, and the university as a whole was judged to be thoroughly *verjudet*, Judaized.[58] Scurla did not, however, reserve his criticism for the Germans in Turkey; he charged the ministry itself with having responded belatedly to Turkey's call for European educators.[59] At the time of his visit, there were only a few

German lecturers working under Auerbach, and the antifascist stance of someone like Fuchs provided an effective barrier against a pro-Nazi curriculum.[60] Scurla came down hard: his report to the German ministry of science and education called for the "rücksichtslose Ausbürgerung . . . nichtarischer Wissenschaftler," the categorical expatriation of all non-Aryan academics.

With or without Scurla's input, many Jewish émigrés indeed lost their German citizenship in 1939. Non-Jewish émigrés were not exempt from this threat; according to Scurla, they, too, needed close monitoring, and anyone accepting a position in Istanbul ought to be threatened with expatriation because leaving the country was "seriously detrimental to German interests."[61] While Scurla's mission was not as successful as the ministry hoped, his detailed report shows that there was a well-developed Nazi network abroad—a powerful sphere of influence exerted by Nazi academics (especially in Ankara) and by Nazi Party members in Turkey as a whole.[62] Scurla's report also shows that, by 1939, the uneasy alliance between émigrés and the German government authorities was effectively at an end. From now on, the émigrés would be effectively cut off from Germany, in many cases by losing their German citizenship, and their position in Turkey would become far more tenuous.

The German ministry of science and education continued its efforts to establish a German department at Istanbul University. Attempting to bar the Nazi ministry from manipulating the teaching of German at the university, Auerbach tried to hire a Germanist through alternative Swiss channels in the early 1940s. His efforts came to nothing, and, in 1943, the notorious Nazi Germanist Hennig Brinkmann assumed control of the German curriculum. Brinkmann's appointment seems somehow anomalous, given that university appointments were made by the largely progressive university administration and the Turkish ministry of education and in consultation with the émigré academics themselves. Yet we find that the university changed over the years, and so did its modernization policies. Where the university might have once exercised a more judicious choice, Auerbach's efforts to forestall the Brinkmann hire were now overwhelmed by a majority of the Istanbul faculty. When Auerbach pointed out that Brinkmann was a Nazi propagandist, some of his Turkish colleagues were outraged, and, in a gesture of irony that was lost at the time, they accused Auerbach of being a racist. In the heated debate that ensued, Auerbach abstained from voting so that only one émigré, the psychologist Wilhelm Peters, was left to vote against the appointment.[63]

As a result, Brinkmann, a specialist in medieval German and Latin literature and the history of the German language, became the inaugural chair of German at Istanbul University. German was, after a full decade of opportunistic interdisciplinarity, now cleaved from Romance, thereby becoming its own autonomous entity. But, we might ask, what sort of department was this, and at what cost was it created?

Even at the time of his appointment, Brinkmann was known for using his philological work as a platform for Nazi ideology. He had joined the SA (Sturmabteilung), the Nazi paramilitary organization, in 1933 and became a member of the party itself a few years later. Within a year, he was also declaring his intellectual allegiances: in a publication on contemporary German poetry, he claimed in typically florid terms that, thanks to the "National Socialist breakthrough in 1933 . . . a literature foreign to the German *Volk* went under. This literature had obscured the Germans' vision of their own eternal power. With its demise, a poesy emerged into the light, a poesy that had, for years, lain waiting ready to contribute to the reconstruction of inner German life."[64] Like many of his contemporaries in Nazi Germany, Brinkmann firmly believed that Jews subverted other cultures because they lacked their own true mother tongue; to him they were simply "a negation of the healthy human life-force."[65] This was also the way in which Nazis viewed Jewish émigrés in Turkey, namely, as antithetical to German interests. Brinkmann thus took it upon himself to remove German courses from what he referred to as the "influence of the Jew Auerbach."[66]

Brinkmann's appointment at Istanbul University was, of course, a coup for the German Foreign Office and the Nazi functionaries in Istanbul. After years of false starts and backroom dealings, they had finally succeeded in giving German a significant institutional presence. Why the Turks condoned this is more difficult to explain. There are several possible explanations for what I have identified as the shift in university policy. For one thing, the university conceived of itself as European. On the other hand, the very concept of Europe was represented by an overwhelming number of German professors. The university and the ministry of education sent many of the university's students to Germany to round out their education and gain firsthand experience in the West. In the academic year 1940–1941, for example, the Turkish ministry of education granted eighty stipends to students studying abroad. Although this figure seems relatively small and does not include students who studied without financial support from the ministry, it is striking that more than 70 percent of these students were sent to Germany.[67] German institutions, too, culti-vated the education of Turkish students in Germany.[68] The influence of Nazi academics on Turkish students was not deemed problematic. Hav-ing completed their training at German institutions, returning academics were often awarded prominent positions at Turkish universities. As one émigré scholar in Istanbul would complain, some were so influenced by Nazism that they came back anti-Semites.[69] This does not seem to have impeded their careers, and indeed many of these young academics were well placed at Turkish universities.

If this intellectual exchange paid dividends for young Turkish schol-ars, it also benefited German academics. Brinkmann's appointment, for instance, came about as the result of his prior contact with a Turkish graduate who had completed his doctorate in Germany. In fact, Brink-mann took a leave of absence from his home university in order to take up the position in Istanbul. Permission was granted on the condition that he inspect German language teaching in Istanbul high schools and investi-gate the language departments at Istanbul University.[70] One can only imagine Auerbach's mounting frustration with his colleagues when Brinkmann took over the teaching of German language and literature. Brinkmann would last a year in Istanbul, all the while collecting informa-tion for the German ministry of education. The Germanist visited Ger-man schools and German language programs at high schools in Istanbul, Ankara, and Izmir. To the Nazi ministry, he gave a detailed report in which he disclosed which teacher, assistant, or lecturer was Germano-phile, communist, Jewish, or dönme. Brinkmann was relatively successful in fulfilling his task as an inspector and informant. He managed to get in touch with the translation bureau in Ankara and was happy to find that the world translation series had thus far not published any German émi-gré literature in Turkish. The series included the work of only one German-Jewish writer, namely, Heinrich Heine. In fact, Brinkmann's negotiations with the translation bureau in Ankara were, according to his report, so positive that he walked away thinking that the directorship of a new, Istanbul-based translation bureau might be his for the taking.[71] Before this plan could be realized, however, Brinkmann's activities as a Nazi pro-pagandist and spy were brought to a halt when the Turkish government took a stance against Germany in 1944 and finally joined the Allies.

Auerbach's opposition to Brinkmann shows how, over the course of a decade, the faculty for Western languages and literatures became a site of cultural and political collision: Turkish nationalist reformers, German émigrés, and Nazis all competed for control over departmental structures, curricula, libraries, and the shape of the canon.[72] As I have shown, however, the stakes were much greater. On the one hand, these competing forces were fighting over the image of Germany abroad and a correlated set of economic and political interests. On the other hand, they were fighting over the image of Turkey itself. Calling itself European and allying itself with Nazi Germany might have meant striking a pact with the devil. This was what hung in the balance.

Brinkmann was not an isolated example; Istanbul University also appointed other Nazis to its ranks. He was, however, the first to make a dent in Auerbach's power. The fact that Auerbach was accused of racism by members of the Turkish faculty shows the extent to which anti-Semitism had become commonplace within the academy. It now informed debates about appointments as well as curricula—something that does not come as a surprise when we recall the kind of anti-Semitic policies pursued by both Nazis and Turkish authorities in the early 1940s. The decision to hire Brinkmann would mean that émigrés like Fuchs, Auerbach, and their colleague Heinz Anstock were forced to work closely with Nazis.[73] It must have come as a rude shock to find that anti-Semitism was alive and well in the corridors and classrooms of Istanbul University. This brings home the point that our image of Turkey as a counterpoint to Nazi Germany—a bastion of intellectual and religious free expression—is, to some extent, a false one. Of course, it should also prompt us to ask why Turkish anti-Semitism is consistently downplayed, if not elided altogether, in present-day tellings of this story. The interests that were, and continue to be, served by this view will be taken up in the epilogue of this book.

Brinkmann is accorded no particular significance today—if he is remembered in Istanbul at all, then it is only as the founder of Germanistik who taught at the university for a brief while. We find an example of this revisionist view of Turkish academic life in Şara Sayın's history of Turkish Germanistik. While Sayın confirms that Brinkmann established Germanistik as a national discipline, she claims that the humanist European spirit remained untainted during the Nazi years: "During the academic year 1943–44, the professor [Brinkmann] gave lectures on Romance languages and literature, lectures which always culminated in praise of the German *Volk*. However, the skeptical and critical young teaching faculty and students remained unmoved by them."[74] Perhaps Sayın, who later acted as chair of German in Istanbul, would have viewed the past differently had she known that Brinkmann's appointment was not simply prompted by an invitation from one of his former students but was the work of the Nazi ministry itself.[75]

The university upheld its contradictory hiring policy during the post-war period. The professorship in Germanistik was first filled by the classical philologist and philosopher Walther Kranz, who had left Germany because his wife was Jewish.[76] With the support of the German ministry of education, Kranz was initially hired in Istanbul as professor of classical intellectual and cultural history with an emphasis on its bearings on the present.[77] During his chairmanship of the German department (1945–1950), he established a good working relationship between the philosophy and German departments. After Kranz's return to Germany, the German department attracted a German professor from a whole new constituency.

The de-Nazification process in the Federal Republic prompted Nazi scholars to look for academic positions abroad. Troubled by past political sympathies and the current de-Nazification process, the Nazi Germanist Gerhard Fricke was looking for a position outside of Germany. Like Brinkmann, he managed to be appointed thanks to his earlier dealings with Turkish students in Istanbul. At the time of his appointment, he, too, was known to be an active proponent of Nazism. If anything, Fricke was even more rabidly anti-Semitic than Brinkmann. In 1933, Fricke had been the main speaker at the infamous book burning in Göttingen, where he gave the so-called bonfire speech. He referred to the books on the "black list" as "Schutt und Unrat," trash and garbage, and claimed that they alienated, crippled, and suffocated intellectual life in Germany. Anti-Semitic images like "jüdische Literaturhyänen," Jewish literature-hyenas, also peppered the speech that he published in 1933.[78] In 1940, when the German ministry of science and education declared a "war in the humanities," Fricke rushed to the barricades. The aim of this "war" was to create a new vision for the humanities, something that could be instituted after a German victory in Europe.[79] Fricke, together with Franz Koch, took over the organization of the "academic deployment of Germanists in the war."[80] Their self-appointed task was "to excavate the German core imbedded in the German language and literature." Naturally, this work was infused with the cultural and political ethos of Nazism.[81]

Fricke was not the only Nazi employed in Istanbul after the war. The former dean of Cologne's philosophical faculty Heinz Heimsoeth had also lost his position because of the de-Nazification process and was later hired by Istanbul University.[82] When Fuchs encountered Heimsoeth in Istanbul, he remembered how the latter had reproached him in Cologne for protesting against Spitzer's dismissal. Fuchs thought of Heimsoeth as "a fanatic admirer of Nietzsche's superman philosophy" and decided to avoid him because his "aversion was too strong."[83] In allowing Fricke and Heimsoeth to continue their careers at Istanbul University, Turkish authorities, on the other hand, did not seem concerned by any ideological or moral conflict. Even today, it is not considered problematic that such a notorious Nazi chaired the university's German department between 1950 and 1958. In Turkey there has been little interrogating of history comparable to the process of *Vergangenheitsbewältigung* (coming to terms with the past) in the Federal Republic. This makes Fricke's tenure seem so unproblematic that it plays no part at all in reflections about the history of the disciplines. He is instead remembered as a professor who lectured "like a priest from the pulpit" and was obsessed with Kleist, Hölderlin, and the young Goethe.[84]

For Sayın, who was his doctoral student in the 1950s, Fricke's reasons for glorifying certain authors and neglecting others are never at issue. She goes so far as to praise the fact that students of German were confronted with opposing worldviews and different approaches to literature. Further, she points out that the former socialist Klaus Ziegler—also hired as a Germanist in Istanbul after the war—completed his habilitation under Gerhard Fricke at the height of Nazism.[85] Sayın's argument that the teachings of Nazis, Socialists, and Jews led to a productive "alternating hot and cold bath on a symbolic level" is unpersuasive.[86] Her claim is all the more problematic since she remains quiet about the fact that Fricke was, in fact, confronted with his Nazi past once he returned to Cologne University.[87] So grave were his misdeeds during the war years that he was ultimately forced to withdraw from academic life. Sayın's account is not the only one to exhibit such elisions and selective interpretations. This raises the question as to why histories of Turkish tertiary education elide or play down Nazi influences. There are undoubtedly many ways to answer this question. I suggest, however, that the reasons have less to do with the past than they do with the present. It is because the humanities still play a constitutive role in the construction of Turkish national identity that certain kinds of myths need to be perpetuated. As I show in the epilogue, the problem rests on a great irony: it is Turkey's need to uphold the West as a positive role model that frustrates its very ability to compile a self-critical account of this past.

Leaving Istanbul

During his final years in Istanbul, Auerbach felt a growing disappointment over the slow pace of change at the university and in society at large. He had witnessed the rise of anti-Semitism when the prime minister, Saydam, declared in 1942 that Turkey was not going to provide a home for Jews "unwanted elsewhere."[88] Auerbach had also felt such changes closer to home. Brinkmann's appointment in 1943 undermined the progressive tone that had been set in the initial, more optimistic, years of the university's reform. Specifically, Auerbach was concerned about the fact that, over the years, the Turkish faculty no longer seemed to differentiate between the value of humanistic scholarship as practiced by the émigrés and the political and disciplinary implications of Nazi scholarship.

With the collapse of Turkish-German relations in 1944 and Turkey's declaration of war against Germany, the émigré faculty began to disperse. Irrespective of their stance toward the Nazi state, those who still held German citizenship were threatened with internment, allegedly for their own protection. Faced with this prospect, one of the non-Jewish lecturers in the German Department, Anstock, opted to return to war-torn Germany. Law professor Ernst Hirsch, on the other hand, had been granted Turkish citizenship only a year earlier and was so able to avoid internment. Hirsch had been able to save his mother from the Holocaust by inviting her to live with him and his wife in Istanbul in the 1930s. Tragically, he could not rescue his sister, who wrote to him after her deportation to Theresienstadt. Until Turkey severed diplomatic relationships with Nazi Germany, Hirsch had been able to mail packages to the concentration camp. As he learned after the war, his sister and her family were later murdered in Auschwitz.[89]

For those of Jewish background, living in Turkey in 1944 meant surviving the Holocaust. Even if they were interned as German nationals, the conditions in Turkey were not comparable to the atrocities suffered by Jews, antifascists, and prisoners of war in Europe. Germans who were employed at the German consulate were confined, along with their families, to its premises. Eighty-five Germans were interned at the consulate, while 150 had to live in the German school for several months. Conditions for the internees cannot have been pleasant, and there is no doubt that they suffered from shortages and restrictions, but it is remarkable that in January 1945 the consulate was able to build a sauna on its premises in an effort to improve their living conditions.[90]

Most émigrés were not interned in Istanbul and Ankara, but in the small Anatolian towns Çorum, Yozgat, and Kırşehir. Fuchs had been ordered to join Hitler's army as a reservist, but he categorically refused to return. As a result, he was interned in Çorum for thirteen months.[91] The drawings that Fuchs made during his internment in 1944–1945 provide us with a glimpse into the living conditions for enemies of war. His artwork is now archived in the former Robert College, where he was employed for most of his life after the war.[92] It is evident that the internment in small, rather isolated Anatolian towns was unlike any Nazi lager, Soviet gulag, or even British camp for Germans during the war.[93] It was also unlike the camps in which Turkish Jews had been forced to work in 1942. There were restrictions as to where German internees could go and with whom they could communicate, but essentially they lived in regular houses among the locals. Although there was a ban on leaving Çorum, Fuchs and Cornelius Bischoff, who later became Yaşar Kemal's main German translator, found occasions to explore the rural landscape around town.[94] Fuchs used his time to portray the everyday life and natural surroundings of Çorum. He also started teaching art to interned children. Other émigrés, too, tried to make the best of being confined in an Anatolian town. Walter Ruben, the Indologist at the University of Ankara and later chair of East Berlin's Orient Institute, decided to apply his anthropological background to the study of Kırşehir, where he was interned with his family. The outcome of Ruben's research, now of historical value, was published quite recently.[95]

Some émigrés, like Ritter and Auerbach, could avoid internment altogether. Possibly because he was indispensable to the university, Auerbach was exempt from internment and hence able to complete the writing of *Mimesis* from his Bebek home. After the war, Auerbach waited anxiously for the publication of his book in Bern and for a chance to leave Turkey. He resigned from his position as chair of the faculty for Western languages and literatures, considered academic appointments in Germany, and weighed his prospects in the United States. The atmosphere in Turkey had become intellectually oppressive in the immediate postwar period, with Yücel's humanist reforms targeted by the anticommunists. This had an impact on academic life across the country and led to the dismissal of scholars like classical philologist and humanist Erhat. Before

Traugott Fuchs (1906–1997), *Getting a Scrubbing in a Turkish Bath* (Çorum). By permission of Herrmann Fuchs.

Traugott Fuchs, *The Concert* (Çorum). By permission of Herrmann Fuchs.

Traugott Fuchs, *There Was also This: A Foreigner Who Committed Suicide* (Çorum). By permission of Herrmann Fuchs.

leaving Turkey in 1947, however, Auerbach made one final effort to counter the influence of Nazism on the department and to promote intellectual exchange among the Western European philologies. He revived the Romance journal that he had cofounded in Istanbul, now called *Garp Filolojileri Dergisi* (the *Journal of Western Philology*). In his preface to the journal we see glimmers of nostalgia for the early days of the Romance Seminar at Istanbul University, a time when just a handful of students learned several languages, obtained a comprehensive knowledge of Western European culture, and cultivated specialist interests.

We can read Auerbach's editorial work in Turkey as an attempt to uphold the dual value of comprehensive humanist training and specialist knowledge.[96] I make this point keeping in mind Auerbach's influential essay of 1952, "Philology and World Literature," in which he characterizes the ideal scholar as someone capable of striking that perfect balance between specialization and general knowledge. The journal is, however, important for another reason as well, for here Auerbach speaks directly to the future. "We hope, he says in the preface, "that this journal which we have started to reissue will serve the intellectual development of Turkey and continue the work that contributes to the study of international philology."[97] Similar to comparatists like René Wellek in the United States after the war, Auerbach cast himself as a kind of international ambassador, with the aim of encouraging productive collaboration among the faculty. Having witnessed the havoc wrought by extreme nationalism, his academic agenda, one might say, was now once again directed toward transcending the nation as the main organizing principle of intellectual life.[98]

Reflecting on his influence on tertiary education after eleven years in Istanbul, Auerbach stressed that the émigrés had indeed accomplished something, "just not nearly as much as might have been possible."[99] He held the university's vacillating policies accountable for the émigrés' limited success. Disillusioned, he concluded that it was difficult to Europeanize a non-European country in so short a time because of the great danger of practical and moral anarchy.[100] Concluding that he was only the chair of the faculty for Western languages and literatures "on paper," the disappointed Auerbach withdrew from his position.[101] The transitional phase had, he believed, produced nothing better than a vacuum, because "irresponsible, dilettantish, and half-baked experiments" had made the whole process so difficult.[102] Auerbach was not alone in his critique but—for reasons explained in chapter 3—he would always have difficulty expressing such views publicly.[103] In contrast, Turkish colleagues like Ahmet Hamdi Tanpınar, professor for modern Turkish literature at Istanbul University, were outspoken critics of the many new beginnings and ruptures that characterized the late Ottoman and early Turkish periods. Reflecting later on the reforms, Tanpınar concluded that the discontinuity in cultural affairs had had a highly deleterious effect on society at large.[104]

As I argue throughout this book, it is necessary to think of exile not only as an act of dislocation, but also as one of relocation. Exile brings with it loss and discontinuity but also processes of reorientation, accommodation, and, indeed, new forms of belonging. Only by acknowledging exile's dual character can we properly evaluate its epistemological implications. For these reasons, I find it necessary to contextualize the study of exile by examining the broader cultural and historical picture. Above all, it seems important to examine the political climate not only at the point of departure, but also at the point of arrival. Thus we find that the politics of Auerbach's exilic home—the competing interests of Turkish nationalist reformers, German émigrés, Nazis, and the German community at large—were at least as important to his stance as a critic as the mere fact of his displacement.

5

Writing *Mimesis* in Istanbul

"UNFORTUNATELY, THERE WERE ALMOST NO BOOKS," claimed Leo Spitzer, long after he had left Istanbul and established himself as a scholar in the United States. Asking the dean at Istanbul University about the shortage, the dean apparently replied, "We don't bother with books. They burn."[1] Odd as the statement seems, Spitzer conceded that the dean may have had a point: the city was built atop a seismic fault, making for frequent cataclysms, the buildings were mostly of wood, and the fire department was hopelessly disorganized. How sad this must have seemed to Spitzer, who had fled a country where books were deliberately set ablaze and their authors deprived of all vestiges of human dignity.

It is often said that Istanbul had few books. Perhaps the statement is repeated so often because it seems revelatory—it suggests Istanbul's difficulties to modernize or seems to tell us something about the city's vulnerability to the forces of nature and social disorganization; perhaps it is oft repeated because the lack of books implies the lack of an intellectual sphere and Istanbul as a kind of tabula rasa.[2] Since the war, such suggestions have come to signify not just the conditions of exilic scholarship in Istanbul, but the general state of scholarship at Europe's periphery. The implication is that Western scholarship could be exported to the periphery, yet nothing was learned in exchange. This is implied in two terms still current in Germany—*Wissenstransfer* (knowledge transfer) and *Bildungshilfe* (educational aid)—terms that are routinely used to describe Turkish-German relations between 1933 and 1945.[3] These terms strike me as problematic because they suggest a unidirectional flow of information and skills. It is as

133

though knowledge were dispensed exclusively by Europeans, and non-Europeans were its desperate recipients. What of the possibility that the Turkish academy may have had a reciprocal bearing on German émigré scholarship?

In this chapter, I argue against one-sided notions of knowledge transfer and, instead, direct attention to conditions on the ground. Only by examining the context in which knowledge arises can we draw meaningful conclusions about how chains of influence, appropriation, and adaptation operate. We might begin by taking a closer look at the person who opens this chapter, the university dean who seemed so cavalier about books. He has passed into Western history as an unnamed source, but actually his identity is not hard to uncover: at the time of Spitzer's hire, the dean of the faculty for literature was literary historian Mehmet Fuat Köprülü, one of the few scholars not to have been dismissed when the old Darülfünun became Istanbul University. As the founder of the university's first Türkiyat Enstitüsü, Institute of Turcology, in the 1920s, Köprülü collected some sixteen thousand volumes on Turkish language, literature, and history during the course of the decade.[4] In fact, his association with books and collecting antedate this: he came from an old Ottoman family of grand viziers who had established a reading house for the poor and a public library that would become one of the most important Ottoman libraries.[5]

It seems indisputable that this most prolific and influential of literary critics and historians was a bibliophile, and if there was irony in Köprülü's remarks to Spitzer, then the Austrian obviously missed it. But perhaps the remarks were meant more cynically than ironically. The city had certainly suffered some disastrous book losses caused by fires like the one that annihilated the Darülfünun library in the 1860s. We can also think of Köprülü's invocation of fire in metaphorical terms. Fires posed a literal threat to the city's old wooden buildings, as Spitzer himself noted, but their destructive force also encapsulated the troubled relationship between the new Turkish Republic and the Ottoman Empire. While the republic was supposed to rise like Phoenix from the ashes, the charred ruins of the empire generated an unprecedented sense of despair during the early republican period. We see these sentiments expressed by writers like Ahmet Hamdi Tanpınar. In his 1946 essay on Istanbul, Tanpınar showed how the rupture between the Ottoman past and the Turkish present impacted the urban landscape. He admitted to an uncomfortable mix of pleasure and despair, as he watched the vestiges of the Ottoman Empire disappear. It was, he said, like Nero watching Rome burn.[6] This senti-ment is echoed in Orhan Pamuk's more recent *Istanbul: Memories and the City*, a work that centers on the concept of *hüzün*, collective melancholia. Pamuk describes *hüzün* as one of the defining characteristics of the city's inhabitants. Recalling his own feelings watching old Ottoman buildings burn in the 1950s and 1960s, he writes: "Ours was the guilt, loss, and jeal-ousy felt at the sudden destruction of the last traces of a great culture and a great civilization that we were unfit or unprepared to inherit, in our frenzy to turn Istanbul into a pale, poor, second-class imitation of a west-ern city."[7]

For Pamuk and his literary predecessors, fire invokes memories of the past, melancholy, transformation, and even modernization. These sorts of allusions suggest various interpretations for the remarks I cited at the beginning of the chapter. To take dean Köprülü's response to Spitzer literally is to miss the point that the fires that destroyed traces of Ottoman imperialism simultaneously created an uneasy, but unique, cultural land-scape in the rapidly modernizing Turkish Republic. Notwithstanding fire's destructive force—a metaphor for erasing a rich Ottoman culture and history—we will find that Istanbul libraries were, in fact, modern-ized, expanded, and, indeed, established anew.

Scholars in the West have long been preoccupied with the question of whether Istanbul impeded or advanced the work of German émigrés dur-ing the war. To be sure, Istanbul exile resulted in great scholarship. And answering the question of whether this was accomplished despite or be-cause of their surroundings would seem to tell us something about both Turkey and the condition of exile. Alternatively, it might tell us something about those few German-Jewish scholars who managed to produce work of rare genius in the face of the worst kind of psychic deprivation. Auer-bach's *Mimesis* has legendary status, in part, because most Western critics emphasize that it was written between 1942 and May 1945 outside of Eu-rope and in the absence of adequate research material. Paradoxically, Istan-bul is regarded as a place that was intellectually productive through its very lack of books. This view was put forth by Auerbach himself, who com-mented on the paucity of research material in the epilogue to *Mimesis*:

The book was written during the war and at Istanbul, where the libraries are not well equipped for European studies. International communications were impeded; I had to dispense with almost all periodicals, with almost all the more recent investigations,

Anonymous, sixteenth century, *The Great Fire of Constantinople*. Codex Cicogna. Museo Correr, Venice, Italy. Photo: Cameraphoto Arte, Venice. By permission of Art Resource, New York.

and in some cases with reliable critical editions of my texts . . . it is quite possible that the book owes its existence to just this lack of a rich and specialized library. If it had been possible for me to acquaint myself with all the work that has been done on so many subjects, I might have never reached the point of writing.[8]

This is, in effect, how Auerbach justified his sparse use of footnotes and secondary literature, something that was atypical among his generation of philologists, who often marshaled vast screeds of secondary literature in support of their arguments. Critics have been fascinated by Auerbach's suggestion that this seminal book owed its very existence to a lack of adequate resources. Indeed, this authorial imprimatur has come to legitimize a position not only on *Mimesis* but on Istanbul itself, a site that is unquestioningly construed as having been thinly populated by books, ideas, and intellectuals themselves. Edward Said, for one, took Auerbach to mean that there were "no Western research libraries" at all. Such a library, Said suggested, turning the lack into a gain, might have otherwise "swamped" Auerbach with material. In reconstructing Auerbach's modus operandi, Said assumed that Auerbach had his own limited library of primary sources but that he "relied mainly on memory and what seems like an infallible interpretive skill for elucidating relationships between books and the world they belong to."[9]

That *Mimesis* is a unique achievement is indisputable, and my purpose here is to question neither the author's skill nor the work's originality. Rather, I mean to take a fresh look at its site of production. Contrary to what was claimed by Auerbach and reiterated by generations of subsequent readers, Istanbul offered a rich intellectual life, numerous libraries, and other cultural resources. Moreover, the city was gripped by a sense of excitement about its identity as a European city, and this was, in fact, highly conducive to writing a magnum opus that took the history of Europe as its subject. Offering a corrective to the reception of *Mimesis* not only tells us more about Auerbach and Istanbul during the war period. It also tells us about how intellectual production operates within the transnational context. Most importantly, perhaps, it shows that the kinds of distinctions we like to insist upon—Europe and non-Europe; intellectual and anti-intellectual; attachment at home and detachment in exile—are often hyperboles within political rhetoric. By questioning these distinctions and insisting on a more nuanced account of transnational intellectual production, it will perhaps be possible to arrive at more fertile forms of exchange.

Critics today overlook the fact that, unlike Spitzer, Auerbach never said that there were "almost no books" in Istanbul. Auerbach merely said that "in some cases" he had to work without "reliable critical editions" of his texts. He pointed specifically to the dearth of professional journals, rather than books, from Western Europe. From his correspondence we learn that the philologist tried to keep abreast of recent scholarship—at least until the outbreak of the war—by exchanging print material with scholars in Germany, Turkey, and elsewhere. Since Nazi scholarship was of little value to his project, we can assume that there would have been few wartime publications that interested him in Germany anyway. He would probably have wanted to read the work of Romance scholars like Victor Klemperer and Werner Krauss, intellectuals who survived under inhumane conditions in Nazi Germany but were hindered from publishing. This brings me to my thesis that the catalyst for *Mimesis* was not, in fact, the insufficiency of source material, but its very sufficiency. As we already know from previous chapters, the Dante-scholar found a circle of colleagues and students who were acutely interested in the kinds of questions he was asking. While Auerbach was in exile, the first Turkish translation of the *Commedia* appeared in print, and the idea of a Turkish Renaissance generated an interesting debate about Europe's cultural heritage. Auerbach was surrounded by print material, a vibrant intellectual circle, and the tremendous weight carried by humanist scholarship in his home away from home. With this in mind, I investigate three things that have come to encapsulate the originality of Auerbach's authorship, namely, the unavailability of books, the poor state of scholarship and intellectual dialogue, and, finally, detachment as a precondition for critical thinking.

Books

It is true that libraries in Istanbul were not comparable to the well-stocked and catalogued Prussian State Library in Berlin, where Auerbach had worked for some years as a librarian. In Berlin, he had the resources he needed to establish himself as a medievalist and write his professorial thesis on Dante. But Istanbul was not without its own rich resources. In fact, when American Orientalist Harry Howard did a survey of the Istanbul libraries and archives in the late 1930s, he estimated that at least one hundred thousand ancient manuscripts were preserved in Istanbul, and these manuscripts spanned the Greek, Roman, Byzantine, Islamic, Ottoman, and

Turkish periods of history.[10] This led Howard to characterize Istanbul as "one of the richest cities in the world in its archival and library resources, rivaling the known treasures of Rome."[11] The museums in Istanbul, he added, contained not only Ottoman relics, but also Greek, Roman, and Byzantine artifacts. The comparatist Liselotte Dieckmann, who first worked with Spitzer at the Istanbul faculty and later immigrated to the United States, confirms this observation. She emphasized that humanists could avail themselves of "the most beautiful old manuscripts."[12]

In the early days of the university reform, the library at Istanbul University still had some catching up to do. The introduction of the Latin alphabet in 1928 meant that there were simply not enough books in the new script to fill the shelves. However, the university made rapid progress setting up the library and purchased vast numbers of books from Europe. In his biography, Ernst Hirsch remembers the moment he walked into an "extraordinarily huge" room in the law department. It was designated as the departmental library but had hardly any books in European languages or modern Turkish. In view of the thoroughgoing legal reform in the Turkish Republic, he regarded books in Ottoman script as outdated. "A university without a library is like a barracks without an arsenal," he said, and decided to build up the departmental library with the help of generous funds set aside by the ministry of education.[13] Following Albert Malche's earlier call to improve the state of the library, the university acquired twenty thousand books during the first year of the tertiary reform alone. This meant that in 1934, the library's total holdings stood at some one hundred and thirty-two thousand items.[14] From Hirsch's memoir we also learn that in 1938 a considerable number of sealed book boxes were found under a staircase. The books had been donated by German institutions in late Ottoman times and had simply been forgotten in the political turmoil caused by the transition. With the help of students and assistants, Hirsch spent months cataloguing the books and setting up the library.[15]

There were also other émigrés actively engaged in improving the conditions for academic productivity in exile. Later we will find out more about Auerbach's close colleague Alexander Rüstow, who spared neither time nor money in buying books for his personal library and improving the holdings of the Istanbul University library. In order to exert some control over its holdings, Rüstow decided to become an acquisitions advisor.[16] How ironic that, in the 1930s, buying books from Germany was cheap and easy. Hirsch tells us that anti-Semitic laws in Nazi Germany meant that well-known antiquarian dealers in Leipzig had to liquidate their businesses and look for ways to sell vast quantities of books cheaply. Quite simply, there was no demand for them anymore. As a result, numerous boxes of books arrived to fill the empty bookshelves.[17] While professors often took personal responsibility for setting up departmental libraries, Gerhard Kessler and later Walter Gottschalk were in charge of establishing the university's central library—these were émigrés who, as one might expect, attended to the needs of their German colleagues.[18] Given the country's newfound interest in humanism and Western literature specifically, we can assume that many of their acquisitions were European classics.

We learn more about the state of the university library from a report by the German library advisor, Jürgens, who had been sent in an official capacity to Istanbul in 1934. The library advisor was charged with inspecting the city's German book trade and evaluating the availability of German books in Turkish libraries. Jürgens reported to the German research foundation in Berlin that Istanbul's university library holdings were far better than he had been led to believe—especially when it came to philosophy and Germanistik. The library owned the "Kürschner edition of national literature, the selection of the best editions of our classics, and the works of our philosophers which are still regarded as standard editions." Furthermore, Jürgens identified "a strong foundation of German books" "in all subject areas."[19] The American scholar Harry Howard, who visited Istanbul a few years later, reported on the availability of modern books in collections other than the university's central library. The newly founded İnkilap Library in Istanbul was, he wrote, "essentially confined to modern books in French, English, German, Greek, and Armenian, as well as Turkish, and is devoted especially to the nineteenth century. The library contains an important collection of books in French and English and Turkish bequeathed by the late Muallim Cevdet Bey. Here will be found magazines, printed materials, old papers and books."[20]

Indeed, we know that Auerbach actually used collections like these. This point is confirmed by Süheyla Bayrav, who worked as his assistant and translator for a number of years. In an interview about the origins of philology in Turkey, she pointed out that Auerbach benefited from the collection in the department of French philology, as well as drawing on his own rich library, when writing *Mimesis*.[21] Whatever material Auerbach could not find at the university, he tried to find in the personal libraries of other émigrés, in various libraries around Istanbul, and in the city's many bookstores. The Librarie Hachette in Pera, an old European district of Istanbul, was the largest bookstore carrying predominantly French but also German literature. Jürgens's report tells us that the Librarie Hachette displayed German émigré literature in its store windows. The bookstores Kalis and Kapp, in contrast, were both run by Nazis and thus boycotted by Jews and antifascists. The owner of Kalis complained that he lost up to 40 percent of his customers thanks to this boycott of Nazi-owned stores in Istanbul.[22] For the boycotters, the city offered other alternatives when it came to European literature. Besides an Italian bookstore, there were two German bookstores that occupied a significant place in Istanbul's intellectual life. First, the bookstore Karon—owned by Isidor Karon, a German Jew from Alsace who had immigrated to Istanbul in 1914—sold publications important to German émigrés. These included the newspapers *Pariser Tageblatt* and *Das andere Deutschland*, and, in the 1930s, Karon was able to order books from Leipzig directly. During the war, however, he sent his book orders mainly to Switzerland. Naturally, his store was one of the important meeting places for émigrés.[23]

In addition to Karon's more established store, there was also the new bookstore Münchhausen-Halberstädter, which was known for its leftist and scholarly leanings.[24] Indeed, we can assume that German-language bookstores were still in business almost a decade after Jürgens's inspection in 1934. Certainly, Hennig Brinkmann, the Nazi professor whom we heard from in chapter 4, had no difficulty building up a German departmental library in 1943. Brinkmann said that he only took a few books from the university's Romance library; the remainder he was able to stock from the Istanbul bookstores.[25]

In 1938, Auerbach complained in a letter about the lack of a *vernünftige Bibliothek*, a "reasonable library." *Leider kann hier eigentlich nur ein Orientalist arbeiten*, "unfortunately, only an Orientalist can really work here," he wrote to the Dante-scholar Johannes Oeschger.[26] For all his vociferousness about the state of the libraries, Auerbach neglected to mention that he had access to the library of the Dominican monastery of San Pietro di Galata (St. Peter and Paul) in Istanbul, which possesses Jacques-Paul Migne's complete nineteenth-century *Patrologia*. From other letters and memoirs we gather that émigrés could draw on many types of sources dispersed throughout the libraries and archives in Istanbul. Canonical texts, important critical editions, even Greek and Roman manuscripts were within reach. The *Patrologia Latina* in the Dominican monastery contains, alone, more than two hundred volumes of Latin ecclesiastical writing, spanning over a thousand years of theological, philosophical, historical, and literary history from Tertullian to Pope Innocent III. Another vast set of volumes in the Dominican library covered Greek texts and their Latin translations. Long after the publication of *Mimesis*, Auerbach—now in the United States—acknowledged this important find in a footnote to the "Epilegomena" of *Mimesis*. Here, he wrote that it was Roncalli who provided him with access to indispensable sources: "I was able to write the works on *figura* and *passio* because an entire set of Migne's *Patrologia* was located in an attic-level library room of the Dominican monastery of San Pietro di Galata."[27]

Monsignor Roncalli, the later Pope John XXIII, granted the Jewish scholar the privilege of working in the monastery's library in the 1930s. Auerbach had him to thank for this, but in the years 1943–1944 the Vatican representative did something even more remarkable when he helped some thousands of Jews survive the Holocaust.[28] It is not clear whether Auerbach was aware of Roncalli's conversations with Jewish rescue organizations and, most importantly, with Chaim Barlas, director of the Jewish Agency for Palestine in Istanbul.[29] We only have a 1956 letter from Roncalli to Auerbach in which he thanks him for sending a copy of *Mimesis*. Roncalli, whose papacy began two years later, acknowledged the scholarly work as proof of "universal brotherhood" and recalled their "pleasant and friendly conversations of 1937 in Turkey."[30] The letter provides no further indication as to whether theirs was a scholarly relationship or whether they talked theology and politics. What we do know from Auerbach himself, however, is that he would not have been able to formulate some of his most influential ideas without access to the Dominican library. Theologian John Dawson shows that in the *Patrologia*, Auerbach found "a rich tradition of Christian figural reading of the Old Testament in which the historical reality of ancient Jews had been preserved rather than superseded." This finding, Dawson argues, enabled Auerbach to begin writing *Mimesis*.[31] In many ways, Turkish exile marked a turning point for Auerbach. While studying the *Patrologia* in the Dominican library, the philologist concluded that the concept of history in Dante's *Commedia* was informed by a figural interpretation of reality. It was not the Hegelian notion of history—events giving rise to new events—that helps us understand the apprehension of time and reality in the Middle Ages, Auerbach suggested, but the vertical linking of events to a divine order.[32]

These insights into the Istanbul libraries undermine Auerbach's assertion that *Mimesis* owed its genesis to the lack of "a rich and specialized library." Indeed, information about Istanbul's libraries allows us to interpret his oft-quoted claim differently—namely, as a rhetorical gesture. It is through hyperbole—emphasis produced by exaggeration—that Auerbach legitimizes his pioneering approach to literary criticism and staves off criticism from tradition-bound readers.[33] Breaking with philological tradition, Auerbach takes short literary excerpts as points of departure, *Ausgangspunkte*, and highlights distinct modes of representation spanning three millennia.[34]

Auerbach's epilogue has, as we have seen, also been used to indict Istanbul as a place of absence, a nowhere place. We can likewise think of this as a form of hyperbole or even litotes, a rhetorical gesture belonging to the long tradition of Western travel writing. We find it used, for example, in Homer's description of the Cyclops's island, where there are said to exist no laws, no assemblies, no cultivation—nothing, in short, that the civilized arrivee might expect and want.[35] With its strongly normatizing character, this is a rhetorical device that Jonathan Lamb calls a "seesaw between all and nothing, sufficiency and deficiency."[36] More to our purpose, we find another form of negation in an eighteenth-century text that Auerbach translated into German prior to emigrating, namely, Giambattista Vico's *Scienza Nuova* (*New Science*). Vico, whose ideas remained central to all of Auerbach's work, had claimed that, for the purpose of studying the philosophy of history, it was "necessary to proceed as if there were no books in the world."[37] This feat of intellectual negation allowed Vico to envision a clean slate for his own philosophy of history and, by implication, to emphasize the originality of his own work.

The Intellectual Network: Islam, Dante, and the Making of Europe

Not every scholar working on his magnum opus in Turkey drew on these rhetorical devices. Alexander Rüstow, for instance, took a different approach when he drafted *Ortsbestimmung der Gegenwart* (*Localization of the Present*).[38] Rüstow had accepted an academic position as an economist in Turkey in 1933, where he continued to resist the Nazi regime. His scholarly interests were channeled into writing a comprehensive critique of civilization.[39] In the preface to *Ortsbestimmung*, Rüstow summed up the conditions that enabled him to complete his comprehensive cultural-historical study. The first condition for writing "this German book" was, he noted, leaving Hitler's suffocating Germany. Second, he defined the émigré's task as an ethical responsibility to explain the "catastrophic" present within the context of world history. And third, Rüstow pointed out that he, along with many other émigrés, had been enlisted to facilitate Turkey's metamorphosis into a Western culture. Unlike Auerbach, Rüstow acknowledged in his exilic work that the *kameradschaftliche Zusammenarbeit*, "collegial collaboration," alleviated some of the difficulties posed by exile.[40] In his private correspondence, we see him expressing a range of feelings related to exile in Turkey. Rüstow complained about the impossibility of putting down roots in Istanbul and the feeling of being "out of place," but he also acknowledged that his living conditions were rather conducive to his work.[41]

The economist was part of a lively intellectual circle, the so-called Privatakademie, founded soon after the arrival of émigrés in Istanbul. The group met regularly, organized interdisciplinary colloquia, and patronized the Karon bookstore. Among the group's members in the early 1930s were Spitzer, the legal scholar Andreas Schwarz, economists Fritz Neumark, Gerhard Kessler, and Alfred Isaac, archeologist Kurt Bittel, botanists Heilbronn and Brauner, zoologist Kosswig, astronomers Freundlich and Rosenberg, and chemists Arndt and Breusch.[42] Not much is known about the activities of this group in the late 1930s, but as an unswerving humanist, Rüstow was an important intellectual companion to Auerbach. From Auerbach's and Rüstow's personal correspondence, some of which is now archived in the Literaturarchiv Marbach, we learn how Auerbach benefited from Rüstow's acquaintance: they exchanged books and drafts of their writing and discussed scholarly matters pertinent to their work.

Paul Bové rightly claims that *Mimesis* "owes much to its academic cultural context," a point hinted at in one of Auerbach's letters yet elided from his published work.[43] Perhaps it was also Harry Levin's article on Spitzer and Auerbach, an article published shortly after the latter's death in 1957, that established the notion of Istanbul as a place that precluded possibilities for intellectual exchange between Turkish and émigré intellectuals. According to Levin, it was because Istanbul lacked adequate scholarly institutions that it marked the point of divergence for the two scholars: Istanbul "drew a sharp line between the two approaches within the same field: the infra-scholarship of Spitzer and the para-scholarship of Auerbach."[44] Levin argued that Turkish exile turned out to be a "blessing in disguise" for Auerbach because the gaps in his library allowed him to generate an "imaginary museum of . . . European civilization."[45] He "found himself perforce in the position of writing a more original kind of book than he might otherwise have attempted, if he had remained within easy access to the stock professional facilities."[46] Levin took this argument one step further, claiming that it was not only the want of an adequate library but the ignorance of Auerbach's Turkish contemporaries that plunged him into a void, from whence he emerged with *Mimesis*. To exemplify this point, Levin related an anecdote about Auerbach's encounter with the Turkish translator of the *Commedia*:

One of his anecdotes casts a comic light upon the sense of disconnection from which he [Auerbach] must have suffered. On taking up his official duties at Istanbul, he was introduced to various Turks with whom, it was presumed, he would have much in common. One of them, understandably, was the Turkish translator of Dante, whose rendering of the *Commedia* had been accomplished in less than two years; indeed it would have been completed sooner, he boasted, had he not also been translating potboilers during the same interim. When Auerbach congratulated him on his grasp of the language, this colleague blandly confessed that he knew no Italian at all. His brother did; but that was scarcely of help, since the brother had been away at the time. To Auerbach's obvious question, his informant replied that he had worked from a French translation. Auerbach, doing his best to keep his eyebrows from twitching, asked which one. "I don't recall the name," said the Turk, "but it was a large brown book." What could be expected, under these circumstances, from so highly qualified a *Gelehrter* as Auerbach? He would be working, as he liked to put it, "*dans un grenier*." After he had used up his backlog of notes, he would have to suspend his medieval researches. In the absence of learned journals, compilations, and commentaries, how could one continue to be a scholar?[47]

Characterizing the Turk, an ignorant translator of potboilers, as the very antithesis of German erudition is what makes this story so entertaining. Indeed, the anecdote must have accomplished its rhetorical purpose because it elicited sympathy for the beleaguered German scholar, and even today the story, with all its intensifications and drollery, is allowed to stand. But since it remains unclear how Levin dramatized the anecdote for comic effect, I propose that we examine it from another angle. It strikes me as significant, for instance, that the teller focuses on the mechanics of translation but overlooks the importance of the translation project per se. And it is this project—translating Dante for a Turkish audience—that I now wish to examine in some detail.

In a society that had only recently taken leave of its Ottoman past, the publication of Dante's *Commedia* was nothing short of revolutionary. The work, we recall, portrays Dante and Virgil's encounter with Mohammed and Ali in the ninth circle of hell, where they are being punished as "sowers of scandal and schism."[48] The depiction is particularly offensive to Muslim believers because of its characterization of the prophets. (In fact, only Judas, Brutus, and Cassius separate Mohammed and his son-in-law Ali from Satan, and this triumvirate receives its punishment in the subsequent circle of hell.) The scene in question describes, in graphic detail, the brutal torture of Ali and of Mohammed, who is disemboweled and split into two. The torture scene was considered so inflammatory that earlier translators like Musurus Paşa, the Ottoman ambassador to London who translated the *Commedia* into modern Greek in 1882, simply omitted this episode.[49] Religious norms governing the representation of Islam dictated that the *Inferno*, the first part of the *Commedia*, not be translated, and consequently there was scarcely any Ottoman reception of Dante during this period. To all intents and purposes, the *Commedia* did not exist for most Ottoman readers.

As I pointed out earlier, Levin used Auerbach's encounter with the translator to encapsulate the poor conditions suffered by the German émigré in Istanbul. But to readers familiar with the cultural history of Turkey, the 1938 Dante translation is evidence of something else: it shows, namely, that exciting new intellectual possibilities accompanied the secularization of Turkey, possibilities that impacted the world of publishing. Thus, instead of dismissing the "ignorant Turk," along with the supposedly bibliophobic dean we heard from earlier, I think it is worth uncovering the identities of these people and finding out something about them. The name of the translator was Hamdi Varoğlu. In 1938, he published the first prose translation of the *Commedia* into Turkish, and this was followed and improved on by a number of successive translators. At the time, Varoğlu was one of the most productive translators in the country and best known for his Zola translations; he also rendered into Turkish works by Stendhal, Rousseau, Zweig, Cervantes, Plato, and Euripides—certainly not, or not only, the potboilers mentioned by Levin. This is not the place to discuss the quality of these translations, nor do I wish to discuss questions of translatability, the legitimacy of using an intermediary language, and the theory and ethics of translation. Rather, I wish to remind the reader of the significance of these translations for Turkey's secular, humanist project generally. The 1938 prose translation of the *Commedia* anticipated the much larger translation project initiated by the minister of education, Yücel.

Dante's reception in modern Turkey begins with Nüshet Haşim Sinanoğlu's study on Dante. Published in 1934, the author gave a brief summary of each of the punishments suffered in the various circles of the *Inferno*. As Sinanoğlu pointed out, the twelfth-century Egyptian Sultan Salahaddin, famous for his generosity and heroism, is among the great Greek and Roman philosophers and poets caught in limbo.[50] Together with the unbaptized, this group is trapped at the edge of Dante's hell, not as sinners, but because they are not Christian. Although Sinanoğlu specifically names one of the three Muslims in limbo (the others being the philosophers Avicenna [980–1037] and Averroës [1126–1198], whom Dante honored by placing them here, too), Sinanoğlu passed over Mohammed and Ali in the ninth circle of hell. To be more precise, Sinanoğlu describes the punishment meted out to schismatics but does not disclose their identities. He merely reports that the cleft figure in the ninth circle is "the founder of the religion that caused many wars for the Christians."[51]

Given that Sinanoğlu considered Turkish readers circa 1934 not yet ready for the schismatics in Dante's *Inferno*, we can see the significance of Hamdi Varoğlu's translation just a few years later. Certainly, Varoğlu and his publisher, İbrahim Hilmi Çığıraçan, were careful in their approach. The translation of the *Commedia* included a preface in which the writer M. Turhan Tan impressed on readers the need to interpret Dante's portrayal of hell and paradise from an aesthetic, not religious, point of view.[52] Tan ascribed the irreverent, ridiculing portrayal of other religions to Dante's need to appease the Catholic Church. Only thus, Tan said, could Dante produce his masterpiece.[53] Although Varoğlu was not threatened with censorship like the earlier Greek-Ottoman translator Musurus Paşa, Tan's preface shows that the *Commedia* elicited serious concerns about the work's reception. For the first time, Turkish readers would be confronted by the image of Mohammed in the *Inferno*, a passage that I cite here from Varoğlu's Turkish prose translation and Mark Musa's English verse translation:

Dibi çıkan veya bir tahtası kopan hiç bir fıçı yoktur ki, benim gördüğüm, çenesinden şercine kadar yarılmış bir günahkâr derecesinde delinmiş olsun. Bağırsakları bacaklarının arasında sallanıyor, ahşası ve yenilen şeyleri necasete tahvil eden murdar kese meydanda görünüyordu. Ben, sabit nazarlarla ona bakarken, o da bana baktı ve göğsünü elile açarak, dedi ki:

　　—Bak, nasıl vücudumu paralıyorum; bak Muhammed nasıl alil oldu. Önümden ağlayarak giden Alinin yüzü, çenesinden kafatasına kadar yarıktır. Ve burada gördüğün bütün diğerleri, yeryüzünde, nifak ve itizal saçmışlardır, onun için böyle yarıldılar. Arkamızda bir zebani var ki, bu elem yolunu bir kere devrettiğimiz zaman, bizi keskin kılıncı ile bir kere daha zalimane biçiyor; zira, onun önüne varmadan evvel yaralarımız tekrar kapanmış bulunuyor.[54]

No wine cask with its stave or cant-bar sprung
　　was ever split the way I saw someone
　　ripped open from his chin to where we fart.
Between his legs his guts spilled out, with the heart
　　and other vital parts, and the dirty sack
　　that turns to shit whatever the mouth gulps down.
While I stood staring into his misery,
　　he looked at me and with both hands he opened
　　his chest and said: "See how I tear myself!"
See how Mohamet is deformed and torn!
　　In front of me, and weeping, Ali walks,
　　his face cleft from his chin up to the crown.
The souls that you see in passing in this ditch
　　were all sowers of scandal and schism in life,
　　and so in death you see them torn asunder.
A devil stands back there who trims us all
　　in this cruel way, and each one of this mob
　　receives anew the blade of the devil's sword
each time we make one round of this sad road,
　　because the wounds have all healed up again
　　by the time each one presents himself once more.[55]

Concerned that Dante's views might be taken for his own, Varoğlu felt it necessary to add a lengthy footnote distancing himself from the portrayal of Mohammed and Ali. To press home his point, he also cited a poem in which the Ottoman poet Abdülhak Hamid (Tarhan) criticized Dante's treatment of Mohammed and Ali. In the poem, Abdülhak Hamid addresses the Italian poet with a measure of irony and contempt: "Oh Dante! Is it you? Great ingenious slanderer!"[56] Lest we think that things have changed, let me point out that all Turkish translations that I have read (including the more recent translation by Rekin Teksoy) show in one way or another that translators still feel the need to distance themselves from Dante's representation of the Muslim prophet.[57] Ultimately, this reminds us that Turhan Tan's 1938 injunction to regard the *Commedia* as an aesthetic rather than religious text remains pertinent even to this day. It also indicates that the Turkish secular reform—introduced almost ninety years ago to separate state and religion and guarantee freedom of thought—is yet to achieve its goal.[58]

One wonders how Auerbach, as a German-Jewish Dante-scholar, dealt with the tensions generated by Dante's work. The publications and translations suggest that there was a fragile market for Dante, just as there was public interest in the social and cultural conditions that gave rise to the Renaissance. Spitzer capitalized on this interest, giving lectures on

Giovanni da Modena (fl. 1409–1455), *The Prophet Mohammed*, detail of the fresco of Hell, inspired by Dante, circa 1410. Bolognini Chapel. S. Petronio, Bologna, Italy. Photo: Scala. By permission of Art Resource, New York.

Boccaccio, Rabelais, and Cervantes at the university.[59] In each of these three lectures, Spitzer touched on Dante's impact on the Renaissance. Yet like Sinanoğlu, neither Spitzer nor his successor Auerbach, who discussed *Commedia* in his *Introduction to Romance Languages and Literature*, published in Turkish in 1944, mentioned Dante's portrayal of Mohammed in the *Inferno*.[60] There may have been pragmatic reasons for skirting Mohammed, but it also strikes me as a missed opportunity: touching on this topic might have sparked a critical discussion about the very translatability of secular humanism from a Christian-dominated society to a Muslim-led one.

In the academic year 1939–1940, the university outreach program hosted an event that might have easily put Auerbach's feet to the fire. Unlike Spitzer's earlier lectures on the Renaissance, Auerbach's talk was the first to focus on Dante's *Commedia* per se. It was a risky topic, but, as we will duly see, he shied away from controversy, choosing to emphasize what was more palatable to a predominantly Muslim audience. According to Güzin Dino, Spitzer's student and later Auerbach's assistant, these events reached a large public. In an interview that I conducted with her in Paris in 2007, she remembered having simultaneously translated one of Spitzer's lectures from French into Turkish. On this occasion, she recalled, the audience consisted of some three thousand students, faculty, and visitors to the university.[61] The outreach program provided the émigrés with an opportunity for introducing their pioneering work to the Turkish public: Paul von Aster, for instance, talked about the concept of free will, Wilhelm Peters discussed the history of European universities, Gerhard Kessler lectured on politics and ethics, Alexander Rüstow reflected on the past and future of the proletariat, Alfred Heilbronn delved into the origins and purpose of sexuality, and Philipp Schwartz dealt with Freud and psychoanalysis.

Auerbach himself gave a total of at least seven lectures in this series, lectures that were subsequently published in Turkish: "On Yedinci Asırda Fransız 'Public'i" (The French Public in the Seventeenth Century, 1937), "Jean Jacques Rousseau" (1939), "XVIıncı asırda Avrupada Milli Dillerin Teşekkülü" (The Formation of National Languages in Sixteenth-Century Europe, 1939), "Dante" (1940), "Edebiyat ve Harp" (Literature and War, 1941–1942), "XIXuncu Asırda Avrupada Realism" (Realism in Nineteenth-Century Europe, 1942), and "Montesquieu ve Hürriyet Fikri" (Montesquieu and the Notion of Liberty, 1945).[62] Most of these lectures, which were translated into Turkish from either French or German, have not been available in any other language.[63] For the purpose of this book, Victoria Holbrook translated two lectures by Auerbach from Turkish into English—the lecture on nineteenth-century realism and a speech on literature and war that he presented after the outbreak of World War II (see the appendix to this volume). What makes Auerbach's Turkish lectures so compelling is that here we see him reflecting on topics that resonated strongly with his times and the reforms in Turkey—the increasing connectedness of the world, the emergence of the Renaissance, the relationship between nationhood and vernacular language, the concept of liberty, and the rise of the bourgeoisie. Other topics explored in the lectures, including the relationship between literature, nation building, and war or the impact of colonialism on literature, show Auerbach as a compelling but cautious political figure.

These lectures differ from Auerbach's other work because in them he fills in contextual gaps for the benefit of his Turkish audience. In *Mimesis*, historical and sociopolitical context is undoubtedly relevant, but in the Turkish lectures, literature's sociopolitical context assumes a more central role. The annual lectures thus provide valuable insights into the ways in which Auerbach developed his ideas for *Mimesis*, and they tell us something about his relationship with his audience. As part of a series intended to reach a nonacademic but highly educated public, his lectures served the purpose rather well: focusing on politically relevant topics within a historicized framework, they introduced the audience to the cultural and literary history of Europe from the middle ages to the nineteenth century.

The exiled philologist opened his public lecture on Dante with the remark, "Dante Alighieri, the greatest poet of Europe's Middle Ages, was born in Florence in 1265, according to the Islamic calendar in 633, and died in exile at the age of 56."[64] This opening conjures up an image of Dante and Auerbach sharing the "eternal and changeless fate" of exile—a point that has been made by David Damrosch, Seth Lerer, and Kathleen Biddick in reference to Auerbach's later treatment of Dante in *Mimesis*.[65] Summarizing the poet's life and the reasons that forced him into exile, Auerbach shed light on the historical and political background of thirteenth-century Italy. At the same time, his lecture, which referenced Varoğlu's recently published translation, served as a general introduction to Dante as catalytic for the Renaissance.

What seems unusual about the opening of the lecture is Auerbach's reference to both the Christian and Muslim calendars—something that was no longer common among secular scholars in the late 1930s, more than a decade after the transition to the Christian calendar. From this opening gesture, one would expect Auerbach to have continued with a broader contextualization of Dante and his times: Italy and the Islamic world were after all connected not only by the geography of the Mediterranean, by trade and travel; they were also linked by the preservation, translation, and interpretation of classical Greek texts by Muslim philosophers, most importantly by Aristotelians Avicenna and Averroës, whom Dante clearly acknowledged. Auerbach did concede only a few references to the Islamic world that were pertinent to his Istanbul audience. He explained, for example, that the crusades served to unify Europe against Islam, and he pointed out the significance of Oriental trade for a city like Florence.

What Auerbach did not bring up was Mohammed's bloody evisceration in hell. Would the audience have fallen still on hearing this? Would it have murmured its disapproval and left en masse? We do not know how listeners would have reacted, for they were not openly challenged. It would be interesting to think, though, that had Auerbach taken the risk, at least some of his listeners might have reflected critically on the medieval view of Islam. Why, they might have asked, is Dante considered central for the emergence of European secular humanism? And what prospects could secular humanism then have in a Muslim-dominated society? So much for speculative history: the émigré did not take this chance. We understand his reticence but, in sidestepping the issue, he also bypassed a discussion of the Islamic influences on the *Commedia* itself. To some extent at least, Auerbach had acknowledged indirect Islamic influences on Dante in his pre-exilic work. Can we assume that Auerbach consciously elided the issue in his lecture at Istanbul University? He invited his audience to situate Dante's work in a shared Muslim-Christian world, but he withheld contextual information that would have been productive for Dante's Turkish reception. More importantly, such a discussion would have meant rethinking the making of modern Europe as a process marked by the interrelationship between Christianity, Judaism, and Islam.

The influence of Islam on Dante is, in fact, not so far-fetched. As Auerbach knew, early twentieth-century Dante-scholars vigorously discussed the overlap between Islam and Christianity in the *Commedia*: on

Ascension of the Prophet Mohammed on Buraq (a mythical horse), miniature, nineteenth
century. North Provincial style, copied in Turkey. Inv. Ms. or. oct. 952, f. 9a. Staatsbibliothek zu Berlin, Stiftung Preussischer Kulturbesitz, Berlin, Germany. By permission of
Bildarchiv Preussischer Kulturbesitz / Art Resource, New York.

the one hand, they were interested in the influence of the Arab world on Provençal poetry and, hence, on Dante. On the other hand, they suggested that the *Commedia* combined Islamic and Christian eschatological ideas. In his 1919 study, *La Escatología musulmana en la Divina Comedia* (*Islam and the Divine Comedy*, 1926), Miguel Asín Palacios argued, for example, that the Muslim notion of Mohammed's nocturnal journey (*isra*) to the infernal regions, and his subsequent ascension (*miraj*) to celestial regions, was "a prototype of Dante's conception" in the *Commedia*.[66] Of Dante, the Arabist Asín argued that Mohammed and Ali's sufferings coincided with depictions in Islam—the torture, for example, of sinners like the "bloodthirsty general Al-Hajjaj, whom tradition represented . . . walking in hell with their bowels dangling between their legs."[67] Asín also pointed to parallels between the portrayals of purgatory by Dante and the Muslim philosopher Ibn Arabi (1165–1240), who imagined purgatory to have a certain number of enclosures, stations, and passages.[68] Such a detailed and precise description of purgatory could not, according to Asín, be found in Christian eschatology before Dante.[69]

From Leonardo Olschki we know that the question of Dante's influences was discussed in a "tense and passionate mood . . . in different countries and circles" between the two world wars.[70] An interesting role is played by the idea that the Mediterranean itself contributed to the making of Western Europe. In a 1924 review essay, for example, the Romance scholar Werner Mulertt acknowledged that Asín made an important contribution to Western scholarship when he incorporated Arabic material previously unknown to Dante-scholars. Although Mulertt did not completely deny intersections between Muslim and Dantean views of the apocalypse, he roundly dismissed Asín's work as ideologically driven and warned of the dangers of its selective method.[71] The Mediterranean, Mulertt acknowledged, provided various notions of the afterworld, but he saw a problem in tracing a genealogy between Muslim apocalyptic views and Dante's.[72] The debate between Danteists and Arabists did also not go unnoticed by Karl Vossler, who published his major study on Dante, *Die Göttliche Komödie* (The Divine Comedy), in 1925. Vossler, mentioning Asín's work in a mere footnote, sought to justify the common traits between Dante's and Muslim notions of the afterworld by pointing to the Judeo-Christian roots of Muslim apocalypticism. However, Vossler also acknowledged that "some of its fragments might have flooded back into the medieval apocalypticism of the Occidental world, possibly via Sicily and Spain."[73] Like Mulertt, Vossler at least entertained the idea that the Mediterranean was a space for cross-cultural and cross-religious fertilization and that this might have had a bearing on the formation of Europe.

The question of Europe's origins and the idea of the Mediterranean also interested Auerbach in his pre-exilic work. In his 1929 professorial thesis on Dante, Auerbach acknowledged that the general idea and many of the mythical details in Dante's work stem from the "rich treasure of mythology of Eastern as well as Western origin that had accumulated over centuries in the countries of the Mediterranean basin." This treasure, Auerbach suggested, was accessible to Dante without recourse to literary models; he took them in like "the air he breathed."[74] As Suzanne Marchand points out, 1920s Western scholarship did not typically emphasize its debts to the East.[75] In light of this, Auerbach's concession to the existence of cultural contact and exchange between countries that made up the "Mediterranean basin" is all the more important. Yet, his concession was strictly circumscribed: Auerbach ruled out the possibility that Muslim literary culture, exemplified through Ibn Arabi, had any direct impact on Dante. The problem of Oriental influences on European literature did, however, preoccupy Auerbach in later years, as we can discern from one of his manuscripts, the undated manuscript of a lecture titled "Provenzalen 1" (Provençal 1).

Auerbach wrote this lecture in German and in it referred to studies that appeared several years before he left for Turkey—publications by, for example, Konrad Burdach, Samuel Singer, Alfred Jeanroy, Gaston Paris, and Hennig Brinkmann. The presentation was likely intended for Auerbach's students in Marburg. The lecture deals with the roots of eleventh- and twelfth-century Provençal literature and its bearing on Dante's style and his use of the vernacular language. Auerbach disagreed with Konrad Burdach's thesis that the Spanish-Arabic world had influenced Provençal poetry: he thought it unsubstantiated. But, as in his 1929 study of Dante, Auerbach did not deny Oriental influences altogether. The lecture points out that in the early medieval period, there were subterranean connections between the Christian, classical, Germanic, and Arab traditions existing in myths, stories, and institutions.[76] Arguing that the ancient Greco-Roman world was influenced by Egyptian, Babylonian, Persian, and other Oriental cultures, Auerbach portrayed Europe as being in perpetual flux—constantly transformed as the result of diverse currents and influences. Out of this *Völker- und Mythengewimmel*, "throng of peoples and myths," under Roman rule all later Occidental and Muslim Arab cultures were born.[77]

In contradistinction to this pre-exilic work, Auerbach's later scholarship does not uphold what he referred to here as the *allgemeine Verbundenheit der Kulturen*, "the general interconnectedness of cultures." In his later work, the Muslim world seems to fall away. It is as if Turkish exile made him draw the boundaries of Europe tighter, making it impregnable to Muslim influences. Instead of adhering to the idea of a "Mediterranean basin" as a site for the emergence of Judaism, Christianity, and Islam, Auerbach ultimately presented a bounded Judeo-Christian world in *Mimesis*. In fact, none of Auerbach's exilic work on Dante—neither the 1944 *Neue Dantestudien* (New Dante Studies), which included an essay on his concept of *figura*, nor the Dante chapter in *Mimesis*—dealt with the *Berührungspunkte* or "meeting points" between Islam and Christianity in the Middle Ages and Renaissance.

How strange it seems that, having moved to Turkey, Auerbach retreated into a Eurocentric mindset and downplayed the world of Islam. Even so, he continued to be needled by questions about Dante's amalgamation of Muslim and Christian notions of the afterlife. As a letter from Rüstow to Auerbach in the summer of 1942 shows, Rüstow challenged Auerbach by asking what was "renaissance-like" and "non-medieval" (*renaissancehaft, unmittelalterlich*) in Dante's work. Rüstow did not mince words when he called Auerbach a *Danteanbeter*, "a worshiper of Dante," and criticized the *hemmungslose Rachsucht*, the "uninhibited vindictiveness," of the *Inferno*.[78] The tenor of the letter suggests that the economist and the philologist enjoyed an intellectual relationship that was fraught with political disagreement. Driving his point home, Rüstow reminded Auerbach that Goethe had disapproved of the Italian poet because of his *widerwärtiger, oft abscheulicher Grossheit* ("repulsive, and often disgusting greatness"). Interestingly, this is the exact phrase that Auerbach uses in the Dante chapter of *Mimesis*, when he acknowledges that many important critics have been understandably troubled by Dante's *allzu harten Gegenwartsnähe im Erhabenen*, "closeness to the actual in the realm of the sublime." As if directly responding to Rüstow's letter, Auerbach further acknowledged that the *Commedia* made "later Humanists and men of humanistic training ill at ease."[79]

Rüstow's letter and Auerbach's Dante chapter provide evidence of a lively dialogue among émigrés in Istanbul, a point that Auerbach never mentions in his remarks about the working conditions in exile. Their exchange also illustrates the importance of their physical location for renewed discussions about the interplay between the Muslim and Christian worlds. Rüstow asked Auerbach whether he owned Carra de Vaux's *Fragments d'eschatologie musulmane* (Fragments of the Muslim Eschatology, 1895) and Miguel Asín Palacios's work, probably his *La Escatología musulmana en la Divina Comedia* (1919). Rüstow may not have known that Auerbach was already familiar with Asín's work even before he went to Turkey. Perhaps he hoped such studies would encourage his colleague to reconsider the intersections between Islam and Christianity in Dante. Dante's merging of Muslim and Christian notions of the afterworld would, Rüstow assumed, elicit a reaction from the Catholic front. And, provoking his colleague further, Rüstow concluded that Dante-enthusiasts like Auerbach were responsible for "silencing" this part of history.

My aim here is not to argue for the Muslim precedents for Dante's work—a still highly contested claim. Rather, my point is that Auerbach made some unexpected intellectual choices while in exile. Surprising, to me at least, is the fact that his Dante treatment leaves out the debate between the Danteists and Arabists. We can only speculate as to why Auerbach may have elided this debate over the origins of Dante's work. But such elisions, however motivated, constituted a lost opportunity for promoting discussion between the Judaic, Christian, and Islamic worlds. This view of Auerbach questions Said's endorsement of the philologist as "a Prussian Jewish scholar in Turkish, Muslim, non-European exile handling (perhaps even juggling) charged, and in many ways irreconcilable, sets of antinomies."[80] Auerbach did, of course, improvise a new life in a foreign place and juggled all manner of contradictory impulses. Yet, in contradistinction to some of his fellow exiles, he did not synthesize all of these impulses and, to extend Said's metaphor, in exile he simply let some of the balls drop. Concerned with the survival of the Jewish legacy within European culture, he broadened the conception of Europe by emphasizing its Hellenic and Judaic origins. As Geoffrey Hartman points out, when Auerbach taught at Yale in the 1950s, Judaic studies did not yet exist and "even a purely cultural interest in Judaism was merely tolerated by Yale's distinctive, if quietly assumed, Christian ethos."[81] To be sure, Auerbach's pioneering approach changed the way we think about European literary culture today. However, it is also important to recognize that Auerbach did not contribute to the kind of secular humanism that acknowledged

Islam along with cultural and religious traditions like Hellenism, Judaism, and Christianity.

We might have expected a critic like Said to have taken Auerbach to task for eliding Islam from discussions of Western European literature. Instead, as Apter rightly points out, we witness Said's "noticeable lack of attention to Auerbach's Eurocentrism."[82] Apter implies that it would not have been in Said's interests to harp on the limitations of Auerbach's Eurocentric humanism. Instead, Said employed the exiled philologist to argue that "humanism provides futural parameters for defining secular criticism in a world increasingly governed by a sense of identitarian ethnic destiny and competing sacred tongues."[83] While Said may indeed have remedied the humanism of earlier scholars like Auerbach, it is worth remembering that secular criticism was already a realistic possibility in 1930s and 1940s Turkey. We see this in the work of some of Auerbach's Turkish, as well as émigré, colleagues. In chapter 4, I showed that philologists like Rosemarie Burkart, for example, expanded the notion of Europe and found common ground between Muslim and Judeo-Christian histories. Auerbach, in contrast, abandoned the possibility of this kind of productive intellectual network and presented a Judeo-Christian world that was essentially disconnected from Islam. Auerbach left Germany as a Dante-scholar and became a comparatist in Turkish exile. He did so partly because he wanted to rescue from oblivion a world that was being destroyed by the Nazis and partly because his designated role in Turkey was that of a Europeanist, not a Romance scholar. The paradox here is, however, that he helped propagate an idea of Europe that bypassed the very context in which he found himself.[84]

We can conclude that Auerbach's intellectual context in Turkey is far more complex than Harry Levin's anecdote suggests. It is a story of diversions and elisions that can also be traced in *Mimesis* itself. When Auerbach opens the first chapter of *Mimesis* with Homer's *Odyssey* and the biblical story of Abraham and Isaac, he does not make any reference to the fact that both texts are linked to modern Turkey. During Auerbach's time in Istanbul, Homeric Greece was already integrated into Turkey's vision of humanism and, because of the geographical overlap between the Homeric world and Turkey, considered part of Turkey's own past. We can say that the reforms of the 1930s and 1940s tested humanism's compatibility with a predominantly Muslim, secularized society. Yücel's reforms culminated in visions of an Anatolian humanism that not only celebrated

Abraham and Isaac, painting from Safed, Palestine, nineteenth century. The inscription asks to remember "the binding of Isaac" on Rosh Hashanah. Watercolor, nineteenth century. Collection of Isaac Einhorn, Tel Aviv, Israel. Photo: Erich Lessing. By permission of Art Resource, New York.

Homer as Anatolia's scion but traced the seeds of Turkey's own cultural origin to Troy.[85]

The story of Abraham, analyzed by Auerbach in his first chapter, is likewise of central importance to Turkey. Abraham's test of faith is commemorated every year through the sacrifice of a sheep on a religious holiday called *kurban bayramı*, the feast of the sacrifice.[86] The Turkish word *kurban* goes back to the Hebrew *korban*, meaning sacrifice. Even the most isolated scholar in Turkey could not have missed Abraham's significance for Islam. But in *Mimesis*, there is no space for Abraham as a prophet of Islam. Abraham either signifies an essentially Jewish story, as in the opening chapter of *Mimesis*, or appears—via Proust—as an Orientalized figure in the book's final chapter.[87] My interest in the next section, then, is to further investigate the ways in which *Mimesis* itself is structured by a kind of instrumental amnesia regarding the influence of Islam. We will find that exclusive, hermetic spaces like attics, islands, and lighthouses serve as metaphors for Auerbach's exilic authorship.

Attics, Islands, and Lighthouses

If there is a counterexample to Auerbach in Turkey, it is, arguably, Rüstow. Whereas Rüstow actively engaged with his immediate surroundings, Auerbach claimed to inhabit a world that was both temporally and spatially disjunctive from Europe. As we know from Harry Levin's anecdote, the philologist compared his years of Istanbul exile to working *dans un grenier*, "in an attic."[88] Rather than dismissing the remark, we can investigate it as a trope. The attic is, after all, one of the common tropes in modern Western literature. Auerbach's reference to the *grenier* recalls, for instance, both Virginia Woolf's character Mrs. Dalloway, who retreats to her attic for reflection, and the author's own call for a room of one's own. Auerbach's emphasis on his spatiotemporal detachment from Europe as a condition for writing *Mimesis* is, I suggest, not unlike the way in which Woolf or Proust linked memory and authorship to a sense of spatial or temporal detachment from everyday life.

In Auerbach's final chapter of *Mimesis*, "The Brown Stocking," we find that tropes of detachment are central not only to literary modernism but also to Auerbach's own methodology. When, in the last chapter of *Mimesis*, Auerbach takes up the question of Woolf's and Proust's remembrance of things past, he does so in order to reflect on his own philological method in relation to modernity. In typical fashion, the chapter uses these literary excerpts as points of departure for a careful unfolding of his argument about the representation of reality. The "Brown Stocking" begins with an excerpt from Woolf's *To the Lighthouse* that shows the Ramsay family at their seaside resort, a "good-sized summer house on one of the Hebrides islands," as Auerbach writes.[89] The scene in question begins shortly after Mr. Ramsay, a philosophy professor, announces to his family and visitors that the much-anticipated trip from the Scottish island to the lighthouse might have to be postponed because of bad weather. James, the youngest son, is deeply disappointed. While Mrs. Ramsay tries to console James, she measures the stocking that she is knitting for the lighthouse-keeper's son against her own son's leg. Occupied by this simple task, she plunges into a lengthy reflection on the meaning of the rundown holiday house for its summer residents:

Never mind: the rent was precisely twopence halfpenny; the children loved it; it did her husband good to be three thousand, or if she must be accurate, three hundred miles from his library and his lectures and his disciples; and there was room for visitors. Mats, camp beds, crazy ghosts of chairs and tables whose London life of service was done—they did well enough here; and a photograph or two, and books. Books, she thought, grew of themselves. She never had time to read them. Alas! Even the books that had been given her, and inscribed by the hand of the poet himself: "For her whose wishes must be obeyed . . ." "The happier Helen of our days . . ." disgraceful to say, she had never read them. And Croom on the Mind and Bates on the Savage Customs of Polynesia ("My dear, stand still," she said)—neither of those could one send to the Lighthouse.[90]

The scene shows Mrs. Ramsay, sitting by the window, while her mind wanders from the interior of the house to its surroundings. In the continuation of this scene, Mrs. Ramsay takes in "the whole room from floor to ceiling," listening into the space so as to hear whether the doors and windows of the house are open. Her thoughts arrive at the Swiss maid looking out of one of the windows while thinking of her dying father back home. In the following passage, we once again follow the thought flow of Mrs. Ramsay and one of her visitors—only to be repeatedly returned to the moment when Mrs. Ramsay measures the stocking against her fidgety son's leg. In the latter part of the excerpt quoted by Auerbach, an unidentified character, or narrative voice, remarks repeatedly that "Never did anybody look so sad." It is the sight of Mrs. Ramsay, seeming to conceal her tears, that prompts this remark, which, as Auerbach says, "verges upon the realm beyond reality" because we cannot identify the person who made the remark.[91] In the analysis of this scene, Auerbach argues that contemporary reality is represented "by means of numerous subjective impressions received by various individuals."[92]

While in this last chapter he discusses the multilayered character of the modern consciousness, Auerbach simultaneously uses the scene for localizing—to use Rüstow's term—his own present and his condition as an intellectual in exile. It is thus no coincidence that Auerbach chose this specific passage from *To the Lighthouse*. The reference to the Swiss maid gazing into space while mourning her dying father at home becomes, for the reader of *Mimesis*, an uncanny reminder of the immeasurable grief suffered by those surviving the Holocaust in exile. In this scene, as elsewhere in the book, disjunctions of time are linked to disjunctions of space, and being far from home conjures up memories of the past. This is the case not only for Mr. and Mrs. Ramsay and the Swiss maid but also, on a meta-level, for Auerbach himself, who was writing the final chapter of his book while horrific news from liberated Europe was arriving in Turkey.

Mr. Ramsay's sense of separation from London—his library, lectures, and students—turns out to be beneficial to the philosopher who is puzzling over questions about the human condition. In Auerbach's account of the scene, the lighthouse is described as no place for "erudite volumes"—it suggests a space of reflection and creative energy, yet one unconstrained by intellectualism. This image of the bookless lighthouse resonates with Auerbach's description of Istanbul in the epilogue to *Mimesis*. Here, too, Auerbach implies that there is a relationship between place and thought, between his own place of exile and the method in which he approaches the past. In *Mimesis*, there is no further elaboration of the lighthouse as a peripheral, bookless place. Nonetheless, it is precisely this idea of the detached place that adds depth to Auerbach's concluding chapter. The lighthouse constitutes the turning point in Woolf's novel; it is thence that Mr. Ramsay finally travels with his youngest son and daughter many years after Mrs. Ramsay's death and the tragic losses wrought on the family by World War I; a place that, once reached, generates a sense of unity and harmony through recollection. For artist Lily Briscoe, the trip to the lighthouse becomes central to her vision of art in the modern age. We can think, then, of detached places such as lighthouses, islands, and attics as signifying both recollection and modernity.

In order to make his point about the symbolic *Jederzeitlichkeit*, or "omnitemporality of an event fixed in a remembering consciousness," Auerbach cites a passage from Proust's *Remembrance of Things Past*: the narrator vividly recalls a moment in his childhood when he felt deeply consoled.[93] This scene illustrates the multiple layers of time that structure Proust's narrative: the narrator informs the reader that he was a highly strung child who craved motherly affection, and, unlike Abraham "telling Hagar that she must tear herself away from Isaac," his father allowed his mother to soothe him.[94] Without analyzing the passage in detail, Auerbach highlights the point that Proust's technique for recalling the past reveals the "layered structure of consciousness."[95] By echoing some of the motifs that

Auerbach discusses in the first chapter of his work, the Proust and Woolf passages reveal the layered structure of *Mimesis* itself. The excerpt from *To the Lighthouse* allows Auerbach's readers to recall the themes and narrative devices of Homer's *Odyssey*. In his discussion of Woolf and Homer, for instance, Auerbach deals with a deferred trip that promises reconciliation; he emphasizes prosaic details (e.g., the washing of feet or the measuring of a stocking) that prompt recollection or reflection; and he deals with digression as a narrative device. The excerpt from *Remembrance of Things Past*, on the other hand, weaves in the story of Abraham and Isaac to illustrate the creation of historical depth through interpretation and prefiguration in Genesis.[96] In so doing, Auerbach frames Western European literature as a textual corpus that is historically connected by recurring motifs, narrative devices, and explicit intertextual references.

While Auerbach's first chapter distinguishes between the Homeric and biblical styles to demonstrate that the representation of the present and the notion of history are inextricable, the final chapter of *Mimesis* focuses on the relationship between the representation of reality, time, space, and the flow of consciousness. Auerbach argues that, in contradistinction to the Homeric style, the biblical one refrains from making the time and place of narration explicit. This in effect strengthens the universal-historical claims of the Bible. The concluding chapter is interested in Woolf's treatment of time and points to the incongruity between the randomness of external events and the intensity of inner processes. Auerbach emphasizes the fact that an insignificant event "releases ideas and chains of ideas which cut loose from the present of the exterior occurrence and range freely through the depths of time."[97] Taking this thought further, he argues that, by detaching himself from his own present, the modern artist thereby "comes face to face with his own past."[98] Here, Auerbach draws on ethnographic terminology, which renders detachment productive for the writer/ethnographer, who is at once participant and observer of the object under study. We can apply this thought to Auerbach's own project and say that he saw detachment from his own present as a precondition for writing an account of his literary and cultural past.

At the end of the final chapter, Auerbach presents his readers with a vision that is as memorable as Lily Briscoe's decisive brushstroke at the end of *To the Lighthouse*: "Perhaps it will be too simple to please those who, despite all its dangers and catastrophes, admire and love our epoch for the sake of its abundance of life and the incomparable historical vantage point which it affords. But they are few in number, and probably they will not live to see much more than the first forewarnings of the approaching unification and simplification."[99]Auerbach's elegy for the depth and vitality of modernity is not altogether dystopian. Against the atmosphere of universal doom, the "blatant and painful cynicism" of James Joyce's *Ulysses*, Auerbach upholds Woolf's *To the Lighthouse* as a novel "filled with good and genuine love but also, in its feminine way, with irony, amorphous sadness, and doubt of life."[100] Needless to say, Auerbach's gender politics holds problems for us today.[101] Yet it is interesting that Auerbach juxtaposes the standardization of culture against the "wealth of reality and depth of life" in random moments of the everyday.[102] His method of exploring the depth of humanity in a literary excerpt that he claims to have chosen more or less "at random" parallels the modernist author's emphasis on the random and prosaic as instances that reveal the depths of the human soul.[103] Auerbach hopes that attention to these instances of the everyday will counter the forces that tend toward the "unification and simplification" of culture.[104]

The philologist regards these random moments as largely independent of the political and social order over which people "fight and despair."[105] After the poststructuralist turn, we can no longer sustain the idea that something—a moment of everyday life, an exilic space, an island, an attic, or a lighthouse—exists outside political or discursive regimes. However, our notion of critical distance is related to these modern images of spatial and temporal displacement. The image of working *dans un grenier* in Istanbul exile must be seen as a modernist trope of authorship, a trope that continues to have some traction to this day. The "grenier" is a peripheral space that facilitates memory for the very reason that it is detached from its immediate surroundings. We see this also reflected in Spitzer's conception of the humanist. The humanist, he argued, "should live among his fellowmen" but "not lose contact with them, for then he would be no longer humane himself; but he should live somewhat removed from them. He [the humanist] stands at the window of our national civilizations before which opens the vista of other civilizations. And he *is* that window, which looks outside, not into the room."[106] This is the habitus that Spitzer and Auerbach, during the postwar period, promoted as productive for interpreting the literary and cultural history of Europe.

"*Mimesis* is quite consciously a book that a particular person, in a particular situation, wrote at the beginning of the 1940s," wrote Auerbach in his "Epilegomena to Mimesis" (1953).[107] Here, he portrayed his space of authorship as an irreproducible point of departure for the recollection of Europe's cultural and literary history. We could say that Auerbach derives his methodology from the ontology of exile. Scholars had long been pre-occupied with the question of how significant experience was to the mak-ing of knowledge. They asked, as Vanessa Agnew points out, whether traveling to the *Schauplätze der Geschichte*, the historical settings, might not be necessary for the writing of history, or whether the journey might not endow the traveler with a privileged, comparative perspective.[108] In the aftermath of World War II, we find, however, precisely the opposite move: Auerbach implies in his epilegomena that it is not the experience of a historical setting but one's very detachment from it that serves as the basis for intellectual production.

Notwithstanding the specificity of his "historical vantage point," Auerbach's Turkish exile has become a trope for critical inquiry in the postwar period. This trope was almost dogma among the first readers and reviewers of *Mimesis*. The debate about the inadequacy of Istanbul librar-ies versus the breadth and depth of *Mimesis* metamorphosed into a debate about the methodology Auerbach developed during his years in Turkey. Victor Klemperer's 1948 review of *Mimesis*, "Philologie im Exil," already shows the germ of this debate. Here, Klemperer suggested that exile en-abled Auerbach to lay aside the *Scheuklappen*, the blinkers, of his disci-pline and simultaneously assume the perspective of an aesthetician, histo-rian, and sociologist.[109] Klemperer argued that it was exile, rather than Auerbach's location in Istanbul per se, that was necessary for exploding disciplinary boundaries.[110] The idea has persisted ever since, that the place of exile would have either no impact on the exilic work or be influential only in its absence, alienation, or negation. This is how Auerbach became the figure of the writer "in political withdrawal: a Dantesque figure of our time, an Ovid of mid-century."[111] He became the quintessential émigré scholar in the postwar period because critics externalized, as Seth Lerer rightly points out, his Turkish exile, turning it into either a research prob-lem or a "badge of honor."[112]

In this chapter, we have seen that wartime exile in Istanbul was not, in and of itself, an obstacle to fine scholarship—Auerbach could benefit from a variety of libraries, a productive interdisciplinary network of émigré scholars, and the value that Turkish humanists saw in his teachings. It is thus misleading to see exile solely in terms of alienation and detachment.

Exile has a double side: while it triggers reflection and recollection and prompts comparisons between the familiar and the unfamiliar, it also demands new affiliations with the place of exile. Detachment from one place does not, after all, preclude émigrés from availing themselves of new, if temporary, attachments. Whatever positive that is born of exile—innovation, improvisation—is not born from a condition of stasis and lack. I thus disagree with those who insist that intellectual productivity arises because the exile is somehow frozen in time and space. Although exiles like Auerbach never truly immigrated and remained in a state of limbo, they were nonetheless drawn into an everyday world that bore the "wealth of reality and depth of life," to use Auerbach's own words.[113] This brings me to conclude that the trope of the isolated exile emerged in conjunction with tropes of literary modernism. By the same token, I doubt that ontology is directly correlated to epistemology. The assumption—that the loss of home necessarily confers an "epistemological advantage" over those who remain behind—is, I think, false.[114] It wrongly implies that critical thinking is first made possible by the trauma of deracination and, hence, cannot be learned.

If we look at current Turkish literature, we find that Orhan Pamuk introduces a concept of authorship that shows us something different. Suggesting that we live in an age defined by "mass migration and creative immigrants," Pamuk says that it is difficult to explain why he has stayed in Istanbul. Contrasting himself to Conrad, Nabokov, and Naipaul, whose "imaginations were fed by exile," he emphasizes that his own creative imagination is, in fact, nourished by constantly "gazing at the same view."[115] As Pamuk notes in *Istanbul: Memories and the City*, he has never left the world of his childhood. But the notion of detachment is not irrelevant to his authorship—the difference in his reflections about Istanbul's late Ottoman and early republican past is that his sense of detachment and estrangement is temporal rather than spatial. Moreover, his authorial position integrates the view of the Western traveler and the exile into his own vision. Pamuk's example of settled authorship is thus connected to exilic forms of cultural production and shows that in the twenty-first century the boundaries between the intellectual exile, migrant, and transnational scholar/author are often blurred. Likewise, it proves that representations of Istanbul are always the product of mimetic appropriations between what we have come to call East and West.

Epilogue: Turkey's Humanist Legacy

THIS BOOK RAISES QUESTIONS that extend beyond the historical specificities of Auerbach and his colleagues in exile. It asks whether Turkish humanism—for all its state sponsorship, native optimism, and foreign support—was flawed because of its inherent Eurocentrism. What are the prospects for secularism worldwide in the twenty-first century? At a time when fundamentalism and the spread of global capital steer foreign policy, this book also asks whether modernization and secularization—still regarded as history's apogee—must inevitably follow Western models. If *East West Mimesis* provides no clear answers, let it be understood as a prompt to critical reflection and further discussion.

Although the era of secular humanism in Turkey faced its official end in 1947, humanism continued to do its work in literary circles and institutions of higher learning. Onetime students of Auerbach, Spitzer, and Rohde enjoyed lasting influence as translators, scholars, and writers. Many of those who had been trained by the émigrés now became the country's leading scholars and public intellectuals—classical philologists Azra Erhat and Suat Sinanoğlu, Romance scholar Süheyla Bayrav, literary critics and writers Sabahattin Eyüboğlu, Adnan Benk, and Güzin Dino, English professors Mina Urgan and Berna Moran, and Germanist Şara Sayın, to name but a few.[1] While Eyüboğlu and Erhat promoted a brand of Anatolian humanism based on the Trojan legacy in Asia Minor, others highlighted humanism's very compatibility with Islam.[2] In 1971, the Turkish minister of culture, Talât Sait Halman, revived the mystic poet Yunus Emre (d. ca. 1321) as a representative of this homegrown tradition.[3] Translating Yunus Emre's poetry into English, Halman stressed the sympathies between Western humanism and an indigenous Eastern form. Güzin Dino, too, translated the Sufi mystic's poetry into French and English and pointed out that Europe's great heroes of humanism—Erasmus and Martin Luther—had in fact been aware of Yunus Emre's poetry. They referred to Yunus Emre, she said, as "a pre-humanist forerunner who sought . . . to modify man's traditional concept of himself and the world."[4] It was Yunus Emre who believed that God is reflected in every human being, and this kind of worldliness distinguished him from other Sufi mystics of his time.

Halman went so far as to compare Yunus Emre's legacy with Dante's.[5] The comparison between the Anatolian mystic and the Italian poet is intriguing: the two men died in the same year, but, more significantly, Yunus Emre became to Turkish literature what Dante was to Italian. Unlike other Sufi mystics versed in Persian and Arabic, Yunus Emre was the first to write in the Turkish vernacular, marking a turning point for literary Turkish in the late thirteenth and early fourteenth centuries. We can say, too, that both Dante's and Yunus Emre's poetry was inspired by the notion of *gurbet*, the sense of exilic longing and search for divine love. While Dante's banishment was, in the first instance, politically motivated, Yunus Emre, from the outset, construed the spiritual journey as an attempt to overcome alienation: the human being was, by very definition, cut off from his spiritual home. We can think of this condition as *hüzün*—something that Orhan Pamuk more recently defines as the all-pervading melancholia that is rooted in the Koran. Hüzün is the Sufi mystic's response to humankind's sense of estrangement, a kind of "spiritual anguish" that arises from not being close enough to God.[6] Because in Yunus Emre's worldview the human being is made in God's image, human beings long to "return to God's reality," and their lives are characterized by "the tragic plight of exile."[7] Exile and estrangement, we can thus say, characterize the spirituality of Islamic mysticism, and it is this mysticism that—in Halman's view—underpins the Turkish humanist tradition.

During the Cold War, scholars and writers invoked Turkey's humanist heritage as a way of promoting secularism and social concord. Violent clashes between ultranationalists and leftists in the 1970s deeply affected Turkey's academic elite, prompting classicist Suat Sinanoğlu, for one, to champion the earlier set of ideals. At the height of the conflict, Georg Rohde's former student tried to persuade his countrymen of the renewed relevance of the humanist tradition to secularism, democracy, and freedom of speech.[8] Humanist education, Sinanoğlu argued, creates a kind of "intellectual habitus" that is indispensable for promoting human dignity and ethical freedom.[9] These efforts to overcome political factionalism and revive Turkey's early vision were, however, short-lived. Sinanoğlu had planned to establish a new School of Classics and an Institute for Humanist Research in Ankara, but there was a sudden turn in the political tide.[10] On September 9, 1980, the Turkish army—already for the third time in the course of twenty years—overthrew the government and put a stay on democracy. The universities, often the battleground for violent armed clashes between students at extreme ends of the political spectrum, suffered a backlash as a result of the military coup. For more than a decade, freedom of speech was strictly curtailed; Turkish universities lost the autonomy they had enjoyed under the humanist reformer Yücel, and tertiary education was, after the military coup of 1980, once again placed under central governmental control. Scores of leftist intellectuals, journalists, activists, and politicians were censored, imprisoned, tortured, and killed. When the democratization process made headway in the 1990s, the face of Turkey was transformed from an ethnically and religiously homogeneous to a more heterogeneous one.

This change came in the wake of cultural and political turmoil and decades of forced assimilation for Turkey's many ethnicities. The notion that the country's Muslim citizens were ethnically Turkish was eventually countered by Kurds agitating for political and cultural autonomy and by a movement that brought the country to the brink of civil war in the 1980s. Thousands of Kurdish activists living in European—often German—exile drew international attention to the institutionalized racism of the Turkish government, the forced deportations and military violence in the eastern Kurdish-dominated provinces, and the ongoing pressure to assimilate to mainstream Turkish culture. Once the seal had been broken, human rights activists within Turkey and abroad began to expose the governmental and military atrocities against Kurds, other ethnic minorities, and leftists.

In the 1990s, intellectual and political restrictions were slowly eased: questions of marginality, ethnicity, multiculturalism, multilingualism, and gender were taken up by nongovernmental organizations, and scholars in the humanities found their way back to central cultural debates. After many years of civil resistance and critique, the government slowly reestablished limited civil liberties and granted, for the first time in its history, some rights to the Kurdish-speaking community. Official acknowledgment of the Kurds caused a chain reaction among other ethnic minorities. Turkey's cultural landscape was henceforth transformed by the expression of new bifurcated forms of identity—Kurdish-Turkish, Armenian-Turkish, Greek-Turkish, and Jewish-Turkish.[11]

Jews also underwent a change in status in the 1990s. Following the quincentennial commemoration of the Sephardic immigration to the Ottoman Empire, Jewish citizens gained new visibility, reestablishing Istanbul as a center of Jewish life. When historians Avner Levi and Rıfat Bali assessed the history of Jews in the Ottoman Empire and Turkey, they directed attention to the role of German-Jewish academics in the 1930s.[12] We recall that Reşit Galip, the minister of education responsible for hiring expelled academics, had not connected the late fifteenth-century exodus of Jews from the Iberian Peninsula to the twentieth-century exodus of Jews from Germany. But, beginning in the 1990s, books, exhibits, conferences, and films dealing with the history of the country's Jewish citizens suddenly construed these as analogous historical events. Post-commemoration, émigré intellectuals of the 1930s were, so to speak, rediscovered as Jews and instated as figures of modernity within Turkish cultural history. In 2001, for example, the first Jewish museum in Istanbul was opened with the aim of displaying seven hundred years of "amity between Jews and Turks."[13] Here museum curator Naim Güleryüz chose to emphasize positive aspects of Jewish-Muslim relations. The museum exhibit interprets the hiring of German-Jewish academics as an act of great humanity on the part of the Turkish government. In so doing, it responds to the current political need to emphasize peaceful interactions between Jews and Muslims in Turkey, and yet it distorts the historical record.

The past decade has seen even greater interest in the intellectual emigration from Germany to Turkey. Istanbul Technical University, in cooperation with the Goethe Institute, mounted the first exhibition highlighting anti-Semitism as the prime reason for emigration from Nazi Germany. In honor of Berlin sculptor Rudolf Belling (1886–1972), the exhibition was housed in his former atelier at Istanbul Technical University.[14] The bilingual exhibition Haymatloz: Exil in der Türkei 1933–1945 (Homeless: Exile in Turkey 1933–1945) opened in Istanbul in 1998, but shortly thereafter, the Aktives Museum Faschismus und Widerstand (Active Museum Fascism and Resistance), a Berlin organization dedicated to the research and remembrance of Nazi atrocities, became involved in the project. What began as Istanbul Technical University's initiative to show the influence of

German emigration on the arts and sciences in Turkey was transformed into an international endeavor involving several Turkish and German institutions. Two years after the Istanbul exhibition, a second, expanded version opened at the Akademie der Künste (Academy of the Arts) in Berlin and subsequently toured Germany. The exhibition catalogue, initially published in Germany, became available in Turkish translation a few years later—but with disconcerting changes.[15] The Turkish translation censored the German original in significant ways: it cut articles showing Turkey in a problematic light and excluded any reference to Turkey's role in supplying chromite for Nazi Germany's war efforts.[16]

In Turkey, there followed other exhibitions on German emigration, but these mounted a negligible challenge to the official rhetoric. Two exhibitions concentrated on Traugott Fuchs, Spitzer's onetime assistant who remained in Istanbul until his death in 1997. Having taught French and German under Spitzer and Auerbach, Fuchs was employed by Boğaziçi University, formerly the American Robert College. The philologist left behind a rich archive of letters and artwork dating from the time of his emigration in 1934 and covering the end of the war, three military coups in the postwar period, and the slow revival of democracy toward the end of his life. With Auerbach's emigration to the United States, his wife, Marie, kept up a lively correspondence with Fuchs, an exchange that continued even after Erich's death in 1958. Fuchs also stayed in touch with the Orientalist and longtime Istanbul resident Hellmut Ritter, who, like himself, was homosexual. Ritter had moved to Istanbul in 1925 after being dismissed from his professorship in Hamburg on the grounds of homosexuality. Although none of the exhibitions and publications on Fuchs emphasizes this point, it seems possible that Fuchs's sexual orientation had some bearing on his initial decision to go into Turkish exile. The much-reiterated view, that the young, loyal Fuchs followed his professor Spitzer to Istanbul out of protest against anti-Semitism, still holds true.[17] However, there may also be another, hitherto unacknowledged, side to the story. Hopefully, researchers at the Fuchs archive, now housed at Boğaziçi University, will shed more light on the status and contribution of gay men in Turkish exile.[18]

To date, exile is linked in the scholarly, as well as public, imaginations to the flight from fascism. There has been little recognition of the fact that exile was, on occasion, also motivated by factors other than anti-Semitism, factors like sexual orientation and socialist convictions. This neglect speaks, I think, to a pervasive, if unspecified, attitude that tolerates homosexuality so long as it is not spoken of openly. The neglect of socialist émigrés, in turn, seems to derive from a kind of vestigial anticommunism. Post–Cold War, there are few political interests to be mobilized by reviving this particular story. The Jewish affiliation of scholars like Auerbach and Spitzer, in contrast, has been brought into ever-closer focus. Recent Turkish investigations into the impact of émigrés on modernization stress the fact that most émigré scholars were part of an intellectual German-Jewish minority. Yet, as I have argued throughout this book, their "comeback" calls for a more nuanced historical understanding. Grasping the role of German-Jewish émigrés in accounts of twentieth-century Turkish cultural history means differentiating between the ways they were construed in Turkey at the time of exile and the way they have come to be seen at the turn of the millennium. Turkish reformers, as we know from chapter 3, embraced Nazi Germany's Jewish outcasts as representatives of modern Europe. In the decade he spent in Turkey, Auerbach was respected primarily as an erudite European scholar who could help revive the humanist heritage of old Constantinople.

In recent years, however, leading Kemalists have privileged the connection between the humanist reform movement and the Jewishness of most émigrés. During the present reform process, initiated primarily in an effort to join the European Union, Kemalists are looking for ways to burnish Turkey's image in Europe. The accession negotiations place the government under pressure to—among other things—improve the country's human rights record, protect the secular foundations of the republic, and promote equality among its citizens. Construing Turkey as a European country, Kemalists once again uphold humanism as an important guarantor of freedom of thought, secularism, and enlightenment. Ahmet Saltık, board member of the Atatürkçü Düşünce Derneği (Association for Kemalist Thought), for instance, celebrates Atatürk as a humanist statesman with a role in saving scholars from Nazi Germany. Building Turkish humanism on the humanitarianism of the early reformers is, like the example of the Jewish museum exhibit, an essentially political move.

History may always be the product of narration, but sometimes its bias is acute. This is to say, particular ideological interests are served when the history of modern education at Turkish universities is construed as a story of Turks rescuing Jews from Nazi death camps. Süleyman Demirel, president of Turkey from 1993 to 2000, gave a speech to the European University Association in 2006, in which he highlighted European influences on Turkey's tertiary education. In the speech, Demirel reminded his audience that it was thanks to Jewish professors from Germany that Istanbul University could become one "of the leading centers of learning in the world. [The fact that] the newly founded university was able to open its doors to an influx of a large number of Jewish professors at a time when European powers were rushing to appease Hitler is one of the proudest periods in our history."[19] Demirel presented the hiring of Jewish scholars as proof of Turkey's salutary qualities, and even of its capacity to surpass the Western model: when Europe failed its Jewish citizens, it was Turkey that stepped up to save them. With this distorted representation of Turkish-German relations, Demirel asserted Turkey's civilized nature over and against Germany's barbaric past. Turkey, he implied, was true to its ideals, even when Europe was not. Turkey's Europeanness is, in other words, said to have evolved through its capacity to help exiled Jews survive the Holocaust. As I have shown in this book, at best, such a vision of Turkish-German relations misrepresents the past; at worst, it deliberately distorts the historical record for contemporary political purposes. The result is the papering over of Turkish anti-Semitism, the country's role in the death of refugees in Turkish waters, and atrocities against its Greek, Armenian, and Kurdish citizens.

It is perhaps unsurprising that these claims are being mobilized at a time when Turkey is yet again trying to emphasize its Europeanness. Corresponding anxieties about what it means to be Turkish have intensified during the past decade. In 2005, the infamous article 301 was, for instance, incorporated into the penal code in an effort to safeguard the notion of Turkishness as a fundament of the republic. The article defined the act of publicly "denigrating Turkishness, the Republic, and the Grand National Assembly of Turkey" as a criminal one. As a result, the law seriously inhibited the country's capacity to deal with long-silenced episodes in its history. However, owing to the proliferation and misuse of the charge and the diffuse nature of the term *Turkishness*, along with international pressure and civil disobedience campaigns in Turkey itself, the penal code was slightly modified. In 2008, it was "denigrating the Turkish nation," rather than "denigrating Turkishness," that became punishable. Notwithstanding this amendment, the article continues to hamstring critical revisions of Ottoman and Turkish history. Official recognition of the Armenian genocide in 1915 and, consequently, the revision of Ottoman history has become a kind of litmus test for Turkey's entry into the European Union.

One way Turkish authorities respond to such charges is by pointing out that the country played a role in saving thousands of European Jews from the Holocaust. The notion of Turks as perpetrators of the Armenian genocide is thus countered by the image of Turks as saviors in the Jewish genocide. This image is promulgated by, for example, a recently published biography of Behiç Erkin, the Turkish ambassador to France, who is said to have saved thousands of Turkish Jews from French deportation to the concentration camps.[20] At the present time, Turkish authorities are making concerted efforts to identify such ambassadors and consuls—the so-called Turkish Schindlers—and bring them to international attention. This involves, for instance, funding the production of a Hollywood film about ambassador Erkin and his role in saving an alleged 18,000 Jews by enabling them to travel to Turkey in the early 1940s. Betraying a kind of defensiveness, along with the underlying motive for the film, one of the producers said: "At a time when Islam and Turkey are under attack, this is yet more proof that when Europe was indifferent and silent, it was a Muslim and a Turk who made a difference and did not remain silent to the inhumanity taking place in the heart of Europe."[21] Such flagrant politicization of the past is not uncommon; it also has historical precedents. As Margaret Anderson shows, the trope of Turkish tolerance toward Jews was invoked by German Turcophiles in response to the charge of Ottoman mass killings of Armenians in the 1890s.[22]

My contention, then, is that the tropes and narratives celebrating Turks as saviors of Jews obscure other atrocities, just as they conceal the fact that aid was withheld from thousands of others. The Political Archive in Berlin houses documents confirming great acts of humanity by individual Turkish officials; but it also houses ample evidence of Turkish authorities' indifference to the Nazi persecution of Jews. Recall Prime Minister Saydam announcing in 1942 that Turkey was not going to become a home for Jews who were "unwanted elsewhere."[23] In other words, a Turkish-American film company might aim to produce a film that shifts the international perception of Turks as murderers of Armenians to one of Turks as saviors of Jews, but there are also other, more balanced voices backed by persuasive archival research, oral interviews, and firsthand testimony. The Turkish-French film director Meta Akkuş, for instance, has begun work on a documentary on Erkin, called *Son Tren* (The Last Train). The film draws on interviews with Jewish survivors who were able to escape France with the ambassador's assistance. Paris-based Akkuş claims that she is not interested in telling the story of a Turkish hero but rather in documenting the hitherto neglected accounts of survivors.[24]

Revisiting Auerbach's Exile

In the context of the seventy-fifth anniversary of the founding of the Turkish Republic, Germanist Şara Sayın wrote an essay on the beginnings of philology at Turkish universities and drew attention to the far-reaching impact of German-Jewish scholars like Auerbach.[25] Her essay does not address the fact that Turkish reformers did not always differentiate between the kind of German scholarship—exiled or National Socialist—that was imported into the Turkish context. As I argued in chapter 4, the ambiguous relationship between the German ministry of education and Turkish academic institutions shows the extent to which Nazi teachings were tolerated and, in some instances, even welcomed in Turkey. Turkish anti-Semitism during World War II and the ideological stamp left by Hennig Brinkmann and Gerhard Fricke on Istanbul's Germanistik curriculum have yet to be fully examined. The fact that Auerbach and other émigré scholars had to work side by side with Nazi scholars is something that is often played down in Turkish accounts so as to emphasize Turkey as the antipode to Nazi Germany.

Beginning in the 1990s, Turkish publications dealing with Auerbach's work suggest that there is renewed interest in his work across the disciplines. Some of the lectures given by Auerbach in Istanbul have been republished in journal form, and in planning are several books on the philologist's work in Turkey. The first Turkish translation of *Mimesis* is under way.[26] The comparatist's legacy in Turkey today is felt not only in these scholarly endeavors but also in the literary domain: the most prominent and influential Kurdish-Turkish author Mehmed Uzun (1953–2007) chose Auerbach's Turkish exile as the basis for his novel *Heviya Auerbach* (Auerbach's Hope). Persecuted in Turkey as a Kurdish separatist, Uzun sought exile in Sweden in 1977, where he had the liberty to write and publish in his native Kurdish, a language outlawed in Turkey until only recently. For three decades, the Kurdish writer lived as a political activist and public intellectual seeking to reestablish Kurdish as a literary language. Uzun died in 2007 before completing his novel on Auerbach. However, he left behind various interviews, essays, and diary entries that explain his interest in Auerbach as a Jewish exile in a predominantly Muslim world. While reflecting on Auerbach's experience, Uzun articulated his own agenda as a minority intellectual negotiating the religious and cultural divide between East and West. The links he construed between himself and Auerbach are many and various, but what he singled out especially was the critical distance that seemed to spring from exile. Two years before his death, he was invited by the European Union parliament to present a paper at a conference on the relations among Turkey, its Kurdish citizens, and the European Union, and here Uzun hailed Auerbach as an exile who managed to build the foundations of an East West relationship. He said that what inspired him to write a novel on Auerbach was this:

> I am of Eastern origin from a Muslim family whose ancestors trace back to Mesopotamia. I am [the] product of Aegean, Anatolian and Mediterranean cultures. . . . I fled from Turkey . . . , emigrated to the West, and settled as a political refugee in Sweden. Like Auerbach I also lived the life of exile, I was an intellectual trying to stay alive and establish a path for myself. I became a literary writer. Meeting the west, living in the west and writing modern Kurdish novels enabled me to pursue a life for myself. If I had not lived in the west, I would have always viewed things through an eastern culture and my writing would not have been as successful.[27]

In Uzun's view, Auerbach occupied the position of an exiled, minority intellectual navigating the Jewish, Christian, and Muslim worlds—an experience that Uzun himself invoked in order to reflect on the significance of the accession negotiations for improving minority rights within Turkey. If Auerbach's exile allowed him to forge an East West relationship, Uzun saw his own exile as an opportunity for furthering the dialogue.[28]

Germans, too, have been invested in commemorating the émigrés in Istanbul—albeit for different political ends. Entering the gates of Istanbul University today, we find on the left-hand side a plaque that was placed there in 1986 to memorialize the exiled German scholars. The plaque dates back to an initiative by Federal Republic president Richard von Weizsäcker. Voicing what he referred to as the gratitude of "the German people," he thanked Turkey for having granted refuge to German scholars. As we might guess, the timing of the commemoration was critical. The president's visit to Turkey coincided with the 1986 general election campaign in the Federal Republic, a campaign waged over the question of whether asylum law ought to be upheld in its original form. Increasing numbers of asylum seekers in the Federal Republic meant that conservative politicians had begun to demand restrictions on the right to asylum. This right had been enshrined in the 1949 constitution, partly as an expression of remorse for the crimes of the Holocaust and partly as a reciprocal gesture for the exile granted to victims of Nazi persecution. With the plaque at the university's gate, Weizsäcker sent a signal to election campaigners who were trying to undermine the constitutional right to asylum. His signal was not heeded for very long: it is now very difficult to receive asylum in Germany.

Welcoming the Newcomer

Turkey's accelerated process of Westernization in the twenty-first century and its standing as Europe's political ally in the Muslim world has not erased the cleft between what it means to be European or Europeanized. These issues remain critical because of the debates concerning Turkey's integration into the European Union and the status of two million people of Turkish origin who now live in Germany. In light of contemporary debates about the status of immigrants in Europe, Auerbachian exile suggests something about models of integration and assimilation, just as it does about the historicity of these models. The benefits of cultural assimilation generally go unquestioned in Western European countries: almost every Western European country vehemently insists that Muslim migrants must moderate or even suspend their indigenous cultural practices in favor of those of the host country. The case of Auerbach shows, however, that the exact converse was deemed necessary for promoting the national project in Turkey: the newcomer was required to preserve his cultural difference rather than adapt to the majority culture. How fresh, even peculiar, this injunction now seems.

Tracing the reverse route of migration from Turkey to Germany in the postwar period, we find that assimilation becomes legally and socially mandated yet, I would argue, effectively unattainable. Migrants from Turkey, considered temporary "guest workers" in the 1960s, came to be regarded as "foreigners" in the 1970s and "Muslims" after 9/11. These shifts in terminology have been accompanied by changes in legislation intended to facilitate migrants' integration into German society.[29] Since 2000, nonnative members of German society can achieve full citizenship after passing language and citizenship tests. But while ever more migrants and their descendants are in fact granted citizenship, they are generally not perceived as German. In official parlance, they are *Deutsche mit Migrationshintergrund*, "Germans with a migration background"; colloquially, they remain "foreign." It seems sadly ironic that in light of the holocaustal German past, religion and ethnicity once again dominates perceptions about the failure, or refusal, to assimilate. After all, assimilation never was the happy answer to national belonging that it is now claimed to be. Over and against the

Erich Auerbach at Princeton University, 1949/1950. By permission of the Literary Archive Marbach.

German models of foreigner and guest worker, or the Turkish models of eternal guest, mimic, and dönme, how much better it would be if national belonging, and citizenship could be divorced entirely from both religion and ethnicity.

Exiles as well as immigrants bear, I have argued throughout this book, multiple national affiliations.[30] These historically contingent affiliations can, as I have shown in Auerbach's case, create dilemmas as well as open new avenues. This insight, at the heart of the book, reflects the social, cultural, political, and epistemological transformations that arise when people, whether by desperation or self-design, traverse the globe. What enables these transformations are, ultimately, gestures of hospitality. The Ottoman Empire and Turkey welcomed exiles of almost every religious, ethnic, and political stripe: this *omnigatherum* included fifteenth-century Sephardic Jews and nineteenth-century Poles; twentieth-century Czarists fleeing the socialist revolution but also Trotsky fleeing Stalin; Jews escaping anti-Semitism as well as Nazis eluding de-Nazification. According to the popular historian Demirtaş Ceyhun, at the heart of such indiscriminate receptivity lies a notion of hospitality that views the unexpected guest as a godsend, a *tanrı misafiri*.[31] Turkish hospitality is characterized, he claims, by the guest's privileged status and by the host's obligation to offer only the best there is. While I do not subscribe to these essentializing notions of hospitality, it does seem worthwhile rethinking hospitality and reciprocity in terms of transnational exchange, cosmopolitanism, and exile.[32] Auerbach, after all, opened *Mimesis* with the evocative scene of Odysseus returning from Troy in the guise of a stranger. Knowing neither his identity nor his intentions, Euryclea washes the stranger's feet, and in this generous welcome lies the revelation of Odysseus's true history. Readers of the *Odyssey* will remember that *xenos* means foreigner; it also means guest-friend.

Appendix: Lectures by Erich Auerbach in Turkey

Translated by Victoria Holbrook

Realism in Europe in the Nineteenth Century[1]

Esteemed Rector, Ladies, Gentlemen,

Everyone knows what literary realism is, but would, I believe, find it difficult to explain, let alone define. This should come as no surprise. Terms having a general definition and mode of thought or artistic integrity, like individualism, symbolism, and romanticism, lose fixed meaning to the extent they make themselves accepted in precise and circumscribed definitions. Terms much used become indefinable, like ancient coins whose inscriptions and edges have been worn away.

Therefore I will not begin by defining what I think realism is. This is rather the goal than the starting point of my lecture: in so far as possible, to have a concrete knowledge of realism in the nineteenth century. In order to grasp this we will investigate the basis of realism, most importantly, the genre of the novel in its specific nineteenth-century manifestation.

Everyone read novels in the nineteenth century, and everyone still reads novels; although our age is not as inclined to read as that of our fathers and grandfathers, and methods of access to artistic performances and knowledge of the outside world are much changed, the novel always occupies an important position. In the nineteenth century, the most widespread literary form, or as an economist might put it, the literary form which to a great extent occupied production and found the most consumers, was the novel. And the realist novel made up the majority of these novels.

Let me make a provisional statement of what this means. These novels dealt with contemporary subjects, telling the stories of individuals living in the same time in similar environments. The story of a teacher, for example, or a villager, doctor, industrialist, aristocrat, or artist. As the hero's life was followed in the novel, social conditions were often discussed; the topic could be ordinary as long as it was contemporary. The terms "contemporary" and "ordinary" are in need of precise definition.

For something to be "contemporary" means not only that it is materially contemporaneous. For a topic to be contemporary in the realistic sense, it must be modern in the way I have just stated and must not be distant from the reader's environment.

Those of our contemporaries who are still living at a civilizational level we have already surpassed, for example, the Ethiopians of Africa or Australian aborigines, cannot be subjects of the realist novel. They could be subjects only of an exotic novel. This distinction is in itself quite obscure and relative. For Frenchmen living in 1835, the customs of Spaniards and the inhabitants of the Isle of Corsica described by Mérimée were so different from their own that Colomba or Carmen seemed more exotic than realistic. However, today a Parisian doctor may find the life story of a laborer in San Francisco to be a contemporary tale. We rightly consider the wonderful Chinese novels of Madame Pearl Buck to be realist novels.

As time goes on the life of human beings on earth presents a commonality due, if not due to similarity, to the fact that an event concerning one individual immediately affects another, so that today a contemporary novel is naturally a realist novel. It is getting harder and harder to write an exotic novel.

So, a realist novel must be contemporary in such a way that the reader understands its subject to be a part of the life which shares a commonality with his own experience; that modern life which has begun to be shared in common by all humanity was in the nineteenth century common only to Europe, or a part of Europe.

We have said that the topic of a realist novel may be ordinary as long as it is contemporary. The term "ordinary" must also be explained, for it has a specific meaning here. The characters in a realist novel may be ordinary, but do not have to be.

An ordinary baker, sailor, man of state, or journalist may be one of the main characters of a realist novel if invented by the author rather than being a known person.

For if a person who has played a role in history—such as Atatürk, Roosevelt, or Einstein, or even a baker who becomes generally known because he is mixed up in an important court case—is chosen as the hero of a novel, the work cannot be considered a realist novel. It would be viewed more as a fictionalized life story.

The term "ordinary" has a broader scope; works of tragedy from the past, and especially the age of French classicism, never took up ordinary subjects. An elite subject was required; the heroes of such works had to exist outside of everyday, ordinary life, they had to be kings, princes, Casanovas, or shepherds in love; everyday life could not enter into poetry. The contrary has been true for a century now. In modern realism there are no elite environments; an ordinary environment is compulsory. We will discuss this again.

I believe we now know what a realist novel is. These are novels which tell the life stories of contemporary, ordinary persons. We can go further and say that in realist literature, the qualities of each thing are understood because the subject is contemporary and ordinary.

But if I say we have reached our goal and finish my lecture here, you will not be satisfied. Several issues have yet to be resolved.

Why did realism, especially the realist novel, occupy such an important position in the nineteenth century, a position it had never been able to claim before? Was it technique and material circumstance that provided greater possibilities relative to earlier centuries? Or was the event of nineteenth-century realism a new event, different and more compelling to people than others known before?

Let us first discuss the situation of technique. The novel is a product; it must be manufactured, and for this there must be sufficient consumers to ensure a profit for the manufacturer. The production of novels requires not only that they be written; they must also be printed.

You know that printing was discovered in the fifteenth century, but this was at first a craft; the technical development which allowed for publication on a large scale at relatively little cost occurred gradually; the mechanical press was invented around the year 1800, and this helped to make possible the development of journalism as well as the publication of books on a grand scale; there were almost no daily newspapers in the eighteenth century; the modern printing press was invented in the nineteenth century. The serial novel also emerged during this period and enjoyed widespread demand.

But the issue is even more important when analyzed from the point of view of the consumer. In order for novels to be purchased in great numbers, great numbers of people had to be able to read them easily, without difficulty; only then could they enjoy books of three hundred to five hundred pages.

You know that even in European countries, primary education became universal only in the nineteenth century; at the end of the century there were people even in the most civilized countries who could read only very slowly and with difficulty.

In the eighteenth century the art of reading and writing was confined to a large but specific coterie, one not sufficient to form the mass readership of the realist novel. One should remember that the economic phenomenon of an author able to earn a living by sale of his books has come about only in recent times. In the seventeenth century writers who had no personal wealth and were not members of the clergy lived by patronage of the king or a great aristocrat.

By the eighteenth century this situation had gradually changed. The number of writers in France and England making a living by their writings, selling their books or having them sold, was increasing. But their number was not so many as it would be in the nineteenth century. The tastes of readers, whose number was much smaller than in the nineteenth and twentieth centuries, were more the refined tastes of nobility.

Readers came not only from the aristocracy. On the contrary, the bourgeoisie, wielding power due to superior manners, wealth, intelligence, and position, also represented a great proportion of the readership. But bourgeois readers formed a tiny portion of the nation; in the economic world which had been emerging in Europe since the fifteenth century, they were the rich; they had not yet sufficiently comprehended the independence of their class to demand equality under the law, not yet gotten free of the tyrannical patterns of feudalism, and while bound to its thought and taste, would occasionally, without being conscious of it, give rise to important transformations.

They could not constitute the type of reader appropriate to the realist novel in the modern sense. The emergence of this type of reader required a broader, self-conscious, informed readership which was interested in the modern life of its peers—the life shared in common—and which derived a personal pleasure from reading. This mass readership had been formed by the nineteenth century. It was first of all a French, English, German, Russian readership; later it became a European readership, and now it is more or less a world readership. Let me say right now that the realist novel would have a brighter future in times to come if it were not for the art of cinema, which rivals it in the field of realism with its documents, homogeneous and diverse, fixing every moment in time.

The pleasure of reading novels is something the individual experiences alone. Contemporary people read in order to gain information more quickly or to broaden their knowledge; their tastes, even their intellectual tastes, are satisfied more through the event of seeing, and when they are part of a group. Realism as we understand it today, whether in the novel, the cinema, or something else, could not have emerged prior to the nineteenth century, for there was no readership that could understand it.

Those among you who know a bit about European literature may assert that realism existed before the nineteenth century. Scarron, Molière, Boileau, Lesage, and many more were realists; the bourgeois novel existed in England in the eighteenth century; there was a strong realism in the literary movement begun in Germany by Lessing, Goethe, and Schiller during the second half of the eighteenth century. So it may be said that in the eighteenth century a limited readership read and enjoyed the writings of realist authors; but this was something completely different; there are profound differences between the realism of the seventeenth and eighteenth centuries and the realism which developed from 1830 with the novels of Stendhal and Balzac. I will try to clarify this for you with an example. Some in my audience will remember Molière's masterpiece *The Miser* and Père Grandet, the perfectly modern miser Balzac portrayed in his novel *Eugénie Grandet*.

To be sure, Molière is as much a realist as Balzac. But his style is completely different. His miser, Harpagon, is always miserly; Harpagon's passion for material wealth, like that of Grandet, has destroyed all his feeling. He, too, is a pater familias. But the ties of Molière's character to his time are scarcely shown; Molière gave us no idea of Harpagon's socioeconomic situation. He is rich, he is a miser and a usurer, and that is all. These attributes may apply to misers of all historical periods. We do not know if Harpagon earned his fortune himself or inherited it, or how he manages it; the information given to us about his fortune is of such a general nature that if the play had not been written in seventeenth-century French, we could assume that Harpagon had lived in some other country, in a different era.

The complete contrary is the case with Père Grandet of Balzac's novel. The political and economic history of France from 1789 to 1830, from the time of the revolution to Louis Philippe's ascension to the throne, is related within the story of Père Grandet and his fortune. In former times while Grandet was a cooper and winegrower in the town of Turenne, he had bought an aristocratic estate very cheaply at auction with the little money he had saved and his wife's dowry. He passed as an ardent republican during the revolution and got himself elected mayor; taking advantage of his position, he had roads built which eased the delivery of his goods, and established a procedure of taxation which served his interests; he himself determined the value of his land and the taxes due upon it. By the time of Napoleon he had been a purveyor to armies and become a very wealthy, influential old man dominating the markets for wheat, wood, and wine.

What I have told you here in a few words summarizes a great deal of the detail that constitutes Grandet's personality. This detail ties him to the historical period contemporary with Balzac, to Turenne at the time of the Restoration; the whole atmosphere of the period is brought alive in the novel. You see the difference between Molière and Balzac. It sometimes happened that Molière showed more of the environment and of contemporary life than he did in *The Miser*, and it is in fact hazardous to compare the genre of the theatrical play, which offers little place for action and description, with that of the novel. Several novels written in the seventeenth and early eighteenth centuries which discuss the special qualities of the lives of petit bourgeois and actors in the theater give the social atmosphere of the time in a clear enough manner. There are even those among them, like Lesage's novel *Gil Blas*, which take their characters from all levels of society in order to portray manners in detail.

But nineteenth-century realism is completely different. The social, political, and economic developments we call historical movements, which move people to action, are felt nowhere in these novels; neither is life as it is lived by the reader; the hidden voice of the writer does not say to him, "I am describing your life, for even if you are living in a different country, and your circumstances are different than the heroes, I am talking about you." He does not say, "We are all, you, your family and friends, bound by the historical destiny which is increasingly our shared life." That is why the influence of manners and customs of centuries past remains pleasantly alive while superficial; we do not see man within life as he lives it, directly and profoundly; issues of the milieu are not under discussion. It is assumed that social life is organized in a static and absolute manner. The realism of the seventeenth and eighteenth centuries addressed completely different readers.

The manners this realism described were related in order to enter-tain a particular coterie of readers, a coterie which, rightly or wrongly, saw itself as superior to the people whose lives were narrated in a realistic form. The style of life described was not their own, and they had no connections with those masses. While the people in this coterie assumed in a general way that all share the same virtues and sins, they did not perceive their own lives in the lives being narrated. And this brings us in contact with the profound differences between nineteenth-century realism and the re-alism of previous centuries. Seventeenth-century French classicism ac-cepted the aesthetic principle Greek and Roman theoreticians called "the separation of genres," and applied it extravagantly. This thesis put forth the argument that tragedy and realism were incompatible; everything re-alistic was naturally comic, and everything comic condescended in so far as it was realistic.

Those among you who know a bit about seventeenth-century litera-ture will recall that descriptions of a doctor, a lawyer, a laborer, or villager were always grotesque; in tragedy there is no place for realistic detail. The existing personalities were all either princes or great aristocrats, and in this respect had only a general symbolic character; in their world meals are not eaten, no one sleeps, and the weather is never mentioned. The re-nowned unity of time and place is either arbitrary, inclusive of all times, or external to the concept of time.

This is something extraordinary, and played a greater role in the emergence of works of personal poetry than any other factor. But as a re-sult, the real, concrete, and contemporary side of life played no serious role in the art of the diary; in order for a person to enter into the atmosphere of tragedy in this poetic world, he had to put aside his personal, profes-sional, particular, and everyday attributes; realistic problems had no place in the realm of tragedy.

I will not expound here upon the origins of this theory, the reasons for its re-emergence in the seventeenth century, its particulars and extent. It is enough for us to know that it dominated French classical poetry and, thanks to the great influence of classicism, reigned throughout Europe in the seven-teenth and eighteenth centuries. This mode began to gradually lose its hege-mony in the eighteenth century, and in the second half of the century rebel-lion against the tyranny of classical principles broke out everywhere. The strongest movement was Sturm und Drang, which coincided with Goethe and Schiller's youth; there were similar movements in England and France.

In France it was Denis Diderot rather than Jean-Jacques Rousseau who championed the mixture of genres. But that was only the beginning.

It was only after the revolution, after the Napoleonic period, that is, after the breakdown of the old society and the absolute victory of the fully developed, self-conscious bourgeois class in its struggle with the undifferentiated masses, which is to say around 1830, that the separation of genres disappeared and tragic realism could be born.

You will read in the handbooks that Victor Hugo, France's greatest Romantic poet, accomplished this revolution. He himself claimed it was so and took pride in it. He claimed to have democratized poetry, likening himself to Danton and Robespierre. This is not quite correct, and from the point of view of realism, not correct at all; what Victor Hugo wanted to do, and did, was to mix the sublime and the grotesque.

But this is extremely distant from real life. It can only bring forth poetry which, like Victor Hugo's, is romantic, rhetorical, very entertaining, and full of unexpected detail; it can never portray life as it is lived, for life is rarely sublime or grotesque, only always real. It is full of ordinary truths, and can be tragic.

It was Stendhal and Balzac who first portrayed the seriousness and tragedy of real life. One in *The Red and the Black*, published in 1830, the other in *The Human Comedy*, whose first volumes were published in the same year.

It is customary to esteem Stendhal for the keenness of his psychology and the freedom of his thought. In contrast to the obscurity, exaggeration and confessionalism of contemporary romantics, Stendhal's attentive analyses and the always self-reflective devotion to freedom he called "egoism" made him a harbinger of the positivist mentality and the individualism of Nietzsche.

This is all true. Those who approve of his style, which was understood and appreciated only fifty years later, as that of a harbinger are completely correct. But if Stendhal's value were of this nature alone, the interest shown in him would have been of a very particular kind and would have given a select, precious pleasure only to those seeking aesthetic experiences. Stendhal would have had no historical importance, he would have been considered a personality of no influence, alone in his time.

But Stendhal does not interest us merely as a person alone in his time, which we may explain by his belonging to a great pre-revolutionary bourgeois family, his having lived in France, Italy, Germany, and Russia, by his experiences of the revolutionary and Napoleonic wars, and especially his courageous and Epicurean personality. This made the new reactionary capitalist society founded after Napoleon's revolution seem grotesque and disgusting to him. He was not more than thirty years old at the time; his youth had been filled with adventure and dissipation. In spite of this his solitariness did not shake his courage, as it did that of others.

In spite of his lack of money, he continued to live as he liked and wished. The society in which he lived bored and alienated him. His efforts were not servile and ignominious, as those of men at home in that society were. But he had a fixed purpose, and understood that only with that sense of purpose could he be successful in the new environment. This environment consisted of hardworking, scandalmongering, reactionary people who hated the modern, hated adventure, lived in continual fear of the state and, probably, of revolution.

Stendhal was ambitious; but what he wanted was love, passion, power, and perhaps fame. He was far from the humble bourgeois type; he was very different from the men of the new society, and he could not have been successful. Only in Italy, living on the remains of its old society, could he be comfortable. But the richness of his personality created a body of work which described the forms of this enemy society he hated yet could not destroy and whose advance he witnessed with every passing day.

Stendhal was the first to see modern society, in all its ordinary reality, with its political, economic, and religious roots, with all its serious problems, as the subject of a tragic work of art. *The Red and the Black*, the story of Julien Sorel, describes Stendhal's personal struggle against his age; this struggle displayed that age to him in a more profound way than his contemporaries; the work represents the mixture of genres; full of ordinary events, serious, it contains the problematic or tragic life shared in common, the realism, of nineteenth- and twentieth-century men.

If Stendhal's work, with its virtues, faults, and flaws, is the result of hatred for the age in which he lived, and a struggle against it, Balzac's was on the contrary born of the exuberant excitement he felt at the complex, multifarious life, full of movement and action, which he saw all around him.

Balzac was sixteen years younger than Stendhal and had not seen the old society or the revolution. He was of the generation of Vigny and Hugo. He was as romantic as he was realist; the two styles may conform, for the same idea emerges from its separate interpretations; the idea is shared: the idea of the mixing of genres.

As Balzac, with his superhuman capacity for work, described all aspects of contemporary life, he often let his pleasure in the extraordinary, the melodramatic and strange run away with him; these are the negative aspects of his poetic nature. For he was a poet, in spite of his lack of economy; his admirers rightly compare his work with *The Thousand and One Nights*. It is the greatest epic of contemporary life.

It was conceived more broadly than Stendhal's. Balzac's work grasps the economic details of modern life more closely; the complex forms, actions, and practices of society, with their tendencies and flaws, have been analyzed more accurately, and a more complete tableau of society has been painted; if its ebullient imagery and the tastelessly crude and grotesque exaggerations of its style sometimes make the reader uncomfortable, the strength of its vision is so suggestive that its flaws do not affect the general judgment.

One must agree that despite his excesses, Balzac knew what he wanted to do: To his work which minutely describes the human heart, social position, and social and historical events which are not imaginary but take place everywhere, he gave the name *Comédie Humaine*.

You will read in the handbooks that it was the great romantic poet Victor Hugo who accomplished the revolution of democratizing literature that is called the mixture of genres. This is not correct; what Victor Hugo did, as he himself said, was to mix the sublime and the grotesque. What realism required was not this; for life is rarely sublime or grotesque, but always subject to an everyday, concrete reality; each day it is beset with problems, and can be tragic.

Life does not give us the sublime or the grotesque. It gives us something more serious: everyday reality. And it was not Victor Hugo but his contemporaries, the two writers Stendhal and Balzac, who gave us that. One gave us realism with his novel *The Red and the Black*, published in 1830, and the other with his compilation *The Human Comedy*, whose first volumes were published in the same year. One comprehended this reality through the hatred and resentment he felt toward the society in which he lived, and the other through the ardent love he felt for the life full of action and passion around him. Stendhal and Balzac are the true inventors of modern realism.

You may be amazed that I attribute the source of modern realism to two French writers alone, without mentioning the literatures of other countries. This does not come of my being a specialist in Romance languages and literatures. The late eighteenth- and early nineteenth-century development in several other European countries was slower and less eventful than that of France, and it was possible to solve problems in a more composed manner. For political and economic reasons, these countries grasped nineteenth-century realism much later.

Germany, for example, came to know this realism mixed with tragedy when Goethe and Schiller were young. But because of the political and economic circumstances of the country, this realism had a pastoral and idyllic character throughout the nineteenth century. Only around the year 1900 did realism find a place in prominent works like the dramas of Hauptmann and the novels of Thomas Mann. And it was present in the pastoral fragments of Stifter, Keller, Storm, and Fontane.

The situation for England is different, and many would have me give place to Thackeray and Dickens beside Balzac and Stendhal. Without a doubt, these were great realist writers. But I hesitate to consider them as much creators of realism as Stendhal and Balzac. Neither the satirical moralism of Thackeray nor the poetic irony of Dickens gives me the concept of modern life. I do not find in them the best understanding of the political and economic entities which characterize the new forms of tragic realism. Although everyday life in England is very modern, the vantage point on life is very backward.

For another nation of Europe, the Russian nation, the problem is the reverse. All throughout the nineteenth century, Russia failed to get free of the political and economic order which blocked its development; it was the most backward nation in Europe. Its government was based on tyranny; its economic life had not arrived at a capitalist form in the precise sense, it was not free of feudalistic patterns. Yet Russia greatly aided the development of tragic realism in Europe.

Although the realist art of such as Gogol, Tolstoy, and Dostoyevsky first emerged under the influence of Europe, it was freed of this influence at the end of the nineteenth century and, bravely, with profound, rich works, extricated the bourgeois realism of Europe from the narrow framework of its first period. This period corresponded to the publications of Balzac, Flaubert, and their contemporaries in France.

Although the French realists abandoned the separation of genres and related contemporary and ordinary subjects in a tragic and profound style, they spoke only of the self-conscious class, that is, the bourgeoisie; the masses could enter their works only in a fleeting and superficial manner. The masses were not seen with their own independent and particular life, they were viewed from above, with the desire to pity, despise, or school them, and sometimes with an idealistic socialism.

Socialism, as a leveling movement within the society which appeared in a state of becoming in Europe from 1850, first showed itself in the economic and political rather than the artistic field. It had no long-lasting influence because the bold and hard-working Emile Zola, who was the first to try to apply it to art, was unable to free his view of man from an exclusively economic and biological understanding.

The Russians had this influence; it is a bit difficult to explain why. It is probably due to the nature of the subjects, pertaining to the bourgeoisie and aristocrats rather than the masses, even Gorky could not help but deal with. This is because the psychological chasm between the bourgeoisie and the masses did not exist in Russia as it did in Europe. If in Europe the various classes within nations were separated by position and wealth, and by long-standing traditions, as had been the case in the Middle Ages, they had the same culture, religion and views on morality. These classes understood one another intuitively and instantly. They could be likened to rungs on the same ladder. In the great novels of Tolstoy and Dostoyevsky all the nation's classes were welded together, and this gave them an atmosphere completely different from that of the French novels; they were much broader and pertained more to the masses.

We know that the Russian realists, particularly Dostoyevsky, found depths to the psyche which had until then remained unknown; in them psychology had a shocking, complex character which was not to be easily understood. But the capacity to understand had no connection with the class to which the reader belonged. The writing is about humanity and sometimes very Russian; one can easily understand it being human, and sometimes Russian.

The Russian writers represented a new reality in western realism. They broadened and deepened its scope. Various influences difficult to sort out in a lecture were added to the movements we have mentioned; the art of realism is in a developing state, and works to show forth to the mind our life on earth and its increasing tendency to become a life shared in common.

Those who understand this should not be shaken by the tragic events occurring today. History is manifested through catastrophic events and ruptures. That which is being prepared today, that which has been in preparation for a century, is the tragic realism I have discussed, modern realism, the life shared in common which grants the possibility of life to all people on earth.

Erich Auerbach
Professor Ordinarius
1941–1942

Literature and War[2]

There are two types of war literature. One is the literature comprised of short pieces of the lyric genre which come into being with wars: prayers for victory, songs urging soldiers to heroism, satires condemning and scorning the enemy, folk songs honoring victory and thanking the gods. There are many existing examples of all of these.

The most ancient are from the Children of Israel residing in Palestine: the song of victory sung by Deborah upon the defeat of the Canaanites, mentioned in the Bible; and from the oldest works of Greek literature, the elegies of Tyrtaeus exhorting the Spartans to victory over their neighbors the Peloponnesians. He was the first to articulate the well-known and oft-repeated idea that "it is a beautiful thing to die fighting in the front ranks for one's country."

You find this type of literature in every European nation which has embraced the cause of war.

Much has changed since the crusader songs of the twelfth century and the religious and war songs of the sixteenth. We are now indifferent to the subjects of those struggles. But when we read the texts of the songs we can still sense the fervor which inspired them. I will remind you of the more recent "Marseillaise," the French song of war and freedom, and the freedom songs sung by Germans during their liberation struggles against Napoleon I.

My aim in this lecture is to better explain songs such as the "Marseillaise." For as I have said, it is both a song of war and a song of freedom; it describes the arming of the entire nation against internal and external enemies. One observes that in France, as in other European nations, the roots of nationalism are in the people and have strong ties to freedom of conscience, economic freedom, and individual freedom, which is to say to its desires.

Now let us move on to the second type of war literature. This may be the more important one from the point of view of art. For there are more existing masterpieces of this genre, and it everywhere forms the basis of national literature. These works are generally long; they are not lyric but epic; they do not speak of a war contemporary with the poet but of a war in the past, and they narrate the heroic exploits of ancestors.

These are first of all national epics, like the *Iliad* of Homer, the *Aeneid* of Virgil, the German *Nibelungen*, the French *Song of Roland* and many more. In more recent times, some of the tragedies of Goethe and Schiller were of this genre, and even some novels. Among novels I will mention Tolstoy's great novel *War and Peace*; its subject is Napoleon's Russian campaign of 1812. It is in my opinion one of the finest books of the nineteenth century, and I recommend that you read it. There is a Turkish translation available.

All the works of this second genre are historical, they do not pertain to the present, as I have said, but they have all (especially the ancient epics) helped to prepare and strengthen national consciousness. Homer's *Iliad* was a powerful factor in the preservation of Greek unity at one of the most perilous moments in its history; the French *Song of Roland* and the Spanish epic of *El Cid* have been just as important.

Works of this second genre can be influential at moments of peril for nations even though their subjects are not of the present. Among the Greeks, the French, and other nations, it has often happened that a few verses from an ancient poet recited onstage created great excitement because they were near to the present sentiments of the audience. During the occupation of Paris in 1871, a lecture Professor Gaston Paris gave on "*The Song of Roland* and French Nationalism" helped greatly to revive the idea of resistance. So the political importance of the second group of works, whose subjects are historical, is no less than that of the first.

But although there were many wars in the seventeenth and eighteenth centuries, which is to say in the age of European absolutism, there was no war literature created by the people, whether of the first type, lyric and pertaining to the present, or the second, epic and pertaining to historical subjects.

Although we have Voltaire's *Henriade*, which narrates the wars of Henri IV in the epic genre, it is a cold work having no connection to the people; there do exist a few more important military songs loved by the people. They were composed for famous generals of the time, such as Eugene of Savoy and the Duke of Marlborough. You may know some of those about Marlborough, who was an ancestor of Prime Minister Churchill. But these songs and marches do not have the seriousness and the ardor of war poetry from other times; they are like dance music, and their lyrics do not express political thoughts or the perilous and heroic duties of defending the homeland. Rather they are gay, at times touching, at times frivolous; this is not the literature of a nation struggling for its existence and its freedom.

What can be the reason for the meagerness in the development of this genre of literature during those two centuries spent in war? It did not come of a general dearth of literature, for we know that European, especially French, literature was very fruitful during the seventeenth and eighteenth centuries; it was the age of the masterpieces of French classicism, the age of Molière, Boileau, La Fontaine, and their imitators in other countries as well as in France.

But this classical literature was not the literature of the people; addressed to a specific coterie in society, highly refined in both meaning and form, it is a literature that did not interest the people at all.

This observation shows us the method which must be followed in order to find the solution to the problem that interests us: in Europe, during the two-centuries-long period of absolutism, the people were mute.

In the Middle Ages and the Renaissance the people played an important and active historical role. Villagers and urban bourgeoisie were an integral and powerful element of public life in guilds and institutions founded by the state. Institutions were not, as in modern democracies, based upon individualistic principles; they were bearers of artisanal and class mentalities, they were very active, and knew their political constituencies. In many countries they were in fact the natural allies of the central power, that is to say the king, in the people's struggle against feudal lords.

This is the basis of national unity and consciousness in France: the king and the people allied against the particularist feudal aristocracy. In those times it was not easy to mount a major war without arousing the interest of the people, without convincing them of its necessity and winning their sympathy. Urban and village populations would often take up arms themselves. But when at the end of the religious wars absolutism won its decisive victory and the feudal aristocrats completely lost their constituents, the central power of the king grew to such an extent that he no longer needed the people. His government definitively ruled the country without need of guilds and people's representatives: wars were the wars of princes, planned, declared, and led from ministerial chambers, and the people participated only by contributing to their costs.

The military participation of the people was removed with developments in the art of war. Firearms, especially cannon, made necessary a military training which could not be given to the people as a whole. Consider that even in Europe at that time, military service and education were not compulsory, and the great majority of Europeans did not know the alphabet. Armies were made up of mercenaries, often from other countries, who chose the military as a profession. These were men who sold their blood.

Among officers there was also a type of soldier who was usually the youngest son of a great family. Because they were deprived of inheritance, they were persons without wealth or position. They offered their services to warring princes, wandering the world in search of adventure and fortune.

We find this type in *Minna von Barnhelm*, a famous eighteenth-century comedy written by the German poet Gotthold Ephraim Lessing. Lieutenant Ricaut de la Martinière, the youngest son of a noble French family, serves in the armies of Holland, the Pope, and the Prussian Frederick the Great until he is forced to make a living at cards.

If this is what becomes of officers, you can imagine what became of infantrymen. Men wandering the various countries of Europe seeking to enter the service of powerful young men, their masters the princes, they gathered up malcontents, persons estranged from their families, vagabonds, paupers, and often murderers; they sometimes duped an inexperienced youth in a moment of drunkenness with the promises they made and made him sign a contract for ten, twelve, even twenty years. It even happened that penniless young princes would sell a few thousand of their subjects to other wealthy and powerful princes.

You see that wars conducted in this fashion could not have been people's wars; they were the business only of royalty and its ministers. The cause of the longest and most important of these conflicts was the struggle between a Bourbon and a Habsburg candidate over the ascension to the empty Spanish throne. Both families were related to the Spanish houses. You see that this was simply a dynastic quarrel. Neither the German nor the French people were directly concerned in it; as for the Spanish people, they were not even asked their opinion.

It would not be correct to say that the kings who conducted such wars did not think of their people at all; they hoped to increase the wealth and prosperity of their people by enlarging their kingdoms and gaining possession of political and economic privileges. It was only that they had lost the habit of asking their people's opinion; they felt no need to do so.

Often they could not gauge the ability of their people to withstand the burdens and costs of long wars. The famous example of Louis XIV shows that even when the King was intelligent, conscientious, and always victorious, he would destroy the economic and political fabric of the country if he tried to decide everything himself, or acted on the advice only of officials he himself chose.

As for the people, they were at first content with their circumstances. In many ways it served their interests to have the administration of the central government, the King, strengthened; they were freed from the lords and barons who had oppressed them for so long. For administration to be institutionalized in the hands of the King and his bureaucracy insured peace within the interior and security of work. Exhausted by religious conflicts, wearied by centuries of chaos, they renounced their rights, gave up the old institutional privileges and were content to be ruled by princes in peace.

But they gradually regretted their renunciations and began to rebel against absolutism. Far from the state administration, burdened by taxes, rebellion against bureaucratic wrongs and corruption gradually rose to take the place of quietude and obedience. When new ideas of national and individual freedoms began to be written down in the eighteenth century, they created a profound reaction first among the French and then the other European peoples.

The French Revolution of 1789 became the first stage of this change; revolution overturned absolutism, established the national sovereignty of the people, and, granting all political responsibility to them, also destroyed the old military institution; it changed ideas of war and created the concept of national defense. Compulsory military service was established after that, and the education of all children by the state was closely connected with it.

There is in Europe a nation whose political development was a century, even a few centuries, ahead of other European states—the British. Their democratic system began not in the eighteenth but the seventeenth century, and even then it appeared as the final stage in a revolution which had begun much earlier. Almost all of the institutions of modern democracies were formed first of all in Britain. But the military institution must be excepted from these; due to the geographical position of the British, for them the problem of national defense took an entirely different form. Until 1914 they conducted all their wars by means of their naval fleets, and often with volunteers made up of the inhabitants of colonies; even now they consider compulsory service an extraordinary measure necessary only when facing a threat to the nation. That is why national reconciliation has its origin not in England but as the sole great democratic institution in France.

If we were to research into the origin of French ideas on the arming of the entire nation in defense of the homeland, which spread immediately throughout the world, we would find them in the social system of Jean-Jacques Rousseau, a political writer of extreme sensitivity who had no affinity for combat. Rousseau never mentions war in his writings, and military victories are doubtless far from the natural framework of his thought. However, the idea of the natural freedoms of man, which he considered a sacred property to be defended by any means necessary, led him to the theory of national sovereignty and unity; and this required that every citizen able to bear arms defend the collective freedom when threatened.

The events of the revolution that ensued ten years after Rousseau's death brought about the discovery of this unknown aspect of his political system. At a moment when the people in rebellion thought, rightly or wrongly, that they were being threatened by the mercenaries of the King, the arming of the entire nation in self-defense was the necessary measure immediately taken, and the same measure was taken later in a moment of peril when neighboring kings and princes sent armies, again made up of professional soldiers, to reestablish absolutism, save the King and destroy the national and individual freedom which had been so decisively won. Although hurriedly roused in 1792 and ill-equipped, this first army formed by the people, who worked miracles in defense of the country, was the basis of Napoleon's army.

This development was of primary importance in human history, and its importance goes beyond the military. A people which becomes conscious of itself and understands that national defense must be performed by the entire nation must also comprehend the intellectual imperatives this duty requires in modern times; in order to defend itself, it must be informed. Military service and compulsory education are closely connected, and complementary. The school is preparation for the barracks. And the barracks often educates and develops the nation not only in the military sense, but professionally and generally.

The French people's acceptance of the national defense measures that successfully brought it into being motivated other European peoples as well. For the troops employed solely for defense at the time of the Revolution were used in the Napoleonic era to invade all of Europe. The national feeling of the others was thereby aroused, and they were forced to defend themselves with the national powers which had crushed them. The

War of 1813–1815, which freed Europe of domination by Napoleon, was a war of nations; it was the arming of nations.

When the Prussian King Frederick Wilhelm III declared war on Napoleon, he addressed his formal published statement to "My people." This address, which appears to us natural in such a situation, was at that time a completely new, unheard-of and extraordinary thing. It shows, in a manner leaving no room for doubt, how entirely things had changed since the days when wars were conducted by kings from ministerial chambers, far from the active participation of the people and without their consent.

Since the French Revolution and the Napoleonic era, ideas of national defense and military service have become deeply rooted in Europe and many other very different nations. The process did not occur without struggle. Various parties have taken up the issue, at times trying to abolish military service and at others to use it for aims far from its national democratic origins. We are not going to discuss the history of such political struggles; they never presented an obstacle to the development of the military institution. The idea of national armament has formed the basis of modern warfare until our times.

It is natural that such a change should have affected literature. The war literature of the nineteenth century is the literature of the struggling nation. It has been so from the beginning. Many poets were appalled by the horrors of the French Revolution and did not look favorably upon the uprising of the masses. They believed that the moral and aesthetic values of civilization as a whole would be wiped out by the tyranny of the exultant masses.

Even Goethe, who was a passionate advocate of freedom and the people when he wrote the Götz von Berlichingen tragedy in his youth, regarded the events taking place in France from 1789 on with shock, anguish, and disgust. In 1792 he participated in the war the German princes launched against revolutionary France. The information he left to us from there is very realistic and, while far from fanatical, betrays no inclination against the revolutionary movement.

However, on the eve of the cannon shelling which caused the German princes to flee the revolutionary army at Valmy, he is supposed to have told anxious friends who came to visit him: "Today a new stage in history has begun and you can say that you were witness to its birth." The statement shows his apprehension. He was not swayed by the hopes of most of his friends into believing that the uprising of nations could be overcome. At the same time, he was not in favor of the uprising he felt sure would be victorious. Until the end of his life (he lived until 1832), he shrank from any movement which resembled an uprising of the people.

The other great classic poet of the Germans, Schiller, who was ten years younger than Goethe, never completely renounced the revolutionary spirit which was the soul of the tragedies he wrote in his youth. The subject of *Wilhelm Tell*, perhaps the best-known of his late tragedies, portrays the early fourteenth-century rebellion of Swiss cantons against the domination of the Habsburgs, whom they regarded as foreign. Schiller took the idea from a folk legend which portrayed as sudden a national rebellion that had in fact been long in preparation. And the ideas of freedom expressed by the characters in the tragedy are more the ideas of Schiller's own time than those of the fourteenth century. The fame of the play became greater for it. Although Schiller was not Swiss and had never seen Switzerland, his tragedy passed into the ranks of Swiss national poetry.

War literature in France in the first half of the nineteenth century was bound up with Napoleon's personality and legend in particular. After his downfall and death he gradually became an epic hero of the people and a nationalistic symbol, a development we can sense in writers like Paul-Louis Courier and Stendhal, who served in the armies of the Empire and took up literature after Napoleon's demise.

Neither Courier nor Stendhal had any love for Napoleon while he was in power. Like many of their contemporaries, they saw him not as a revolutionary but as the destroyer of the revolution. After his downfall, however, when the reactionary government which displayed the pettiness of the Bourbons lost the love of the people, the greatness of Napoleon's ideas and memories of the victory he had bestowed upon France caused the sufferings of his era to be forgotten. He was no longer a despot but a hero who had brought the nation from victory to victory in wars against the reactionary policies of foreign princes and exiled aristocrats.

The memory of the Empire had a particularly great effect upon the bold and adventurous of the younger generation. Courier and Stendhal were swept up in it, somewhat unawares, and wrote fervent pieces about Napoleon containing ideas they would never have held when he was in power. There were many youths who, like them, admired Napoleon although they had no personal memory of him. The most famous of these was the freedom-loving Béranger. He had fame, he loved the Empire, and he was mediocre. But he made a great impression upon his contemporaries because his simple, likable songs expressed the general sentiment.

Populist and democratic nationalism made great strides in Europe around the middle of the nineteenth century. Although Victor Hugo, head of the Romantic movement in France, was a political conservative at first, in time he became a fervent and almost mystic supporter of democracy. In works such as *Les Châtiments, Legendes des siècles*, and later *L'Année terrible*, he brought the full force of his genius to bear upon the people's struggle for freedom. Historians of the Romantic period such as Michelet had the same mentality.

In Germany the democratic group called "Young Germany," which played an important role in the 1848 revolution and prepared the way for German unity, was born as much of democratic as nationalist ideas, and left profound marks on literature. Even in Switzerland the idea of national armament was not separate from democratic ideals; readers of the stories of Gottfried Keller, especially *Das Fähnlein der sieben Aufrechten*, will understand this state of mind.

There were only two nations in Europe that remained distant from the atmosphere of democratic nationalism. One was Britain, the most democratic of all, and the other was Russia, at that time in a condition of tyranny more extreme than that of any other European state. In Britain the democratic state was bound to an unshakable tradition; because the nation was protected by its geographical position, the military form of nationalism was never encouraged and heroism in war played a secondary role in the literature of the nineteenth century.

Thackeray's renowned novel *Vanity Fair*, which deals with the historical events of the Battle of Waterloo, is a very meaningful example. Here the great events are frameworks applied only to set forth individual and social problems. The heroism displayed by the British against Napoleon is rarely mentioned, and Thackeray is insistent that a man capable of great heroism may be morally weak and fond of empty show.

In Russia the situation was quite the opposite. Democratic ideas were entirely foreign to the people there in the nineteenth century; their nationalism was an instinctive expression of their love of the homeland. *War and Peace*, the novel by Tolstoy I mentioned at the beginning of my lecture, which like *Vanity Fair* deals with the final stages of the Napoleonic wars, is dominated by the sense that the entire sacred ground of Russia is rising against the invader, and the will of the land appears to control the people; at their head the calm, patient, tenacious general Kutuzov, apparently an ordinary old man, seems a symbol of that land and its race.

The literature of war lost its importance during the long period of peace in Europe from 1871 to 1914. An increasingly graceful lyric literature dominated everywhere, with spiritual and social concerns. I spent my youth in the last years of that era. And I can say that in my opinion, despite the political crises, despite the debates over a possible war, very few seriously believed there would be a European war in the material sense.

When war did break out in 1914, literature followed it with difficulty. With the exception of a few plays commissioned or brought into being by in fact quite base and transient ambitions, the literature of the war of 1914–1918 is one that came about after the war. This is a magnificent literature. I know only certain examples of it. In fact various judgments may be made about this literature depending on one's personal point of view. I will tell you only my own impressions.

The books pertaining to this war are again dominated by the concept of armed peoples, and dominated more powerfully than ever before. To be sure, the number of books dealing with individual heroes, whether they be generals, pilots, or submarine commanders, is many. But these types of books were not much in demand. The best-written and most-read books were those dealing with ordinary man, books about any ordinary individual in the trenches. You see his symbol everywhere around you in the monuments raised to memorialize the unknown soldier. So, as in the nineteenth century, the dominant element is the people.

But the mentality has changed. More than heroism and great ideals, it is the sufferings of war, the trenches, the mud, the hunger, that are spoken of. And what is it all for? To live and work in freedom, bring up children and for them, assuming people behave rationally, prepare a future in line with the possibilities afforded by our civilization—that is what is desired. Does not the man on the other side calibrating his machine gun to kill me want more or less the same things? Are not his thoughts like mine? Do we have to kill one another for this? These, I believe, were the ideas dominant in Europe after the war. These were the ideas dominant in the books dealing with the Great War.

We can well understand that all peoples dreaded a new war and many states did not want to consider such an eventuality, did not even prepare for it. But despite this state of mind, the present war did break out and is widening as time goes on; perhaps it will surpass the previous war not only in scope but in the changes it will bring about in people's lives. It is early yet to discuss the literature of this war. But certain observations may be made on the role the people will play. I would like to finish my lecture with these observations.

War is now more than ever the business of the entire nation. All individuals must be organized for readiness and conduct of war. In industry, agriculture, aviation, transport, everyone, women and children as well, must actively or inactively accustom themselves to conditions made compulsory by war, conditions far from those of their everyday lives. Although the number of the rank and file in combat in the present situation is not very large, none in the countries taking part in the struggle can live as they normally do.

Victory depends upon the ability of states to organize, and more importantly, upon the people's state of mind. I can even say that the first factor, organization, depends to a great degree upon the people's state of mind. We have seen that a nation determined to defend itself at all costs cannot be easily defeated even if its population is small and its circumstances dire. War cannot be conducted without the help of the whole nation. And if the people are brave and keep a cool head, it cannot be lost.

A second observation: Every war now has the capacity to become a world war. An unresolved issue in a corner of Europe affects the entire world—the Mediterranean, Africa, the Far East, America. In the world as it is at present, everything is connected. There is nothing so difficult as to limit a conflict. While this is an extraordinarily terrifying thing, it also offers hope. The world is a whole which the mind of man has begun to grasp at a glance. World war puts forth the world problem, and because technical development dominates the world in a way we could not even have conceived of thirty years ago, a solution must be found through peaceful as well as military means. Once something has become such an essential and quotidian problem, its solution is not far off. I will not say that this war will be the last war, but as long as human beings do not seek out enemies on other planets, it will be one of the last wars they will see on earth.

All peoples love peace, but every people that comprehends its own being knows how to fight when its independence is at stake.

Erich Auerbach
1941–1942

Chaire de philologie Romane à la Faculté

des lettres.

Entre Monsieur le Professeur Cemil Bilsel, Recteur de l'Université d'Istanbul, agissant au nom du Ministère de l'Instruction
Publique d'une part et Monsieur Auerbach, d'autre part il a été
conclu le contrat suivant:

1 - Monsieur Auerbach est nommé par le Ministère de l'Instruction
Publique Professeur de la philologie Romane à Faculté des Lettres.
Il assumera, outre les cours de sa chaire, la Direction de
l'Ecole des langues dependant de la dite Faculté de l'Université
d'Istanbul. *Tant que les chaires de philologie anglaise et allemande seront vacantes* *Il assumera se charge de la surveillance des études de lettres*
Monsieur Auerbach s'engage à consacrer toutes ses forces au tra-
vail d'enseignement et de recherches qui lui est confié, à donner
lui-même tous les cours nécessaires pour sa branche à procéder
lui-même et à fond à tous les examens relevant de sa chaire.

2 - Il s'engage à fournir un sertificat médical singné de 3 Professeur constatant qu'il n'est sujet à aucune maladie qui l'em-
pêcherait de remplir régulièrement ses fonctions de professeur
et de directeur.

3 - La durée du présent contrat est de cinq ans. Il commence le
15.10.1936 pour expirer le 15.10.1941.

4 - Jusqu'à la fin de la troisième année, l'enseignement peut être
fait dans une langue étrangère (français, allemand, anglais)
Monsieur Auerbach s'engage à faire tout son possible pour enseig-
ner en langue Turque après la troisième année. *apprendre* *la* *dans les délais de 3 ans*

5 - Monsieur Auerbach s'engage, avant la fin de la troisième année
de son contrat, à préparer un manuel exposant tous les aspects
principaux de la philologie romane. Une édition en turc de ce
manuel sera faite avec sa collaboration. *introduisant les philolog* *turcs de à l'étude des aspects principaux de la philologie* *pour*

6 - Monsieur Auerbache, outre ses cours aux étudiants, s'engage à
donner régulièrement et gratuitement des cours de perfectionne-
ment destinés aux professeurs de lycée.

Erich Auerbach's contract with Istanbul University, 1936. By permission of the Literary
Archive Marbach.

La forme et la matière de ces cours sont fixées d'accord avec
le doyen de la Faculté.

7 - Il s'engage à collaborer aux cours d'extention Univairsitaire
destinés au grand public et éventuellement, à y faire participer
les Docents de son service, et les assistantes.

8 - Il s'engage à prendre une part active au développement des orga-
nisations de culture en relation avec son enseignement.

9 - Les frais des voyages de service sont remboursés selon les régle-
ments en viguer pour les fonctionnaires supérieurs de l'Etat.

10 - Le contrat présent ne peut être résilié que d'un commun accord
entres les parties.

11 - Les Parties s'engagent à notifier l'une à l'autre 5 mois avans
l'échéance du contrat, qu'elles n'entendent pas prolonger ce der-
nier. Faute de quoi le contrat est considéré comme renouvelé pour
une année.

12 - Monsieur Auerbach s'engage à s'abstenir de toute activité politique économique et *commerciale* ainsi que toute activité ayant pour but de
faire la propagande d'un gouvernement étranger il ne peut accepter aucune fonction dans des institutions ou établissements étrangers .

13 - Le traitement mansuel de Monsieur Auerbach est de 450 livres
turques nettes, après défalcation de toutes retenues et de tous
impôts sur les traitements, sauf, cependant l'impôt dit d'aérop-
lane qui est de 2 %. Ce traitement subsiste dans tous les cas,
même si une élévation générale des impôts d'Etat sur les traitements ou toute autre restriction de traitement se produisaient.
Au cas où le contrat serait renouvelé pour une nouvelle période
le traitement mensuel de Monsieur le Professeur Auerbach sera
porté à 500 livres turques. Le Payement est mensuel, il sera ver-
sé d'avance.

14 - La chaire de Professeur est liée à la direction complète de son
institut. Les deux fonctions de professeur et de directeur sont
inséparables.

15 - En cas d'empêchement, le professeur a le droit de choisir, et
réserve de l'aprobation du Recteur, ses suppléants ou ses rempla-
çants tant pour les cours que pour les examens.

16 - En cas de maladie, le traitement est payé sans intérruption pendant
6 mois. si la maladie dure plus longtems; le Ministre de l'Instruction Publique peut résilier le contrat.
En cas de décès,-suicide exclus- la veuve ou, à son défaut, les
enfants mineurs, touchent le traitement de 6 mois .

17 - Une indemnité forfaitaire de 1000 livres turques sera versée à
Monsieur Auerbach pour couvrir les frais de déménagements, de son
déplacement et de sa famille. La même disposition sera appliquée si,
à l'expiration de 5 années Monsieur Auerbach quitte la Turqie.

18 - Le tribunal d'Ankara sera comptétent pour tous les litiges qui
surgiraient entre le Ministre et Monsieur Auerbach.

19 - Ce contrat est fait et signé en double exemplaire à Istanbul.

Notes

Introduction

1. The route continued to be significant insofar as it was vital to Ottoman-European trade until the Ottoman surrender to European powers in 1918. For a study dealing with the history of Genoese in Constantinople, see Kate Fleet, *European and Islamic Trade in the Early Ottoman State: The Merchants of Genoa and Turkey* (Cambridge: Cambridge University Press, 1999); Louis Mitler, "Genoese in Galata, 1453–1682," *International Journal of Middle East Studies* 10, no. 1 (1979): 71–91.

2. Louis Mitler gives a brief overview over the history of the church San Pietro e Paolo in "Genoese in Galata, 1453–1682," 88–89.

3. The original letter to Auerbach dated October 16, 1935, is held in the Literary Archive in Marbach.

4. Notwithstanding Turkey's ongoing denial of this crime, the international community now recognizes the mistreatment of the Armenians as an act of genocide. The transnational scholar Taner Akçam, for example, claims that the death of Armenians during World War I constitutes genocide. Taner Akçam, *A Shameful Act: The Armenian Genocide and the Question of Turkish Responsibility* (New York: Metropolitan Books, 2006).

5. In his biography, Ernst Hirsch writes about the difficulties this caused for many German émigrés. Ernst E. Hirsch, *Aus des Kaisers Zeiten durch die Weimarer Republik in das Land Atatürks: Eine unzeitgemäße Autobiographie* (München: Schweitzer, 1982), 197–206.

6. Deniz Kandiyoti and Keith Watenpaugh, for example, resist the argument that the modernization reforms were merely a response to the decline of the Ottoman Empire. Watenpaugh shows the pitfalls of following the lines of a linear narrative of modernization: Keith David Watenpaugh, *Being Modern in the Middle East: Revolution, Nationalism, Colonialism, and the Arab Middle Class* (Princeton, NJ: Princeton University Press,

2006), 7. For a comprehensive study of the Westernization reforms during the Ottoman Empire's decline, see Fatma Müge Göçek, *Rise of the Bourgeoisie, Demise of Empire: Ottoman Westernization and Social Change* (New York: Oxford University Press, 1996); Fatma Müge Göçek, "The Decline of the Ottoman Empire and the Emergence of Greek, Armenian, Turkish, and Arab Nationalisms," in *Social Constructions of Nationalism in the Middle East*, ed. Fatma Müge Göçek (Albany: State University of New York Press, 2002), 15–84.

7. Virginia H. Aksan and Daniel Goffman, *The Early Modern Ottomans: Remapping the Empire* (Cambridge: Cambridge University Press, 2007), 225.

8. For a definition of the terms *modernization* and *Westernization*, see Göçek, *Rise of the Bourgeoisie*, 6–7. For a discussion of the dress codes and clothing reforms, see my article "Ethnomasquerade in Ottoman-European Encounters: Re-enacting Lady Mary Wortley Montagu," *Criticism* 46, no. 3 (2004): 393–414.

9. Trevor Mostyn, *Egypt's Belle Epoque: Cairo and the Age of the Hedonists* (London: Tauris Parke, 2006), 44.

10. Long before the emergence of postcolonial studies, historian Ulrich Trumpener researched the German-Ottoman policies during World War I and came to the conclusion that the alliance treaty of August 1914 between the Germans and the Ottoman Empire was not, as some had claimed, the beginning of "complete" or "almost complete" German domination of the Ottoman Empire. Rather, the alliance was "an arrangement between equals, notwithstanding the enormous disparity between the two countries in terms of military, economic, and financial power." The Germans, Trumpener argues, could neither convert their alliance with the Ottomans into a "rider-horse" relationship nor convert it into a "satellite of the Reich." Instead, Trumpener shows that the Ottoman Empire hoped to regain its status as a fully sovereign power during the war and reconquer some of its previously lost provinces. Ottoman leaders even hoped to acquire new territories in the Caucasus and Russian Central Asia. Ulrich Trumpener, *Germany and the Ottoman Empire, 1914–1918* (Princeton, NJ: Princeton University Press, 1968), 21, 370. For articles on the nature of Ottoman imperialism, see Ussama Makdisi, "Ottoman Orientalism," *American Historical Review* 107, no. 3 (2002): 768–796; Selim Deringil, "'They Live in a State of Nomadism and Savagery': The Late Ottoman Empire and the Post-Colonial Debate," *Society for Comparative Study of Society and History* 45, no. 2 (2003): 311–342.

11. For a comprehensive article on the process of secularization, see Fuat Keyman, "Modernity, Secularism, and Islam," *Theory, Culture & Society* 24, no. 2 (2007): 215–234.

12. For an article on the emergence of the "New Turkish Woman" as a result of the transition from the Ottoman Empire to the Turkish Republic, see Deniz Kandiyoti, "End of Empire: Islam, Nationalism and Women in Turkey," in *Feminist Postcolonial Theory: A Reader*, ed. Reina Lewis and Sara Mills (New York: Routledge, 2003), 263–284.

13. Saliha Paker summarizes the translation practices and institutions in Ottoman and Turkish times in "Turkish Tradition," in *Routledge Encyclopedia of Translation Studies*, ed. Mona Baker and Kirsten Malmkjær (London: Routledge, 1998), 571–582.

14. Suraiya Faroqhi, *The Later Ottoman Empire, 1603–1839*, vol. 3 of *The Cambridge History of Turkey* (Cambridge: Cambridge University Press, 2006), 61. Faroqhi writes that the translation chamber was established in 1822. Saliha Paker, on the other hand, points out that the first kind of these translation offices was established in 1833. Paker, "Turkish Tradition," 577.

15. Hasan Ali Yücel, "Önsöz," *Tercüme* 1, no. 1–2 (1940): 1.

16. Bryan Turner also argues that the Turkish reforms were "consciously mimetic in that it took Europe as its specific model of adaptation." Bryan S. Turner, *Weber and Islam* (London: Routledge, 1998), 168. For other scholarly work on cultural mimesis, see Michael Taussig, *Mimesis and Alterity: A Particular History of the Senses* (New York: Routledge, 1993); Barbara Fuchs, *Mimesis and Empire: The New World, Islam, and European Identities* (Cambridge: Cambridge University Press, 2001).

17. Richard Maxwell, Joshua Scodel, and Katie Trumpener, "Editors' Preface," *Modern Philology* 100, no. 4 (2003): 510.

18. Erich Auerbach, *Mimesis: The Representation of Reality in Western Literature*, trans. Willard R. Trask (Princeton, NJ: Princeton University Press, 2003), 443.

19. Leo Spitzer, "The Addresses to the Reader in the *Commedia*," *Italica* 32, no. 3 (1955): 144.

20. Ahmet Hamdi Tanpınar, *Yahya Kemal* (Istanbul: Dergah Yayınları, 1982).

21. In 1932 Yakup Kadri and other writers launched the state-sponsored journal *Kadro* that "propagated realism and the treatment of social issues in literature." Şehnaz Tahir Gürçağlar, *The Politics and Poetics of Translation in Turkey, 1923–1960* (Amsterdam: Rodopi, 2008), 146. The Orientalist Otto Spies also reflected upon the realist and nationalist trend in Turkish literature: Otto Spies, *Die türkische Prosaliteratur der Gegenwart* (Leipzig: Otto Harrasowitz, 1943), 2.

22. Makdisi, "Ottoman Orientalism," 783.

23. Cited in Suzanne L. Marchand, *Down from Olympus: Archaeology and Philhellenism in Germany, 1750–1970* (Princeton, NJ: Princeton University Press, 1996), 192. For a discussion of the German involvement in the archeological projects in the Ottoman Empire, see chapter 6 in Marchand's *Down from Olympus*.

24. Makdisi, "Ottoman Orientalism," 783.

25. Emily Apter, "Global *Translatio*: The 'Invention' of Comparative Literature, Istanbul, 1933," *Critical Inquiry* 29, no. 2 (2003): 261. See also Jane Newman, "Nicht am 'falschen Ort': Saids Auerbach und die 'neue' Komparatistik," in *Erich Auerbach: Geschichte und Aktualität eines europäischen Philologen*, ed. Karlheinz Barck and Martin Treml (Berlin: Kulturverlag Kadmos, 2007), 341–356; Seth Lerer, *Error and the Academic Self: The Scholarly Imagination, Medieval to Modern* (New York: Columbia University Press, 2002), 4, 241; Deringil, "'They Live in a State of Nomadism and Savagery,'" 314.

26. Gerd Gemünden and Anton Kaes, "Introduction to Special Issue on Film and Exile," *New German Critique* 89 (2003): 3–8. Kaplan discusses Auerbach and Said in her section on "Traveling Theorists": Caren Kaplan, *Questions of Travel: Postmodern Discourses of Displacement* (Durham, NC: Duke University Press, 1996). Bammer edited a collection

of articles on the relationship between displacement and cultural identity: Angelika Bammer, ed., *Displacements: Cultural Identities in Question* (Bloomington: Indiana University Press, 1994). See also Alexander Stephan, ed., *Exile and Otherness: New Approaches to the Experience of Nazi Refugees* (Oxford: Peter Lang, 2005). With regard to *diaspora*, Braziel and Mannur also argue that the term must be historically grounded: Jana Evans Braziel and Anita Mannur, eds., *Theorizing Diaspora: A Reader* (Cornwall, UK: Blackwell Publishing, 2003). I agree with Sophia A. McClennen, who criticizes that in many scholarly works, the term *exile* is "empty of history and an association with materiality." Sophia A. McClennen, *The Dialectics of Exile: Nation, Time, Language, and Space in Hispanic Literatures* (West Lafayette, IN: Purdue University Press, 2004), 1.

27. See, for example, Emily Apter, *Translation Zone: A New Comparative Literature* (Princeton, NJ: Princeton University Press, 2006); William V. Spanos, "Humanism and the Studia Humanitatis after 9/11/01: Rethinking the Anthropologos," *symploke* 7, no. 1–2 (2005): 219–262; Debjani Ganguly, "Edward Said, World Literature, and Global Comparatism," in *Edward Said: The Legacy of a Public Intellectual*, ed. Ned Curthoys and Debjani Ganguly (Melbourne: Melbourne University Press, 2007), 176–202; Djelal Kadir, "Comparative Literature in a World Become Tlön," *Comparative Critical Studies* 3, no. 1–2 (2006): 125–138; Aamir R. Mufti, "Critical Secularism: A Reintroduction for Perilous Times," *Boundary 2* 31, no. 2 (2004): 1–9.

28. Abdul R. JanMohamed, "Worldliness-without-World, Homelessness-as-Home: Toward a Definition of the Specular Border Intellectual," in *Edward Said: A Critical Reader*, ed. Michael Sprinker (Oxford: Blackwell, 1992), 98–99.

29. Azade Seyhan, "German Academic Exiles in Istanbul: Translation as the Bildung of the Other," in *Nation, Language and the Ethics of Translation*, ed. Sandra L. Bermann and Michael Wood (Princeton, NJ: Princeton University Press, 2005), 285.

30. Edward W. Said, *The World, the Text, and the Critic* (London: Vintage, 1991), 6.

31. For a discussion of Said's ahistoricism, see Maria Todorova, who also argues that the "Saidian fallacy is rooted in the tension between his attraction to Erich Auerbach (as a thinker and existential role model of the intellectual exile) and Said's simultaneous, and incompatible, attraction to Foucault." Maria Todorova, *Imagining the Balkans* (New York: Oxford University Press, 1997), 9. For Nina Berman's critique of Said's approach, see Nina Berman, "Ottoman Shock-and-Awe and the Rise of Protestantism: Luther's Reactions to the Ottoman Invasions of the Early Sixteenth Century," *Seminar* 41, no. 3 (2005): 226–245.

32. Said writes that Auerbach could turn the executive value of exile into effective use. Said, *The World, the Text, and the Critic*, 8.

33. Erich Auerbach, "Epilegomena zu Mimesis," *Romanische Forschungen* 65, no. 1/2 (1953): 18. For the English translation, see Auerbach, *Mimesis*, 574.

34. Said, *The World, the Text, and the Critic*, 8. For a critique of Said's take on Auerbach, see also Newman, "Nicht am 'falschen Ort,'" 341–356.

35. JanMohamed, "Worldliness-without-World," 96–120.

36. Aamir R. Mufti, "Auerbach in Istanbul: Edward Said, Secular Criticism, and the Question of Minority Culture," in *Edward Said and the Work of the Critic: Speak-*

ing Truth to Power, ed. Paul A. Bové (Durham, NC: Duke University Press, 2000), 229–256.

37. Erich Auerbach, Letter to Johannes Oeschger, May 27, 1938, Nachlass Fritz Lieb, Universitätsbibliothek Basel (Handschriftenabteilung), NL 43 (Lieb) Ah 2,1. I thank Martin Vialon for sharing this letter with me before he published it with his commentary in Martin Vialon, "Wie das Brot der Fremde so salzig schmeckt: Hellsichtiges über die Widersprüche der Türkei: Erich Auerbachs Istanbuler Humanismusbrief," *Süddeutsche Zeitung*, October 14, 2008, 16. The letter will also be published in Martin Vialon, "Erich Auerbach: Gesammelte Briefe 1922–1957" (forthcoming).

38. Emily Apter makes a compelling argument about Auerbach's *Literary Language and Its Public*. She writes that it is a "matter of speculation as to whether or not the standardization of modern Turkish directly inspired" this work, but "it seems safe to assume that Turkey's self-colonizing policy of *translatio imperii* afforded compelling parallels to imperial Rome." Apter, "Global *Translatio*," 268.

39. Scott Spector's study of Kafka in Prague served as a model for studying the cultural history of Istanbul and the rhetorical figures that appear in the diverse material that I dealt with. For the outline of his method, see Scott Spector, *Prague Territories: National Conflict and Cultural Innovation in Franz Kafka's Fin de Siècle* (Berkeley: University of California Press, 2002), 25–35.

40. Erich Auerbach, *Neue Dantestudien: Sacrae scripturae sermo humilis; Figura; Franz von Assisi in der Komödie. Dante Hakkında Yeni Araştırmalar*, ed. Robert Anhegger, Walter Ruben, and Andreas Tietze, Istanbuler Schriften—Istanbul Yazıları (Istanbul: İbrahim Horoz Basımevi, 1944), 47. Hayden White illuminates Auerbach's notion of figural causation and modernist historicism in *Figural Realism: Studies in Mimesis Effect* (Baltimore: Johns Hopkins University Press, 1999), 87–100.

41. It is Said who is concerned with the question of how Auerbach's exile became "converted from a challenge or a risk, or even from an active impingement on his European selfhood, into a positive mission, whose success would be a cultural act of great importance." Said, *The World, the Text, and the Critic*, 7.

Chapter 1

1. Karlheinz Barck, "Erich Auerbach in Berlin: Spurensicherung und ein Porträt," in *Erich Auerbach: Geschichte und Aktualität eines europäischen Philologen*, ed. Karlheinz Barck and Martin Treml (Berlin: Kadmos, 2007), 201. Barck cites the historical information about Charlottenburg in Berthold Grzywatz, *Die historische Stadt: Charlottenburg*, vol. 1 (Berlin: Nicolai, 1987), 414. According to Grzywatz, the number of Charlottenburg's Jewish residents increased between 1895 and 1910 from 4,678 to 22,580.

2. Gert Mattenklott suggests that, because the options for Jews interested in pursuing a university career were restricted, Auerbach might have decided to study law. Gert Mattenklott, "Erich Auerbach in den deutsch-jüdischen Verhältnissen," in *Wahrnehmen Lesen Deuten: Erich Auerbachs Lektüre der Moderne*, ed. Walter Busch, Gerhart Pickerodt, and Markus Bauer (Frankfurt am Main: Vittorio Klostermann, 1998), 16.

3. Auerbach volunteered in December 1914 and fought as a soldier until April 1918. He first joined the "2. Ulanenregiment" and subsequently the "Infanterieregiment 466." See his Marburg curriculum vitae in Barck, "Erich Auerbach in Berlin," 199. Auerbach, as he notes in a letter to Martin Hellweg in 1939, fought in northern France during the war. Martin Elsky, Martin Vialon, and Robert Stein, "Scholarship in Times of Extremes: Letters of Erich Auerbach (1933–46), on the Fiftieth Anniversary of His Death," *Publications of the Modern Language Association of America* 122, no. 3 (2007): 755.

4. Bauer notes that Auerbach was injured in the foot. Markus Bauer, "Die Wirklichkeit und ihre literarische Darstellung: Form und Geschichte—der Essayist Erich Auerbach beschäftigt weiterhin seine Exegeten," *Neue Zürcher Zeitung*, February 2, 2008, http://www.nzz.ch/nachrichten/kultur/literatur_und_kunst/die_wirklichkeit_und_ihre_ literarische_darstellung_1.663957.html (accessed May 15, 2008).

5. David Damrosch, "Auerbach in Exile," *Comparative Literature* 47, no. 2 (1995): 97–115; Vassilis Lambropoulos, *The Rise of Eurocentrism: Anatomy of Interpretation* (Princeton, NJ: Princeton University Press, 1993); Seth Lerer, *Error and the Academic Self: The Scholarly Imagination, Medieval to Modern* (New York: Columbia University Press, 2002); James I. Porter, "Auerbach and the Scar of Philology," in *Classics and National Culture*, ed. Susan Stephens and Phiroze Vasunia (Oxford: Oxford University Press, forthcoming); Djelal Kadir, *Memos from the Besieged City: Lifelines for Cultural Sustainability* (Stanford, CA: Stanford University Press, 2011). My thanks to Djelal Kadir for sharing the chapter titled "Auerbach's Scar" from his manuscript.

6. Erich Auerbach, *Literary Language and Its Public in Late Latin Antiquity and in the Middle Ages*, trans. Ralph Manheim (New York: Pantheon Books, 1965), 5.

7. Mattenklott, "Erich Auerbach," 24.

8. Auerbach, *Literary Language and Its Public*, 5.

9. Compare Auerbach's 1924 preface and 1949 article: Giambattista Vico, *Die neue Wissenschaft über die gemeinschaftliche Natur der Völker*, trans. Erich Auerbach, 2nd ed. (Berlin: Walter de Gruyter, 2000), 31; Erich Auerbach, "Vico and Aesthetic Historism," *Journal of Aesthetics and Art Criticism* 8, no. 2 (1949): 116. Auerbach's German translation is based on Vico's last edition of *Scienza Nuova* in 1744. Auerbach saw in Vico a precursor of Herder, Rousseau, and the early Romantics. See his introduction, "Purpose and Method," in Auerbach, *Literary Language and Its Public*, 13–14. For a discussion of the relationship between Auerbach and Vico, see, for example, Luiz Costa Lima, "Erich Auerbach: History and Metahistory," *New Literary History* 19, no. 3 (1988): 467–499; Timothy Bahti, "Vico, Auerbach, and Literary History," *Philological Quarterly* 60, no. 2 (1981): 235–255.

10. "Der leidige Katholizismus [liess Vico] den modernen Begriff des Fortschritts nicht finden." Auerbach's preface to Vico, *Die neue Wissenschaft*, 39. In his epilogue to the reprint of Vico in German translation, Wilhelm Schmidt-Biggemann suggests that Auerbach's selection from *Scienza Nuova* pinpoints the eighteenth-century scholar specifically as the founder of the modern, secular philosophy of history: Vico, *Die neue Wissenschaft*, 455.

11. The first German translation of *Scienza Nuova* by Wilhelm Ernst Weber appeared in 1822. For an introduction to Vico's philosophy of history, see Anne Eusterschulte, "Kulturentwicklung und -verfall: Giambattista Vicos kulturgeschichtliche Anthropologie," in *Humanismus in Geschichte und Gegenwart*, ed. Richard Faber and Enno Rudolph (Tübingen: Mohr Siebeck, 2002), 17–44.

12. Auerbach, "Vico and Aesthetic Historism," 117–118.

13. Vico's view was formative for R. G. Collingwood's (1889–1943) and Benedetto Croce's (1866–1952) philosophy of history. Ned Curthoys discusses the influence of Vico and Auerbach on Edward Said in "Edward Said's Unhoused Philological Humanism," in *Edward Said: The Legacy of a Public Intellectual*, ed. Ned Curthoys and Debjani Ganguly (Melbourne: Melbourne University Press, 2007), 152–175.

14. Auerbach claims in his introduction titled "Purpose and Method" that his purpose was always to write history: Auerbach, *Literary Language and Its Public*, 20.

15. The letter is dated March 5, 1924. Quoted in Barck, "Erich Auerbach in Berlin," 208.

16. For an article on the relationship between Auerbach and Benjamin, see Robert Kahn, "Eine 'List der Vorsehung': Erich Auerbach und Walter Benjamin," in *Erich Auerbach: Geschichte und Aktualität eines europäischen Philologen*, ed. Martin Treml and Karlheinz Barck (Berlin: Kulturverlag Kadmos, 2007), 153–166. For a discussion of the topographical and intellectual intersections between Auerbach and Benjamin, see also Barck, "Erich Auerbach in Berlin," 195–214.

17. Carlo Ginzburg, "Auerbach und Dante: Eine Verlaufsbahn," in *Erich Auerbach: Geschichte und Aktualität eines Philologen*, ed. Karlheinz Barck and Martin Treml (Berlin: Kadmos, 2007), 33; Barck, "Erich Auerbach in Berlin," 210.

18. Robert Kahn discusses the early reception of Proust by Ernst Robert Curtius, Erich Auerbach, and Walter Benjamin in Kahn, "Eine 'List der Vorsehung,'" 154–155.

19. "Image of Proust" appeared in English in Walter Benjamin, *Illuminations: Essays and Reflections*, ed. Hannah Arendt (New York: Schocken Books, 1969), 201–215.

20. The article, titled "Marcel Proust: Der Roman von der verlorenen Zeit," reappeared in Erich Auerbach, *Gesammelte Aufsätze zur Romanischen Philologie* (Bern: Francke Verlag, 1967), 296–300. For a discussion of this passage, see Kahn, "Eine 'List der Vorsehung,'" 156.

21. "*Die Suche nach der verlorenen Zeit* ist eine Chronik aus der Erinnerung—in der an Stelle der empirischen Zeitenfolge die geheime und oft vernachlässigte Verknüpfung der Ereignisse tritt, die der rückwärts blickende und in sich selbst blickende Biograph der Seele als die eigentliche empfindet." Auerbach, *Gesammelte Aufsätze zur Romanischen Philologie*, 300.

22. See Auerbach's preface in Vico, *Die neue Wissenschaft*, 14.

23. ". . . unabhängig von der Atmosphäre seiner Zeit und seiner Umgebung." See Auerbach's preface in ibid., 16. "Ist es überhaupt vorzustellen, daß ein Mensch völlig vereinzelt und außerhalb seiner Zeit lebt? Letzten Endes natürlich nicht." Vico, *Die neue Wissenschaft*, 18.

24. Erich Auerbach, *Dante: Poet of the Secular World* (Chicago: University of Chicago Press, 1961), 83, 175.

25. "... seine innere Leidenschaft zur Wahrheit und seine fanatische Versunkenheit waren so stark, daß er wie im Traum durch das irdische Leben ging." See Auerbach's preface in Vico, *Die neue Wissenschaft*, 15.

26. "... läuft der ungeheure Roman zwischen seinen wenigen Motiven und Ereignissen wie in einem Käfig, ohne die Welt, die dicht daran vorbeiströmt, zu sehen und ohne ihren Lärm zu hören." Auerbach, *Gesammelte Aufsätze zur Romanischen Philologie*, 297. Compare also Kahn, "Eine 'List der Vorsehung,'" 156.

27. "In eine neue Welt, deren Fremdheit so durchtränkt ist von der Erinnerung des Wirklichen, daß sie als die eigentliche, das Leben aber als ein Fragment und als Traum erscheint, bannt Dante seine Hörer, und in dieser Einheit aus Wirklichkeit und Entrückung liegen die Wurzeln seiner psychagogischen Macht." Erich Auerbach, *Dante als Dichter der irdischen Welt*, 2nd ed. (Berlin: Walter de Gruyter, 2001), 211–212. Compare Manheim's misleading translation of this passage in Auerbach, *Dante: Poet of the Secular World*, 173.

28. Benjamin nonetheless published his thesis as Walter Benjamin, *Zum Ursprung des deutschen Trauerspiels* (Berlin: Ernst Rowohlt, 1928). Auerbach also dealt with the question of realism and the bourgeois drama in the *Mimesis* chapter titled "Miller the Musician."

29. An anthology investigates the fate of persecuted Romance scholars in Germany and Austria: Hans Helmut Christmann and Frank-Rutger Hausmann, eds., *Deutsche und Österreichische Romanisten als Verfolgte des Nationalsozialismus* (Tübingen: Stauffenburg Verlag, 1989). For biographical essays on a number of Romance scholars, including Auerbach, see Hans Ulrich Gumbrecht, *Vom Leben und Sterben der großen Romanisten: Carl Vossler, Ernst Robert Curtius, Leo Spitzer, Erich Auerbach, Werner Krauss*, ed. Michael Krüger (München: Carl Hanser Verlag, 2002).

30. For studies of German emigration to the United States, see Werner Berthold, Brita Eckert, and Frank Wende, *Deutsche Intellektuelle im Exil: Ihre Akademie und die "American Guild for German Cultural Freedom"* (München: Saur, 1993); Martin Jay, *Permanent Exiles: Essays on the Intellectual Migration from Germany to America* (New York: Columbia University Press, 1985); Helge Pross, *Die Deutsche Akademische Emigration nach den Vereinigten Staaten 1933–1941* (Berlin: Dunckner & Humboldt, 1955); Laura Fermi, *Illustrious Immigrants: The Intellectual Migration from Europe, 1930–1941* (Chicago: University of Chicago Press, 1968). The emigration of certain disciplines consitutes the focus in Herbert A. Strauss, Klaus Fischer, Christhard Hoffmann, and Alfons Söllner, *Die Emigration der Wissenschaften nach 1933: Disziplingeschichtliche Studien* (München: Saur, 1991). Exile in Turkey is the subject of Jan Cremer and Horst Przytulla, *Exil Türkei: Deutschsprachige Emigranten in der Türkei 1933–1945* (München: Verlag Karl M. Lipp, 1991); Horst Widmann, *Exil und Bildungshilfe: Die deutschsprachige akademische Emigration in die Türkei nach 1933* (Bern: Herbert Lang, 1973). For a study of German exile in Los Angeles focusing on Thomas Mann, Bertolt Brecht, Theodor W. Adorno, Arnold Schönberg, and others, see Ehrhardt

Bahr, *Weimar on the Pacific: German Exile Culture in Los Angeles and the Crisis of Modernism* (Berkeley: University of California Press, 2007).

31. "Ich bin Preuße, jüdischer Konfession und wohne in Berlin-Charlottenburg," wrote Auerbach in his curriculum vitae that he sent to the University Greifswald in 1921. Cited in Martin Treml, "Auerbachs imaginäre jüdische Orte," in *Erich Auerbach: Geschichte und Aktualität eines europäischen Philologen*, ed. Karlheinz Barck and Martin Treml (Berlin: Kulturverlag Kadmos, 2007), 235. His dissertation on early renaissance novellas in Italy and France was published as Erich Auerbach, *Zur Technik der Frührenaissancenovelle in Italien und Frankreich* (Heidelberg: C. Winter, 1921).

32. Mattenklott, "Erich Auerbach," 15–30; James I. Porter, "Auerbach and the Judaizing of Philology," *Critical Inquiry* 35 (2008): 115–147; Treml, "Auerbachs imaginäre jüdische Orte," 230–251.

33. Erich Auerbach in a letter to Erich Rothacker, professor of philosophy, sociology, and psychology at the University of Bonn, January 29, 1933. Elsky, Vialon, and Stein, "Scholarship in Times of Extremes," 745.

34. The correspondence between Auerbach and Krauss was first published in Karlheinz Barck, "Eine unveröffentlichte Korrespondenz: Erich Auerbach/Werner Krauss," *Beiträge zur Romanischen Philologie* 26, no. 2 (1987): 301–326; Karlheinz Barck, "Eine unveröffentlichte Korrespondenz (Fortsetzung): Erich Auerbach/Werner Krauss," *Beiträge zur Romanischen Philologie* 27, no. 1 (1988): 161–186.

35. "Er hat in den Tagen des Anfangs der Judenhetze sich so von diesem Leid zu distanzieren, ja sogar persönlich zu jubilieren gewußt—empörte, aber zuverlässige Berichte haben es mir mitgeteilt—, daß ich, nun er einsehen gelernt hat daß er mit uns allen anderen auf einer Galeere sitzt, schwerlich zu ihm finden kann: wer in entscheidenden Augenblicken nicht weiß wo er zu stehen hat, darf sich nicht wundern wenn er weiter als Fremdling behandelt wird. Sie wissen daß ich kein 'überzeugter Jude' bin, ja daß ich das Beste dem christlichen Einfluß verdanke—aber es gibt doch so etwas wie ein 'atavistisches Solidaritätsgefühl' in der Not." Leo Spitzer, "Letter to Karl Löwith on 21 April 1933" (Literaturarchiv Marbach, A: Löwith 99.17.113/1).

36. Karl Löwith, *Mein Leben in Deutschland vor und nach 1933: Ein Bericht* (Stuttgart: Metzler, 1986), 107. Also see Spitzer's letters to Karl Jaspers in which he discusses Löwith's prospects for a position in Istanbul: Leo Spitzer, "Letter to Karl Jaspers, 5 December 1935" (Literaturarchiv Marbach, A: Jaspers 75.14541).

37. Letter to Karl Vossler from Siena on September 15, 1935. Published by Elsky, Vialon, and Stein, "Scholarship in Times of Extremes," 747.

38. Klemperer tried to make himself attractive to potential employers by saying that in addition to Romance literatures he could also teach German and comparative literature. May 2, 1935, Victor Klemperer, *Ich will Zeugnis ablegen bis zum letzten*, vol. 1: *Tagebücher 1933–1941*, ed. Walter Nowojski (Berlin: Aufbau-Verlag, 1996), 196.

39. May 15, 1935, ibid., 201.

40. On August 12, 1935, Klemperer wrote: "'Es liegt zwar am äußeren Rande—man sieht nach Asien hinüber—, aber es liegt doch in Europa,' hat mir Dember gesagt, als er

mir vor zwei Jahren von seiner Berufung an die Universität Istanbul berichtete." Victor Klemperer, *LTI: Notizbuch eines Philologen* (Berlin: Aufbau-Verlag, 1947), 168. See Emily Apter's reference to Harry Dember's letter to Klemperer in Emily Apter, "Global *Translatio*: The 'Invention' of Comparative Literature, Istanbul, 1933," *Critical Inquiry* 29, no. 2 (2003): 266.

41. Klemperer, *Ich will Zeugnis ablegen*, 168.

42. Klemperer, *LTI*, 169.

43. Ibid.

44. July 8, 1936: "ein langer Brief von Blumenfelds in Lima: ich beneide sie, und sie fühlen sich im Exil." Klemperer, *Ich will Zeugnis ablegen*, 280.

45. "Wie kann man Sehnsucht haben nach einem Europa, das keines mehr ist?" Klemperer, *LTI*, 169.

46. July 21, 1935, Klemperer, *Ich will Zeugnis ablegen*, 211.

47. In a biographical essay, Gumbrecht discusses Curtius's ambivalent position during the Nazi regime: Gumbrecht, *Vom Leben und Sterben*, 49–70. See also Walter Boehlich, "Ein Haus, in dem wir atmen können: Das Neueste zum Dauerstreit um den Romanisten Ernst Robert Curtius," *Die Zeit* 50 (1996): 52. On Curtius, see also a brief passage in Apter, "Global *Translatio*," 260. For a discussion of inner emigration and German literature, see Cathy Gelbin, "Elisabeth Langgässer and the Question of Inner Emigration," in *Flight of Fantasy: New Perspectives on Inner Emigration in German Literature, 1933–1945*, ed. Neil H. Donahue and Doris Kirchner (New York: Berghahn, 2003), 269–276; Stephen Brockmann, "Inner Emigration: The Term and Its Origins in Postwar Debates," in *Flight of Fantasy: New Perspectives on Inner Emigration in German Literature, 1933–1945*, ed. Neil H. Donahue and Doris Kirchner (New York: Berghahn, 2003), 11–26.

48. Letter to Karl Vossler from Siena on September 15, 1935. Elsky, Vialon, and Stein, "Scholarship in Times of Extremes," 747.

49. Robert Kahn suggests that this was Bertolt Brecht's address. Kahn, "Eine 'List der Vorsehung,' " 161.

50. Letter to Walter Benjamin from Rome on October 23, 1935. Elsky, Vialon, and Stein, "Scholarship in Times of Extremes," 747. Originally, the letters by Erich Auerbach to Walter Benjamin were found and published by Karlheinz Barck, "5 Briefe Erich Auerbachs an Walter Benjamin in Paris," *Zeitschrift für Germanistik* 9, no. 6 (1988): 688–694. The first English translation appeared in Karlheinz Barck and Anthony Reynolds, "Walter Benjamin and Erich Auerbach: Fragments of a Correspondence," *Diacritics* 22, no. 3/4 (1992): 81–83.

51. "Regarding your Paris book, I've known it for a long time—at one point it was to be called 'Paris Passages.' That will be a real document, if only there are still people who read documents." Letter to Walter Benjamin from Florence on October 6, 1935. Elsky, Vialon, and Stein, "Scholarship in Times of Extremes," 748.

52. Walter Benjamin, *Berliner Kindheit um neunzehnhundert: Mit einem Nachwort von Theodor W. Adorno* (Frankfurt am Main: Suhrkamp, 1987).

53. Ibid.

54. Auerbach, *Dante: Poet of the Secular World*, 83.

55. Ibid., 76.

56. Ibid., 99. I changed the English translation by Kurt Flasch. See original in Auerbach, *Dante als Dichter der irdischen Welt*, 124.

57. Letter to Karl Vossler dated September 15, 1936. Elsky, Vialon, and Stein, "Scholarship in Times of Extremes," 747.

58. This is suggested by Elsky, Vialon, and Stein in ibid., 759.

59. One of the first two articles Auerbach published in Turkey was a study of mimesis in Flaubert, Stendhal, and Balzac. Erich Auerbach, "Über die ernste Nachahmung des Alltäglichen," *Romanoloji Semineri Dergisi* 1 (1937): 262–294. This article overlaps to some extent with the chapter "In the Hôtel de la Mole" of *Mimesis*.

60. Erich Auerbach, *Neue Dantestudien: Sacrae scripturae sermo humilis; Figura; Franz von Assisi in der Komödie. Dante Hakkında Yeni Araştırmalar*, ed. Robert Anhegger, Walter Ruben, and Andreas Tietze, Istanbuler Schriften—Istanbul Yazıları (Istanbul: İbrahim Horoz Basimevi, 1944), 66.

61. Klemperer obtained this information from an Italian lecturer. July 17, 1936. Klemperer, *Ich will Zeugnis ablegen*, 286.

62. July 16, 1936. Ibid., 281. Under the Nuremberg laws, Klemperer was deemed a Jew. That he had been baptized a Christian was of no interest to the Nazis, who sought to "cleanse" Europe of all Jews. Klemperer was spared deportation from Dresden to a death camp possibly because his wife, Eva, was considered Aryan by the Nazis. Trapped in Nazi Germany, he fought "the hardest battle for my Germanness. . . . I must hold on to this: I am German, the others are un-German," he wrote in his diary. "The spirit is decisive, not blood." Victor Klemperer, *I Will Bear Witness: A Diary of the Nazi Years, 1942–1945* (New York: Random House, 1998), 51.

63. July 17, 1936. Klemperer, *Ich will Zeugnis ablegen*, 286.

64. The French is transcribed as written. The committee argued here in favor of Auerbach because he worked on French and Italian literary history and dealt with the major civilizational impulses. The committee tried to convince university administrators that Auerbach was able to see the "Occidental civilization" from a distanced perspective. The search committee submitted the report to the university administration in May 1936. Istanbul Üniversitesi Arşivi (Istanbul University Archive), Auerbach Dosyası.

65. "19 haziran 1936, Kültür Bakanlığı Onuruna. Profesör Spitzer'in yerine Profesör Auerbach veya Rheinfelder'den birinin seçilmesi meselesinde Berlin Talebe Ispekterimiz Reşat Şemsettin ve Elçimiz Hamdi ile görüştüm. Elçimiz müsavi şartlar altında bile Almanya ile münasebeti kesilmiş bir profesörün alınmasının Üniversite lehine olduğu kanaatindedir. Müsavi olmıyan şartlarda ise üstün yahudinin tercih edilmesine, almanların hiçbir şey diyemiyeceklerini ve demediklerini söylemiştir. Profesör Hellmanda uğradığımız dezillüsion göz önünde tutularak bu işe Yüksek Vekâletlerince çabuk karar verilmesini, saygılarımla dilerim. Üniversite Rektörü." Ibid.

66. Henri Peyre defines Auerbach as an agnostic, too. Henri Peyre, "Erich Auerbach," in *Marburger Gelehrte in der ersten Hälfte des 20. Jahrhunderts*, ed. Ingeborg Schnack (Marburg: Veröffentlichungen der Historischen Kommission für Hessen, 1987), 10–11. In

his discussion of Peyre's text, Martin Treml also speaks of Auerbach's agnosticism and his secular lifestyle: Treml, "Auerbachs imaginäre jüdische Orte," 236.

67. Robert Grudin, "Humanism," *Encyclopædia Britannica Online*, http://search.eb .com.proxy.lib.umich.edu/eb/article-11769 (accessed July 14, 2008).

68. Victor Klemperer, *Der alte und der neue Humanismus* (Berlin: Aufbau-Verlag, 1953), 8.

69. James Harvey Robinson, ed., *Petrarch: The First Modern Scholar and Man of Letters* (New York: Knickerbocker Press, 1898), 308.

70. Grudin, "Humanism."

71. On reenactment as a way of approaching the past, see Vanessa Agnew, "Introduction: What Is Reenactment?" *Criticism* 46, no. 3 (2004): 327–339; Vanessa Agnew, "History's Affective Turn: Historical Reenactment and Its Work in the Present," *Rethinking History* 11, no. 3 (2007): 299–312.

72. Erich Auerbach, *Introduction to Romance Languages and Literature: Latin, French, Spanish, Provençal, Italian*, trans. Guy Daniels from French (New York: Capricorn Books, 1961), 131.

73. Klemperer, *Der alte und der neue Humanismus*, 8.

74. Auerbach, *Introduction to Romance Languages and Literature*, 131f. Nancy Bisaha shows the effect of the fall of Constantinople and the emigration of Byzantine scholars to Italy. See her chapter "Straddling East and West: Byzantium and Greek Refugees," in Nancy Bisaha, *Creating East and West: Renaissance Humanists and the Ottoman Turks* (Philadelphia: University of Pennsylvania Press, 2004), 94–134.

75. Auerbach, *Introduction to Romance Languages and Literature*, 131.

76. *Humanitas* implied not only qualities associated with the modern word *humanity*—understanding, benevolence, compassion, mercy—but also fortitude, judgment, prudence, eloquence, and love of honor. Grudin, "Humanism."

77. Klemperer, *Der alte und der neue Humanismus*, 17.

78. Ibid., 23.

79. There are, of course, other elements that contributed to the decline of humanism. Among these are the effects of scientific and technological progress, archeological discoveries, and fundamental shifts in political and economic structures worldwide.

80. Suzanne Marchand, "Nazism, Orientalism and Humanism," in *Nazi Germany and the Humanities*, ed. Wolfgang Bialas and Anson Rabinbach (Oxford: Oneworld, 2007), 273. Marchand identifies Germandom, classical antiquity, and Orientalistik as the three major cultural reference points in the early twentieth century.

81. Ibid., 271. For a chapter on the decline of philhellenism in Nazi Germany, see Suzanne L. Marchand, *Down from Olympus: Archaeology and Philhellenism in Germany, 1750–1970* (Princeton, NJ: Princeton University Press, 1996), 341–354.

82. I thank Julia Hell for drawing my attention to the Paris conference. Marchand notes that few non-Jewish humanists stayed on in Nazi Germany; those that did lapsed back into "despotic humanism." Marchand, "Nazism, Orientalism and Humanism," 272.

83. Wolfgang Klein, ed., *Paris 1935: Erster Internationaler Schriftstellerkongreß zur Verteidigung der Kultur. Reden und Dokumente. Mit Materialien der Londoner Schriftstellerkonferenz 1936* (Berlin: Akademie-Verlag, 1982), 9–10.

84. For the conference call, see ibid., 36.

85. "Sie ist unser gemeinsames Gut, sie ist uns allen gemein, ist international." Ibid.

86. Unable to travel to Paris, Maxim Gorki wrote a message in which he reflected on the underlying assumptions of the congress. See Maxim Gorki, "Von den Kulturen," *Internationale Literatur: Zentralorgan der Internationalen Vereinigung Revolutionärer Schriftsteller* 5, no. 9 (1935): 10. Cited in Klein, *Paris 1935*, 24.

87. "Der sozialistische Humanismus ist der komplexe und komplette Gegensatz des Faschismus." See Klaus Mann's speech in Klein, *Paris 1935*, 156.

88. See Paul Nizan's speech in ibid., 192.

89. Ibid., 23–25, 457–458.

90. The significance of addresses in Dante's *Commedia* occupied both Auerbach and Spitzer. For an exemplary article on this subject, see Leo Spitzer, "The Addresses to the Reader in the *Commedia*," *Italica* 32, no. 3 (1955): 143–165. In his 1953 lecture, Klemperer argued that with the opening address "To All" in the October revolution of 1917, Lenin eliminated racial, national, and gender differences among the people of the republic. Klemperer, *Der alte und der neue Humanismus*, 18. Klemperer emphasized the significance of school reforms and the literacy campaign for Soviet citizens in the wake of the revolution. For Klemperer, there was something redeemable in the "old" humanism that socialist reforms of the twentieth century put into practice, namely, the commitment to develop "earthly-human faculties of the senses and the intellect." Klemperer, *Der alte und der neue Humanismus*, 21.

91. I thank Wolfgang Klein for providing me with information about the congress. For the program in which Yakup Kadri is mentioned, see the revised French edition of the conference proceedings.

92. Klein, *Paris 1935*, 221.

93. In 1937, in the aftermath of the congress in Paris, Yakup Kadri published a novel titled *Bir Sürgün* (*Exile*), which narrates the story of an exiled Ottoman intellectual in Paris at the turn of the century. In his reflections about the differences between East and West, the protagonist also reflects on the Greco-Roman grounds of European culture. For an analysis of the novel, see Beatrix Caner, *Türkische Literatur: Klassiker der Moderne* (Hildesheim: Georg Olms, 1998), 230.

94. For Talat Paşa's role in the Armenian genocide, see Taner Akçam, *A Shameful Act: The Armenian Genocide and the Question of Turkish Responsibility* (New York: Metropolitan Books, 2006).

95. Having seen mutilated and starving Armenian children in Damascus, the Austrian Jewish author decided to tell the story of the "unfathomable fate of the Armenian people." See the preface of 1933 in Franz Werfel, *Die vierzig Tage des Musa Dagh* (Frankfurt am Main: Fischer, 2006).

96. Anderson examines German responses to the killings of Armenians in the 1890s and 1910s. For various political reasons, she argues, Germans on the left gave the mass murders less publicity than their counterparts in other European countries. Margaret Lavinia Anderson, " 'Down in Turkey Far Away': Human Rights, the Armenian Massacres, and Orientalism in Wilhelmine Germany," *Journal of Modern History* 79, no. 1 (March 2007): 93.

97. Isaak Behar, *Versprich mir, daß Du am Leben bleibst: Ein jüdisches Schicksal* (Berlin: Ullstein, 2002), 21–22.

98. With the birth of their son in 1924, the young family moved to an apartment on Steinplatz—the square where Talat Paşa had been killed only three years earlier.

Chapter 2

1. "Berlin dışında en büyük Alman Üniversitesi." Necdet Sakaoğlu, *Cumhuriyet Dönemi Eğitim Tarihi* (Istanbul: Iletişim Yayınları, 1993), 77.

2. Forty scholars were hired in 1933 alone. According to the German consular report in Istanbul, the number of German scholars at Istanbul University in 1935 was forty-six. Five of these were sent by the German ministry of education to Istanbul. The report, dated May 22, 1935, is archived in the Politisches Archiv des Auswärtigen Amts, Akten des Generalkonsulats Istanbul, GK Istanbul 164, Band III 1935–1936.

3. Traugott Fuchs, *Çorum and Anatolian Pictures* (Istanbul: Boğaziçi Üniversitesi, Cultural Heritage Museum Publications, 1986), 13.

4. In the postwar period, Heinz Anstock became the principal of the Deutsche Schule Istanbul.

5. For a discussion of Rüstow's interpretation of history, see Kathrin Meier-Rust, *Alexander Rüstow: Geschichtsdeutung und liberales Engagement* (Stuttgart: Klett-Cotta, 1993). While in exile, Ernst von Aster wrote a brief inquiry into the role of Turks in the history of philosophy, Clemens Bosch published on the history of Hellenism, and Alexander Rüstow worked on a universal cultural history: Clemens Bosch, *Helenizm Tarihinin Anahatları*, Edebiyat Fakültesi Yayınlarından (Istanbul: Istanbul Üniversitesi, 1942/1943); Alexander Rüstow, *Ortsbestimmung der Gegenwart: Eine universalgeschichtliche Kulturkritik* (Erlenbach: Eugen Rentsch Verlag, 1952); Ernst von Aster, *Die Türken in der Geschichte der Philosophie* (Istanbul: Devlet Basımevi, 1937).

6. Hans Reichenbach, *Experience and Prediction: An Analysis of the Foundations and the Structure of Knowledge* (Chicago: University of Chicago Press, 1938). Upon publication of his book in the United States in 1938, Reichenbach left Turkey.

7. In a farewell letter to Auerbach in 1947, Hellmut Ritter, founder of the Orient Institute in Istanbul, summed up the factors such as the common cultural heritage that connected the émigrés to one another over the years. Hellmut Ritter, "Letter to Erich and Marie Auerbach, 1947," Literaturarchiv Marbach, A: Nachlaß Auerbach.

8. "Betrachtete man die Köpfe, so war die Mannigfaltigkeit und Unterschiedlichkeit der Schädelformen und Physiognomien frappierend. An dieser lebendigen Wirklichkeit gemessen wurde die nationalsozialistische Rassentheorie zur Farce. Hier, in dem auf

der 'Koprü' brodelnden Neben- und Miteinander von Menschentypen, lebte nicht nur das Osmanische Reich als Vielvölkerstaat weiter, sondern es tauchten Gesichtszüge aus dem Altertum auf, deren Ähnlichkeit mit Abbildungen babylonischer, hethitischer, ja ägyptischer, hellenistischer und römischer Skulpturen verblüffend war. Die vieltausend-jährige Völkergeschichte Kleinasiens zog an meinen Augen vorüber." Ernst E. Hirsch, *Aus des Kaisers Zeiten durch die Weimarer Republik in das Land Atatürks: Eine unzeit-gemäße Autobiographie* (München: Schweitzer, 1982), 181–182.

9. Martin Elsky, Martin Vialon, and Robert Stein, "Scholarship in Times of Ex-tremes: Letters of Erich Auerbach (1933–46), on the Fiftieth Anniversary of His Death," *Publications of the Modern Language Association of America* 122, no. 3 (2007): 750–751.

10. For Şehnaz Tahir Gürçağlar, who offers the most comprehensive study of the translation movement to date, the translations indicate a way to establish a new literary habitus. Şehnaz Tahir Gürçağlar, *The Politics and Poetics of Translation in Turkey, 1923–1960* (Amsterdam: Rodopi, 2008), 311–312.

11. Edward W. Said, *The World, the Text, and the Critic* (London: Vintage, 1991), 6.

12. In his reflections on Auerbach in Istanbul, Aamir Mufti points out that Said interprets Auerbach "in a rigorous sense as a Jewish figure, as a member of minority, of *the* minority par excellence" and as a "paradigmatic figure for modern criticism." Aamir R. Mufti, "Auerbach in Istanbul: Edward Said, Secular Criticism, and the Question of Minority Culture," in *Edward Said and the Work of the Critic: Speaking Truth to Power*, ed. Paul A. Bové (Durham, NC: Duke University Press, 2000), 236–237.

13. For a critique of Said's approach within the German-language context, see Nina Berman, "Ottoman Shock-and-Awe and the Rise of Protestantism: Luther's Reactions to the Ottoman Invasions of the Early Sixteenth Century," *Seminar* 41, no. 3 (2005): 242.

14. Emily Apter, "Global *Translatio*: The 'Invention' of Comparative Literature, Is-tanbul, 1933," *Critical Inquiry* 29, no. 2 (2003): 263.

15. Erich Auerbach, Letter to Johannes Oeschger, May 27, 1938, Nachlass Fritz Lieb, Universitätsbibliothek Basel (Handschriftenabteilung), NL 43 (Lieb) Ah 2,1 (Martin Vialon made this letter available). "Es sind nicht nur die Hügel am Ufer mit ihren meist verfallenen Palästen, nicht nur die Moscheen, Minarets, die Mosaiken, Miniaturen, Kunstschriften und Koranversen; sondern auch die unbeschreiblich vielfältigen Menschen mit ihren Lebens-und Kleidungsweisen, die Fische und Gemüse, die man zu essen bekommt, der Kaffee und die Cigaretten, der Rest islamischer Frömmigkeit und Formvollendung. Es ist Istanbul im Grunde noch immer eine hellenistische Stadt, denn das arabische, armenische, jüdische und auch das nun herrschende türkische Element verschmelzen oder leben nebeneinander in ei-nem Ganzen, das doch wohl von der alten hellenistischen Form des Kosmopolitismus zusammengehalten wird. Freilich ist alles schlimm modernisiert und barbarisiert, und wird es immer mehr. Die im Ganzen doch wohl sehr kluge und geschickte Regierung kann nichts anderes tun als den Prozess der modernen Barbarisierung beschleunigen."

16. David Lawton, "History and Legend: The Exile and the Turk," in *Postcolonial Moves: Medieval through Modern*, ed. Patricia Clare Ingham and Michelle R. Warren (New York: Palgrave Macmillan, 2003), 192.

17. Timothy Brennan points out that "One's judgment of cosmopolitanism's value or desirability . . . is affected by whose cosmopolitanism or patriotism one is talking about—whose definitions of prejudice, knowledge, or open-mindedness one is referring to. Cosmopolitanism is *local* while denying its local character. This denial is an intrinsic feature of cosmopolitanism and inherent to its appeal while denying its local character." Timothy Brennan, "Cosmo-Theory," *South Atlantic Quarterly* 100, no. 3 (Summer 2001): 659–660.

18. Rönesans, "ümmet ruhunun çöküşüyle millet ruhunun teşkili arasında geçmesi zaruri bir dünya vatandaşlığı . . . , bir insancılık devresidir. Rönesans, Yunan ve Latin medeniyetine dönüş manasındadır. Ortaçağdaki canlılığı kaybettirilmiş bir dine karşı tepki hareketi başlamış, laik . . . ahlaka, laik medeniyete iştiyak artmıştır." Ziya Gökalp, "Tevfik Fikret ve Rönesans," in *Makaleler V* (Ankara: Kültür Bakanlığı, 1981), 173–175. The essay was first published in 1917. Quoted in Yümni Sezen, *Hümanizm ve Atatürk Devrimleri* (Istanbul: Ayışığıkitapları, 1997), 187.

19. For Gökalp's influence on concepts of national education in republican Turkey, see also Sam Kaplan, *The Pedagogical State: Education and the Politics of National Culture in Post-1980s Turkey* (Stanford, CA: Stanford University Press, 2006), 39–42.

20. Ziya Gökalp, *Millî Terbiye ve Maarif Meselesi* (Ankara: Diyarbakır Tanıtma ve Turizm Derneği Yayınları, 1964), 108. The essay in question is titled "Maarif Meselesi" and originated in 1916.

21. According to Müge Göçek, Gökalp's vision "gave advantage to the westernized Muslim Turks of the empire over the other social groups, excluded Ottoman religious minorities, and created an ethnically based Turkish nationalism." Fatma Müge Göçek, "The Decline of the Ottoman Empire and the Emergence of Greek, Armenian, Turkish, and Arab Nationalisms," in *Social Constructions of Nationalism in the Middle East*, ed. Fatma Müge Göçek (Albany: State University of New York Press, 2002), 38.

22. Ziya Gökalp, *Turkish Nationalism and Western Civilization*, trans. and ed. Niyazi Berkes (New York: Columbia University Press, 1959), 252. Gökalp made this remark specifically with regard to family structures and notions of womanhood. I have slightly changed the translation.

23. Niyazi Berkes gives an early overview of the origins of sociology as a discipline in Turkey and describes Gökalp's adaptation of Durkheim's approach. Niyazi Berkes, "Sociology in Turkey," *American Journal of Sociology* 42, no. 2 (1936): 238–246.

24. Gökalp, *Millî Terbiye ve Maarif Meselesi*, 113.

25. Ibid.

26. "Fransada tenkid edebiyattan doğmuş iken Almanyada edebiyat tenkidden doğdu. Biz de ancak bu usulü takibederek milli zevkimizi bulabiliriz." Ibid., 114. Following the French anthropologist and philosopher Lucien Lévi-Bruhl, Gökalp emphasized the need to promote *tenkid*, criticism, as a genre in Turkey. Gökalp supported Lévi-Bruhl's view that French criticism had originated in literature, while in Germany literature had developed from criticism. The essay is titled "Maarif Meselesi" and was published in 1916.

27. For an article dealing with this question, see Fritz Klein, "Der Einfluß Deutschlands und Österreich-Ungarns auf das türkische Bildungswesen in den Jahren des Ersten Weltkrieges," in *Wegenetz europäischen Geistes: Wissenschaftszentren und geistige Wechselbeziehungen zwischen Mittel- und Südosteuropa vom Ende des 18. Jahrhunderts bis zum Ersten Weltkrieg,* ed. Richard Georg Plaschka and Karlheinz Mack (Wien: Verlag für Geschichte und Politik, 1983), 420–432. Klein argues that German and Austrian intervention in the Ottoman education system was motivated by imperial ambitions.

28. Ernst Jäckh, *Der aufsteigende Halbmond: Auf dem Weg zum deutsch-türkischen Bündnis* (Stuttgart: Deutsche Verlags-Anstalt, 1915), 72.

29. Oktay Aslanapa, *İstanbul Üniversitesi: Edebiyat Fakültesi Tezleri (1920–1946)* (Istanbul: İsar Vakfı Yayınları, Yıldız Yayıncılık, Reklamcılık, 2004), 18. The Germanist Werner Richter (Greifswald University) taught at Darülfünun. Mustafa Gencer, *Jöntürk Modernizmi ve "Alman Ruhu"* (Istanbul: İletişim, 2003), 130. For archival documents about the dispatch of German professors to Darülfünun, see Politisches Archiv des Auswärtigen Amts, Die Universität in Konstantinopel R 64140, Oktober–November 1918; Politisches Archiv des Auswärtigen Amts, Die türkische Universität zu Konstantinopel (Stambul) R 64141, 1919–1922. For insights into Weimar Germany's influence on the educational institutes after the founding of the Turkish Republic, see documents in Politisches Archiv des Auswärtigen Amts, Die Universität zu Konstantinopel R 64142, 1923.

30. "Bu suretle darülfünun içinde yeni ve ecnebi bir kuvvet olmuştu. Bu kuvvet görevine yalnızca Alman kalmak, Alman görünmek ve Almanca çalışmak noktasında yoğunlaştırdı. Darülfünun ıslahatına Türkler tarafından hiç beklenilmeyen tarzda, teferruat ve zevahirle başladılar. Hasta darülfünunun tedavisi ve şifası için zihinsel üretimi gerek görmeden, daha doğrusu Almanya darülfünuna göre şekil vermek istediler. Belki de az zamanda çok is görmek zaafına uğradılar. Darülfünunun sürüklenmekte olduğu uçuruma onlar da ayaklarını kaptırdılar." Quoted in Tahir Hatiboğlu, *Türkiye Üniversite Tarihi* (Ankara: Selvi Yayınevi, 1998), 52–53.

31. Politisches Archiv des Auswärtigen Amts, Die Deutschen Schulen in der Türkei, Allgemeines, R 62451, 1915–1917. One suggestion was to circumvent the problem by training Ottoman students in Germany. For a detailed report on the failure of the German involvement in Darülfünun, see "Deutsche Universitäts-Professoren in Konstantinopel: Eine Denkschrift," in Politisches Archiv des Auswärtigen Amts, Die Universität in Konstantinopel R 64140, Oktober–November 1918. The competition between France and Germany over Ottoman education is also reflected in the German embassy correspondence of 1914: Politisches Archiv des Auswärtigen Amts, Der Beirat des türkischen Unterrichtsministers R 63442, 1913.

32. Gencer, *Jöntürk Modernizmi ve "Alman Ruhu,"* 133.

33. Gökalp, *Turkish Nationalism and Western Civilization,* 278.

34. On the cultural dualism that dominated the Ottoman education, see Carter Vaughn Findley, *Ottoman Officialdom: A Social History* (Princeton, NJ: Princeton University Press, 1989), 131–173. For another study of the Ottoman education system, see Benjamin

C. Fortna, *Imperial Classroom: Islam, the State, and Education in the Late Ottoman Empire* (Oxford: Oxford University Press, 2002).

35. See Benedict Anderson, *Imagined Communities: Reflections on the Origin and Spread of Nationalism* (London: Verso, 1992), 195–197.

36. Following Anderson's thesis about the significance of time keeping to nationhood, Alev Çınar argues that the creation, homogenization, and nationalization of time in the Turkish Republic is something that "dominates and shapes all perceptions of the past, present, and future." Alev Çınar, *Modernity, Islam, and Secularism in Turkey: Bodies, Places, and Time* (Minneapolis: University of Minnesota Press, 2005), 138–139.

37. "With respect then to both humanistic and naturalistic studies, education should take its departure from this close interdependence. It should aim not at keeping science as a study of nature apart from literature as a record of human interests, but at cross-fertilizing both the natural sciences and the various human disciplines such as history, literature, economics, and politics." John Dewey, *Democracy and Education: The Introduction to the Philosophy of Education* (New York: Macmillan Company, 1922), 334.

38. See Mustafa Ergün, *Atatürk Devri Türk Eğitimi*, Ankara Üniversitesi Dil ve Coğrafya Fakültesi Yayınları, No. 325 (Ankara: Ankara Üniversitesi Basımevi, 1982), 110. For a discussion of his influence in Turkey, see Sabri Büyükdüvenci, "John Dewey's Impact on Turkish Education," *Studies in Philosophy and Education* 13, no. 3–4 (1994): 393–400. See also the "Preliminary Report on Turkish Education" and the "Letter of Transmittal for Preliminary Report on Turkish Education" by Robert Scotten, the first secretary of the U.S. Embassy in Istanbul, in John Dewey, *The Middle Works, 1899–1924,* ed. Jo Ann Boydston, vol. 15: *1923–1924* (Carbondale: Southern Illinois University Press, 1983). Dewey's suggestion that university students be granted study-abroad fellowships in order to secure scholars trained in modern methods was not new. Since the early nineteenth century, the Ottoman Empire had sent its best students to Western Europe in order to accelerate socioeconomic modernization reforms. As early as 1827, Sultan Mahmut II, for instance, sent several hundred students to Western Europe.

39. For a history of Ottoman education, see Necdet Sakaoğlu, *Osmanlı Eğitim Tarihi* (Istanbul: İletişim Yayınları, 1993). See also Benjamin Fortna, who emphasizes Ottoman agency over Orientalist notions of Ottomans as mere victims of the West. The educational policies were, he argues, "informed by a very enlightenment notion of progress that relied heavily on Western European models but cut them with a strong dose of Ottoman and Islamic elements that were deemed capable of meliorating the deleterious side-effects of Western influence." Fortna, *Imperial Classroom*, 3.

40. Reşit Galip claimed that a new vision of history, similar to a nationalist movement, had taken over the country. He argued that three years had to pass before Darülfünun even took an interest in these new developments: "Yeni bir tarih telakkisi, milli bir hareket halinde ülkeyi sardı. Darülfünun'da buna bir alaka uyandırabilmek için üç yıl kadar beklemek ve uğraşmak lazım geldi." Quoted in Ernst Hirsch, *Dünya Üniversiteleri ve Türkiyede Üniversitelerin Gelişmesi*, vol. 1 (Istanbul: Ankara Üniversitesi Yayımları, 1950), 312.

41. For Albert Malche's original report, see ibid., 229–295.

42. In his speech for the inauguration of Istanbul University, Minister of Education Galip announced that the new university had no relationship with Darülfünun. A transcript of the speech can be found in Hatiboğlu, *Türkiye Üniversite Tarihi*, 118.

43. Nazım Irem provides insights into the competing interpretations of Kemalism during this period that led to the dismissal of Turkish faculty. Irem argues that the socialism-oriented *Kadro* circle supported the university reform and the dismissal of conservative faculty. Yakup Kadri Karaosmanoğlu, who in 1935 was invited to the international humanism conference in Paris, was a member of the *Kadro* circle. Nazım Irem, "Turkish Conservative Modernism: Birth of a Nationalist Quest for Cultural Renewal," *International Journal of Middle East Studies* 34, no. 1 (2002): 101–102.

44. Philipp Schwartz, *Notgemeinschaft: Zur Emigration deutscher Wissenschaftler nach 1933 in die Türkei* (Marburg: Metropolis-Verlag, 1995), 48, 66.

45. Jan Cremer and Horst Przytulla, *Exil Türkei: Deutschsprachige Emigranten in der Türkei 1933–1945* (München: Verlag Karl M. Lipp, 1991), 27. The Berlin-based organization *Verein Aktives Museum* estimates that 1,040 Germans emigrated to Turkey between 1933 and 1945. *Mitgliederrundbrief*, vol. 43 (Berlin: Verein Aktives Museum: Faschismus und Widerstand in Berlin, May 2000, http://www.aktives-museum.de/fileadmin/user_upload/Extern/Dokumente/rundbrief-43.pdf (accessed March 20, 2009), 9.

46. Annemarie Schwarzenbach, "Die Reorganisation der Universität von Stambul," *Neue Zürcher Zeitung*, 03. Dezember 1933, Blatt 8 (Sonntagsbeilage).

47. Ibid.

48. The foundation of the University for Agriculture in Ankara (Yüksek Ziraat Üniversitesi) in 1930, for example, was laid by academics dispatched from the Weimar Ministry of Education. For a brief history of this university, see Horst Widmann, *Exil und Bildungshilfe: Die deutschsprachige akademische Emigration in die Türkei nach 1933* (Bern: Herbert Lang, 1973), 37–39.

49. See Erich Auerbach's Istanbul University, Chaire de Philologie Romane à la Faculté des lettres, 11 December 1936, Literaturarchiv Marbach, Nachlaß Erich Auerbach, Zugehörige Materialien.

50. "MUSTAFA KEMAL . . . und seine Freunde hatten grandiose Pläne für die Wiedergeburt des türkischen Volkes ausgearbeitet; sie sahen aber nicht, wie diese ausgeführt werden könnten. Und nun erlaubte ein Zufall, eine groteske Verirrung der Geschichte die Verwirklichung: Ich brachte auserlesene Produkte einer Jahrhunderte alten Tradition, Gelehrte und Forscher, die sich nach einem scheinbaren Zusammenbruch der Welt, zu welcher sie gehörten, in ihrer Mission hier nun bestätigt sehen würden." Schwartz, *Notgemeinschaft*, 46.

51. Galip pointed out that this was an extraordinary day in history: "Als vor fast 500 Jahren Konstantinopel fiel, beschlossen die byzantinischen Gelehrten das Land zu verlassen. Man konnte sie nicht zurückhalten. Viele von ihnen gingen nach Italien. Die Renaissance war das Ergebnis. Heute haben wir uns vorbereitet, von Europa eine Gegengabe zu empfangen. Wir erhofften eine Bereicherung, ja, eine Erneuerung, unserer Nation.

Bringen Sie uns Ihr Wissen und Ihre Methoden, zeigen Sie unserer Jugend den Weg zum Fortschritt. Wir bieten Ihnen unsere Dankbarkeit und unsere Verehrung an." Quoted in ibid., 47. The Turkish original of this passage can be found in Hatiboğlu, *Türkiye Üniversite Tarihi*, 111.

52. In his article on Erich Auerbach and Leo Spitzer, Harry Levin draws a link between the flight of Byzantine scholars from the Ottomans and the flight of Jewish scholars to the United States: "When the history of twentieth-century diaspora is fully chronicled, we should be able to test the parallel it implies with the fifteenth-century influx of catalytic knowledge to western Europe after the fall of Constantinople. Meanwhile, given the scale of events precipitating the latter-day exodus, the number of countries whence the refugees took flight, the brilliance of their talents and the variety of their fields, we make a modest start wherever we can by trying to follow the fortunes of those whose paths have crossed our own. Those losses to European faculties, which have meant such gains for ours, have completed the maturation of American higher learning." Harry Levin, "Two *Romanisten* in America: Spitzer and Auerbach," in *The Intellectual Migration: Europe and America, 1930–1960*, ed. Donald Fleming and Bernard Bailyn (Cambridge, MA: Belknap Press of Harvard University Press, 1969), 480.

53. Sezen, *Hümanizm ve Atatürk Devrimleri*, 187; Gökalp, *Millî Terbiye ve Maarif Meselesi*, 131.

54. For a short biography, see Asım Bezirci, *Nurullah Ataç: Yaşamı, Kişiliği, Eleştiri Anlayışı, Yazıları* (Istanbul: Varlık Yayınları, 1983).

55. Nurullah Ataç, *Diyelim* (Istanbul: Varlık Yayınları, 1954), 40–43.

56. For a discussion of humanism and Westernization, see Tarık Z. Tunaya, *Türkiyenin Siyasi Hayatında Batılılaşma Hareketleri* (Istanbul: Yedigün Matbaası, 1960), 156–158.

57. Kaplan, *Pedagogical State*, 42. For a section discussing the challenge of Islam in the Kemalist State, see Sultan Tepe, *Beyond the Sacred and the Secular: Politics of Religion in Israel and Turkey* (Stanford, CA: Stanford University Press, 2008), 86–98.

58. Yümni Sezen points to the link between humanism and Atatürk's vision of a secular Turkish nation. Sezen, *Hümanizm ve Atatürk Devrimleri*, 196–198.

59. "Hümanizmacı . . . fikirlerin müşterek esası, kendi kendimizi batılı metodlara uyarak tanımak, âdeta *keşfetmek* olarak özetlenebilir." Tunaya, *Türkiyenin Siyasi Hayatında Batılılaşma Hareketleri*, 159.

60. Hirsch, *Dünya Üniversiteleri ve Türkiyede Üniversitelerin Gelişmesi*, 284–285.

61. Ibid.

62. For a discussion of the hiring process, see chapter 1. The report of the search committee is preserved in Istanbul Üniversitesi Arşivi (Istanbul University Archive), Auerbach Dosyası.

63. Cemil Bilsel, "Dördüncü Yıl Açış Nutku," in *Üniversite Konferansları 1936–1937*, İstanbul Üniversitesi Yayınları No. 50 (Istanbul: Ülkü Basımevi, 1937), 9–10.

64. In a letter to Walter Benjamin dated January 3, 1937, Auerbach mentioned the changes he and other scholars made in Istanbul. Karlheinz Barck, "5 Briefe Erich Auerbachs an Walter Benjamin in Paris," *Zeitschrift für Germanistik* 9, no. 6 (1988): 691. For a

dissertation on the institutionalization of philology by Spitzer, Auerbach, and others at Istanbul University, see Şebnem Sunar, "Türkiye Cumhuriyeti'nin Batılılaşma Sürecinde Filolojinin Örgütlenmesi (İstanbul Üniversitesi Alman Filolojisi Örneğinde)" (unpublished dissertation, Istanbul University, 2003). I thank Şebnem Sunar for sharing her work on the beginnings of Germanistik in Istanbul.

65. Lydia H. Liu, *Translingual Practice* (Stanford, CA: Stanford University Press, 1995), xx. With regard to the final phase of the Ottoman Empire, Müge Göçek also argues that "visions of history and literature played a very significant role in creating and determining new meanings and their boundaries, which were then reproduced through the educational system." Göçek, "Decline of the Ottoman Empire," 44.

66. For a critical investigation into the impact of racial thought on the faculty, see Nazan Maksudyan, *Türklüğü Ölçmek: Bilimkurgusal Antropoloji ve Türk Milliyetçiliğinin Çehresi, 1925–1939* (Istanbul: Metis, 2005).

67. Bern Nicolai, *Moderne und Exil: Deutschsprachige Architekten in der Türkei 1925– 1955* (Berlin: Verlag für Bauwesen, 1998), 142. Bruno Taut died in Turkey in 1938. The building was completed two years later.

68. For a recent dissertation on the Greek-Turkish population exchange, see Aslı Iğsız, "Repertoires of Rupture: Recollecting the 1923 Greek-Turkish Compulsory Religious Minority Exchange" (unpublished dissertation, University of Michigan, 2006).

69. During Ottoman times, the young writer Ömer Seyfettin initially opposed this trend. See Suat Sinanoğlu, *Türk Humanizmi* (Ankara: Türk Tarih Kurumu Basımevi, 1980), 92.

70. I am following Yümni Sezen's argument here: Sezen, *Hümanizm ve Atatürk Devrimleri*, 191.

71. Sinanoğlu, *Türk Humanizmi*, 189.

72. Bernard Lewis, *From Babel to Dragomans: Interpreting the Middle East* (Oxford: Oxford University Press, 2004), 426.

73. We can trace the influence of the teachings of émigré German professors in the memoirs of Auerbach's assistant Güzin Dino. Güzin Dino, *Gel Zaman Git Zaman: Anılar* (Istanbul: Can Yayınları, 1991), 87–88.

74. ". . . das herrliche bithynische Brussa, das Sie sich nach Lage und Charakter wie ein islamisches Perugia vorstellen mögen." Auerbach, Letter to Johannes Oeschger, May 27, 1938.

75. Dankwart A. Rüstow, *Politics and Westernization in the Near East* (Princeton, NJ: Princeton University Press, 1956), 15. Dankwart Rüstow made a reference here to his father's exilic work: A. Rüstow, *Ortsbestimmung der Gegenwart*, 127.

76. During World War I, Ritter had served as translator for the German-Ottoman alliance and thus witnessed firsthand the rapid decline of the Ottoman Empire. In 1926, he settled in Istanbul because he had been discharged from his professorship at Hamburg University's Oriental Institute on the grounds of homosexuality.

77. Excerpt from a letter to his mentor C. H. Becker, August 15, 1931. Quoted in Thomas Lier, "Hellmut Ritter in Istanbul 1926–1949," *Die Welt des Islams* 38, no. 3 (1998):

351–352. "Warum kann man nun einmal nicht fassen, dass . . . es eine wissenschaft geben soll, die nicht zu dem schluss kommt, dass die Türken nachkommen der Hetiter sind und dass es nicht unnational ist, das zu bestreiten? Theologie verwandelte sich in nationologie, statt religiöser Ketzer gibt es politische, das ist der ganze unterschied gegen früher. Gebundene marschrute so oder so. Dass in einem volk tiefste religiöse bindung und grösste geistige freiheit nebeneinander leben können, dass man ein modernes volk sein kann und doch historische denkmäler schützen kann, und doch sektiererereien dulden kann, doch den bauern ihre tracht lassen kann, das geht in keinen orientalischen kopf."

78. "Aber er hat alles, was er getan hat, im Kampf gegen die europäischen Demokratien einerseits und gegen die alte mohammedanisch-panislamitische Sultanswirtschaft andererseits durchsetzen müssen, und das Resultat ist ein fanatischer antitraditioneller Nationalismus: Ablehnung aller bestehenden mohammedanischen Kulturüberlieferung, Anknüpfung an ein phantastisches Urtürkentum, technische Modernisierung im europäischen Verstande. . . . Resultat: Nationalismus im Superlativ bei gleichzeitiger Zerstörung des geschichtlichen Nationalcharakters." Barck, "5 Briefe Erich Auerbachs an Walter Benjamin," 692. For the English translation, see Karlheinz Barck and Anthony Reynolds, "Walter Benjamin and Erich Auerbach: Fragments of a Correspondence," *Diacritics* 22, no. 3/4 (1992): 82.

79. The letter is dated June 5, 1938. "Manches, besonders das Verhältnis der gegenwärtig hier herrschenden Richtung zur eigenen Kulturtradition, das ganz negativ ist, ist für unsereinen traurig und sogar manchmal, durch den Vergleich mit dem, was anderswo im gleichen Sinne geschieht, gespenstisch. Aber das ist für die Lage des Landes zunächst zwangsläufig, auf eine allmähliche Reaktion kann man hoffen, wenn erst die dringendsten Modernisierungsaufgaben abgeschlossen sind—und im übrigen muss man schon sagen, dass es hier eine ruhige, zielbewußte und auch nach der Lage der Dinge vergleichsweise freie Regierung gibt." Erich Auerbach, "Ein Exil-Brief Erich Auerbachs aus Istanbul an Freya Hobohm in Marburg—versehen mit einer Nachschrift von Marie Auerbach (1938), Transkribiert und kommentiert von Martin Vialon," *Trajekte* 9 (2004): 11.

80. Ibid.

81. Erich Auerbach, *Gesammelte Aufsätze zur Romanischen Philologie* (Bern: Francke Verlag, 1967), 305.

82. Louis-Jean Calvet, *Language Wars and Linguistic Politics* (Oxford: Oxford University Press, 1998), 186–187.

83. "Freilich ist alles schlimm modernisiert und barbarisiert, und wird es immer mehr. Die im Ganzen doch wohl sehr kluge und geschickte Regierung kann nichts anderes tun als den Prozess der modernen Barbarisierung beschleunigen. Sie muss das arme und nicht arbeitsgewohnte Land organisieren, ihm moderne und praktische Methoden beibringen, damit es leben und sich wehren kann; und wie überall geschieht das im Zeichen eines puristischen Nationalismus, der die lebende Tradition zerstört, und sich teils auf ganz phantastische Urzeitvorstellungen, teils auf modern-rationale Gedanken stützt. Die Frömmigkeit wird bekämpft, die islamistische Kultur als arabische Überfremdung betrachtet, man will zugleich modern und rein türkisch sein, und

es ist so weit gekommen, dass man die Sprache und Abschaffung der alten Schrift, durch Entfernung der arabischen Lehnworte und ihren Ersatz teils durch 'türkische' Neubildungen, teils durch europäische Entlehnungen völlig zerstört hat: kein junger Mensch kann mehr die ältere Literatur lesen—und es herrscht eine geistige Richtungslosigkeit, die äusserst gefährlich ist." Auerbach, Letter to Johannes Oeschger, May 27, 1938.

84. Ataç, *Diyelim*, 98–99.

85. Ibid., 42–43.

86. Orhan Burian, *Denemeler Eleştiriler* (Istanbul: Can Yayınları, 1964), 18.

87. Celâleddin Ezine, "Türk Humanizmasinin İzahı," *Hamle* 1 (1940): 7. "Çünkü milletler, özlerinden bir şey katmadan Latin ve Grek örneklerinin yalnız mukalidleri olabilmişlerdi." ▪

88. Ibid., 10.

89. For a reprint of the series of essays that Tanpınar published in the 1940s, see Ahmet Hamdi Tanpınar, *Edebiyat Üzerine Makaleler* (Istanbul: Milli Eğitim Basımevi, 1969), 61–71.

90. "Kuvvetli bir kesafetli bir tercüme devresi geçirmeyen kültürler, rahmetsiz kalmış topraklar gibi kurumaya, verimsiz kalmaya mahkûmdurlar." Faruk Yücel, "Türkiye'nin Aydınlanma Sürecinde Çevirinin Rolü," *Hacettepe Üniversitesi Edebiyat Fakültesi Dergisi* 23, no. 2 (2006): 216.

91. Necdet Sakaoğlu provides a detailed overview of the structure of the village institutes in Sakaoğlu, *Cumhuriyet Dönemi Eğitim Tarihi*, 89–100.

92. See, for example, the preface to Mina Urgan's translation of Balzac: H. de Balzac, *Otuz Yaşındaki Kadın*, trans. Mina Urgan (Istanbul: Milli Eğitim Basımevi, 1946).

93. Preface to ibid. For a study of the politics of translation and Westernization in Egypt, see Richard Jacquemond, "Translation and Cultural Hegemony: The Case of French-Arabic Translation," in *Rethinking Translation: Discourse, Subjectivity, Ideology*, ed. Lawrence Venuti (New York: Routledge, 1992), 139–158. For the translation of French literature into Arabic in nineteenth-century Egypt, see Carol Bardenstein, *Translation and Transformation in Modern Arabic Literature: The Indigenous Assertions of Muhammad 'Uthman Jalal* (Wiesbaden: Harrassowitz, 2005).

94. This comparison, which takes into consideration all translations until 1966, is based on Adnan Ötüken's bibliography in Adnan Ötüken, *Klasikler Bibliyografyası 1940–1966* (Ankara: Ayyıldız Matbaası, 1967). See also Gürçağlar, *Translation in Turkey*, 166.

95. For a complete bibliography with a list of translators, see Ötüken, *Klasikler Bibliyografyası 1940–1966*.

96. Murat Katoğlu, "Cumhuriyet Türkiye'sinde Eğitim, Kültür, Sanat," in *Cumhuriyet Dönemi Edebiyat Çevirileri Seçkisi*, ed. Öner Yağcı (Ankara: Kültür Bakanlığı Yayınları, 1999), 332. For a complete list of translations between 1940 and 1948, see Adnan Ötüken, *Klasikler Bibliyografyası 1940–1948* (Ankara: Milli Eğitim Basımevi, 1949). Saliha Paker points out that priority was given to Plato over Aristotle. Most translations from Greek and Latin relied on French as the intermediary language. Saliha Paker, "Changing Norms of

the Target System: Turkish Translations of Greek Classics in Historical Perspective," in *Studies in Greek Linguistics: Proceedings of the 7th Linguistics Conference* (Thessaloniki: Aristotelian University of Thessaloniki, 1986), 218. In this article, Paker also reflects on the first Ottoman translations of Homer's *Iliad* and *Odyssey*.

97. "İçinde bulunmaya mecbur olduğumuz medeniyet dünyasının kökü, eski Yunan'dadır. Bu ilkenin duyuluşu demek olan Hümanizma iyi anlaşılmadıkça, bu gerçek, şu veya bu türlü taasupçu fikirlere sapılarak inkâr olunur, bir asırdır beklediğimiz düşünüş kalkınması olamaz veya uçak devrinde kağnınınkine benzer bir ağırlıkta yürür." Quoted in F. Yücel, "Türkiye'nin Aydınlanma Sürecinde Çevirinin Rolü," 215.

98. "Müellif bizden olmıyabilir, bestekâr başka milletten olabilir. Fakat o sözleri ve sesleri anlıyan ve canlandıran biziz. Onun için Devlet Konservatuvarının temsil ettiği piyesler, oynadığı operalar bizimdir, Türktür ve millîdir." An excerpt of the speech in the original and in German translation can be found in Mustafa Çıkar, *Hasan-Âli Yücel und die türkische Kulturreform* (Bonn: Pontes Verlag, 1994), 65–66.

99. Ezine, "Türk Humanizmasinin İzahı," 10.

100. Tunaya, *Türkiyenin Siyasi Hayatında Batılılaşma Hareketleri*, 159; emphasis added.

101. Burian, *Denemeler Eleştiriler*, 43–45. The title of the Atatürk obituary, originally published in 1938, is "Renaissance."

102. "Türk Devrimi . . . İslamlığın dogma'larını kökünden söküp atmıştır." See a 1935 essay titled "Humanizma ve Biz" in ibid., 11–19. The essay was originally published in the journal *Yücel*.

103. Yümni Sezen points out the connection between humanism and Atatürk's vision of a secular Turkish nation in Sezen, *Hümanizm ve Atatürk Devrimleri*, 196–198.

104. For work on cultural mimesis in the colonial encounter, see Barbara Fuchs, who defines cultural mimesis as "the fun-house mirror, the reflection that dazzles, the impersonator, the sneaky copy, the double agent—mimesis, that is, as a deliberate performance of sameness that necessarily threatens, or at least modifies, the original." Fuchs's definition of cultural mimesis is close to Homi Bhabha's view of mimicry's function in a colonial context. Barbara Fuchs, *Mimesis and Empire: The New World, Islam, and European Identities* (Cambridge: Cambridge University Press, 2001), 5.

105. Barck, "5 Briefe Erich Auerbachs an Walter Benjamin," 691.

106. For Prime Minister Refik Saydam's statement regarding Jewish emigration to Turkey, see chapter 3.

107. Apter argues that "it was the volatile crossing of Turkish language politics with European philological humanism that produced the conditions conducive to the invention of comparative literature as a global discipline, at least in its early disguise." Apter, "Global *Translatio*," 263, 277.

108. Prior to his departure to the United States, Auerbach wrote to Werner Krauss in 1947: ". . . ein hiesiger Kollege, der Psycholog Peters, einst Jena, nennt mich, nicht ohne Ironie, den 'Europäologen.'" Karlheinz Barck, "Eine unveröffentlichte Korrespondenz (Fortsetzung): Erich Auerbach/Werner Krauss," *Beiträge zur Romanischen Philologie* 27, no. 1 (1988): 165.

109. For an investigation into the declining status of ancient Greek culture in Germany, see Suzanne L. Marchand, *Down from Olympus: Archaeology and Philhellenism in Germany, 1750–1970* (Princeton, NJ: Princeton University Press, 1996).

110. Ahmet Hamdi Tanpınar, *Yaşadığım Gibi*, 2nd ed. (Istanbul: Dergah Yayınları, 1996), 70. The newspaper column was published on January 1, 1945.

111. "Almanya Roma olmak istiyordu. Kendisini Kartaca yaptı. . . . Bugünkü Avrupa, Roma'nın parçalanmasından doğmuştur. Onun için ikinci bir Roma doğamaz. . . . Valéry, bir yazısında, 'Medeniyetlerin insanlar gibi ölümlü olduğunu artık öğrendik.' der. Medeniyet ağacı hiçbir zaman bu savaşta olduğu kadar kökünden sallanmadı. Çatı ile temelin birbirine karışmasından korkulan günler geçirdik. Bu tecrübenin bir daha tekrarlanmaması lâzımdır." Ibid., 78–79. The newspaper column was published in *Ülkü* on May 16, 1945.

112. For an overview see Erik J. Zürcher, *Turkey: A Modern History* (London: I. B. Tauris & Co., 1998), 209–214.

113. Apter, "Global *Translatio*," 269.

114. Sakaoğlu, *Cumhuriyet Dönemi Eğitim Tarihi*, 99.

115. Uğur Mumcu, *40'ların Cadı Kazanı* (Istanbul: Tekin Yayınevi, 1990), 70, 142.

116. Çıkar, *Hasan-Âli Yücel und die türkische Kulturreform*, 79.

117. The translation project ended in 1950. Sakaoğlu, *Cumhuriyet Dönemi Eğitim Tarihi*, 106. See also Çıkar, *Hasan-Âli Yücel und die türkische Kulturreform*, 59.

118. In the late 1930s, Turkish universities were labeled as propaganda machines of the nation-state. Demands for new tertiary administrative structures were issued but not resolved until Yücel granted them autonomy shortly after the war.

119. Katoğlu, "Cumhuriyet Türkiye'sinde Eğitim, Kültür, Sanat," 332.

120. Tanpınar, *Yaşadığım Gibi*, 32–33. Tanpınar wrote about the significance of translation since the tanzimat period in a column titled "Kültür ve Sanat Yollarında Gösterdiğimiz Devamsızlık," published on January 25, 1951. See also his follow-up column titled "Medeniyet Değiştirmesi ve İç İnsan," published on March 2, 1951 (both can be found in *Yaşadığım Gibi*).

121. For a detailed study of educational politics after the military coup in 1980, see Kaplan, *Pedagogical State*.

122. Sabahattin Eyüboğlu also translated works by Ernst Curtius, Montaigne, Plato, and Shakespeare.

123. Azra Erhat wrote in her memoirs: "Spitzer yaşamımda bir dönüm noktasıdır, hem geleceğime yön veren, hem de öğretisi ve yöntemiyle o gün bu gün çalışmalarıma damgasını veren bilgindir. Leo Spitzer olmasaydı ben bugün ben olamazdım, dünya görüşüm bu olmaz, anılarımı da açık seçik bir dille iletemezdim sana." Azra Erhat, *Gülleylâ'ya Anılar (En Hakiki Mürşit)* (Istanbul: Can Yayınları, 2002), 135.

124. Todorova proposes the analytical category of historical legacy as an alternative to regional or national entities: Maria Todorova, "Spacing Europe: What Is a Historical Region?" *East Central Europe/L'Europe du Centre-Est* 32, no. 1–2 (2005): 59–78. Applied to the Turkish context, Todorova's approach highlights the way in

which Erhat, for example, perceived ancient Anatolian cultures as modern Turkey's historical legacy.

125. See Eyüboğlu's essay "Ilyada ve Anadolu," in Sabahattin Eyüboğlu, *Mavi ve Kara: Denemeler (1940–1966)* (Istanbul: Çan Yayınları, 1967), 283. For the passage in question, see Michael de Montaigne, *Works of Michael de Montaigne: Comprising His Essays, Journey into Italy, and Letters, with Notes from All the Commentators, Biographical and Bibliographical Notices, Etc.*, vol. 2, ed. W. Hazlitt and O. W. Wight (New York: H. W. Derby, 1861), 528.

126. The fifteenth-century manuscript was translated into Ottoman Turkish in 1912. For the English translation see Kritovoulos, *History of Mehmed the Conqueror*, trans. C. T. Riggs (Princeton, NJ: Princeton University Press, 1954), 181–182. I thank Martin Treml for drawing my attention to the account of Mehmed II in Troy. For articles dealing with Mehmed II's visit in Troy see Robert Ousterhout, "The East, the West, and the Appropriation of the Past in Early Ottoman Architecture," *Gesta* 43, no. 2 (2004): 165–176; and Can Bilsel, "Our Anatolia": Organicism and the Making of Humanist Culture in Turkey," *Muqarnas* 24 (2007): 223–241.

127. Eyüboğlu, *Mavi ve Kara*, 284.

128. Eyüboğlu also wrote about Turkey's relationship to ancient Greece in a 1956 essay titled "Bizim Anadolu" and in "Halk," written in 1965. Ibid., 5–11, 14–19.

129. I am indebted to Djelal Kadir, who inspired me to see mimesis not only as representation of reality but also as "mimetic enactment." I also thank him for allowing me to read his chapter on Auerbach in manuscript form: Djelal Kadir, *Memos from the Besieged City: Lifelines for Cultural Sustainability* (Stanford, CA: Stanford University Press, 2011).

130. The difference between the Orient and Occident, according to Tanpınar, was in positioning oneself within a particular reality. In his view, it was the consistency of history that made Western civilization possible. Tanpınar, *Yaşadığım Gibi*. The newspaper column was published in *Cumhuriyet* on September 6, 1960. I was not able to confirm the origin of this quote in Dante's oeuvre.

131. Here I am partly following Franz Bäuml's definition of mimesis. Bäuml argues that mimesis is the representation of an imagined but canonically established reality. By the same token, however, he argues that reality does not itself precede mimesis. Reality is, in Bäuml's view, the result of mimetic reproduction. Franz H. Bäuml, "Mimesis as Model: Medieval Media-Change and Canonical Reality," in *Mimesis: Studien zur literarischen Repräsentation/Studies on Literary Presentation*, ed. Bernhard F. Scholz (Tübingen: Francke Verlag, 1998), 78.

132. As one of the dilemmas of conceptualizing modernity in Indian history, Dipesh Chakrabarty sees the process of equating a certain version of Europe with modernity. Dipesh Chakrabarty, "Postcoloniality and the Artifice of History: Who Speaks for 'Indian' Pasts?" in *The Decolonization Reader*, ed. James D. Le Sueur (New York: Routledge, 2003), 444.

133. Cf. Chakrabarty's stance on non-European history. Ibid.

Chapter 3

1. Albert Einstein, "Einstein on His Theory: Time, Space, and Gravitation," *The Times*, November 28, 1919, 14.

2. ". . . ein von der westlichen Pest unberührtes Land." This image stems from émigrés like Philipp Schwartz, who had close contact with Turkish officials and negotiated the hiring of émigré scholars through the Notgemeinschaft deutscher Wissenschaftler im Ausland (Aid Organization for German Academics Abroad). Schwartz told the minister of education, Reşit Galip, that the arrival of Europeans in Turkey would compensate for the shameful expulsion of scholars from Germany. Philipp Schwartz, *Notgemeinschaft: Zur Emigration deutscher Wissenschaftler nach 1933 in die Türkei* (Marburg: Metropolis-Verlag, 1995), 45.

3. Arnold Reisman, "Jewish Refugees from Nazism, Albert Einstein, and the Modernization of Higher Education in Turkey (1933–1945)," *Aleph: Historical Studies in Science and Judaism* 7 (2007): 264.

4. For the interpretation of archival material regarding this case, see Rıfat Bali, *Sarayın ve Cumhuriyetin Dişçibaşısı Sami Günzberg* (Istanbul: Kitabevi, 2007), 89–107. Bali explores the role of Sami Günzberg, a member of an Ashkenazi family that emigrated from Hungary to the Ottoman Empire in the mid-nineteenth century, as another mediator for Einstein's offer.

5. Gad Freudenthal and Arnold Reisman translated İnönü's letter from French to English. Reisman, "Jewish Refugees," 266–267.

6. The letterhead stated the purpose of the OSE as "Pour la protection de la santé des populations juives."

7. For publications that place the exodus of Sephardic and German Jews within a common context, see Rıfat N. Bali, *Cumhuriyet Yıllarında Türkiye Yahudileri: Bir Türkleştirme Serüveni* (Istanbul: İletişim, 1999); Avner Levi, *Türkiye Cumhuriyeti'nde Yahudiler* (Istanbul: İletişim, 1992); Stanford J. Shaw, *Turkey and the Holocaust: Turkey's Role in Rescuing Turkish and European Jewry from Nazi Persecution, 1933–1945* (Hampshire, UK: Macmillan Press, 1993).

8. Levi, *Türkiye Cumhuriyeti'nde Yahudiler*, 103.

9. Şemseddin Günaltay, "Açış Dersi: Türklerin Ana Yurdu ve Irki Mes'elesi," in *Üniversite Konferansları 1936–1937*, İstanbul Üniversitesi Yayınları No. 50 (Istanbul: Ülkü Basımevi, 1937), xiii.

10. "Kafaları, bedeni teşekkülleri, iltisaki dilleri Türklerin aynı olan Sümerler . . ." Ibid., 10.

11. Günaltay's lecture indicates the direction taken by the study of Turkish history in the 1930s. For a discussion of Atatürk's nation-building project that draws on Benedict Anderson's theoretical framework, see Alev Çınar, *Modernity, Islam, and Secularism in Turkey: Bodies, Places, and Time* (Minneapolis: University of Minnesota Press, 2005). The Institute for Turkish History was founded in 1931.

12. The decoupling of Turkish from Ottoman history was justified by the fact that, to date, Ottoman history had been preoccupied with the genealogy of the sultans and

their military achievements. Turkish history, in contrast, was to be concerned with the history of the people. The debate about the disassociation of Turkish and Ottoman history is one that has broad implications today in view of Turkey's refusal to accept the Armenian genocide as part of its historical legacy.

13. The Persian historian Reşidüddin's name is also transliterated as Rashid ad-Din Tabib, Rashid al-Din, or Rashiduddin. Günaltay refers here to the French eighteenth-century sinologist Joseph de Guignes. Günaltay, "Açış Dersi," 1.

14. "Bu mehareti göstermek, bir yahudi dönmesi olduğu rivayet edilen Reşidüddin için müşkül bir iş olamazdı." Ibid., 4.

15. The dönme can be compared to, but are not to be equated with, the *conversos* in fifteenth-century Spain. Sabbatai Sevi (Shabbatay Tzevi) declared himself the Jewish Messiah and planned to depose the Ottoman sultan. While imprisoned in Istanbul, he converted to Islam. Hundreds of his followers, particularly in Saloniki, also decided to convert to Islam. Gershom Scholem, who first became interested in Sabbatai Sevi in the 1930s, published the first comprehensive history of the Sabbataian movement in Hebrew in 1957. An English publication followed later: Gershom Scholem, *Sabbatai Sevi: The Mystical Messiah, 1626–1676* (Princeton, NJ: Princeton University Press, 1973).

16. For an article on this question, see Marc Baer, "The Double Bind of Race and Religion: The Conversion of the Dönme to Turkish Secular Nationalism," *Comparative Study of History and Society* 46, no. 4 (2004): 682–708.

17. For a brief history of Sabbatai Sevi's and his followers' apostasy, see Avigdor Levy, *The Sephardim in the Ottoman Empire* (Princeton, NJ: Darwin Press, 1992), 84–89. Levy points out that the sect is referred to by Jews as *minim* (sectarian) and by Muslims as *dönme*. For a lengthier discussion of the term, see Abdurrahman Küçük, *Dönmeler (Sabatayistler) Tarihi* (Ankara: Alperen Yayınları, 2001), 181–204. For a comprehensive discussion of the Sabbataian sect in the twentieth century, see Baer, "Double Bind," and Ilgaz Zorlu, *Evet, Ben Selanikliyim: Türkiye Sabetaycılığı* (Istanbul: Belge Yayınları, 1998).

18. In their dictionary of popular political terms, Aslandaş and Bıçakçı establish that the term *dönme* is used to signify a person with a hidden agenda who acts like a Trojan horse. Alper Sedat Aslandaş and Baskın Bıçakçı, *Popüler Siyasi Deyimler Sözlüğü* (Istanbul: İletişim Yayınları, 1995), 196–198. Yalçın Küçük and Soner Yalçın have, in recent years, mobilized the term *dönme* to serve their own reactionary political agenda. See, for example, Yalçın Küçük, *İsimlerin İbranileştirilmesi: Tekelistan-Türk Yahudi İsimleri Sözlüğü* (Istanbul: Salyangoz Yayınları, 2006).

19. Abdurrahman Küçük argues that at times of political crisis, the idea of the dönme as a member of a conspiracy group is remobilized in Turkey. See A. Küçük, *Dönmeler (Sabatayistler) Tarihi*, 441–443.

20. Günaltay, "Açış Dersi," 13.

21. Homi K. Bhabha, *The Location of Culture* (London: Routledge, 1994), 122.

22. By way of alternative, means of becoming a part of Europe were suggested. In 1925, the radical reformist Abdullah Cevdet suggested that intermarriages and the "mixing of blood" would pave the way for Turkey's Europeanization. For this purpose,

he proposed encouraging Italian and German immigration to Turkey. Tarık Z. Tunaya, *Türkiyenin Siyasi Hayatında Batılılaşma Hareketleri* (Istanbul: Yedigün Matbaası, 1960), 81. Abdullah Cevdet's vision of improving the "Turkish race" through hybridizing, however, did not find any support.

23. For an analysis of the "Speak Turkish" campaign, see Bali, *Cumhuriyet Yıllarında Türkiye Yahudileri*, 131–158. This campaign was initiated by a group of law students at Istanbul University. See Yelda, *Istanbul'da, Diyarbakır'da Azalırken* (Istanbul: Belge, 1996), 204. There is an interesting correlation in Turkey and in Germany about language as an assimilatory tool vis-à-vis Jews. See Hutton's discussion of the Nazi linguist Schmidt-Rohr who, in 1917, proposed a relationship between race and language and maintained a vision of the German language as assimilating force: Christopher M. Hutton, *Linguistics and the Third Reich: Mother-Tongue Fascism, Race and the Science of Language* (London: Routledge, 1999), 288–294.

24. For a discussion of Munis Tekinalp's nationalist beliefs, see Ergun Hiçyılmaz and Meral Altındal, *Büyük Sığınak: Türk Yahudilerinin 500 Yıllık Serüveninden Sayfalar* (Istanbul: Belgesel, 1992), 78–82. For a biography of Munis Tekinalp, see Liz Behmoaras, *Bir Kimlik Arayışının Hikayesi* (Istanbul: Remzi Kitapevi, 2005).

25. Seyla Benhabib suggests that the effects of the "Speak Turkish" campaign of the 1920s lasted far into the 1950s and 1960s. Her own efforts to speak Turkish without an accent in public were an outcome of a "leveling and stupefying nationalism and patriotism." Seyla Benhabib, "Traumatische Anfänge, Mythen und Experimente: Die multikulturelle Türkei im Übergang zur reifen Demokratie," *Neue Zürcher Zeitung*, November 26, 2005, 71.

26. Marc Baer argues that a distinction was made between "Turks, members of a primordial nation, and Turkish citizens, members of the Turkish nation-state." Baer, "Double Bind," 694.

27. Ibid., 704.

28. "Der Abschied von Istanbul war ein sehr melancholisches Ereignis. Spürte ich, daß damit ich von eigentlich allem Abschied nahm, was mir ansonsten Familie und Wissenschaft wert ist: deutsches Leben, alte Kultur, *ein* lieber und geliebter Mensch, viele junge Mitarbeiter, verständnisvolle Studenten—und sogar die Türken selbst, die mich doch wie einen deutschen verdienten Professor wegfeierten" ("I felt that I was really taking leave of everything that signified family and scholarship to me: German life, ancient culture, *one* loving and beloved person, many young colleagues, understanding students— and even the Turks themselves, who in fact gave me the send-off worthy of a meritorious German professor"). Letter to the Romance philologist Karl Vossler, dated December 6, 1936, quoted in Hans Ulrich Gumbrecht, *Vom Leben und Sterben der großen Romanisten: Carl Vossler, Ernst Robert Curtius, Leo Spitzer, Erich Auerbach, Werner Krauss*, ed. Michael Krüger (München: Carl Hanser Verlag, 2002), 52.

29. Quoted in Arnold Reisman, *Turkey's Modernization: Refugees from Nazism and Atatürk's Vision* (Washington, DC: New Academia Publishing, 2006), 393.

30. "Die Türken sind für meine Vergangenheit schlechterdings uninteressiert, ich vertrete hier, mag man das in Deutschland wissen wollen oder nicht, gleichviel ob ich

will oder nicht will, in den Augen der Türken nicht die deutsche Orientalistik, sondern die Europas." Ritter to Kahle, March 10, 1933: Thomas Lier, "Hellmut Ritter in Istanbul 1926–1949," *Die Welt des Islams* 38, no. 3 (1998): 347.

31. Avigdor Levy argues that Iberian Jewish culture "was transplanted to, and revitalized on, Ottoman soil" (Levy, *Sephardim in the Ottoman Empire*, 37). See also Levy, *The Jews of the Ottoman Empire* (Princeton, NJ: Darwin Press, 1994), 37–39.

32. For a critical examination of the so-called German-Jewish identity crisis and the concept of assimilation, see Scott Spector, "Forget Assimilation: Introducing Subjectivity to German-Jewish History," *Jewish History* 20, no. 3–4 (2006): 349–361.

33. Report of the Nationalsozialistische Deutsche Arbeiterpartei Auslands–Organisation Hamburg (NSDAP) to the Foreign Office in Berlin, January 8, 1935: "Vermöge ihrer Rasseeigentümlichkeit können sich diese Leute besonders gut der türkischen Mentalität anpassen und erlernen sehr schnell die Sprache des Landes." Politisches Archiv des Auswärtigen Amts, Auswärtiges Amt Abteilung III, Akte Deutsche [Experten ?] in der Türkei 1924–36, R 78630.

34. Proving to Western Europeans that Turks were not just Orientals who merely imitated and appropriated European knowledge, but people who could *be* European, was an endeavor that mutually occupied politicians, scholars, and intellectuals alike. Ottoman travel literature of the nineteenth and early twentieth centuries exemplifies the significance of this effort. Cf. Kader Konuk, "Ethnomasquerade in Ottoman-European Encounters: Re-enacting Lady Mary Wortley Montagu," *Criticism* 46, no. 3 (2004): 393–414.

35. "Die Europäer fürchten sich in diesem Land. Keiner von ihnen wird heimisch, daran ändern Jahre nichts. Man stellt ihnen grosse Aufgaben, sie lösen sie, ohne dass der Erfolg sie zufrieden macht. . . . Man hat hübsche Wohnhäuser, Tennisplätze, einen Klub, gute Pferde. Man besitzt noch dies und jenes, und man lebt in einem Land, welches an die Zukunft glaubt und an die Güter der Vernunft, der Zivilisation und des Fortschritts, die man in Europa so erniedrigend preisgibt. Das Land wird von einer Auswahl geistig hochstehender Männer regiert, von aufrichtigen Demokraten, die kein anderes Ziel kennen, als ihr Volk möglichst bald mündig zu machen. Und die Europäer, die man beruft, um an dieser Aufgabe mitzuwirken, dürfen glauben, dass sie bald überflüssig werden. Keiner zweifelt an dem Land, am Volk. Aber jeder zweifelt an seiner Aufgabe. Das ist die Furcht." Annemarie Schwarzenbach, *Winter in Vorderasien* (Basel: Lenos Verlag, 2002), 22.

36. Law professor Ernst Hirsch also describes this view in his biography. Ernst E. Hirsch, *Aus des Kaisers Zeiten durch die Weimarer Republik in das Land Atatürks: Eine unzeitgemäße Autobiographie* (München: Schweitzer, 1982), 197.

37. Erich Auerbach, May 27, 1938. "Dass 'man' uns von hier vertreiben wird, wenn man die Macht dazu hat, steht fest, und dann werden auch hier die Feinde nicht fehlen. Im Grunde haben wir natürlich viele, obgleich sie zur Zeit schweigen." Erich Auerbach, Letter to Johannes Oeschger, May 27, 1938, Nachlass Fritz Lieb, Universitätsbibliothek Basel (Handschriftenabteilung), NL 43 (Lieb) Ah 2,1.

38. Istanbul University, Chaire de Philologie Romane à la Faculté des lettres, 11 December 1936, Literaturarchiv Marbach, Nachlaß Erich Auerbach, Zugehörige Materialien.

39. Bali, *Cumhuriyet Yıllarında Türkiye Yahudileri*, 513–515.

40. My thanks go to Galit Hasan-Rokem for clarifying this distinction in my work.

41. Galit Hasan-Rokem and Alan Dundes, *The Wandering Jew: Essays in the Interpretation of a Christian Legend* (Bloomington: Indiana University Press, 1986), vii.

42. Edward Timms, *The Wandering Jew: A Leitmotif in German Literature and Politics* (Brighton, UK: University of Sussex, 1994).

43. Elizabeth Grosz, "Judaism and Exile: The Ethics of Otherness," in *Space and Place: Theories of Identity and Location*, ed. Erica Carter, James Donald, and Judith Squires (London: Lawrence & Wishart, 1993), 61.

44. For an essay investigating the changing social structures for Jews in the Ottoman and republican period, see Riva Kastoryano, "From *Millet* to Community: The Jews of Istanbul," in *Ottoman and Turkish Jewry: Community and Leadership*, ed. Aron Rodrigue (Bloomington: Indiana University Press, 1992), 253–277; and Aron Rodrigue, "From Millet to Minority: Turkish Jewry in the 19th and 20th Centuries," in *Paths of Emancipation: Jews within States and Capitalism*, ed. Pierre Birnbaum and Ira Katznelson (Princeton, NJ: Princeton University Press, 1995), 238–261.

45. Avigdor Levy also maintains in this context that in 1892, at the fourth centennial celebration of the settlement of Sephardic Jews in the Ottoman Empire, "sentiments of gratitude were sincere" (Levy, *Sephardim in the Ottoman Empire*, 124). Levy points out that by the mid-sixteenth century, "Ottomans came to regard the Jews in a class by themselves and as playing a special role in the processes of empire-building" (ibid., 66). In the 1920s, Mehmed Karakaşzade Rüşdü, a Turkish nationalist of dönme origin, reinterpreted the motif of the host and the guest and identified "the host and the parasite motif, which was current at the time: the Turks are the unwitting host to a dangerous parasite that can destroy them" (Baer, "Double Bind," 697).

46. For a chapter on Turkey as a transit country to Palestine, see Corry Guttstadt, *Die Türkei, die Juden und der Holocaust* (Berlin: Assoziation A, 2008), 235–257.

47. The German embassy and consulate reported in January and February of 1939 that the Turkish government considered expelling those European Jews from Turkey who were expected to become stateless as a result of the new racial legislation in their native countries. According to the reports in the German archive that have to be verified by other accounts, the Turkish government did not want to host stateless Jews. German-Jewish professors were not going to be affected by this order. Politisches Archiv des Auswärtigen Amts, Konstantinopel / Ankara 540, Akte Judentum Band 2.

48. "Başvekil Refik Saydam'ın Gazetecilerle Hasbıhali," *Vakit*, January 27, 1939, cited in Douglas Frantz and Catherine Collins, *Death on the Black Sea: The Untold Story of the* Struma *and World War II's Holocaust at Sea* (New York: Ecco, 2003), 138–139. Refik Saydam announced that if "they happen to have sisters or families or close relatives in other countries who would wish to come to our country, we would welcome them to enable the experts to work with comfortable minds."

49. On January 23, 1939, the German embassy in Ankara informed the Foreign Office in Berlin that the Turkish government wanted to avoid the settlement of a greater number of Jewish émigrés in Turkey. Along with this, the embassy passed on the information about the proof of Aryan descent now required at Turkish consulates. Politisches Archiv des Auswärtigen Amts, Konstantinopel / Ankara, 539, Akte Judentum 1925–1939. Hellmut Ritter's brother writes in his travel diary in July 1939, too, that he has to verify his Aryan descent to Turkish authorities. Karl Bernhard Ritter, *Fahrt zum Bosporus: Ein Reisetagebuch* (Leipzig: Hegner, 1941), 151.

50. "Şehrimizdeki Alman Musevileri Almanlıktan Çıkardılar," *Yeni Sabah*, 12 August 1939, cited in Bali, *Cumhuriyet Yıllarında Türkiye Yahudileri*, 337.

51. After his naturalization in 1943, Hirsch was not paid the higher salary that was reserved for foreign professors. He received the same salary as his Turkish colleagues. Hirsch, *Aus des Kaisers Zeiten*, 281.

52. Politisches Archiv des Auswärtigen Amts, Akten des Generalkonsulats Istanbul, 3989, Paket 28, Akte 2 Istanbul Emigranten. Toepke's report is dated October 9, 1939; he wrote, "Anträge auf Einbürgerung haben sämtliche Juden und Mischlinge gestellt mit Ausnahme von Professor Auerbach."

53. Corry Guttstadt researched several Turkish and German archives to assess the politics of citizenship with regard to Jews in Turkey. Guttstadt, *Die Türkei*, 224–234.

54. Hirsch, for example, says that the general public continued to regard him and other émigrés who had become Turkish citizens as foreigners. Hirsch, *Aus des Kaisers Zeiten*, 196.

55. See also Martin Vialon, "Kommentar," *Trajekte* 9 (2004): 14.

56. The letter is dated June 5, 1938. Erich Auerbach, "Ein Exil-Brief Erich Auerbachs aus Istanbul an Freya Hobohm in Marburg—versehen mit einer Nachschrift von Marie Auerbach (1938), Transkribiert und kommentiert von Martin Vialon," *Trajekte* 9 (2004): 11.

57. Responsible for this is, after all, Turkey's switch from the Arabic to the Roman alphabet in 1928 and the establishment of the Institute for the Turkish Language in the 1930s that promoted the "purification" of the Turkish language, thereby replacing Arabic and Persian words with Turkish vocabulary. The Arabic script ceased to be taught in schools.

58. Erich Auerbach, *Gesammelte Aufsätze zur Romanischen Philologie* (Bern: Francke Verlag, 1967), 305.

59. Martin Vialon, ed., *Erich Auerbachs Briefe an Martin Hellweg (1939–1950)* (Tübingen: A. Francke Verlag, 1997), 78. The letter is dated May 16, 1947.

60. "Ich bin doch sehr liberalistisch, die von den Umständen mir verliehene Lage hat diese Neigung noch verstärkt; ich geniesse hier die grösste Freiheit des ne pas conclure. Ich konnte mich hier wie nirgends sonst von jeder Bindung freihalten; gerade meine Haltung als nirgends Hingehöriger, grundsätzlich und unassimilierbar Fremder ist das, was man von mir wünscht und von mir erwartet, aber, wo Sie mich hinhaben wollen, erwartet man eine 'Grundbereitschaft.'" Auerbach's letter to Werner Krauss is dated August 27, 1946. Karlheinz Barck, "Eine unveröffentlichte Korrespondenz: Erich

Auerbach/Werner Krauss," *Beiträge zur Romanischen Philologie* 26, no. 2 (1987): 317. I have slightly changed Gumbrecht's translation of this passage in Hans Ulrich Gumbrecht, " 'Pathos of the Earthly Progress': Erich Auerbach's Everydays," in *Literary History and the Challenge of Philology: The Legacy of Erich Auerbach*, ed. Seth Lerer (Stanford, CA: Stanford University Press, 1996), 32.

61. Letter to Werner Krauss dated October 27, 1946: "Mit Gastprofessur sieht es zur Zeit böse aus, da man als passloser Deutscher sich nicht bewegen kann, oder doch nur hinaus, nicht wieder hinein; die Versuche die andere unternommen haben um diese Schwierigkeit zu überwinden waren bisher erfolglos. Sie wären sofort überwunden, wenn wir die türkische Staatsangehörigkeit annähmen, was man uns jetzt anbietet; aber das hat seine Nachteile, und wäre auch nicht anständig, wenn man wegzugehen gedenkt." Nachlaß Erich Auerbach, Literaturarchiv Marbach.

62. Vialon, *Erich Auerbachs Briefe an Martin Hellweg*, 70. The letter is dated May 16, 1947. In a 1946 letter, Auerbach complained to Werner Krauss about the impossibility of moving since he did not have a passport. Barck, "Erich Auerbach/Werner Krauss," 316.

63. Emir Kıvırcık, *Büyükelçi* (Istanbul: Goa, 2007), 10.

64. According to Nazi records, 3,042 Turkish Jews lived in Paris alone in 1942: Politisches Archiv des Auswärtigen Amts, R 100889, Akte Judenfrage in der Türkei 1942–1944, Inland II g 207. A telegram from Paris, dated February 12, 1943, reports that the Turkish General Consul presented Nazi authorities with a list of 631 Turkish Jews whose citizenship he had cleared. A memorandum dated February 17, 1943, states the estimated number of Turkish Jews living in the Western occupied territories as 3,000. Another report, dated March 12, 1943, refers to the departure of 121 Turkish Jews in mid-March. The same record refers to a list of five thousand Turkish Jews, which is not part of the archive. All documents are located in Politisches Archiv des Auswärtigen Amts, Judenfrage in der Türkei, R 99446 1938–1943, Inland II A/B. In *Turkey and the Holocaust*, Stanford Shaw evaluated a different set of archival sources. For a novel dealing with Turkish Jews in France, see Ayşe Kulin, *Nefes Nefese*, 15th ed. (Istanbul: Remzi Kitapevi, 2002).

65. Corinna Görgü Guttstadt, "Depriving Non-Muslims of Citizenship as Part of the Turkification Policy in the Early Years of the Republic: The Case of Turkish Jews and Its Consequences during the Holocaust," in *Turkey beyond Nationalism: Towards Post-Nationalist Identities*, ed. Hans-Lukas Kieser (London: I. B. Tauris, 2006), 56.

66. See, for example, a report from Paris to the Foreign Office in Berlin, June 23, 1943: "Mündlich hat der hiesige türkische Generalkonsul durchblicken lassen, daß die Türkische Regierung auf diese Anfrage keine Antwort erteilen könne, weil sie offiziell einen Unterschied zwischen türkischen Staatsangehörigen jüdischer und anderer Rasse nicht mache." Politisches Archiv des Auswärtigen Amts, Judenfrage in der Türkei, R 99446 1938–1943, Inland II A/B.

67. Memorandum by von Thadden, dated September 22, 1943. Koç, the representative of the Turkish embassy in Berlin, informed von Thadden of the Turkish government's decision: "die türkischen Konsularvertretungen mit der Weisung zu versehen, alle rückkehrwilligen Juden türkischer Staatsangehörigkeit nach Prüfung jedes Einzelfalles in der Türkei zu übernehmen. Hierbei solle davon ausgegangen werden, daß eine Masseneinwanderung von

Juden in die Türkei zu verhindern sei, insbesondere von solchen Juden, die zwar ordnungs-gemäß türkische Papiere hätten, aber bereits seit Jahrzehnten mit der Türkei keinerlei Kontakt mehr hätten." Ibid.

68. Isaak Behar's autobiographical account of his life as a Turkish Jew in Nazi Germany tells a tragic story. Behar writes that, in April 1939, the Turkish government asked his family to verify their citizenship. After handing over their Turkish passports to German authorities, however, the Behar family was left unprotected and eventually declared stateless. Isaak Behar survived by going underground; his parents and two sisters were deported and killed in death camps: Isaak Behar, *Versprich mir, dass Du am Leben bleibst: Ein jüdisches Schicksal* (Berlin: Ullstein, 2002), 73–74.

69. At the time, it was not known that the Soviets sank the *Struma*. Tuvia Friling, *Between Friendly and Hostile Neutrality: Turkey and the Jews during World War II*, vol. 2 (Jerusalem: Tel Aviv University, 2002), 331–333. For other accounts of the *Struma* tragedy, see Hiçyılmaz and Altındal, *Büyük Sığınak*. For the most comprehensive account, see Frantz and Collins, *Death on the Black Sea*.

70. Bali, *Cumhuriyet Yıllarında Türkiye Yahudileri*, 361.

71. Frantz and Collins, *Death on the Black Sea*, 217. See also Bali, *Cumhuriyet Yıllarında Türkiye Yahudileri*, 361.

72. On October 14, 1942, the German embassy provided the Foreign Office in Berlin with a detailed report on the "State of the Jewish Problem in Turkey." The report, by Julius Seiler, showed that there was an increase in anti-Semitism in Turkey—evidenced by tax measures, Saydam's response to Jewish refugees, and labor camps: Politisches Archiv des Auswärtigen Amts, Judenfrage in der Türkei, R 99446 1938–1943, Inland II A/B.

73. Rıfat N. Bali, *The "Varlık Vergisi" Affair: A Study of Its Legacy—Selected Documents* (Istanbul: Isis Press, 2005), 55.

74. For a discussion of the discriminatory nature of the capital tax, see Rıfat Bali's study (ibid., 99), which includes original documents from various national archives. All in all, between the years 1942 and 1943, 1,443 members of minorities were sent to the Aşkale labor camp and were released by December 1943.

75. Sule Toktas, "Citizenship and Minorities: A Historical Overview of Turkey's Jewish Minority," *Journal of Historical Sociology* 18, no. 4 (2005): 404.

76. A. Küçük, *Dönmeler (Sabatayistler) Tarihi*, 43, 438. A renewed interest in the religious practices of dönme is also evident in publications from the war period. İbrahim Alaettin Gövsa suggested in 1940 that twelve thousand Sabbataian families lived in Turkey. See İbrahim Alaettin Gövsa, *Sabatay Sevi: İzmirli Meşhur Sahte Mesih Hakkında Tarihî ve İçtimaî Tetkik Tecrübesi* (Istanbul: S. Lütfi Kitapevi, 1940).

77. See the collection of cartoons in *Yahudi Fıkraları* (Istanbul: Akbaba Yayını, 1943).

78. Nadir Nadi, *Cumhuriyet*, January 23, 1943. Nadi's article is summarized in Bali, *"Varlık Vergisi,"* 266.

79. Public Record Office, FO371/37470/R5698, Report by H. Knatchbull-Hugessen to the Right Honorouble Anthony Eden, M.C., M.P., No. 254 (779/3/43) British Em-

bassy, Ankara, June 21, 1943. Quoted in ibid., 278. I assume that the insertion in brackets ("[450 years ago!]") stems from Knatchbull-Hugessen.

80. Moltke went to Istanbul in July and December 1943, where he also met Paul Leverkuehn, who directed the Istanbul branch of the German intelligence service, and the German ambassador Franz von Papen. Moltke unsuccessfully tried to "dissuade the Allies from the demand of unconditional surrender on the part of the Germans." Freya von Moltke, *Memories of Kreisau and the German Resistance*, trans. Julie M. Winter (Lincoln: University of Nebraska Press, 2005), 38. See also Klemens von Klemperer, *German Resistance against Hitler: The Search for Allies Abroad, 1938–1945* (Oxford: Oxford University Press, 1992), 331.

81. The document can be viewed at http://germanhistorydocs.ghi-dc.org/sub_document.cfm?document_id=1517 (accessed December 1, 2007). For an overview of Moltke's and Rüstow's efforts in Istanbul, see Michael Balfour and Julian Frisby, *Helmuth von Moltke: A Leader against Hitler* (London: Macmillan, 1972), 270–281.

82. "Das Rassebewußtsein ist sehr ausgeprägt. Zita, die Angestellte von Leverkühn, ist Griechin. Sie redet mit keinem Türken. Die Juden sind hier völlige outcasts; sie werden mit Du angeredet und man gibt ihnen weder die Hand noch einen Stuhl, auch wenn sie von Geld strotzen und ganz europäisiert sind. Levantiner sind Kinder aus Mischehen mit Italienern und Griechen. Auch das Kind eines Deutschen mit einer Griechin ist ein Levantiner und steht sozial unter den Türken. Alles ist merkwürdig." Helmuth James von Moltke, *Briefe an Freya 1939–1945* (München: C. H. Beck, 1988), 504. I have slightly changed the translation of the letter in Helmuth James von Moltke, *Letters to Freya: 1939–1945*, trans. Beate Ruhm von Appen (New York: Alfred A. Knopf, 1990), 319. The letter is dated July 7, 1943.

83. "Uns ist es wider jede Wahrscheinlichkeit gut gegangen; die neue Ordnung drang nicht bis zu den Meerengen; damit ist eigentlich alles gesagt. Wir haben in unserer Wohnung gelebt und nichts erlitten als kleine Unbequemlichkeiten und Furcht: bis Ende 42 sah es sehr böse aus, aber dann verzog sich die Wolke allmählich." Vialon, *Erich Auerbachs Briefe an Martin Hellweg*, 69–70.

84. In March 1944, the capital tax debts were released. Bali, "*Varlık Vergisi*," 55.

85. Selim Deringil, *Turkish Foreign Policy during the Second World War: An "Active" Neutrality* (Cambridge: Cambridge University Press, 1989), 184.

86. For Turkey's negotiation with the Allies over the delivery of chromite, see ibid., 168–169.

87. Guttstadt, *Die Türkei*, 255–256.

88. Nurullah Ataç, *Diyelim* (Istanbul: Varlık Yayınları, 1954), 98–99.

Chapter 4

1. C. Busolt, "Deutsch als Weltsprache," *Türkische Post: Tageszeitung für den Nahen Osten*, February 1, 1933, 1–2.

2. Anne Dietrich, *Deutschsein in Istanbul: Nationalisierung und Orientierung in der deutschsprachigen Community von 1843 bis 1956* (Opladen: Leske und Budrich, 1998), 78.

Due to the military alliance between the German and the Ottoman empires in World War I and the decline of the Ottoman Empire, the size of the community varied. In 1926, after the revival of German-Turkish relations, an estimated fifteen hundred Germans lived in Istanbul. By 1938, the German-speaking community in Turkey had swelled to more than two thousand Germans and a thousand Austrians. Dietrich, *Deutschsein in Istanbul*, 177–178.

3. The school still exists and is located in the part of the city that used to be known as Pera. Numerous other German institutions were established, including the Protestant Church School in 1857, the Protestant Church in 1861, the branch of the Deutsche Bank in 1888, and the German Orient Bank in 1906.

4. The Germans living in Istanbul referred to themselves as *Auslandsdeutsche*, that is, Germans abroad; they were organized in the *Bund der Auslandsdeutschen*, the Union for Germans Abroad. Dietrich, *Deutschsein in Istanbul*, 178.

5. Horst Widmann, *Exil und Bildungshilfe: Die deutschsprachige akademische Emigration in die Türkei nach 1933* (Bern: Herbert Lang, 1973), 76. Only places such as the German Hospital, the German Archeological Institute, and the Protestant Church were frequented by both circles, the national socialists and the émigrés. Stanford J. Shaw, *Turkey and the Holocaust: Turkey's Role in Rescuing Turkish and European Jewry from Nazi Persecution, 1933–1945* (Hampshire, UK: Macmillan Press, 1993), 13. See also Widmann, *Exil und Bildungshilfe*, 76. The documentary *Zuflucht am Bosporus* by Nedim Hazar and Pavel Schnabel (Troja Filmproduktion in Koproduktion mit Goethe-Institut Inter Nationes e.V., Deutschland 2001, ZDF) is based on interviews with two children of emigrants, Addi Scholz and Cornelius Bischoff.

6. For a discussion of the *Gleichschaltung* in Istanbul, see Dietrich, *Deutschsein in Istanbul*, 203–256.

7. For a discussion of German media in Turkey, see Johannes Glasneck, *Methoden der deutsch-faschistischen Propagandatätigkeit in der Türkei vor und während des Zweiten Weltkriegs* (Halle: Martin-Luther-Universität Halle, 1966). In 1937, the Nazi propaganda was amplified by the opening of a German news agency in Istanbul.

8. The articles published in the newspaper offer insights into the concerns and aims of Nazi officials in Istanbul. See, for example, F.F.S.D., "Die Heimat," *Türkische Post: Tageszeitung für den Nahen Osten*, April 18, 1933, 1–2; "Auslandsdeutschtum und deutsche Erneuerung," *Türkische Post: Tageszeitung für den Nahen Osten*, April 3, 1933, 1–2; "Reichsregierung und Auslandsdeutschtum," *Türkische Post: Tageszeitung für den Nahen Osten*, March 18, 1933, 1–2.

9. Along with the Istanbul-based newspaper, the magazine *Signal*, edited by Goebbels's ministry for propaganda, circulated in the German community. Dietrich, *Deutschsein in Istanbul*, 193.

10. For a report about the flag-raising festival, the Flaggenfeier, at the consulate and the celebration of Hitler's birthday in the community hall Alemannia, see "Die Hitler-Geburtstagsfeier in Stambul," *Türkische Post: Tageszeitung für den Nahen Osten*, April 22, 1933, 4; "Flaggenfeier," *Türkische Post: Tageszeitung für den Nahen Osten*, March 17, 1933, 4.

11. Letter by Toepke to the Foreign Office, Istanbul, June 27, 1935. Politisches Archiv des Auswärtigen Amts, Berlin, Akten des Generalkonsulats Istanbul, 3977, Paket 9, NSDAP Band I 1933–. Also cited in Dietrich, *Deutschsein in Istanbul*, 171. Forty of the members were Austrian and Czech citizens. Anne Dietrich believes that German émigrés were not included in the count. The Nazis in Ankara reported that, out of 350 Germans, fifty had become members of the Nazi Party.

12. The émigré Nissen attributes this victory to the insecurity of German diplomats after Hitler's rise to power. Rudolf Nissen, *Helle Blätter, dunkle Blätter: Erinnerungen eines Chirurgen* (Stuttgart: Deutsche Verlags-Anstalt, 1969). See also Widmann, *Exil und Bildungshilfe*, 58, 76. Compare Schwartz's memoirs in Philipp Schwartz, *Notgemeinschaft: Zur Emigration deutscher Wissenschaftler nach 1933 in die Türkei* (Marburg: Metropolis-Verlag, 1995), 57.

13. Nissen, *Helle Blätter, dunkle Blätter*, 226.

14. See, for example, Politisches Archiv des Auswärtigen Amts, Berlin, Akten des Generalkonsulats Istanbul, 3970, Paket 1, Akte "Propaganda" 1935–39.

15. Report by Saucken: "Die deutschen Professoren an der Istanbuler Universität." February 28, 1935. Politisches Archiv des Auswärtigen Amts, Berlin, Akten des Generalkonsulats Istanbul, 3976, Paket 8, Akte Geheim Band II, Dezember 1932–1935.

16. Toepke lists five emigrant professors as suspicious—Kantorowisz, Liepmann, Liepschitz, Mieses, and Schwartz. Toepke also notes that, along with the forty-six emigrant scholars, five scholars were sent by the German ministry of education to Istanbul, namely, Schede, Bittel, Bossert, Ritter, and Bodendorf. The report is dated May 22, 1935. Politisches Archiv des Auswärtigen Amts, Berlin, Akten des Generalkonsulats Istanbul, GK Istanbul 164, Band III 1935–1936. See also a later report by German ambassador Keller, dated March 8, 1938. Politisches Archiv des Auswärtigen Amts, Berlin, Akten des Generalkonsulats Istanbul, 3970, Paket 1, Akte: "Kulturpropaganda (Allgemeines), Akte 'Propaganda' besonders" März 1930–.

17. In 1935, Paul Hindemith was invited to Turkey, where he advised Turkish authorities about ideas for musical life in Turkey. For this purpose, he wrote the essay "Vorschläge für den Aufbau des türkischen Musiklebens." Thomas Lier writes about Hellmut Ritter's chamber quartet in Thomas Lier, "Hellmut Ritter und die Zweigstelle der DMG in Istanbul 1928–1949," in *Hellmut Ritter und die DMG in Istanbul*, ed. Angelika Neuwirth and Armin Bassarak (Istanbul: Orient Institut der Deutschen Morgenländischen Gesellschaft, 1997), 40–41.

18. "Sie haben vor einem Jahr in so offener und feinfühliger Weise mit mir über das Emigrantenproblem gesprochen, dass ich mir vielleicht erlauben darf, Ihnen meine Gefühle angesichts des beschämenden Vorgangs neulich in der Deutschen Schule bei dem *Amar*-Konzert auszusprechen. Welchen peinlichen und widerspruchsvollen Eindruck musste es auf die zahlreichen Deutschen und Ausländer machen, die die deutsche Musik lieben und die hier bisher von deutscher Seite kaum so hochwertige Darbietungen gehört haben, – dass die offizielle Vertretung des Deutschen Reiches ein Konzert des jüdischen Künstlers anhörte, aber nicht <u>ihm</u>, sondern seinen Mitarbeitern, die <u>er</u> erst auf diese

künstlerische Höhe gebracht hat, die Hand zu schütteln für richtig befand. Ist der Virus den das Ohr vermittelt, gefahrloser als der des Händedruckes? Will man es ungeschehen machen, dass eine unerwünschte Geige Beethovensche Laute erstehen ließ? Und soll das 'Seid umschlungen, Millionen' durch binnenländische Grenzziehung ersetzt werden? Man sagt, unsere Zeit sei nicht mehr die Beethovens, sie sei die der Eroberer und Realpolitiker. Aber wen kann man so realpolitisch erobern? Keine der beiden deutschen Gruppen kann von diesem Halben, diesem Zuhören und Nicht-Zugehört-Haben-Wollen, diesem Kommen und Diskriminieren befriedigt sein—erst recht nicht die türkischen Zeugen solcher Tragikomik. Beethoven macht die richtige Propaganda: er gewinnt die Herzen. Schwer kann ich die Menschen verstehen, die durch Duldung solcher Kulturwidrigkeiten diese erst richtig herausstellen und ad absurdum führen. Werden sie nicht innerlich zerrissen von der Lüge, die sie mitmachen, und warum treten sie auf eine Bühne, die jede ihrer Bewegungen im Vexierspiegel verzerrt? Bitter für den Deutschen, zu denken, dass er deutsche Musik hier ungestört nur im Robert College, in der Casa d'Italia oder im Fransız Tiyatrosu hören kann! Dies wollte ich aussprechen, verzeihen Sie die Offenheit." The letter, dated December 10, 1935, is archived in the consulate files at the Politisches Archiv des Auswärtigen Amts, Berlin, Akten des Generalkonsulats Istanbul, GK Istanbul 164, Band III 1935–1936.

19. Much as it has been disputed, this strain of Beethoven reception persists into the present. On the universal in German music, see Celia Applegate, "What Is German Music? Reflections on the Role of Art in the Creation of the German Nation," *German Studies Review* 15 (1992): 21–32.

20. For a study of German musicology during the Third Reich, see Pamela Potter, *Most German of the Arts: Musicology: Musicology and Society from the Weimar Republic to the End of Hitler's Reich* (New Haven, CT: Yale University Press, 1998).

21. Victor Klemperer, *LTI: Notizbuch eines Philologen* (Berlin: Aufbau-Verlag, 1947), 169.

22. Spitzer's letter to the vice consul is dated December 12, 1935. Politisches Archiv des Auswärtigen Amts, Berlin, Akten des Generalkonsulats Istanbul, GK Istanbul 164, Band III 1935–1936.

23. Ibid. Toepke wrote on November 26, 1935: Spitzer "machte darauf aufmerksam, daß von den Franzosen bereits jetzt stark darauf hingearbeitet würde, ihn durch einen französischen Professor ersetzen zu lassen. Er hielte eine solche Lösung aus kulturellen und wissenschaftlichen Gründen für unglücklich und frug mich, ob nicht die Möglichkeit bestehe, der Universität einen deutschen Professor vorzuschlagen. Da seinem Eindruck nach sowohl der türkische Kulturminister als auch sein Staatssekretär sehr deutschfreundlich seien, glaube er, daß ein solcher Vorschlag auch Aussicht auf Erfolg haben werde."

24. For another record of a conversation between the consul and Spitzer about the details of German language teaching at Istanbul University, see the report dated May 22, 1935. Ibid.

25. Ibid. Consul Toepke's letter to Ambassador Keller, dated December 13, 1935.

26. See a copy of Spitzer's apology, dated December 16, 1935. The apology has no signature. Ibid.

27. Ali Arslan, *Darülfünun'dan Üniversiteye* (Istanbul: Kitabevi, 1995), 417.

28. For the course offerings in 1936–1937, see *Edebiyat Fakültesi: 1936–7 Ders Yılı Talebe Kılavuzu* (Istanbul: Resimli Ay Basımevi T.L.S., 1936).

29. Among the scholars who emigrated to Turkey with Spitzer's assistance were Heinz Anstock, Eva Buck, Rosemarie Burkart, Herbert Dieckmann, Liselotte Dieckmann, Traugott Fuchs, and Hans Marchand. Among the scholars Auerbach helped to emigrate were Robert Anhegger (Islamic Studies), Ernst Engelberg, Kurt Laqueur, Andreas Tietze (Turkish Studies), and Karl Weiner. See Widmann, *Exil und Bildungshilfe*, 290–291. For a short biography in which Fuchs describes how the SS tried to intimidate him because he collected signatures against Spitzer's dismissal, see Traugott Fuchs, *Çorum and Anatolian Pictures* (Istanbul: Boğaziçi Üniversitesi, Cultural Heritage Museum Publications, 1986), 7–14. Martin Vialon studied Traugott Fuchs's archive now housed at Boğaziçi University and published his research on Fuchs and Auerbach in Martin Vialon, "The Scars of Exile: Paralipomena concerning the Relationship between History, Literature, and Politics—Demonstrated in the Examples of Erich Auerbach, Traugott Fuchs, and Their Circle in Istanbul," *Yeditepe University Philosophy Department: A Refereed Yearbook* 1, no. 2 (2003): 191–246.

30. *Edebiyat Fakültesi.*

31. Emily Apter, "Global *Translatio*: The 'Invention' of Comparative Literature, Istanbul, 1933," *Critical Inquiry* 29, no. 2 (2003): 269–270.

32. Rosemarie Burkart, "Truchement: Histoire d'un mot Oriental en Français," *Romanoloji Semineri Dergisi* 1 (1937): 53.

33. Although her article highlighted the significance of translation processes to human history, she ended with a cautionary note: "L''expositeur' de parlers étrangers a subi des revers que connaît tout homme qui se trouve en marge d'un milieu." Ibid., 55.

34. Azra Erhat, "Üslup Ilminde Yeni bir Usul," *Romanoloji Semineri Dergisi* 1 (1937): 5.

35. "Dass 'man' uns von hier vertreiben wird, wenn man die Macht dazu hat, steht fest, und dann werden auch hier die Feinde nicht fehlen. Im Grunde haben wir natürlich viele, obgleich sie zur Zeit schweigen." Erich Auerbach, Letter to Johannes Oeschger, May 27, 1938, Nachlass Fritz Lieb, Universitätsbibliothek Basel (Handschriftenabteilung), NL 43 (Lieb) Ah 2,1.

36. "Sie haben sich nicht verbittern lassen, sie haben das hingenommen und ertragen mit einem gleichmut, der zur bewunderung zwingt. Ist es weise lebensfilosofie, ist es temparament? Vielleicht ist es beides, das sie befähigt, über vieles leichter hinwegzukommen als manche andere. Sie schoben wohl, so schien es uns oft, mit gelassener hand manch würgende last, die andere fast erdrückte, zur seite und von sich fort. Sie gaben sich nicht hin, Sie liessen sich nicht überwältigen! Sie besassen wohl die magische kraft, die dinge zu reduzieren und manche dämonen unschädlich zu machen, in dem Sie sie, wie der fischer in 1001 nacht, in die flasche zurückzwangen, der sie entstiegen waren, um sich ungebührlich zu Monstern aufzublasen, die die seele bedrücken. Oder schien es uns nur so?

Genug, Sie traten uns allezeit entgegen mit einer seltenen serenität der seele, die Sie nie im stich zu lassen schien, und vielleicht war es gerade dieser zauber der serenität der seele, der uns auch dann wieder zu Ihnen zwang, wenn uns . . . die . . . allzu gelassene hand einmal befremdete?" The German is transcribed as written. Hellmut Ritter's letter to Erich and Marie Auerbach has no specific date but was written in 1947. The original is archived in the Auerbach Nachlaß, Literaturarchiv Marbach.

37. Despite worsening conditions for Jews in Nazi Germany, Auerbach insisted on his right to receive German state benefits while he lived in Turkish exile. Karlheinz Barck, "'Flucht in die Tradition': Erfahrungshintergründe Erich Auerbachs zwischen Exil und Emigration," in *Stimme, Figur: Kritik und Restitution in der Literaturwissenschaft*, ed. Aleida Assman and Anselm Haverkamp (Stuttgart: Metzler, 1994), 57.

38. Letter by Carsten Meves, head of the Nazi Party branch in Istanbul, dated November 25, 1937. Politisches Archiv des Auswärtigen Amts, Berlin, Akten des Generalkonsulats Istanbul, 3977, Paket 9, Akte NSDAP, 1937–1940.

39. Letter by Carsten Meves, head of the Nazi Party branch in Istanbul, to the German consulate in Istanbul, January 18, 1938. See also the letter by Hänni, head of the DAV, to the general consul on February 3, 1938. Ibid.

40. In his letter, Auerbach defended the club: "Lassen Sie sich bitte von maßgebender Stelle belehren, was eine politische Vereinigung überhaupt ist und nehmen Sie zur Kenntnis, daß der 'D.A.V.' weder mit Politik oder dergleichen je etwas zu tun hatte, noch zu tun hat und auch nie haben wird." Letter by Auerbach to Oskar Krenn, April 14, 1939. Ibid.

41. Ibid.

42. See report about the general assembly of the DAV, April 8, 1939. Ibid.

43. Karl Bernhard Ritter was an influential clergyman who traveled to Turkey to visit his brother Hellmut Ritter. Karl Bernhard Ritter, *Fahrt zum Bosporus: Ein Reisetagebuch* (Leipzig: Hegner, 1941), 152. See also chapter 3 in this volume on the legal status of German Jews in Turkey.

44. For an article on this topic, see Barck, "'Flucht in die Tradition,'" 47–60.

45. ". . . sich jeder politischen Betätigung enthält." Seiler also noted that the only significant conflicts he was aware of arose with Halide Edip (Adıvar), the most significant woman politician and writer of the early Turkish Republic who had returned from exile in Britain and now chaired the English department at Istanbul University. Ibid., 57.

46. The report by the German ambassador Keller, dated March 8, 1938, is titled "Erster Kultur-Jahresbericht für die Türkei." Keller wrote: "Die Intensivierung unseres Kultureinflusses muss notgedrungen bei der Propagierung der Sprache einsetzen. Wie das französische Beispiel eindringlich demonstriert, ist die Verbreitung der Sprache auf die Dauer der einzig wirksame Schlüssel zur kulturellen Durchdringung des Landes. Der durch den Krieg bedingte Aufschwung, den die deutsche Sprache hier erfahren hat, müsste mit allen Mitteln gestützt und ausgebaut werden." Politisches Archiv des Auswärtigen Amts, Berlin, Akten des Generalkonsulats Istanbul, 3970, Paket 1, Akte: "Kulturpropaganda (Allgemeines), Akte 'Propaganda' besonders" März 1930–.

47. Report by German ambassador Keller, dated March 8, 1938. Ibid.

48. The director of the reading room, Stumvoll, named these as its financial backers. The consulate report is dated February 26, 1938. Ibid.

49. "Türkiyede Nazi Propagandası," *Haber*, January 1, 1938. "Türkiyede Nazi propagandası yapılması karşısında lakayt kalamayız! Nasyonal-Sosyalist propaganda yatakları üniversitemizin yanıbaşına kadar sokuldu."

50. See Toepke's report, February 26, 1938. Politisches Archiv des Auswärtigen Amts, Berlin, Akten des Generalkonsulats Istanbul, 3970, Paket 1, Akte: "Kulturpropaganda (Allgemeines), Akte 'Propaganda' besonders" März 1930–.

51. Kurt Bodendorf, specialist for pharmaceutical chemistry, who had been sent by the German ministry of science and education to teach at Istanbul University, gathered information about the activities and teachings of émigré scholars and reported to the German consulate. After Bodendorf left Turkey, Consul Toepke requested a substitute from the Foreign Office in Berlin (April 3, 1939). See also Toepke's letter dated May 13, 1939. Politisches Archiv des Auswärtigen Amts, Berlin, Akten des Generalkonsulats Istanbul, GK Istanbul 167, Universität Istanbul Band VI.

52. Consul Toepke's report to the Foreign Office in Berlin, dated August 3, 1937: Politisches Archiv des Auswärtigen Amts, Berlin, Akten des Generalkonsulats Istanbul, 3989, Paket 28, Akte 1 Istanbul Emigranten. Bodendorf wrote: "Auerbach hat sich einmal dienstlich bei mir gemeldet, seither habe ich nicht das Geringste mehr über ihn gehört, da er, wie alle Emigranten, den Verkehr mit hiesigen Deutschen mit Ausnahme der Emigrantenkreise peinlichst meidet."

53. "In das Professorenkollegium einen Keil nationalsozialistisch gesinnter Männer hineinzutreiben." Consul Toepke to the Foreign Office in Berlin on May 25, 1938: Politisches Archiv des Auswärtigen Amts, Berlin, Akten des Generalkonsulats Istanbul, GK Istanbul 166, Band V November 1937–Mai 1939.

54. Yunus Nadi, November 11, 1937, "Les cours de langues étrangères à l'Université." Ibid. The articles, which were also published in Turkey's French-language newspaper, *République*, are also archived in Politisches Archiv des Auswärtigen Amts, Berlin, Akten des Generalkonsulats Istanbul, GK Istanbul 165, Band IV 1936–1937.

55. Ernst Hirsch, *Dünya Üniversiteleri ve Türkiyede Üniversitelerin Gelişmesi*, vol. 1 (Istanbul: Ankara Üniversitesi Yayımları, 1950), 349–473.

56. "Die Tätigkeit deutscher Hochschullehrer an türkischen wissenschaftlichen Hochschulen" was published in Klaus Detlev Grothusen, ed., *Der Scurla-Bericht: Migration deutscher Professoren in die Türkei im Dritten Reich* (Frankfurt: Dagyeli, 1987).

57. ". . . die Stellung der Emigranten an der Universität zu schwächen." Ibid., 117.

58. The faculty comprised Rosemarie Burkart; Fuchs, who had refused to fill out the questionnaire distributed to German émigrés by the German General Consul; Heinz Anstock, whom Scurla charged with being an active communist; Hans Marchand, whose marriage to an Aryan he pointed out; and Ritter, who directed the branch of the German Oriental Society and about whom Scurla was unable to arrive at any definitive conclusions.

59. Grothusen, *Der Scurla-Bericht*, 100, 106.

60. Cf. Politisches Archiv des Auswärtigen Amts, Berlin, Akten des Generalkonsulats Istanbul, 3970, Paket 1, Akte: "Kulturpropaganda (Allgemeines), Akte 'Propaganda' besonders" März 1930–.

61. "... starke Schädigung deutscher Interessen." Grothusen, *Der Scurla-Bericht*, 117.

62. For a more detailed discussion, see Kader Konuk, "Antagonistische Weltanschauungen in der türkischen Moderne: Die Beteiligung von Emigranten und Nationalsozialisten an der Grundlegung der Nationalphilologien in Istanbul," in *Istanbul: Geistige Wanderungen aus der Welt in Scherben?* ed. Faruk Birtek and Georg Stauth (Bielefeld: Transcript, 2007), 191–216.

63. After his arrival in Istanbul, Brinkmann wrote a report about the debate over his hire. Bundesarchiv, Berlin, Reichsministerium für Wissenschaft, Erziehung und Volksbildung, R 4901/13290, Wissenschaftliche Beziehungen zum Ausland, Akte Prof. Dr. Hennig Brinkmann, Univ. Frankfurt a.M., Mai 1943–März 1945. Hennig Brinkmann's thirteen-page report about his trip to Turkey (dated April 29, 1943) is addressed to Oberregierungsrat Dr. Scurla at the ministry of science and education in Berlin. See also Christopher M. Hutton, *Linguistics and the Third Reich: Mother-Tongue Fascism, Race and the Science of Language* (London: Routledge, 1999), 74–77. My thanks to Ludmilla Hanisch, who helped me find Brinkmann's dossier.

64. Hennig Brinkmann, "Deutsche Dichtung der Gegenwart," *Das deutsche Wort: Die literarische Welt* 10, no. 16 (1934): 3. Mit "dem nationalsozialistischen Durchbruch von 1933 ... [versank] ein volksfremdes Schrifttum, das den Blick auf die ewigen Kräfte der Deutschen verdeckte" und eine Dichtung ins Licht rückte, "die seit Jahren bereit stand, am inneren Aufbau des deutschen Lebens gestaltend mitzuwirken." For more biographical information on Brinkmann, see Christoph König, ed., *Internationales Germanistenlexikon 1800–1950* (Berlin: Walter de Gruyter, 2003).

65. Hutton, *Linguistics and the Third Reich*, 242–244.

66. "Es wird danach in Zukunft keine Deutschkurse ausserhalb des Deutschen Seminars geben; sie werden also dem Einfluss des Juden Auerbach entzogen sein": Bundesarchiv, Berlin, Reichsministerium für Wissenschaft, R 4901/13290.

67. Bundesarchiv, Berlin, Reichsministerium für Wissenschaft, Erziehung und Volksbildung, R 4901/6657, Das Schulwesen in der Türkei, 7. Juni 1943, R. Preussners Bericht an das Ministerium, Blatt 67 und 68.

68. In 1938–1939, the German academic exchange service granted only four out of 295 stipends to Turkish students studying in Germany. However, efforts were made to increase the number of Turkish applicants. See Politisches Archiv des Auswärtigen Amts, Berlin, Konstantinopel/Ankara, 729, Akte Studium (türk. Studenten in Deutschland).

69. General Consul Toepke's account "Material zur Abfassung des kulturpolitischen Jahresberichts" is dated February 3, 1939. Politisches Archiv des Auswärtigen Amts, Berlin, Akten des Generalkonsulats Istanbul, 3970, Paket 1, Akte: "Kulturpropaganda (Allgemeines), Akte 'Propaganda' besonders" März 1930–. On page 13 of the report Toepke wrote:

"Ich darf dazu bemerken, dass mir vor kurzem von einem deutschen Emigrantenprofessor mit dem Ausdruck lebhaften Bedauerns mitgeteilt wurde, dass die aus Deutschland zurückkehrenden türkischen Studenten neben der deutschen Sprache auch deutsche politische Anschauungen übernehmen und in ihrem Kreise dafür werben. Dies gilt, wie der Betreffende schmerzlich feststellte, namentlich für die Einstellung zum Judentum."

70. Bundesarchiv, Berlin, Reichsministerium für Wissenschaft, R 4901/13290.

71. Brinkmann's eight-page report to the German ministry of education is dated May 20, 1944. Ibid.

72. For a discussion of Turkish Germanistik, see Kader Konuk, "Istanbuler Germanistik: Grundlegung durch Emigranten und Nationalsozialisten," *Geschichte der Germanistik. Mitteilungen* 27/28 (2005): 30–37.

73. Heinz Anstock's political stance is not quite clear, however. In his report to the German ministry of education, dated May 20, 1944, Brinkmann praises Anstock's assistance in disseminating German propaganda. Bundesarchiv, Berlin, Reichsministerium für Wissenschaft, R 4901/13290.

74. "Im Studienjahr 1943/44 haben nämlich die jungen Lehrkräfte und die Studenten die Romantikvorlesungen, die der Professor hielt, und die immer in dem Lob des deutschen Volkes gipfelten, skeptisch und nachdenklich über sich ergehen lassen." Şara Sayın, "Germanistik an der 'Universität Istanbul,'" in *Germanistentreffen: Tagungsbeiträge Deutschland-Türkei* (Bonn: DAAD, 1995), 30.

75. See the Brinkmann file at Bundesarchiv, Berlin, Reichsministerium für Wissenschaft, R 4901/13290.

76. For a discussion of Kranz's role at Istanbul University, see Arslan Kaynardağ, "Üniversitemizde Ders Veren Alman Felsefe Profesörleri," in *Türk Felsefe Araştırmalarında ve Üniversite Öğretiminde Alman Filozofları* (Istanbul: Türkiye Felsefe Kurumu, 1986), 22–23.

77. In his report to the German ministry of education, Kranz wrote that he saw his main task in Istanbul in demonstrating the significance of Europe's classical heritage for German culture and Europe's intellectual history. Clearly, Kranz used the language of the Nazi ministry in order to cover up his own political stance. His report is dated June 24, 1944. Bundesarchiv, Berlin, Reichsministerium für Wissenschaft, Erziehung und Volksbildung, R 4901/15149, Wissenschaftliche Beziehungen zum Ausland, Akte Prof. Kranz Dez. 1943–Dez. 1944.

78. "... der das geistige Leben Deutschlands überfremdet, gelähmt und erstickt hat." Fricke's career profited from the exile of other academics. Between 1933 and 1941, he headed the German Seminar in Kiel. In 1942, he was designated Ordinarius at the University of Strasburg, where he stayed until 1945. Claudia Albert, ed., *Deutsche Klassiker im Nationalsozialismus: Schiller, Kleist, Hölderlin* (Stuttgart: Metzler, 1994), 264.

79. "... wissenschaftlichen Einsatzes deutscher Germanisten im Kriege." Frank-Rutger Hausmann, *"Deutsche Geisteswissenschaft" im Zweiten Weltkrieg: Die "Aktion Ritterbusch" (1940–1945)*, ed. Holger Dainat, Michael Grüttner, and Frank-Rutger Hausmann (Dresden: Dresden University Press, 1998), 33.

80. Quoted from the letter that was sent to the participants of the first preparatory meeting in Weimar, July 1941. Original to be found in Deutsches Literaturarchiv Marbach, Nachlaß Rehm 74,20 (4 Bl.). Cited in ibid., 171.

81. "... den Wesensgehalt des Deutschen aus dem ihr anvertrauten Bereich deutscher Sprache und Dichtung herauszuarbeiten." Ibid.

82. For a history of the philosophy department, see Arslan Kaynardağ, *Bizde Felsefenin Kurumlaşması ve Türkiye Felsefe Kurumu'nun Tarihi* (Ankara: Türkiye Felsefe Kurumu, 1994); Kaynardağ, "Üniversitemizde Ders Veren Alman Felsefe Profesörleri."

83. Fuchs, *Çorum and Anatolian Pictures*, 12.

84. In contradistinction to the emotions unleashed by the aforementioned authors, a "foreign" writer such as Ibsen met with cool objectivity. "G. Fricke in Istanbul," unpublished dissertation quoted in Gabriele Stilla, "Gerhard Fricke: Literaturwissenschaft als Anweisung zur Unterordnung," in *Deutsche Klassiker im Nationalsozialismus: Schiller-Kleist-Hölderlin*, ed. Claudia Albert (Stuttgart: Metzler, 1994), 24.

85. Sayın, "Germanistik an der 'Universität Istanbul,'" 31. The relationship between Fricke and Ziegler is, however, a particularly complex one that warrants further exploration.

86. "Für Assistenten und Studenten, die nun nach kurzen Abständen mit dem deutschen Idealismus und auch dessen äußerster Kritik konfrontiert wurden, die, kaum dem Fahrwasser der Unbedingtheit hingegeben, an die harte Realität gemahnt wurden, für die meisten Zuhörer war dieses Wechselbad auf symbolischer Ebene nicht unfruchtbar." Ibid.

87. In the Festschrift for Şara Sayın, Nilüfer Kuruyazıcı remarks on the peculiarity of the university's hiring politics but withholds further criticism. She explains the hiring of a Nazi professor by suggesting that from the university's point of view, the professional reputation of German professors might have been more important than their political stance. Nilüfer Kuruyazıcı, "Die deutsche akademische Emigration von 1933 und ihre Rolle bei der Neugründung der Universität Istanbul sowie bei der Gründung der Germanistik," in *Interkulturelle Begegnungen: Festschrift für Şara Sayın*, ed. Şara Sayın, Manfred Durzak, and Nilüfer Kuruyazıcı (Würzburg: Königshausen & Neumann, 2004), 260.

88. Cited in Rıfat N. Bali, *Cumhuriyet Yıllarında Türkiye Yahudileri: Bir Türkleştirme Serüveni* (Istanbul: İletişim, 1999), 361.

89. Hirsch expressed his worries about his sister in a letter to an undisclosed recipient in the summer of 1944. Ernst E. Hirsch, *Aus des Kaisers Zeiten durch die Weimarer Republik in das Land Atatürks: Eine unzeitgemäße Autobiographie* (München: Schweitzer, 1982), 299.

90. For a number of reports about the daily life as an internee in Istanbul, see the consular documents in Politisches Archiv des Auswärtigen Amts, Berlin, Akten des Generalkonsulats Istanbul, 4058, Paket 95.

91. Fuchs, *Çorum and Anatolian Pictures*, 14.

92. During his lifetime, Fuchs published some of his drawings. Ibid.

93. Arnold Reisman was able to compile cases that show how and where German citizens were interned. Reisman also refers to exceptions from internment in *Turkey's Modernization: Refugees from Nazism and Atatürk's Vision* (Washington, DC: New Academia Publishing, 2006), 420–425.

94. Cornelius Bischoff gave an interview to a German newspaper, describing his experiences in Çorum, where he was interned. Maximilian Probst, "Baden im Bosporus," *die tageszeitung*, January 23, 2009, http://www.taz.de/1/archiv/print-archiv/printressorts/digi-artikel/?ressort=ku&dig=2009%2F01%2F23%2Fa0022&cHash=668fab84ed (accessed March 14, 2009). For more about Bischoff in Çorum, see also Kemal Bozay, *Exil Türkei: Ein Forschungsbeitrag zur deutschsprachigen Emigration in die Türkei 1933–1945* (Münster: LIT, 2001), 94, 117–118.

95. Walter Ruben, *Kırşehir: Eine altertümliche Kleinstadt Mittelanatoliens*, ed. Gerhard Ruben (Würzburg: Ergon, 2003). Gerhard Ruben and Cornelius Bischoff describe their experiences of internment in *Mitgliederrundbrief*, vol. 43 (Berlin: Verein Aktives Museum: Faschismus und Widerstand in Berlin, May 2000), http://www.aktives-museum.de/fileadmin/user_upload/Extern/Dokumente/rundbrief-43.pdf (accessed March 20, 2009), 34.

96. This volume is divided into three parts—French, English, and German philology. It includes, along with linguistic studies, essays on literature from Shakespeare to Rainer Maria Rilke. The French section includes a comparative study by Cevdet Perin that deals with the French influence on the nineteenth-century Turkish novel.

97. "Tekrar neşretmeğe başladığımız bu dergiyi, Türkiyenin fikrî gelişmesine hizmet edecek, ve milletler arası filoloji çalışmalarına yardımı dokunacak eserlerin takip edeceğini ümit ederiz." Erich Auerbach, "Önsöz," *Garp Filolojileri Dergisi* 1 (1947), 1.

98. Emily Apter argues that "it was the volatile crossing of Turkish language politics with European philological humanism that produced the conditions conducive to the invention of comparative literature as a global discipline." Apter, "Global Translatio," 263.

99. "An der Universität haben wir wohl einiges erreicht, aber längst nicht so viel als möglich gewesen wäre; die unsichere und oft dilettantische Politik der Verwaltung erschwert die Arbeiten sehr, wobei zuzugeben ist, dass sie es nicht leicht hat." Quoted from a letter to Martin Hellweg, May 16, 1947. Martin Vialon, ed., *Erich Auerbachs Briefe an Martin Hellweg (1939–1950)* (Tübingen: A. Francke Verlag, 1997), 70.

100. ". . . ich habe hier gelernt, wie schwer es ist[,] ein nicht europäisches Land in kurzer Zeit zu europäisieren; die Gefahr der praktischen und moralischen Anarchie ist sehr gross." Ibid.

101. Quoted from a letter by Erich Auerbach to Martin Hellweg, June 22, 1946. Ibid., 70.

102. ". . . verantwortungslose, dilletantische und fortwährend wieder abgebrochene Experimente." Quoted from a letter to Hellweg, May 16, 1947. Ibid., 78.

103. Liselotte Dieckmann—a lecturer who taught at the Faculty for Western Languages and Literatures in the 1930s—also wrote about the problems of rapidly Westernizing

Turkey. See Liselotte Dieckmann, "Akademische Emigranten in der Türkei," in *Verbannung: Aufzeichnungen deutscher Schriftsteller im Exil*, ed. Egon Schwarz and Matthias Wegner (Hamburg: Christian Wegner, 1964), 122–126.

104. Ahmet Hamdi Tanpınar, *Yaşadığım Gibi*, 2nd ed. (Istanbul: Dergah Yayınları, 1996), 32–33.

Chapter 5

1. "Leo Spitzer," *Johns Hopkins Magazine* (April 1952): 26.

2. René Wellek, for example, wrote in his obituary for Leo Spitzer that in Istanbul, he "was put in charge of a large program of modern languages. There was a magnificent palace with a view of the blue Sea of Marmara, and beadles at every door, but almost no books. The dean explained, as Spitzer recalled, 'We don't bother with books.' Fires were part of the tradition at Istanbul." René Wellek, "Leo Spitzer (1887–1960)," *Comparative Literature* 12, no. 4 (1960): 310.

3. See, for example, Horst Widmann, *Exil und Bildungshilfe: Die deutschsprachige akademische Emigration in die Türkei nach 1933* (Bern: Herbert Lang, 1973).

4. Harry N. Howard, "Preliminary Materials for a Survey of the Libraries and Archives of Istanbul," *Journal of the American Oriental Society* 59, no. 2 (1939): 241.

5. Ibid., 235.

6. Orhan Pamuk, *Istanbul: Memories and the City* (New York: Random House, 2006), 209. Ahmet Hamdi Tanpınar's essay on Istanbul originally appeared in 1946. Ahmet Hamdi Tanpınar, *Beş Şehir* (Istanbul: Dergâh Yayınları, 2008), 164.

7. Pamuk, *Istanbul*, 211. Julia Hell analyzes the relationship between imperialism and the aesthetics of ruins in the German context. Julia Hell, "Imperial Ruin Gazers, or Why Did Scipio Weep?" In *Ruins of Modernity*, ed. Julia Hell and Andreas Schoenle (Durham, NC: Duke University Press, 2010), 169–192. See also Julia Hell, "Ruin Travel: Orphic Journeys through 1940s Germany," in *Writing Travel*, ed. John Zilcosky (Toronto: University of Toronto Press, 2008), 123–162.

8. Erich Auerbach, *Mimesis: The Representation of Reality in Western Literature*, trans. Willard R. Trask (Princeton, NJ: Princeton University Press, 2003), 557.

9. Edward W. Said, "Erich Auerbach, Critic of the Earthly World," *Boundary 2* 31, no. 2 (2004): 12.

10. Howard, "Preliminary Materials," 241.

11. Ibid., 227.

12. See Liselotte Dieckmann, "Akademische Emigranten in der Türkei," in *Verbannung: Aufzeichnungen deutscher Schriftsteller im Exil*, ed. Egon Schwarz and Matthias Wegner (Hamburg: Christian Wegner, 1964), 125. "Für die Humanisten gab es zwar die schönsten alten Manuskripte, aber freilich keine Bibliothek. Nur wer eine private Sammlung besaß und sie hatte mitbringen können, konnte über Bücher verfügen."

13. Ernst E. Hirsch, *Aus des Kaisers Zeiten durch die Weimarer Republik in das Land Atatürks: Eine unzeitgemäße Autobiographie* (München: Schweitzer, 1982), 219.

14. Ali Arslan, *Darülfünun'dan Üniversiteye* (Istanbul: Kitabevi, 1995), 500.

15. Hirsch, *Aus des Kaisers Zeiten*, 219, 223. In Hirsch's biography it is unclear whether the gift was made in 1914 or in the 1920s. While conducting research in German archives, I found one folder providing evidence of Weimar Germany's efforts to provide Darülfünun with German books and journals: Politisches Archiv des Auswärtigen Amts, Die Universität zu Konstantinopel R 64142, 1923. It is possible that the German professors employed at Darülfünun in 1914 organized this book supply.

16. Kathrin Meier-Rust, *Alexander Rüstow: Geschichtsdeutung und liberales Engagement* (Stuttgart: Klett-Cotta, 1993), 67–68.

17. Hirsch, *Aus des Kaisers Zeiten*, 220–221.

18. In 1941, Walter Gottschalk was given the task of supervising the libraries of the university's institutes. For an overview of German librarians in Turkey, see Hildegard Müller, "German Librarians in Exile in Turkey, 1933–1945," *Libraries and Culture* 33, no. 3 (1998): 294–305.

19. Jürgens was sent to Turkey by the Bibliotheksausschuß der "Notgemeinschaft der Deutschen Wissenschaft (Deutsche Forschungsgemeinschaft)." The 1934 report is titled "Deutsche wissenschaftliche Stützpunkte in Konstantinopel." Politisches Archiv des Auswärtigen Amts, Akten des Generalkonsulats Istanbul, GK Istanbul 163, Universität Istanbul Band II 1934–1935.

20. Howard, "Preliminary Materials," 241. For a survey of the Istanbul libraries in Turkish, see Muzaffer Gökman, *Istanbul Kütüphaneleri Rehberi* (Istanbul, 1941); Muzaffer Gökman, *Istanbul Kütüphaneleri ve Günkü Vaziyetleri* (Istanbul: Hüsnütabiat Matbaası, 1939).

21. Süheyla Bayrav and Ferda Keskin, "Siz misiniz? Burada İşiniz Ne?" *Cogito* 23 (2000): 150. Other accounts such as Liselotte Dieckmann's also emphasize the importance of private book collections for émigrés. See Dieckmann, "Akademische Emigranten in der Türkei," 125.

22. Politisches Archiv des Auswärtigen Amts, Akten des Generalkonsulats Istanbul, GK Istanbul 163, Universität Istanbul Band II 1934–1935.

23. A very short biography of Isidor Karon can be found in Jüdisches Museum München, "Orte des Exils / Sürgün Yerleri: Münih ve Istanbul" (München: Jüdisches Museum München, 2008), 22. Ernst Hirsch describes how, on his second day in Istanbul, he discovered the bookstore and met Karon, who promised that he could order law books for him from Germany and Switzerland. Hirsch, *Aus des Kaisers Zeiten*, 182.

24. Politisches Archiv des Auswärtigen Amts, Akten des Generalkonsulats Istanbul, GK Istanbul 163, Universität Istanbul Band II 1934–1935. As a result of his detailed report, "Buchhandel in Istanbul," dated July 31, 1934, Jürgens suggested centralizing the vending of German books.

25. While in Istanbul, Brinkmann waited for the delivery of books through the German book exchange program. The books, which were shipped from Marburg, arrived in Istanbul after Brinkmann's departure and were, because of Turkey's stance against Nazi Germany, stored in the German consulate. In his report to the ministry of education dated May 20, 1944, Brinkmann wrote about his achievements in Istanbul. Bundesarchiv,

Berlin, Reichsministerium für Wissenschaft, Erziehung und Volksbildung, R 4901/13290, Wissenschaftliche Beziehungen zum Ausland, Akte Prof. Dr. Hennig Brinkmann, Univ. Frankfurt a.M., Mai 1943–März 1945.

26. Erich Auerbach, Letter to Johannes Oeschger, May 27, 1938, Nachlass Fritz Lieb, Universitätsbibliothek Basel (Handschriftenabteilung), NL 43 (Lieb) Ah 2,1. See also Auerbach's letter to Martin Hellweg, dated May 22, 1939, in which he remarks that the university lacks a functional library: "Uns dreien geht es gut. Es fehlt auch jetzt nicht an Unsicherheit und an Unruhe. Aber das Leben ist vorhand bezaubernd hier.—Nur Bücher, d.h. eine brauchbare UB, fehlen, und Reisen ist unmöglich." Martin Vialon, ed., *Erich Auerbachs Briefe an Martin Hellweg (1939–1950)* (Tübingen: A. Francke Verlag, 1997), 58.

27. Erich Auerbach, "Epilegomena zu Mimesis," *Romanische Forschungen* 65, no. 1/2 (1953): 10. See a translation of this essay in the fiftieth-anniversary edition of *Mimesis.*

28. Hannah Arendt acknowledges Roncalli in Hannah Arendt, "Angelo Giuseppe Roncalli: Der christliche Papst," in *Menschen in finsteren Zeiten*, ed. Ursula Ludz (München: Piper, 1989), 75–88.

29. For his role in saving European Jews in the years 1943 and 1944, see Margaret Hebblethwaite, *John XXIII: Pope of the Century* (New York: Continuum International Publishing Group, 2005), 82–95.

30. A short letter to Auerbach from Pope John XXIII, dated June 23, 1956, is preserved in the Erich Auerbach archive in Marbach.

31. John David Dawson, "Figural Reading and the Fashioning of Christian Identity in Boyarin, Auerbach and Frei," *Modern Theology* 14, no. 2 (1998): 186.

32. The English translation of "Figura" can be found in Erich Auerbach, *Scenes from the Drama of European Literature* (Gloucester, MA: Peter Smith, 1973), 72.

33. Cf. James I. Porter, "Auerbach and the Scar of Philology," in *Classics and National Culture*, ed. Susan Stephens and Phiroze Vasunia (Oxford: Oxford University Press, forthcoming). See also James Porter, "Auerbach and the Judaizing of Philology," *Critical Inquiry* 35 (2008): 115–147.

34. In his letter to Martin Hellweg in 1939, Auerbach describes his method as starting out from an *Einzelphänomen*, a specific phenomenon, "perhaps the history of a word or an interpretation of a passage. The specific phenomenon can never be small and concrete enough, and it should never be a concept introduced by us or other scholars but rather something the subject matter itself presents." Martin Elsky, Martin Vialon, and Robert Stein, "Scholarship in Times of Extremes: Letters of Erich Auerbach (1933–46), on the Fiftieth Anniversary of His Death," *Publications of the Modern Language Association of America* 122, no. 3 (2007): 756. For an edition of the Auerbach-Hellweg correspondence, see Vialon, *Erich Auerbachs Briefe an Martin Hellweg.*

35. Homer, *Odyssey*, trans. Albert Cook (New York: Norton, 1993), 94.

36. Jonathan Lamb, *Preserving the Self in the South Seas, 1680–1840* (Chicago: University of Chicago Press, 2001), 13. Lamb analyzes litotes as a rhetorical device of significance in actual as well as imaginary travel writing. See also his review essay: Jonathan Lamb,

"Coming to Terms with What Isn't There: Early Narratives of New Holland," *Eighteenth-Century Life* 26, no. 1 (2002): 147–155. For another discussion of litotes and travel writing, see Vanessa Agnew, *Enlightenment Orpheus: The Power of Music in Other Worlds* (New York: Oxford University Press, 2008), 166.

37. Giambattista Vico, *New Science* (London: Penguin Classics, 1999), 119. See chapter 1 for a discussion of Vico's influence on Auerbach.

38. For an English translation, see Alexander Rüstow, *Freedom and Domination: A Historical Critique of Civilization*, trans. Salvator Attanasio (Princeton, NJ: Princeton University Press, 1980).

39. Helmuth James von Moltke, the leading member of the resistance group named Kreisau Circle, was in touch with Rüstow when he visited Turkey in 1943. Rüstow had contact with the U.S. intelligence service OSS (Office of Strategic Services) and passed on Moltke's offer for an early peace agreement to the Allies. Stanford J. Shaw, *Turkey and the Holocaust: Turkey's Role in Rescuing Turkish and European Jewry from Nazi Persecution, 1933–1945* (Hampshire, UK: Macmillan Press, 1993), 304. See also Michael Balfour and Julian Frisby, *Helmuth James Graf von Moltke, 1907–1945*, trans. Freya von Moltke (Berlin: Henssel, 1984), 260–271.

40. Alexander Rüstow, *Ortsbestimmung der Gegenwart: Eine universalgeschichtliche Kulturkritik* (Erlenbach: Eugen Rentsch Verlag, 1952), 9.

41. Meier-Rust studied Rüstow's correspondence now archived at the Bundesarchiv Koblenz. Meier-Rust, *Alexander Rüstow*, 64, 67, 77.

42. Fritz Neumark, *Zuflucht am Bosporus: Deutsche Gelehrte, Politiker und Künstler in der Emigration 1933–1953* (Frankfurt am Main: Verlag Josef Knecht, 1980), 180.

43. A. Paul Bové, *Intellectuals in Power: A Genealogy of Critical Humanism* (New York: Columbia University Press, 1986), 79. See also a letter Auerbach wrote to Martin Hellweg after the end of the war. Vialon, *Erich Auerbachs Briefe an Martin Hellweg*, 70.

44. In Levin's view, Spitzer distilled continuities and essential elements in his comparatist analysis, while Auerbach emphasized the aspect of transformation, taking a rather relativistic perspective. Harry Levin, "Two *Romanisten* in America: Spitzer and Auerbach," in *The Intellectual Migration: Europe and America, 1930–1960*, ed. Donald Fleming and Bernard Bailyn (Cambridge, MA: Belknap Press of Harvard University Press, 1969), 472.

45. Ibid., 466, 471.

46. Ibid., 466.

47. Ibid., 465–466.

48. Dante Alighieri, *The Divine Comedy*, vol. 1: *Inferno*, trans. Mark Musa (New York: Penguin Books, 2003), 326.

49. Paget Jackson Toynbee, *Dante Studies* (London: Clarendon Press, 1921), 112. Musurus Paşa, "as a subject of the Sultan [Abdülhamid], thought it incumbent upon him to omit Dante's uncomplimentary references to the founder of Islam." Toynbee reminds his readers that Dante was on the index because he dared to assert that the authority of the emperor was derived from God. Toynbee sees Musurus Paşa's omission of the passage

within the context of other "mutilations of the text," such as an eighteenth-century Latin translation.

50. Nüshet Haşim Sinanoğlu, *Dante ve Divina Commedia: Dante ile İlk Temas* (Istanbul: Devlet Matbaası, 1934), 63.

51. "Bu, hıristiyanlar için birçok muharebelere sebep olan dinin müessisi idi." Ibid., 74.

52. See M. Turhan Tan's preface in Dante Alighieri, *İlâhî Komedi (Divina commedia) Cehennem–Âraf–Cennet,* trans. Hamdi Varoğlu (Istanbul: Hilmi Kitapevi, 1938), xxvi. "Cennetle cehennem hakkında, dinî değil, bediî bir fikir edinmek ve bir şaheser okumak isteyenler bu nefis kitaptan mutlaka birer nüsha edinmelidirler." The editor of the publishing house himself, İbrahim Hilmi Çığıraçan, also added a preface that covered Dante's life and work. See his introduction in Dante Alighieri, *İlâhî Komedi,* v–xx. In 1938, Hamdi Varoğlu also published a forty-page book on Dante's life and work: Hamdi Varoğlu, *Dante Alighieri: Hayatı, Eserleri ve İlahi Komedi* (Istanbul: Cumhuriyet Matbaası, 1938).

53. See Turhan Tan's preface in Dante Alighieri, *İlâhî Komedi,* xxvi.

54. Ibid., 132–133.

55. Dante Alighieri, *Divine Comedy,* vol. 1: *Inferno,* 326.

56. Dante Alighieri, *İlâhî Komedi,* 132. The poem was originally published in his collection titled "Tayflar Geçidi" (Passage of Apparitions).

57. See, for example, Feridun Timur's footnote in Dante Alighieri, *İlâhi Komedya,* trans. Feridun Timur (Ankara: Maarif Basımevi, 1959), 346–347. Edward Said, for example, offered his critical reading of this passage in *Orientalism* and writes that Mohammed's repulsive punishment "spares the reader none of the eschatological detail that so vivid a punishment entails. Mohammed's entrails and his excrement are described with unflinching accuracy." Edward Said, *Orientalism* (New York: Vintage Books, 1979), 68. For a critique of Said's treatment of Dante and his historical periodization, see Kathleen Biddick, "Coming Out of Exile: Dante on the Orient(alism) Express," *American Historical Review* 105, no. 4 (2000): 1234–1249.

58. For a study of secularism as a historical process evolving since the Ottoman eighteenth century see Niyazi Berkes, *The Development of Secularism in Turkey* (Montreal: McGill University Press, 1964). In his work, Berkes discusses the particular valence of the terms "secularism" and "laicism" in Christian and Muslim societies.

59. All three of these lectures were published in Turkish translation. Leo Spitzer, "Bocaccio," in *Üniversite Konferansları 1935–1936* (Istanbul: Ülkü Basımevi, 1937); Leo Spitzer, "Cervantes," in *Üniversite Konferansları 1935–1936* (Istanbul: Ülkü Basımevi, 1937); Leo Spitzer, "Rabelais yahut Rönesans'ın Dehası," in *Üniversite Konferansları 1935–1936* (Istanbul: Ülkü Basımevi, 1937).

60. Erich Auerbach, *Roman Filolojisine Giriş,* trans. Süheyla Bayrav, İstanbul Üniversitesi Edebiyat Fakültesi Yayınlarından, No. 236 (Istanbul: İbrahim Horoz Basımevi, 1944). Auerbach's new studies on Dante were also published in 1944 in Istanbul but not translated into Turkish. Erich Auerbach, *Neue Dantestudien: Sacrae scripturae sermo humilis; Figura; Franz von Assisi in der Komödie. Dante Hakkında Yeni Araştırmalar,* ed. Robert

Anhegger, Walter Ruben, and Andreas Tietze, Istanbuler Schriften—Istanbul Yazıları (Istanbul: İbrahim Horoz Basımevi, 1944).

61. Interview with Güzin Dino in Paris, October 26, 2007. Cemil Bilsel notes in the preface to the published university lectures of 1935–1936 that the interest in these lectures was so great that hundreds of people had to stand in the crowded auditorium.

62. For Auerbach's lectures in Turkey see Erich Auerbach, "On Yedinci Asırda Fransız 'Public'i," in *Üniversite Konferansları*, İstanbul Üniversitesi Yayınları, No. 50 (Istanbul: Ülkü Basımevi, 1937), 113–123; Erich Auerbach, "Jean Jacques Rousseau," in *Üniversite Konferansları 1938–1939*, İstanbul Üniversitesi Yayınları, No. 96 (Istanbul: Ülkü Basımevi, 1939), 129–139; Erich Auerbach, "XVIıncı asırda Avrupada Milli Dillerin Teşekkülü," in *Üniversite Konferansları 1937–1938*, İstanbul Üniversitesi Yayınları, No. 93 (Istanbul: Ülkü Basımevi, 1939), 143–152; Erich Auerbach, "Dante," in *Üniversite Konferansları 1939–1940*, İstanbul Üniversitesi Yayınları, No. 125 (Istanbul: Ülkü Basımevi, 1940), 62–70; Erich Auerbach, "Edebiyat ve Harp," *Cogito* 23 (2000): 219–230; Erich Auerbach, "XIXuncu Asırda Avrupada Realism," in *Üniversite Konferansları 1941–1942*, İstanbul Üniversitesi Yayınları, No. 172 (Istanbul: Kenan Basımevi, 1942); Erich Auerbach, *Dante Hakkında Yeni Araştırmalar*, İstanbul Üniversitesi Edebiyat Fakültesi Yayınları, No. 5 (Istanbul: İstanbul Üniversitesi, 1944); Erich Auerbach, "Montesquieu ve Hürriyet Fikri," in *Üniversite Konferansları 1943–1944*, İstanbul Üniversitesi Yayınları, No. 273 (Istanbul: Kenan Matbaası, 1945): 39–49; Erich Auerbach, "Voltaire ve Burjuva Zihniyeti," *Garp Filolojileri Dergisi* I (1947): 123–134; Erich Auerbach, "Kötünün Zaferi: Pascal'in Siyasi Nazariyesi Üzerine bir Deneme," *Cogito* 18 (1999): 279–299. The article on Pascal was signed with the date May 19, 1941, translated by Fikret Elpe, and originally published in the newly initiated journal *Felsefe Arkivi* I (1946): 2–3. An English version with the title "The Triumph of Evil" first appeared in the *Hudson Review* in the same year. The German version of the essay was published under the title "Über Pascals Politische Theorie" in Erich Auerbach, *Vier Untersuchungen zur Geschichte der französischen Bildung* (Bern: Francke, 1951). The English translation of the essay was published in 1973 in Auerbach, *Scenes from the Drama of European Literature*, 101–129.

63. A few of those published in the 1930s and 1940s have been reprinted in Turkish journals in recent years.

64. "1265, hicrî 633 senesinde Floransada doğan 1321 de 56 yaşında menfada ölen Dante Aligüieri [Alighieri] Orta Zaman Avrupasının en büyük şairi idi." Auerbach, "Dante," 62.

65. David Damrosch, "Auerbach in Exile," *Comparative Literature* 47, no. 2 (1995): 107–109. In *Mimesis*, Erich Auerbach writes that Farinata's and Cavalcante's "eternal and changeless fate is the same" (192).

66. Miguel Asín Palacios, *Islam and the Divine Comedy* (London: John Murray, 1926), xiii. This argument has also been supported in René Guénon, *L'Ésotérisme de Dante* (Paris: Bosse, 1925). Translated into English as René Guénon, *The Esoterism of Dante*, trans. C. B. Bethell (Paris: Gallimard, 1996).

67. Asín Palacios, *Islam and the Divine Comedy*, 104.

68. Ibid., 114.

69. Ibid., 112.

70. Olschki dismissed Asín's work by suggesting that the Arabist wanted to "claim for Spain, even if Moorish, a considerable amount of Dante's glory," something that induced him to "overestimate his findings and to magnify his conclusions." Leonardo Olschki, "Mohammedan Eschatology and Dante's Other World," *Comparative Literature* 3, no. 1 (1951): 1. One year after the publication of Olschki's article in *Comparative Literature*, Theodore Silverstein critically reviewed Asín Palacios's methodology and polemics for the *Journal for Near Eastern Studies* but, unlike Olschki, reconsidered parallels between Christian and Islamic traditions on the basis of newly discovered material. Theodore Silverstein, "Dante and the Legend of the Mi'raj: The Problem of Islamic Influence on the Christian Literature of the Otherworld," *Journal of Near Eastern Studies* 11, no. 2 (1952): 89–110. For a later review of this debate, see Vicente Cantarino, "Dante and Islam: History and Analysis of a Controversy," in *A Dante Symposium*, ed. William de Sua and Gino Rizzo (Chapel Hill: University of North Carolina Press, 1965), 175–198; Paul A. Cantor, "The Uncanonical Dante: The Divine Comedy and Islamic Philosophy," *Philosophy and Literature* 20, no. 1 (1996): 138–153. Paul Cantor adds to the debate by showing that Dante's *Commedia* did not portray Muslims only as schismatic. Cantor pointed out that Dante also set two Muslim figures in a positive light, namely, the medieval Islamic philosophers Avicenna and Averroës.

71. Werner Mulertt, "Asíns Dantebuch," *Islam* 14 (1924): 119.

72. Ibid., 115.

73. Karl Vossler, *Die Göttliche Komödie*, vol. 2 (Heidelberg: Carl Winters Universitätsbuchhandlung, 1925), 510.

74. Erich Auerbach, *Dante als Dichter der irdischen Welt*, 2nd ed. (Berlin: Walter de Gruyter, 2001), 102. For the English translation see Erich Auerbach, *Dante: Poet of the Secular World* (Chicago: University of Chicago Press, 1961), 81f. Acknowledging these influences did not stop Auerbach from insisting on the distinctiveness of Provençal poetry, the precursor to Dante's style. To make his point, Auerbach took recourse to a florid language and employed romantic notions of "Heimatfreude" (joy of homeland) and "Einheit von Landschaft und Lebensform" (union of landscape and lifestyle) along with concepts of "Blutmischung" (blood mixing) and "unterirdische Kulturtradition" (cultural undercurrents). The English translation tones down some of the language and translates "Blutmischung" as "ethnic mixture." Compare Auerbach, *Dante als Dichter der irdischen Welt*, 21, and Auerbach, *Dante: Poet of the Secular World*.

75. See, for example, Suzanne L. Marchand, *Down from Olympus: Archaeology and Philhellenism in Germany, 1750–1970* (Princeton, NJ: Princeton University Press, 1996); Suzanne Marchand, "Nazism, Orientalism and Humanism," in *Nazi Germany and the Humanities*, ed. Wolfgang Bialas and Anson Rabinbach (Oxford: Oneworld, 2007).

76. Erich Auerbach, "Provenzalen 1" (Literaturarchiv Marbach, Nachlass Auerbach), 8.

77. "In die antike griechisch-römische Kultur strömen nämlich noch während ihrer Blütezeit aus ägyptische, babylonische, persische, syrische und andere orientalische Kulturen, und aus dem Völker- und Mythengewimmel der römischen Weltherrschaftszeit sind alle späteren okzidentalischen Kulturen geboren worden—vor allem das Christentum in seiner historisch-herrschenden Gestalt, aber auch die mohammedanisch-arabischen Kulturen." Ibid., 9–10.

78. Alexander Rüstow, Letter to Erich Auerbach, June 16, 1942, Literaturarchiv Marbach, Nachlaß Auerbach.

79. Auerbach, *Mimesis*, 182.

80. Ibid., xviii.

81. Geoffrey Hartman, *A Scholar's Tale: Intellectual Journey of a Displaced Child of Europe* (New York: Fordham University Press, 2007), 104. Hartman also argues, however, that "It must remain a question whether Auerbach could have drawn a similar perspective from his own tradition's exegetical literature had he known it better." Hartman, *Scholar's Tale*, 174.

82. Emily Apter, "Saidian Humanism," *Boundary 2* 31, no. 2 (2004): 40.

83. Ibid., 45.

84. In his book manuscript *The Chinese Taste in Eighteenth-Century England*, David Porter suggests links between Thomas Percy's sinological research and his ballad collection *Reliques of English Poetry*. Porter argues that the "significance either in the simultaneity of the projects or in their formal resemblance has been overlooked" and demonstrates that Percy's conception of English literary and cultural history and identity is reflected "in the face of plainly superior Chinese cultural achievements." I thank David Porter for sharing a chapter from his manuscript to discuss parallel structures of "historical amnesia" in Percy and Auerbach. David L. Porter, *The Chinese Taste in Eighteenth-Century England* (Cambridge: Cambridge University Press, forthcoming).

85. See Eyüboğlu's essay titled "Ilyada ve Anadolu," in Sabahattin Eyüboğlu, *Mavi ve Kara: Denemeler (1940–1966)* (Istanbul: Çan Yayınları, 1967), 283–291.

86. While the structure of the father–son story is essentially the same, it is not Isaac whom God asks Abraham to sacrifice in the Islamic narrative, but Ishmael.

87. For a discussion of Abraham, Isaac, Hagar, and Sarah in relationship to *Mimesis*, see Damrosch, "Auerbach in Exile."

88. Levin, "Two *Romanisten* in America," 466.

89. Auerbach, *Mimesis*, 528.

90. Ibid., 525–526.

91. Ibid., 532.

92. Ibid., 536.

93. Ibid., 544.

94. Ibid.

95. Ibid., 542.

96. For a critical analysis of the polarity between the Homeric and biblical styles in *Mimesis*, see Vasillis Lambropoulos, *The Rise of Eurocentrism: Anatomy of Interpretation*

(Princeton, NJ: Princeton University Press, 1993). Lambropoulos argues that Auerbach is not fighting against Christianity in *Mimesis*, but against the "non-Biblical: the Homeric, the pagan, the Greek" (14). Compare also James Porter, who views the juxtaposition of the Homeric and the biblical tradition as a polemical one. Porter, "Auerbach and the Scar of Philology."

97. Auerbach, *Mimesis*, 540.

98. Ibid., 542.

99. Ibid., 543.

100. Ibid., 542.

101. David Damrosch discusses the construction of femininity in Auerbach's *Mimesis* in "Auerbach in Exile," 114. Damrosch argues that Euryclea and Mrs. Ramsay form a "feminine frame" for *Mimesis*, one that is "in turn paired with the patriarchal binding of Isaac, first in its biblical form and then in its metaphorical recreation in Proust." Seth Lerer reads *Mimesis* as a "paternalistic text" that revolves around the parent–child relationship. Within this context, he also critically reviews the gender politics of *Mimesis*. Seth Lerer, *Error and the Academic Self: The Scholarly Imagination, Medieval to Modern* (New York: Columbia University Press, 2002), 255–256.

102. Auerbach, *Mimesis*, 552.

103. Ibid., 556. David Damrosch questions Auerbach's claim about the randomly chosen texts as a basis for *Mimesis*: Damrosch, "Auerbach in Exile," 106.

104. Auerbach, *Mimesis*, 553.

105. Ibid., 552. In the German original, Auerbach writes: "gerade der beliebige Augenblick ist vergleichsweise unabhängig von den umstrittenen und wankenden Ordnungen, um welche die Menschen kämpfen und verzweifeln." By orders I understand Auerbach to mean political or social orders.

106. "Leo Spitzer," 27.

107. The epilegomena is translated in Auerbach, *Mimesis*, 574.

108. Agnew, *Enlightenment Orpheus*, 29–31. Agnew also discusses the practice of traveling to the *Schauplätze der Geschichte* in Vanessa Agnew, "Genealogies of Space in Colonial and Postcolonial Re-enactment," in *Settler and Creole Re-enactment*, ed. Vanessa Agnew and Jonathan Lamb (Basingstoke, UK: Palgrave, 2010), 294–318.

109. Victor Klemperer, "Philologie im Exil," in *Vor 33 nach 45: Gesammelte Aufsätze* (Berlin: Akademie Verlag, 1956). Klemperer's article was first published in 1948: Victor Klemperer, "Philologie im Exil," *Aufbau* 4, no. 10 (1948): 863–868.

110. Klemperer, who had unsuccessfully sought to become Spitzer's successor at Istanbul University, had only limited knowledge regarding the conditions under which Auerbach worked in Istanbul. His reference point might have been the inaccessibility of libraries for himself and the inner exile into which he retreated during the Holocaust, out of which he had emerged with his diaries and the *Lingua Tertii Imperii*.

111. Lerer, *Error and the Academic Self*, 241.

112. Ibid., 4.

113. Auerbach, *Mimesis*, 552.

114. For a discussion about travel, epistemology, and the traveler's vantage point, see Agnew, *Enlightenment Orpheus*, 29–31. Caren Kaplan discusses the problematic of standpoint theory and critically reflects upon Said's appropriation of Auerbach's vantage point. Kaplan argues that exile has become "the situation par excellence for the cultural critic—distance and alienation enable profound insight." Caren Kaplan, *Questions of Travel: Postmodern Discourses of Displacement* (Durham, NC: Duke University Press, 1996), 115.

115. Pamuk, *Istanbul*, 6.

Epilogue

1. Süheyla Bayrav wrote her dissertation on French literature under Spitzer's supervision and defended it when Auerbach became chair of the Faculty for Western Languages and Literatures. She worked closely with Auerbach as his assistant and translator of his introductory textbook to Romance philology, which he wrote specifically for students in Turkey. Influenced by Spitzer's methodology, Bayrav approached languages from a comparatist point of view. Later in her career, she became the principal authority on structuralism and semiotics in Turkey. Until 1980, she chaired the department of Romance languages and literatures at Istanbul University. For a discussion of Bayrav's work, see Emily Apter, "Global *Translatio*: The 'Invention' of Comparative Literature, Istanbul, 1933," *Critical Inquiry* 29, no. 2 (2003): 262; Osman Senemoğlu, "1933 Üniversite Reformunda Batı Dilleri ve Prof. Dr. Süheyla Bayrav," *Alman Dili ve Edebiyatı Dergisi* 11 (1998): 59–64. For a reflection of Azra Erhat's and Mina Urgan's role as avant-garde Kemalist women scholars, see Erika Glassen, "Töchter der Republik: Gazi Mustafa Kemal Pasa (Atatürk) im Gedächtnis einer intellektuellen weiblichen Elite der ersten Republikgeneration nach Erinnerungsbüchern von Azra Erhat, Mina Urgan und Nermin Abadan-Unat," *Journal of Turkish Studies–Türklük Bilgisi Araştırmaları* 26, no. 1 (2002): 239–264. Interesting is specifically Güzin Dino's work on Namık Kemal's (1840–1888) literature written in exile. Approaching Turkish literature from a Marxist point of view, she argues in *The Birth of the Turkish Novel* that Kemal's *Intibah* (Awakening) is the precursor of the Turkish novel set in a pre-bourgeois Ottoman society. Pointing out Kemal's inspiration by nineteenth-century French literature, Dino shows that Kemal departs from the supernatural dimension of traditional Turkish prose narratives and introduces realism to Turkish literature. Güzin Dino, *Türk Romanının Doğuşu* (Istanbul: Cem Yayınevi, 1978). Güzin Dino's *Towards Realism in Literature after the Tanzimat Period* provides a broad analysis of the influence of French realism on Ottoman literature: Güzin Dino, *Tanzimattan Sonra Edebiyatta Gerçekçiliğe Doğru* (Ankara: Türk Tarih Kurumu Basımevi, 1954).

2. Eyüboğlu's appropriation of Homer and Troy for his vision of Anatolian humanism is most striking in his 1962 essay "Ilayada ve Anadolu," reprinted in Sabahattin Eyüboğlu, *Mavi ve Kara: Denemeler (1940–1966)* (Istanbul: Çan Yayınları, 1967), 283–291. The compatibility of Islam with humanism is also addressed by more recent scholarship. See, for example, Kim Sitzler, "Humanismus und Islam," in *Humanismus in Geschichte und Gegenwart*, ed. Richard Faber and Enno Rudolph (Tübingen: Mohr Siebeck, 2002), 187–212.

3. Halman was Turkey's first minister of culture in 1971. He translated Yunus Emre's poetry into English and published widely on the interconnections between Sufism and humanism: Talât Sait Halman, *The Humanist Poetry of Yunus Emre* (Istanbul: Istanbul Matbaası, 1972).

4. See Dino's short foreword to Yunus Emre, *The Wandering Fool: Sufi Poems of a Thirteenth-Century Turkish Dervish*, trans. Edouard Roditi (San Francisco: Cadmus, 1987), 1. Dino points out that Georgius de Hungaria, who was imprisoned by Turks from 1438 to 1458, wrote about Yunus Emre in his widely read *Tractatus de Moribus, conditionibus et nequitia Turcorum.*

5. Talât Sait Halman, "Turkish Humanism and the Poetry of Yunus Emre," *Tarih Araştırmaları Dergisi / Review of Historical Research* 6, no. 10–11 (1968): 235. Eyüboğlu made this comparison a few years earlier, in a 1965 essay entitled "Halktan Yana": Eyüboğlu, *Mavi ve Kara*, 27.

6. Orhan Pamuk, *Istanbul: Memories and the City* (New York: Random House, 2006), 90.

7. Halman, "Turkish Humanism," 235.

8. Suat Sinanoğlu, *Türk Humanizmi* (Ankara: Türk Tarih Kurumu Basımevi, 1980), 82, 101.

9. Ibid., 101.

10. Ibid., 100.

11. For the shift in the literary discourse with regard to the Greek-Turkish community, see Aslı Iğsız, "Repertoires of Rupture: Recollecting the 1923 Greek-Turkish Compulsory Religious Minority Exchange" (unpublished dissertation, University of Michigan, 2006). For an overview over the correlation between ethnicity and Turkish literature, see Kader Konuk, *Identitäten im Prozeß: Literatur von Autorinnen aus und in der Türkei in deutscher, englischer und türkischer Sprache* (Essen: Die Blaue Eule, 2001), 30–47.

12. See, for example Rıfat N. Bali, *Cumhuriyet Yıllarında Türkiye Yahudileri: Bir Türkleştirme Serüveni* (Istanbul: İletişim, 1999); Avner Levi, *Türkiye Cumhuriyeti'nde Yahudiler* (Istanbul: İletişim, 1992).

13. The museum was opened in the former Zulfaris Synagogue in Karaköy, Istanbul. For the English-language Web site of the Quincentennial Foundation Museum of Turkish Jews, see http://www.muze500.com/content/view/285/253/lang,en/ (accessed February 16, 2009).

14. Belling arrived in Istanbul in 1937 and later managed to bring his son, who was persecuted as a "half-Jew" in Nazi Germany.

15. Sabine Hillebrecht, ed., *Haymatloz: Exil in der Türkei 1933–1945* (Berlin: Verein Aktives Museum, 2000).

16. Corry Guttstadt, "'Haymatloz'—Der Weg in die Zensur?" *Aktives Museum: Faschismus und Widerstand* 58: 14–17. For a discussion of Turkey's chromite delivery to Germany, see Selim Deringil, *Turkish Foreign Policy during the Second World War: An "Active" Neutrality* (Cambridge: Cambridge University Press, 1989), 168–169.

17. This, certainly, is the view of Fuchs's nephew Herrmann Fuchs. On the relationship between Auerbach and Traugott Fuchs, see Martin Vialon, "The Scars of Exile: Paralipomena concerning the Relationship between History, Literature, and Politics—Demonstrated in the Examples of Erich Auerbach, Traugott Fuchs, and Their Circle in Istanbul," *Yeditepe University Philosophy Department: A Refereed Year-book* 1, no. 2 (2003): 191–246.

18. For James Baldwin's experiences in 1960s Istanbul, see Magdalena J. Zaborowska, *James Baldwin's Turkish Decade: Erotics of Exile* (Durham, NC: Duke University Press, 2008).

19. Süleyman Demirel, "European University Association (EUA)," meeting in Istanbul at Technical University of Istanbul, February 2, 2006, http://www.eua.be/eua/jsp/en/upload/demirel.1142257241117.pdf (accessed May 20, 2006).

20. Emir Kıvırcık, *Büyükelçi* (Istanbul: Goa, 2007). See also Stanford J. Shaw's study of Turkey as the savior of Jews, *Turkey and the Holocaust: Turkey's Role in Rescuing Turkish and European Jewry from Nazi Persecution, 1933–1945* (Hampshire, UK: Macmillan Press, 1993). For a criticism of Shaw's study, see Corry Guttstadt, *Die Türkei, die Juden und der Holocaust* (Berlin: Assoziation A, 2008).

21. Duygu Güvenç, "Turkey Battles Genocide Claims in Hollywood," *Turkish Daily News*, February 13, 2007, http://www.turkishdailynews.com.tr/article.php?enewsid=66071 (accessed March 19, 2007).

22. The journalist Hans Barth, for example, used the Sephardic immigration to Constantinople as proof of Turkish tolerance and campaigned against what he regarded as *Türkenhetze*, Turk baiting. Margaret Lavinia Anderson, " 'Down in Turkey Far Away': Human Rights, the Armenian Massacres, and Orientalism in Wilhelmine Germany," *Journal of Modern History* 79, no. 1 (March 2007): 97. Margaret Anderson also points out that "to an extent that undercuts simple notions of Orientalism, German spokesmen succeeded in diluting sympathy for the victims and shifting it to the perpetrators. After offering some hypotheses to explain why German responses took this exceptional turn, I will conclude with more general reflections provoked by these responses to the Armenian-Turkish conflict: on the inevitable weakness of the category 'human'; on the kaleidoscopic nature of 'right here' and 'far away'; and on the permeable boundaries of Germany's (and our) 'Europe' and 'Orient.' " Anderson, " 'Down in Turkey Far Away,' " 83.

23. Bali, *Cumhuriyet Yıllarında Türkiye Yahudileri*, 361.

24. N.N., "1 film, 4 ülke, 500 hayat," *Cumhuriyet* (September 25, 2008), http://www.cumhuriyet.com.tr/?im=yhs&hn=7080&kn=12 (accessed February 12, 2009). For a fictional account dealing with Turkish Jews in occupied France, see Ayşe Kulin, *Nefes Nefese* (Istanbul: Remzi Kitapevi, 2002).

25. Şara Sayın, "Germanistik an der 'Universität Istanbul,' " in *Germanistentreffen: Tagungsbeiträge Deutschland -Türkei* (Bonn: DAAD, 1995), 29–36.

26. Ender Ateşman (Hacettepe Üniversitesi) is in the process of translating *Mimesis*.

27. Mehmed Uzun, "The Dialogue and Liberties of Civilizations" (paper presented at the Second International Conference in the European Union Parliament on the European Union, Turkey, and the Kurds, September 19–21, 2005), http://www.eutcc.org/articles/8/20/document217.ehtml (accessed February 10, 2009).

28. In an essay dated March 15, 2001, Mehmed Uzun reflected on a number of exiled writers and scholars, including Auerbach, whose locations of exile he visited in order to explore the commonalities of living in exile. Mehmed Uzun, *Ruhun Gökkuşağı*, 2nd ed. (Istanbul: İthaki, 2007), 214.

29. Rita Chin investigated the history of Turkish immigration to West Germany in *The Guest Worker Question in Postwar Germany* (Cambridge: Cambridge University Press, 2007). For a comprehensive analysis of German literature of Turkish migration, see Leslie Adelson, *The Turkish Turn in Contemporary German Literature: Toward a New Critical Grammar of Migration* (New York: Palgrave Macmillan, 2005). The dynamic between Turkish immigrants, Germans, and Jews is a particularly interesting one that the Turkish German journalist, essayist, and novelist Zafer Şenocak addressed in numerous venues. For an analysis of this dynamic see Leslie Adelson, "Touching Tales of Turks, Germans, and Jews: Cultural Alterity, Historical Narrative, and Literary Riddles for the 1990s," *New German Critique* 80 (2000): 93–124. Andreas Huyssen investigates how the Turkish minority in Germany negotiates the memory of the Holocaust: Andreas Huyssen, "Diaspora and Nation: Migration into Other Pasts," *New German Critique* 88 (2003): 147–164. See also my article on the remembrance of the Holocaust and the Armenian genocide in Turkish German literature: Kader Konuk, "Taking on German and Turkish History: Emine Sevgi Özdamar's *Seltsame Sterne*," *Gegenwartsliteratur: German Studies Yearbook* 6 (2007): 232–256.

30. For a discussion of transnationalism and cosmopolitanism, see Timothy Brennan, "Cosmo-Theory," *South Atlantic Quarterly* 100, no. 3 (Summer 2001): 659–691; Ulrich Beck, "The Truth of Others: A Cosmopolitan Approach," *Common Knowledge* 10, no. 3 (2004): 430–449; Bruce Robbins, "Comparative Cosmopolitanism," *Social Text* 31–32 (1992): 169–186; Thomas Faist and Eyüp Özveren, *Transnational Social Spaces: Agents, Networks and Institutions* (Aldershot, UK: Ashgate, 2004).

31. Demirtaş Ceyhun, *Ah Şu 'Biz Karabıyıklı' Türkler* (Istanbul: E Yayınları, 1988), 267.

32. The question of hospitality in contemporary Europe concerns, for instance, Seyla Benhabib, *The Rights of Others: Aliens, Residents, and Citizens* (Cambridge: Cambridge University Press, 2004); Jacques Derrida, *Of Hospitality: Anne Dufourmantelle Invites Jacques Derrida to Respond*, trans. Rachel Bowlby (Stanford, CA: Stanford University Press, 2000); Mireille Rosello, *Postcolonial Hospitality: The Immigrant as Guest* (Stanford, CA: Stanford University Press, 2001).

Appendix

1. Translator's note: This lecture appeared in Turkish in *Üniversite Konferansları* [University Lectures] *1941–1942*, İstanbul Üniversitesi Yayınları, No. 172 (Istanbul: Kenan

Basımevi ve Klişe Fabrikası, 1942). It is obviously a translation, though no translator is named. Given that French terms are occasionally provided in parentheses within the Turkish text, it seems the translation was done from French, and given the repetitions in the text, from a recording of the lecture rather than from a source written for publication.

2. Translator's note: This lecture first appeared in Turkish in *Üniversite Konferansları* [University Lectures] *1940–1941*, İstanbul Üniversitesi Yayınları, No. 159 (Istanbul: Kenan Basımevi ve Klişe Fabrikası, 1941), and was reprinted in *Cogito* No. 23 (2000). It is obviously a translation, though no translator is named. Given that French terms are occasionally provided within parentheses in others of the series, it seems the translation was done from French, and given the style, from a recording of the lecture rather than from a source written for publication.

References

Adelson, Leslie. "Touching Tales of Turks, Germans, and Jews: Cultural Alterity, Historical Narrative, and Literary Riddles for the 1990s." *New German Critique* 80 (2000): 93–124.

——. *The Turkish Turn in Contemporary German Literature: Toward a New Critical Grammar of Migration*. New York: Palgrave Macmillan, 2005.

Agnew, Vanessa. *Enlightenment Orpheus: The Power of Music in Other Worlds*. New York: Oxford University Press, 2008.

——. "Genealogies of Space in Colonial and Postcolonial Re-enactment." In *Settler and Creole Re-enactment*, ed. Vanessa Agnew and Jonathan Lamb. Basingstoke, UK: Palgrave, 2010, 294–318.

——. "History's Affective Turn: Historical Reenactment and Its Work in the Present." *Rethinking History* 11, no. 3 (2007): 299–312.

——. "Introduction: What Is Reenactment?" *Criticism* 46, no. 3 (2004): 327–339.

Akçam, Taner. *A Shameful Act: The Armenian Genocide and the Question of Turkish Responsibility*. New York: Metropolitan Books, 2006.

Aksan, Virginia H., and Daniel Goffman. *The Early Modern Ottomans: Remapping the Empire*. Cambridge: Cambridge University Press, 2007.

Albert, Claudia, ed. *Deutsche Klassiker im Nationalsozialismus: Schiller, Kleist, Hölderlin*. Stuttgart: Metzler, 1994.

Anderson, Benedict. *Imagined Communities: Reflections on the Origin and Spread of Nationalism*. London: Verso, 1992.

Anderson, Margaret Lavinia. "'Down in Turkey Far Away': Human Rights, the Armenian Massacres, and Orientalism in Wilhelmine Germany." *Journal of Modern History* 79, no. 1 (March 2007): 80–113.

Applegate, Celia. "What Is German Music? Reflections on the Role of Art in the Creation of the German Nation." *German Studies Review* 15 (1992): 21–32.

Apter, Emily. "Global *Translatio*: The 'Invention' of Comparative Literature, Istanbul, 1933." *Critical Inquiry* 29, no. 2 (2003): 253–281.

———. "Saidian Humanism." *Boundary 2* 31, no. 2 (2004): 35–53.

———. *Translation Zone: A New Comparative Literature.* Princeton, NJ: Princeton University Press, 2006.

Arendt, Hannah. "Angelo Giuseppe Roncalli: Der christliche Papst." In *Menschen in finsteren Zeiten*, ed. Ursula Ludz. München: Piper, 1989, 75–88.

Arslan, Ali. *Darülfünun'dan Üniversiteye.* Istanbul: Kitabevi, 1995.

Asín Palacios, Miguel. *Islam and the Divine Comedy.* London: John Murray, 1926.

Aslanapa, Oktay. *İstanbul Üniversitesi: Edebiyat Fakültesi Tezleri (1920–1946).* Istanbul: İsar Vakfı Yayınları, Yıldız Yayıncılık, Reklamcılık, 2004.

Aslandaş, Alper Sedat, and Baskın Bıçakçı. *Popüler Siyasi Deyimler Sözlüğü.* Istanbul: İletişim Yayınları, 1995.

Aster, Ernst von. *Die Türken in der Geschichte der Philosophie.* Istanbul: Devlet Basımevi, 1937.

Ataç, Nurullah. *Diyelim.* Istanbul: Varlık Yayınları, 1954.

Auerbach, Erich. "Dante." In *Üniversite Konferansları 1939–1940.* İstanbul Üniversitesi Yayınları, No. 125. Istanbul: Ülkü Basımevi, 1940, 62–70.

———. *Dante: Poet of the Secular World.* Chicago: University of Chicago Press, 1961.

———. *Dante als Dichter der irdischen Welt.* 2nd ed. Berlin: Walter de Gruyter, 2001.

———. *Dante Hakkında Yeni Araştırmalar.* İstanbul Üniversitesi Edebiyat Fakültesi Yayınları, No. 5. Istanbul: İstanbul Üniversitesi, 1944.

———. "Edebiyat ve Harp." *Cogito* 23 (2000): 219–230.

———. "Ein Exil-Brief Erich Auerbachs aus Istanbul an Freya Hobohm in Marburg— versehen mit einer Nachschrift von Marie Auerbach (1938). Transkribiert und kommentiert von Martin Vialon." *Trajekte* 9 (2004): 8–17.

———. "Epilegomena zu Mimesis." *Romanische Forschungen* 65, no. 1/2 (1953): 1–18.

———. *Gesammelte Aufsätze zur Romanischen Philologie.* Bern: Francke Verlag, 1967.

———. *Introduction to Romance Languages and Literature: Latin, French, Spanish, Provençal, Italian.* Trans. Guy Daniels from French. New York: Capricorn Books, 1961.

———. "Jean Jacques Rousseau." In *Üniversite Konferansları 1938–1939.* İstanbul Üniversitesi Yayınları, No. 96. Istanbul: Ülkü Basımevi, 1939, 129–139.

———. "Kötünün Zaferi: Pascal'in Siyasi Nazariyesi Üzerine bir Deneme." *Cogito* 18 (1999): 279–299.

———. Letter to Johannes Oeschger, May 27, 1938. Nachlass Fritz Lieb, Universitätsbibliothek Basel (Handschriftenabteilung), NL 43 (Lieb) Ah 2,1.

———. Letter to Oskar Krenn, April 14, 1939. Politisches Archiv des Auswärtigen Amts, Berlin, Akten des Generalkonsulats Istanbul, 3977, Paket 9, Akte NSDAP, 1937–1940.

———. *Literary Language and Its Public in Late Latin Antiquity and in the Middle Ages.* Trans. Ralph Manheim. New York: Pantheon Books, 1965.

———. *Mimesis: The Representation of Reality in Western Literature.* Trans. Willard R. Trask. Princeton, NJ: Princeton University Press, 2003.

————. "Montesquieu ve Hürriyet Fikri." In *Üniversite Konferansları 1943–1944.* İstanbul Üniversitesi Yayınları, No. 273. Istanbul: Kenan Matbaası, 1945, 39–49.

————. *Neue Dantestudien: Sacrae scripturae sermo humilis; Figura; Franz von Assisi in der Komödie. Dante Hakkında Yeni Araştırmalar.* Ed. Robert Anhegger, Walter Ruben, and Andreas Tietze. Istanbuler Schriften—Istanbul Yazıları. Istanbul: İbrahim Horoz Basımevi, 1944.

————. "Önsöz." *Garp Filolojileri Dergisi* 1 (1947): 1–4.

————. "On Yedinci Asırda Fransız 'Public'i'." In *Üniversite Konferansları.* İstanbul Üniversitesi Yayınları, No. 50. Istanbul: Ülkü Basımevi, 1937, 113–123.

————. "Provenzalen 1." Literaturarchiv Marbach, Nachlass Auerbach.

————. *Roman Filolojisine Giriş.* Trans. Süheyla Bayrav. İstanbul Üniversitesi Edebiyat Fakültesi Yayınlarından, No. 236. Istanbul: İbrahim Horoz Basımevi, 1944.

————. *Scenes from the Drama of European Literature.* Gloucester, MA: Peter Smith, 1973.

————. "Über die ernste Nachahmung des Alltäglichen." *Romanoloji Semineri Dergisi* 1 (1937): 262–294.

————. "Vico and Aesthetic Historism." *Journal of Aesthetics and Art Criticism* 8, no. 2 (1949): 110–118.

————. *Vier Untersuchungen zur Geschichte der französischen Bildung.* Bern: Francke, 1951.

————. "Voltaire ve Burjuva Zihniyeti." *Garp Filolojileri Dergisi* 1 (1947): 123–134.

————. "XIXuncu Asırda Avrupada Realism." In *Üniversite Konferansları 1941–1942.* İstanbul Üniversitesi Yayınları, No. 172. Istanbul: Kenan Basımevi, 1942.

————. "XVIıncı asırda Avrupada Milli Dillerin Teşekkülü." In *Üniversite Konferansları 1937–1938.* İstanbul Üniversitesi Yayınları, No. 93. Istanbul: Ülkü Basımevi, 1939, 143–152.

————. *Zur Technik der Frührenaissancenovelle in Italien und Frankreich.* Heidelberg: C. Winter, 1921.

"Auslandsdeutschtum und deutsche Erneuerung." *Türkische Post: Tageszeitung für den Nahen Osten,* April 3, 1933, 1–2.

Baer, Marc. *The Dönme: Jewish Converts, Muslim Revolutionaries, and Secular Turks.* Stanford, CA: Stanford University Press, 2009.

————. "The Double Bind of Race and Religion: The Conversion of the Dönme to Turkish Secular Nationalism." *Comparative Study of History and Society* 46, no. 4 (2004): 682–708.

Bahr, Ehrhardt. *Weimar on the Pacific: German Exile Culture in Los Angeles and the Crisis of Modernism.* Berkeley: University of California Press, 2007.

Bahti, Timothy. "Vico, Auerbach, and Literary History." *Philological Quarterly* 60, no. 2 (1981): 235–255.

Balfour, Michael, and Julian Frisby. *Helmuth James Graf von Moltke, 1907–1945.* Trans. Freya von Moltke. Berlin: Henssel, 1984.

————. *Helmuth von Moltke: A Leader against Hitler.* London: Macmillan, 1972.

Bali, Rıfat N. *Cumhuriyet Yıllarında Türkiye Yahudileri: Bir Türkleştirme Serüveni.* Istanbul: İletişim, 1999.

———. *Sarayın ve Cumhuriyetin Dişçibaşısı Sami Günzberg.* Istanbul: Kitabevi, 2007.

———. *The "Varlık Vergisi" Affair: A Study of Its Legacy—Selected Documents.* Istanbul: Isis Press, 2005.

Balzac, H. de. *Otuz Yaşındaki Kadın.* Trans. Mina Urgan. Istanbul: Milli Eğitim Basımevi, 1946.

Bammer, Angelika, ed. *Displacements: Cultural Identities in Question.* Bloomington: Indiana University Press, 1994.

Barck, Karlheinz. "Eine unveröffentlichte Korrespondenz: Erich Auerbach / Werner Krauss." *Beiträge zur Romanischen Philologie* 26, no. 2 (1987): 301–326.

———. "Eine unveröffentlichte Korrespondenz (Fortsetzung): Erich Auerbach / Werner Krauss." *Beiträge zur Romanischen Philologie* 27, no. 1 (1988): 161–186.

———. "Erich Auerbach in Berlin: Spurensicherung und ein Porträt." In *Erich Auerbach: Geschichte und Aktualität eines europäischen Philologen,* ed. Karlheinz Barck and Martin Treml. Berlin: Kadmos, 2007, 195–214.

———. " 'Flucht in die Tradition': Erfahrungshintergründe Erich Auerbachs zwischen Exil und Emigration." In *Stimme, Figur: Kritik und Restitution in der Literaturwissenschaft,* ed. Aleida Assman and Anselm Haverkamp. Stuttgart: Metzler, 1994, 47–60.

———. "5 Briefe Erich Auerbachs an Walter Benjamin in Paris." *Zeitschrift für Germanistik* 9, no. 6 (1988): 688–694.

Barck, Karlheinz, and Anthony Reynolds. "Walter Benjamin and Erich Auerbach: Fragments of a Correspondence." *Diacritics* 22, no. 3/4 (1992): 81–83.

Barck, Karlheinz, and Martin Treml, eds. *Erich Auerbach: Geschichte und Aktualität eines europäischen Philologen.* Berlin: Kadmos, 2007.

Bardenstein, Carol. *Translation and Transformation in Modern Arabic Literature: The Indigenous Assertions of Muhammad 'Uthman Jalal.* Wiesbaden: Harrassowitz, 2005.

"Başvekil Refik Saydam'ın Gazetecilerle Hasbıhali." *Vakit,* January 27, 1939.

Bauer, Markus. "Die Wirklichkeit und ihre literarische Darstellung: Form und Geschichte—der Essayist Erich Auerbach beschäftigt weiterhin seine Exegeten." *Neue Zürcher Zeitung,* February 2, 2008. http://www.nzz.ch/nachrichten/kultur/literatur_und_kunst/die_wirklichkeit_und_ihre_literarische_darstellung_1.663957.html (accessed May 15, 2008).

Bäuml, Franz H. "Mimesis as Model: Medieval Media-Change and Canonical Reality." In *Mimesis: Studien zur literarischen Repräsentation / Studies on Literary Presentation,* ed. Bernhard F. Scholz. Tübingen: Francke Verlag, 1998, 77–86.

Bayrav, Süheyla, and Ferda Keskin. "Siz misiniz? Burada İşiniz Ne?" *Cogito* 23 (2000): 146–154.

Beck, Ulrich. "The Truth of Others: A Cosmopolitan Approach." *Common Knowledge* 10, no. 3 (2004): 430–449.

Behar, Isaak. *Versprich mir, dass Du am Leben bleibst: Ein jüdisches Schicksal.* Berlin: Ullstein, 2002.

Behmoaras, Liz. *Bir Kimlik Arayışının Hikayesi*. Istanbul: Remzi Kitapevi, 2005.

Benhabib, Seyla. *The Rights of Others: Aliens, Residents, and Citizens*. Cambridge: Cambridge University Press, 2004.

———. "Traumatische Anfänge, Mythen und Experimente: Die multikulturelle Türkei im Übergang zur reifen Demokratie." *Neue Zürcher Zeitung*, November 26, 2005, 71.

Benjamin, Walter. *Berliner Kindheit um neunzehnhundert: Mit einem Nachwort von Theodor W. Adorno*. Frankfurt am Main: Suhrkamp, 1987.

———. *Illuminations: Essays and Reflections*. Ed. Hannah Arendt. New York: Schocken Books, 1969.

———. *Zum Ursprung des deutschen Trauerspiels*. Berlin: Ernst Rowohlt, 1928.

Berkes, Niyazi. *The Development of Secularism in Turkey*. Montreal: McGill University Press, 1964.

———. "Sociology in Turkey." *American Journal of Sociology* 42, no. 2 (1936): 238–246.

Berman, Nina. "Ottoman Shock-and-Awe and the Rise of Protestantism: Luther's Reactions to the Ottoman Invasions of the Early Sixteenth Century." *Seminar* 41, no. 3 (2005): 226–245.

Berthold, Werner, Brita Eckert, and Frank Wende. *Deutsche Intellektuelle im Exil: Ihre Akademie und die "American Guild for German Cultural Freedom."* München: Saur, 1993.

Bezirci, Asım. *Nurullah Ataç: Yaşamı, Kişiliği, Eleştiri Anlayışı, Yazıları*. Istanbul: Varlık Yayınları, 1983.

Bhabha, Homi K. *The Location of Culture*. London: Routledge, 1994.

Biddick, Kathleen. "Coming Out of Exile: Dante on the Orient(alism) Express." *American Historical Review* 105, no. 4 (2000): 1234–1249.

Bilsel, Can. "Our Anatolia": Organicism and the Making of Humanist Culture in Turkey." *Muqarnas* 24 (2007): 223–241.

Bilsel, Cemil. "Dördüncü Yıl Açış Nutku." In *Üniversite Konferansları 1936–1937*, İstanbul Üniversitesi Yayınları No. 50. Istanbul: Ülkü Basımevi, 1937, 3–16.

Bisaha, Nancy. *Creating East and West: Renaissance Humanists and the Ottoman Turks*. Philadelphia: University of Pennsylvania Press, 2004.

Boehlich, Walter. "Ein Haus, in dem wir atmen können: Das Neueste zum Dauerstreit um den Romanisten Ernst Robert Curtius." *Die Zeit* 50 (1996): 52.

Bosch, Clemens. *Helenizm Tarihinin Anahatları*. Edebiyat Fakültesi Yayınlarından. Istanbul: Istanbul Üniversitesi, 1942/1943.

Bové, Paul, A. *Intellectuals in Power: A Genealogy of Critical Humanism*. New York: Columbia University Press, 1986.

Bozay, Kemal. *Exil Türkei: Ein Forschungsbeitrag zur deutschsprachigen Emigration in die Türkei 1933–1945*. Münster: LIT, 2001.

Braziel, Jana Evans, and Anita Mannur, eds. *Theorizing Diaspora: A Reader*. Cornwall, UK: Blackwell Publishing, 2003.

Brennan, Timothy. "Cosmo-Theory." *South Atlantic Quarterly* 100, no. 3 (Summer 2001): 659–691.

Brinkmann, Hennig. "Deutsche Dichtung der Gegenwart." *Das deutsche Wort: Die literarische Welt* 10, no. 16 (1934): 3.

Brockmann, Stephen. "Inner Emigration: The Term and Its Origins in Postwar Debates." In *Flight of Fantasy: New Perspectives on Inner Emigration in German Literature, 1933–1945*, ed. Neil H. Donahue and Doris Kirchner. New York: Berghahn, 2003, 11–26.

Bundesarchiv, Berlin. Reichsministerium für Wissenschaft, Erziehung und Volksbildung, R 4901/6657, Das Schulwesen in der Türkei, 7. Juni 1943, R. Preussners Bericht an das Ministerium, Blatt 67 und 68.

———. Reichsministerium für Wissenschaft, Erziehung und Volksbildung, R 4901/13290, Wissenschaftliche Beziehungen zum Ausland, Akte Prof. Dr. Hennig Brinkmann, Univ. Frankfurt a.M., Mai 1943–März 1945.

———. Reichsministerium für Wissenschaft, Erziehung und Volksbildung, R 4901/15149, Wissenschaftliche Beziehungen zum Ausland, Akte Prof. Kranz Dez. 1943–Dez. 1944.

Burian, Orhan. *Denemeler Eleştiriler*. Istanbul: Can Yayınları, 1964.

Burkart, Rosemarie. "Truchement: Histoire d'un mot Oriental en Français." *Romanoloji Semineri Dergisi* 1 (1937): 51–56.

Busolt, C. "Deutsch als Weltsprache." *Türkische Post: Tageszeitung für den Nahen Osten*, February 1, 1933, 1–2.

Büyükdüvenci, Sabri. "John Dewey's Impact on Turkish Education." *Studies in Philosophy and Education* 13, no. 3–4 (1994): 393–400.

Calvet, Louis-Jean. *Language Wars and Linguistic Politics*. Oxford: Oxford University Press, 1998.

Caner, Beatrix. *Türkische Literatur: Klassiker der Moderne*. Hildesheim: Georg Olms, 1998.

Cantarino, Vicente. "Dante and Islam: History and Analysis of a Controversy." In *A Dante Symposium*, ed. William de Sua and Gino Rizzo. Chapel Hill: University of North Carolina Press, 1965, 175–198.

Cantor, Paul A. "The Uncanonical Dante: The Divine Comedy and Islamic Philosophy." *Philosophy and Literature* 20, no. 1 (1996): 138–153.

Ceyhun, Demirtaş. *Ah Şu 'Biz Karabıyıklı' Türkler*. Istanbul: E Yayınları, 1988.

Chakrabarty, Dipesh. "Postcoloniality and the Artifice of History—Who Speaks for 'Indian' Pasts?" In *The Decolonization Reader*, ed. James D. Le Sueur. New York: Routledge, 2003, 429–448.

Chin, Rita. *The Guest Worker Question in Postwar Germany*. Cambridge: Cambridge University Press, 2007.

Christmann, Hans Helmut, and Frank-Rutger Hausmann, eds. *Deutsche und Österreichische Romanisten als Verfolgte des Nationalsozialismus*. Tübingen: Stauffenburg Verlag, 1989.

Çıkar, Mustafa. *Hasan-Âli Yücel und die türkische Kulturreform*. Bonn: Pontes Verlag, 1994.

Çınar, Alev. *Modernity, Islam, and Secularism in Turkey: Bodies, Places, and Time*. Minneapolis: University of Minnesota Press, 2005.

Cremer, Jan, and Horst Przytulla. *Exil Türkei: Deutschsprachige Emigranten in der Türkei 1933–1945*. München: Verlag Karl M. Lipp, 1991.

Curthoys, Ned. "Edward Said's Unhoused Philological Humanism." In *Edward Said: The Legacy of a Public Intellectual*, ed. Ned Curthoys and Debjani Ganguly. Melbourne: Melbourne University Press, 2007, 152–175.

Damrosch, David. "Auerbach in Exile." *Comparative Literature* 47, no. 2 (1995): 97–115.

Dante Alighieri. *The Divine Comedy*, vol. 1: *Inferno*. Trans. Mark Musa. New York: Penguin Books, 2003.

———. *İlâhî Komedi (Divina commedia) Cehennem–Âraf–Cennet*. Trans. Hamdi Varoğlu. Istanbul: Hilmi Kitapevi, 1938.

———. *İlâhi Komedya*. Trans. Feridun Timur. Ankara: Maarif Basımevi, 1959.

Dawson, John David. "Figural Reading and the Fashioning of Christian Identity in Boyarin, Auerbach and Frei." *Modern Theology* 14, no. 2 (1998): 181–196.

Demirel, Süleyman. "European University Association (EUA)." Meeting in Istanbul at Technical University of Istanbul, February 2, 2006. http://www.eua.be/eua/jsp/en/upload/demirel.1142257241117.pdf (accessed May 20, 2006).

Deringil, Selim. "'They Live in a State of Nomadism and Savagery': The Late Ottoman Empire and the Post-Colonial Debate." *Society for Comparative Study of Society and History* 45, no. 2 (2003): 311–342.

———. *Turkish Foreign Policy during the Second World War: An "Active" Neutrality*. Cambridge: Cambridge University Press, 1989.

Derrida, Jacques. *Of Hospitality: Anne Dufourmantelle Invites Jacques Derrida to Respond*. Trans. Rachel Bowlby. Stanford, CA: Stanford University Press, 2000.

Dewey, John. *Democracy and Education: The Introduction to the Philosophy of Education*. New York: Macmillan Company, 1922.

———. *The Middle Works, 1899–1924*, vol. 15: *1923–1924*. Ed. Jo Ann Boydston. Carbondale: Southern Illinois University Press, 1983.

Dieckmann, Liselotte. "Akademische Emigranten in der Türkei." In *Verbannung: Aufzeichnungen deutscher Schriftsteller im Exil*, ed. Egon Schwarz and Matthias Wegner. Hamburg: Christian Wegner, 1964, 122–126.

"Die Hitler-Geburtstagsfeier in Stambul." *Türkische Post: Tageszeitung für den Nahen Osten*, April 22, 1933, 4.

Dietrich, Anne. *Deutschsein in Istanbul: Nationalisierung und Orientierung in der deutschsprachigen Community von 1843 bis 1956*. Opladen: Leske und Budrich, 1998.

Dino, Güzin. *Gel Zaman Git Zaman: Anılar*. Istanbul: Can Yayınları, 1991.

———. *Tanzimattan Sonra Edebiyatta Gerçekçiliğe Doğru*. Ankara: Türk Tarih Kurumu Basımevi, 1954.

———. *Türk Romanının Doğuşu*. Istanbul: Cem Yayınevi, 1978.

Edebiyat Fakültesi: 1936–7 Ders Yılı Talebe Kılavuzu. Istanbul: Resimli Ay Basımevi T.L.S., 1936.

Einstein, Albert. "Einstein on His Theory: Time, Space, and Gravitation." *The Times*, November 28, 1919, 13–14.

Elsky, Martin, Martin Vialon, and Robert Stein. "Scholarship in Times of Extremes: Letters of Erich Auerbach (1933–46), on the Fiftieth Anniversary of His Death." *Publications of the Modern Language Association of America* 122, no. 3 (2007): 742–762.

Ergün, Mustafa. *Atatürk Devri Türk Eğitimi*. Ankara Üniversitesi Dil ve Coğrafya Fakültesi Yayınları, No. 325. Ankara: Ankara Üniversitesi Basımevi, 1982.

Erhat, Azra. *Gülleylâ'ya Anılar (En Hakiki Mürşit)*. Istanbul: Can Yayınları, 2002.

———. "Üslup Ilminde Yeni bir Usul." *Romanoloji Semineri Dergisi* 1 (1937): 1–6.

Eusterschulte, Anne. "Kulturentwicklung und -verfall: Giambattista Vicos kulturgeschichtliche Anthropologie." In *Humanismus in Geschichte und Gegenwart*, ed. Richard Faber and Enno Rudolph. Tübingen: Mohr Siebeck, 2002, 17–44.

Eyüboğlu, Sabahattin. *Mavi ve Kara: Denemeler (1940–1966)*. Istanbul: Çan Yayınları, 1967.

Ezine, Celâleddin. "Türk Humanizmasinin İzahı." *Hamle* 1 (1940): 6–10.

Faist, Thomas, and Eyüp Özveren. *Transnational Social Spaces: Agents, Networks and Institutions*. Aldershot, UK: Ashgate, 2004.

Faroqhi, Suraiya. *The Later Ottoman Empire, 1603–1839. The Cambridge History of Turkey*, vol. 3. Cambridge: Cambridge University Press, 2006.

Fermi, Laura. *Illustrious Immigrants: The Intellectual Migration from Europe, 1930–1941*. Chicago: University of Chicago Press, 1968.

F.F.S.D. "Die Heimat." *Türkische Post: Tageszeitung für den Nahen Osten*, April 18, 1933, 1–2.

Findley, Carter Vaughn. *Ottoman Officialdom: A Social History*. Princeton, NJ: Princeton University Press, 1989.

"Flaggenfeier." *Türkische Post: Tageszeitung für den Nahen Osten*, March 17, 1933, 4.

Fleet, Kate. *European and Islamic Trade in the Early Ottoman State: The Merchants of Genoa and Turkey*. Cambridge: Cambridge University Press, 1999.

Fortna, Benjamin C. *Imperial Classroom: Islam, the State, and Education in the Late Ottoman Empire*. Oxford: Oxford University Press, 2002.

Frantz, Douglas, and Catherine Collins. *Death on the Black Sea: The Untold Story of the Struma and World War II's Holocaust at Sea*. New York: Ecco, 2003.

Friling, Tuvia. *Between Friendly and Hostile Neutrality: Turkey and the Jews during World War II*, vol. 2. Jerusalem: Tel Aviv University, 2002.

Fuchs, Barbara. *Mimesis and Empire: The New World, Islam, and European Identities*. Cambridge: Cambridge University Press, 2001.

Fuchs, Traugott. *Çorum and Anatolian Pictures*. Istanbul: Boğaziçi Üniversitesi, Cultural Heritage Museum Publications, 1986.

Ganguly, Debjani. "Edward Said, World Literature, and Global Comparatism." In *Edward Said: The Legacy of a Public Intellectual*, ed. Ned Curthoys and Debjani Ganguly. Melbourne: Melbourne University Press, 2007, 176–202.

Gelbin, Cathy. "Elisabeth Langgässer and the Question of Inner Emigration." In *Flight of Fantasy: New Perspectives on Inner Emigration in German Literature, 1933–1945*, ed. Neil H. Donahue and Doris Kirchner. New York: Berghahn, 2003, 269–276.

Gemünden, Gerd, and Anton Kaes. "Introduction to Special Issue on Film and Exile." *New German Critique* 89 (2003): 3–8.

Gencer, Mustafa. *Jöntürk Modernizmi ve "Alman Ruhu."* Istanbul: İletişim, 2003.

Ginzburg, Carlo. "Auerbach und Dante: Eine Verlaufsbahn." In *Erich Auerbach: Geschichte und Aktualität eines Philologen*, ed. Karlheinz Barck and Martin Treml. Berlin: Kadmos, 2007, 33–45.

Glasneck, Johannes. *Methoden der deutsch-faschistischen Propagandatätigkeit in der Türkei vor und während des Zweiten Weltkriegs*. Halle: Martin-Luther-Universität Halle, 1966.

Glassen, Erika. "Töchter der Republik: Gazi Mustafa Kemal Pasa (Atatürk) im Gedächtnis einer intellektuellen weiblichen Elite der ersten Republikgeneration nach Erinnerungsbüchern von Azra Erhat, Mina Urgan und Nermin Abadan-Unat." *Journal of Turkish Studies–Türklük Bilgisi Araştırmaları* 26, no. 1 (2002): 239–264.

Göçek, Fatma Müge. "The Decline of the Ottoman Empire and the Emergence of Greek, Armenian, Turkish, and Arab Nationalisms." In *Social Constructions of Nationalism in the Middle East*, ed. Fatma Müge Göçek. Albany: State University of New York Press, 2002, 15–84.

———. *Rise of the Bourgeoisie, Demise of Empire: Ottoman Westernization and Social Change*. New York: Oxford University Press, 1996.

Gökalp, Ziya. *Millî Terbiye ve Maarif Meselesi*. Ankara: Diyarbakır Tanıtma ve Turizm Derneği Yayınları, 1964.

———. "Tevfik Fikret ve Rönesans." In *Makaleler V*. Ankara: Kültür Bakanlığı, 1981, 173–175.

———. *Turkish Nationalism and Western Civilization*. Trans. and ed. Niyazi Berkes. New York: Columbia University Press, 1959.

Gökman, Muzaffer. *Istanbul Kütüphaneleri Rehberi*. Istanbul, 1941.

———. *Istanbul Kütüphaneleri ve Günkü Vaziyetleri*. Istanbul: Hüsnütabiat Matbaası, 1939.

Gorki, Maxim. "Von den Kulturen." *Internationale Literatur: Zentralorgan der Internationalen Vereinigung Revolutionärer Schriftsteller* 5, no. 9 (1935): 10.

Gövsa, İbrahim Alaettin. *Sabatay Sevi: İzmirli Meşhur Sahte Mesih Hakkında Tarihî ve İçtimaî Tetkik Tecrübesi*. Istanbul: S. Lütfi Kitapevi, 1940.

Grosz, Elizabeth. "Judaism and Exile: The Ethics of Otherness." In *Space and Place: Theories of Identity and Location*, ed. Erica Carter, James Donald, and Judith Squires. London: Lawrence & Wishart, 1993, 57–72.

Grothusen, Klaus Detlev, ed. *Der Scurla-Bericht: Migration deutscher Professoren in die Türkei im Dritten Reich*. Frankfurt: Dagyeli, 1987.

Grudin, Robert. "Humanism." *Encyclopædia Britannica Online*. http://search.eb.com.proxy.lib.umich.edu/eb/article-11769 (accessed July 14, 2008).

Grzywatz, Berthold. *Die historische Stadt: Charlottenburg*, vol. 1. Berlin: Nicolai, 1987.

Guénon, René. *The Esoterism of Dante*. Trans. C. B. Bethell. Paris: Gallimard, 1996.

———. *L'Ésotérisme de Dante*. Paris: Bosse, 1925.

Gumbrecht, Hans Ulrich. "'Pathos of the Earthly Progress': Erich Auerbach's Every-days." In *Literary History and the Challenge of Philology: The Legacy of Erich Auerbach*, ed. Seth Lerer. Stanford, CA: Stanford University Press, 1996, 13–35.

———. *Vom Leben und Sterben der großen Romanisten: Carl Vossler, Ernst Robert Curtius, Leo Spitzer, Erich Auerbach, Werner Krauss*. Ed. Michael Krüger. München: Carl Hanser Verlag, 2002.

Günaltay, Şemseddin. "Açış Dersi: Türklerin Ana Yurdu ve Irki Mes'elesi." In *Üniversite Konferansları 1936–1937*. İstanbul Üniversitesi Yayınları No. 50. Istanbul: Ülkü Basımevi, 1937, i–xiv.

Gürçağlar, Şehnaz Tahir. *The Politics and Poetics of Translation in Turkey, 1923–1960*. Amsterdam: Rodopi, 2008.

Guttstadt, Corinna Görgü. "Depriving Non-Muslims of Citizenship as Part of the Turki-fication Policy in the Early Years of the Republic: The Case of Turkish Jews and Its Consequences during the Holocaust." In *Turkey beyond Nationalism: Towards Post-Nationalist Identities*, ed. Hans-Lukas Kieser. London: I. B. Tauris, 2006, 50–56.

———. *Die Türkei, die Juden und der Holocaust*. Berlin: Assoziation A, 2008.

———. "'Haymatloz'—Der Weg in die Zensur?" *Aktives Museum: Faschismus und Widerstand* 58: 14–17.

Güvenç, Duygu. "Turkey Battles Genocide Claims in Hollywood." *Turkish Daily News*, February 13, 2007. http://www.turkishdailynews.com.tr/article.php?enewsid=66071 (accessed March 19, 2007).

Halman, Talât Sait. *The Humanist Poetry of Yunus Emre*. Istanbul: Istanbul Matbaası, 1972.

———. "Turkish Humanism and the Poetry of Yunus Emre." *Tarih Araştırmaları Dergisi / Review of Historical Research* 6, no. 10–11 (1968): 231–240.

Hartman, Geoffrey. *A Scholar's Tale: Intellectual Journey of a Displaced Child of Europe*. New York: Fordham University Press, 2007.

Hasan-Rokem, Galit, and Alan Dundes. *The Wandering Jew: Essays in the Interpretation of a Christian Legend*. Bloomington: Indiana University Press, 1986.

Hatiboğlu, Tahir. *Türkiye Üniversite Tarihi*. Ankara: Selvi Yayınevi, 1998.

Hausmann, Frank-Rutger. *"Deutsche Geisteswissenschaft" im Zweiten Weltkrieg: Die "Aktion Ritterbusch" (1940–1945)*. Ed. Holger Dainat, Michael Grüttner, and Frank-Rutger Hausmann. Dresden: Dresden University Press, 1998.

Hebblethwaite, Margaret. *John XXIII: Pope of the Century*. New York: Continuum International Publishing Group, 2005.

Hell, Julia. "Imperial Ruin Gazers, or Why Did Scipio Weep?" In *Ruins of Modernity*, ed. Julia Hell and Andreas Schoenle. Durham, NC: Duke University Press, 2010, 169–192.

———. "Ruin Travel: Orphic Journeys through 1940s Germany." In *Writing Travel*, ed. John Zilcosky. Toronto: University of Toronto Press, 2008, 123–162.

Hiçyılmaz, Ergun, and Meral Altındal. *Büyük Sığınak: Türk Yahudilerinin 500 Yıllık Serüveninden Sayfalar*. Istanbul: Belgesel, 1992.

Hillebrecht, Sabine, ed. *Haymatloz: Exil in der Türkei 1933–1945*. Berlin: Verein Aktives Museum, 2000.

Hirsch, Ernst E. *Aus des Kaisers Zeiten durch die Weimarer Republik in das Land Atatürks: Eine unzeitgemäße Autobiographie*. München: Schweitzer, 1982.

———. *Dünya Üniversiteleri ve Türkiyede Üniversitelerin Gelişmesi*, vol. 1. Istanbul: Ankara Üniversitesi Yayımları, 1950.

Homer. *Odyssey*. Trans. Albert Cook. New York: Norton, 1993.

Howard, Harry N. "Preliminary Materials for a Survey of the Libraries and Archives of Istanbul." *Journal of the American Oriental Society* 59, no. 2 (1939): 227–246.

Hutton, Christopher M. *Linguistics and the Third Reich: Mother-Tongue Fascism, Race and the Science of Language*. London: Routledge, 1999.

Huyssen, Andreas. "Diaspora and Nation: Migration into Other Pasts." *New German Critique* 88 (2003): 147–164.

Iğsız, Aslı. "Repertoires of Rupture: Recollecting the 1923 Greek-Turkish Compulsory Religious Minority Exchange." Unpublished dissertation, University of Michigan, 2006.

Irem, Nazım. "Turkish Conservative Modernism: Birth of a Nationalist Quest for Cultural Renewal." *International Journal of Middle East Studies* 34, no. 1 (2002): 87–112.

İstanbul Üniversitesi Arşivi (Istanbul University Archive), Auerbach Dosyası.

Istanbul University. Chaire de Philologie Romane à la Faculté des lettres, December 11, 1936. Literaturarchiv Marbach, Nachlaß Erich Auerbach, Zugehörige Materialien.

Jäckh, Ernst. *Der aufsteigende Halbmond: Auf dem Weg zum deutsch-türkischen Bündnis*. Stuttgart: Deutsche Verlags-Anstalt, 1915.

Jacquemond, Richard. "Translation and Cultural Hegemony: The Case of French-Arabic Translation." In *Rethinking Translation: Discourse, Subjectivity, Ideology*, ed. Lawrence Venuti. New York: Routledge, 1992, 139–158.

JanMohamed, Abdul R. "Worldliness-without-World, Homelessness-as-Home: Toward a Definition of the Specular Border Intellectual." In *Edward Said: A Critical Reader*, ed. Michael Sprinker. Oxford: Blackwell, 1992, 96–120.

Jay, Martin. *Permanent Exiles: Essays on the Intellectual Migration from Germany to America*. New York: Columbia University Press, 1985.

Jüdisches Museum, München. "Orte des Exils/Sürgün Yerleri: Münih ve Istanbul." München: Jüdisches Museum München, 2008.

Kadir, Djelal. "Comparative Literature in a World Become Tlön." *Comparative Critical Studies* 3, no. 1–2 (2006): 125–138.

———. *Memos from the Besieged City: Lifelines for Cultural Sustainability*, Stanford, CA: Stanford University Press, 2011.

Kahn, Robert. "Eine 'List der Vorsehung': Erich Auerbach und Walter Benjamin." In *Erich Auerbach: Geschichte und Aktualität eines europäischen Philologen*, ed. Martin Treml and Karlheinz Barck. Berlin: Kulturverlag Kadmos, 2007, 153–166.

Kandiyoti, Deniz. "End of Empire: Islam, Nationalism and Women in Turkey." In *Feminist Postcolonial Theory: A Reader*, ed. Reina Lewis and Sara Mills. New York: Routledge, 2003, 263–284.

Kaplan, Caren. *Questions of Travel: Postmodern Discourses of Displacement*. Durham, NC: Duke University Press, 1996.

Kaplan, Sam. *The Pedagogical State: Education and the Politics of National Culture in Post-1980s Turkey*. Stanford, CA: Stanford University Press, 2006.

Kastoryano, Riva. "From *Millet* to Community: The Jews of Istanbul." In *Ottoman and Turkish Jewry: Community and Leadership*, ed. Aron Rodrigue. Bloomington: Indiana University Press, 1992, 253–277.

Katoğlu, Murat. "Cumhuriyet Türkiye'sinde Eğitim, Kültür, Sanat." In *Cumhuriyet Dönemi Edebiyat Çevirileri Seçkisi*, ed. Öner Yağcı. Ankara: Kültür Bakanlığı Yayınları, 1999, 331–332.

Kaynardağ, Arslan. *Bizde Felsefenin Kurumlaşması ve Türkiye Felsefe Kurumu'nun Tarihi*. Ankara: Türkiye Felsefe Kurumu, 1994.

———. "Üniversitemizde Ders Veren Alman Felsefe Profesörleri." In *Türk Felsefe Araştırmalarında ve Üniversite Öğretiminde Alman Filozofları*. Istanbul: Türkiye Felsefe Kurumu, 1986.

Keyman, Fuat. "Modernity, Secularism, and Islam." *Theory, Culture & Society* 24, no. 2 (2007): 215–234.

Kıvırcık, Emir. *Büyükelçi*. Istanbul: Goa, 2007.

Klein, Fritz. "Der Einfluß Deutschlands und Österreich-Ungarns auf das türkische Bildungswesen in den Jahren des Ersten Weltkrieges." In *Wegenetz europäischen Geistes: Wissenschaftszentren und geistige Wechselbeziehungen zwischen Mittel- und Südosteuropa vom Ende des 18. Jahrhunderts bis zum Ersten Weltkrieg*, ed. Richard Georg Plaschka and Karlheinz Mack. Wien: Verlag für Geschichte und Politik, 1983, 420–432.

Klein, Wolfgang, ed. *Paris 1935: Erster Internationaler Schriftstellerkongreß zur Verteidigung der Kultur. Reden und Dokumente. Mit Materialien der Londoner Schriftstellerkonferenz 1936*. Berlin: Akademie-Verlag, 1982.

Klemperer, Klemens von. *German Resistance against Hitler: The Search for Allies Abroad, 1938–1945*. Oxford: Oxford University Press, 1992.

Klemperer, Victor. *Der alte und der neue Humanismus*. Berlin: Aufbau-Verlag, 1953.

———. *Ich will Zeugnis ablegen bis zum letzten*, vol. 1: *Tagebücher 1933–1941*. Ed. Walter Nowojski. Berlin: Aufbau-Verlag, 1996.

———. *I Will Bear Witness: A Diary of the Nazi Years, 1942–1945*. New York: Random House, 1998.

———. *LTI: Notizbuch eines Philologen*. Berlin: Aufbau-Verlag, 1947.

———. "Philologie im Exil." *Aufbau* 4, no. 10 (1948): 863–868.

———. "Philologie im Exil." In *Vor 33 nach 45: Gesammelte Aufsätze*. Berlin: Akademie Verlag, 1956, 224–229.

König, Christoph, ed. *Internationales Germanistenlexikon 1800–1950*. Berlin: Walter de Gruyter, 2003.

Konuk, Kader. "Antagonistische Weltanschauungen in der türkischen Moderne: Die Beteiligung von Emigranten und Nationalsozialisten an der Grundlegung der Nationalphilologien in Istanbul." In *Istanbul: Geistige Wanderungen aus der Welt in Scherben?* ed. Faruk Birtek and Georg Stauth. Bielefeld: Transcript, 2007, 191–216.

———. "Ethnomasquerade in Ottoman-European Encounters: Re-enacting Lady Mary Wortley Montagu." *Criticism* 46, no. 3 (2004): 393–414.

———. *Identitäten im Prozeß: Literatur von Autorinnen aus und in der Türkei in deutscher, englischer und türkischer Sprache.* Essen: Die Blaue Eule, 2001.

———. "Istanbuler Germanistik: Grundlegung durch Emigranten und Nationalsozialisten." *Geschichte der Germanistik. Mitteilungen* 27/28 (2005): 30–37.

———. "Taking on German and Turkish History: Emine Sevgi Özdamar's *Seltsame Sterne*." *Gegenwartsliteratur: German Studies Yearbook* 6 (2007): 232–256.

Kritovoulos. *History of Mehmed the Conqueror.* Trans. C. T. Riggs. Princeton, NJ: Princeton University Press, 1954.

Küçük, Abdurrahman. *Dönmeler (Sabatayistler) Tarihi.* Ankara: Alperen Yayınları, 2001.

Küçük, Yalçın. *İsimlerin İbranileştirilmesi: Tekelistan-Türk Yahudi İsimleri Sözlüğü.* Istanbul: Salyangoz Yayınları, 2006.

Kulin, Ayşe. *Nefes Nefese.* Istanbul: Remzi Kitapevi, 2002.

Kuruyazıcı, Nilüfer. "Die deutsche akademische Emigration von 1933 und ihre Rolle bei der Neugründung der Universität Istanbul sowie bei der Gründung der Germanistik." In *Interkulturelle Begegnungen: Festschrift für Şara Sayın,* ed. Şara Sayın, Manfred Durzak, and Nilüfer Kuruyazıcı. Würzburg: Königshausen & Neumann, 2004, 253–267.

Lamb, Jonathan. "Coming to Terms with What Isn't There: Early Narratives of New Holland." *Eighteenth-Century Life* 26, no. 1 (2002): 147–155.

———. *Preserving the Self in the South Seas, 1680–1840.* Chicago: University of Chicago Press, 2001.

Lambropoulos, Vassilis. *The Rise of Eurocentrism: Anatomy of Interpretation.* Princeton, NJ: Princeton University Press, 1993.

Lawton, David. "History and Legend: The Exile and the Turk." In *Postcolonial Moves: Medieval through Modern,* ed. Patricia Clare Ingham and Michelle R. Warren. New York: Palgrave Macmillan, 2003, 173–194.

"Leo Spitzer." *Johns Hopkins Magazine* (April 1952): 19–27.

Lerer, Seth. *Error and the Academic Self: The Scholarly Imagination, Medieval to Modern.* New York: Columbia University Press, 2002.

Levi, Avner. *Türkiye Cumhuriyeti'nde Yahudiler.* Istanbul: İletişim, 1992.

Levin, Harry. "Two *Romanisten* in America: Spitzer and Auerbach." In *The Intellectual Migration: Europe and America, 1930–1960,* ed. Donald Fleming and Bernard Bailyn. Cambridge, MA: Belknap Press of Harvard University Press, 1969, 463–484.

Levy, Avigdor. *The Jews of the Ottoman Empire.* Princeton, NJ: Darwin Press, 1994.

———. *The Sephardim in the Ottoman Empire.* Princeton, NJ: Darwin Press, 1992.

Lewis, Bernard. *From Babel to Dragomans: Interpreting the Middle East.* Oxford: Oxford University Press, 2004.

Lier, Thomas. "Hellmut Ritter in Istanbul 1926–1949." *Die Welt des Islams* 38, no. 3 (1998): 334–385.

————. "Hellmut Ritter und die Zweigstelle der DMG in Istanbul 1928–1949." In *Hellmut Ritter und die DMG in Istanbul*, ed. Angelika Neuwirth and Armin Bassarak. Istanbul: Orient Institut der Deutschen Morgenländischen Gesellschaft, 1997, 17–49.

Lima, Luiz Costa. "Erich Auerbach: History and Metahistory." *New Literary History* 19, no. 3 (1988): 467–499.

Liu, Lydia H. *Translingual Practice*. Stanford, CA: Stanford University Press, 1995.

Löwith, Karl. *Mein Leben in Deutschland vor und nach 1933: Ein Bericht*. Stuttgart: Metzler, 1986.

Makdisi, Ussama. "Ottoman Orientalism." *American Historical Review* 107, no. 3 (2002): 768–796.

Maksudyan, Nazan. *Türklüğü Ölçmek: Bilimkurgusal Antropoloji ve Türk Milliyetçiliğinin Çehresi, 1925–1939*. Istanbul: Metis, 2005.

Marchand, Suzanne L. *Down from Olympus: Archaeology and Philhellenism in Germany, 1750–1970*. Princeton, NJ: Princeton University Press, 1996.

————. "Nazism, Orientalism and Humanism." In *Nazi Germany and the Humanities*, ed. Wolfgang Bialas and Anson Rabinbach. Oxford: Oneworld, 2007, 267–305.

Mattenklott, Gert. "Erich Auerbach in den deutsch-jüdischen Verhältnissen." In *Wahrnehmen Lesen Deuten: Erich Auerbachs Lektüre der Moderne*, ed. Walter Busch, Gerhart Pickerodt, and Markus Bauer. Frankfurt am Main: Vittorio Klostermann, 1998, 15–30.

Maxwell, Richard, Joshua Scodel, and Katie Trumpener. "Editors' Preface." *Modern Philology* 100, no. 4 (2003): 505–511.

McClennen, Sophia A. *The Dialectics of Exile: Nation, Time, Language, and Space in Hispanic Literatures*. West Lafayette, IN: Purdue University Press, 2004.

Meier-Rust, Kathrin. *Alexander Rüstow: Geschichtsdeutung und liberales Engagement*. Stuttgart: Klett-Cotta, 1993.

Mitgliederrundbrief. Vol. 43. Berlin: Verein Aktives Museum: Faschismus und Widerstand in Berlin, May 2000. http://www.aktives-museum.de/fileadmin/user_upload/Extern/Dokumente/rundbrief-43.pdf (accessed March 20, 2009).

Mitler, Louis. "Genoese in Galata, 1453–1682." *International Journal of Middle East Studies* 10, no. 1 (1979): 71–91.

Moltke, Freya von. *Memories of Kreisau and the German Resistance*. Trans. Julie M. Winter. Lincoln: University of Nebraska Press, 2005.

Moltke, Helmuth James von. *Briefe an Freya 1939–1945*. München: C. H. Beck, 1988.

————. *Letters to Freya: 1939–1945*. Trans. Beate Ruhm von Appen. New York: Alfred A. Knopf, 1990.

Montaigne, Michael de. *Works of Michael de Montaigne: Comprising His Essays, Journey into Italy, and Letters, with Notes from All the Commentators, Biographical and Bibliographical Notices, Etc.*, vol. 2. Ed. W. Hazlitt and O. W. Wight. New York: H. W. Derby, 1861.

Mostyn, Trevor. *Egypt's Belle Epoque: Cairo and the Age of the Hedonists*. London: Tauris Parke, 2006.

Mufti, Aamir R. "Auerbach in Istanbul: Edward Said, Secular Criticism, and the Question of Minority Culture." In *Edward Said and the Work of the Critic: Speaking Truth to Power*, ed. Paul A. Bové. Durham, NC: Duke University Press, 2000, 229–256.

———. "Critical Secularism: A Reintroduction for Perilous Times." *Boundary 2* 31, no. 2 (2004): 1–9.

Mulertt, Werner. "Asíns Dantebuch." *Islam* 14 (1924): 114–123.

Müller, Hildegard. "German Librarians in Exile in Turkey, 1933–1945." *Libraries and Culture* 33, no. 3 (1998): 294–305.

Mumcu, Uğur. *40'ların Cadı Kazanı*. Istanbul: Tekin Yayınevi, 1990.

N., N. "1 film, 4 ülke, 500 hayat." *Cumhuriyet* (September 25, 2008).

Neumark, Fritz. *Zuflucht am Bosporus: Deutsche Gelehrte, Politiker und Künstler in der Emigration 1933–1953*. Frankfurt am Main: Verlag Josef Knecht, 1980.

Newman, Jane. "Nicht am 'falschen Ort': Saids Auerbach und die 'neue' Komparatistik." In *Erich Auerbach: Geschichte und Aktualität eines europäischen Philologen*, ed. Karlheinz Barck and Martin Treml. Berlin: Kulturverlag Kadmos, 2007, 341–356.

Nicolai, Bern. *Moderne und Exil: Deutschsprachige Architekten in der Türkei 1925–1955*. Berlin: Verlag für Bauwesen, 1998.

Nissen, Rudolf. *Helle Blätter, dunkle Blätter: Erinnerungen eines Chirurgen*. Stuttgart: Deutsche Verlags-Anstalt, 1969.

Olschki, Leonardo. "Mohammedan Eschatology and Dante's Other World." *Comparative Literature* 3, no. 1 (1951): 1–17.

Ötüken, Adnan. *Klasikler Bibliyografyası 1940–1948*. Ankara: Milli Eğitim Basımevi, 1949.

———. *Klasikler Bibliyografyası 1940–1966*. Ankara: Ayyıldız Matbaası, 1967.

Ousterhout, Robert. "The East, the West, and the Appropriation of the Past in Early Ottoman Architecture." *Gesta* 43, no. 2 (2004): 165–176.

Paker, Saliha. "Changing Norms of the Target System: Turkish Translations of Greek Classics in Historical Perspective." In *Studies in Greek Linguistics: Proceedings of the 7th Linguistics Conference*. Thessaloniki: Aristotelian University of Thessaloniki, 1986, 411–426.

———. "Turkish Tradition." In *Routledge Encyclopedia of Translation Studies*, ed. Mona Baker and Kirsten Malmkjær. London: Routledge, 1998, 571–582.

Pamuk, Orhan. *Istanbul: Memories and the City*. New York: Random House, 2006.

———. "The Two Souls of Turkey." *New Perspectives Quarterly* 24, no. 3 (2007): 10–11.

Peyre, Henri. "Erich Auerbach." In *Marburger Gelehrte in der ersten Hälfte des 20. Jahrhunderts*, ed. Ingeborg Schnack. Marburg: Veröffentlichungen der Historischen Kommission für Hessen, 1987, 10–21.

Politisches Archiv des Auswärtigen Amts, Berlin. Akten des Generalkonsulats Istanbul, 3970, Paket 1, Akte: "Kulturpropaganda (Allgemeines), Akte 'Propaganda' besonders" März 1930–.

———. Akten des Generalkonsulats Istanbul, 3970, Paket 1, Akte "Propaganda" 1935–39.

———. Akten des Generalkonsulats Istanbul, 3976, Paket 8, Akte Geheim Band II, Dezember 1932–1935.

———. Akten des Generalkonsulats Istanbul, 3977, Paket 9, Akte NSDAP, 1937–1940.

————. Akten des Generalkonsulats Istanbul, 3977, Paket 9, NSDAP Band I 1933–.

————. Akten des Generalkonsulats Istanbul, 3989, Paket 28, Akte 1 Istanbul Emigranten.

————. Akten des Generalkonsulats Istanbul, 3989, Paket 28, Akte 2 Istanbul Emigranten.

————. Akten des Generalkonsulats Istanbul, 4058, Paket 95.

————. Akten des Generalkonsulats Istanbul, GK Istanbul 163, Universität Istanbul Band II 1934–1935.

————. Akten des Generalkonsulats Istanbul, GK Istanbul 164, Band III 1935–1936.

————. Akten des Generalkonsulats Istanbul, GK Istanbul 165, Band IV 1936–1937.

————. Akten des Generalkonsulats Istanbul, GK Istanbul 166, Band V November 1937–Mai 1939.

————. Akten des Generalkonsulats Istanbul, GK Istanbul 167, Universität Istanbul Band VI.

————. Auswärtiges Amt Abteilung III, Akte Deutsche [Experten?] in der Türkei 1924–36, R 78630.

————. Der Beirat des türkischen Unterrichtsministers R 63442, 1913.

————. Die Deutschen Schulen in der Türkei, Allgemeines, R 62451, 1915–1917.

————. Die türkische Universität zu Konstantinopel (Stambul) R 64141, 1919–1922.

————. Die Universität in Konstantinopel R 64140, Oktober–November 1918.

————. Die Universität zu Konstantinopel R 64142, 1923.

————. Judenfrage in der Türkei, R 99446 1938–1943, Inland II A/B.

————. Konstantinopel / Ankara, 539, Akte Judentum 1925–1939.

————. Konstantinopel / Ankara 540, Akte Judentum Band 2.

————. Konstantinopel / Ankara, 729, Akte Studium (türk. Studenten in Deutschland).

————. R 100889, Akte Judenfrage in der Türkei 1942–1944, Inland II g 207.

Porter, David L. *The Chinese Taste in Eighteenth-Century England.* Cambridge: Cambridge University Press, forthcoming.

Porter, James I. "Auerbach and the Judaizing of Philology." *Critical Inquiry* 35 (2008): 115–147.

————. "Auerbach and the Scar of Philology." In *Classics and National Culture*, ed. Susan Stephens and Phiroze Vasunia. Oxford: Oxford University Press, forthcoming.

Potter, Pamela. *Most German of the Arts: Musicology and Society from the Weimar Republic to the End of Hitler's Reich.* New Haven, CT: Yale University Press, 1998.

Probst, Maximilian. "Baden im Bosporus." *die tageszeitung*, January 23, 2009. http://www.taz.de/1/archiv/print-archiv/printressorts/digi-artikel/?ressort=ku&dig=2009%2F01%2F23%2Fa0022&cHash=668fab84ed (accessed March 14, 2009).

Pross, Helge. *Die Deutsche Akademische Emigration nach den Vereinigten Staaten 1933–1941.* Berlin: Dunckner & Humboldt, 1955.

Reichenbach, Hans. *Experience and Prediction: An Analysis of the Foundations and the Structure of Knowledge.* Chicago: University of Chicago Press, 1938.

"Reichsregierung und Auslandsdeutschtum." *Türkische Post: Tageszeitung für den Nahen Osten*, March 18, 1933, 1–2.

Reisman, Arnold. "Jewish Refugees from Nazism, Albert Einstein, and the Modernization of Higher Education in Turkey (1933–1945)." *Aleph: Historical Studies in Science and Judaism* 7 (2007): 253–281.

———. *Turkey's Modernization: Refugees from Nazism and Atatürk's Vision.* Washington, DC: New Academia Publishing, 2006.

Reitter, Paul. "Comparative Literature in Exile: Said and Auerbach." In *Exile and Otherness: New Approaches to the Experience of Nazi Refugees*, ed. Alexander Stephan. Oxford: Peter Lang, 2005, 21–30.

Ritter, Hellmut. "Letter to Erich and Marie Auerbach, 1947." Literaturarchiv Marbach, A: Nachlaß Auerbach.

Ritter, Karl Bernhard. *Fahrt zum Bosporus: Ein Reisetagebuch.* Leipzig: Hegner, 1941.

Robbins, Bruce. "Comparative Cosmopolitanism." *Social Text* 31–32 (1992): 169–186.

Robinson, James Harvey, ed. *Petrarch: The First Modern Scholar and Man of Letters.* New York: Knickerbocker Press, 1898.

Rodrigue, Aron. "From Millet to Minority: Turkish Jewry in the 19th and 20th Centuries." In *Paths of Emancipation: Jews within States and Capitalism*, ed. Pierre Birnbaum and Ira Katznelson. Princeton, NJ: Princeton University Press, 1995, 238–261.

Rosello, Mireille. *Postcolonial Hospitality: The Immigrant as Guest.* Stanford, CA: Stanford University Press, 2001.

Ruben, Walter. *Kırşehir: Eine altertümliche Kleinstadt Mittelanatoliens.* Ed. Gerhard Ruben. Würzburg: Ergon, 2003.

Rüstow, Alexander. *Freedom and Domination: A Historical Critique of Civilization.* Trans. Salvator Attanasio. Princeton, NJ: Princeton University Press, 1980.

———. Letter to Erich Auerbach, June 16, 1942. Literaturarchiv Marbach, Nachlaß Auerbach.

———. *Ortsbestimmung der Gegenwart: Eine universalgeschichtliche Kulturkritik.* Erlenbach: Eugen Rentsch Verlag, 1952.

Rüstow, Dankwart A. *Politics and Westernization in the Near East.* Princeton, NJ: Princeton University Press, 1956.

Said, Edward W. "Erich Auerbach, Critic of the Earthly World." *Boundary 2* 31, no. 2 (2004): 11–34.

———. *Orientalism.* New York: Vintage Books, 1979.

———. *The World, the Text, and the Critic.* London: Vintage, 1991.

Sakaoğlu, Necdet. *Cumhuriyet Dönemi Eğitim Tarihi.* Istanbul: İletişim Yayınları, 1993.

———. *Osmanlı Eğitim Tarihi.* Istanbul: İletişim Yayınları, 1993.

Sayın, Şara. "Germanistik an der 'Universität Istanbul.'" In *Germanistentreffen: Tagungsbeiträge Deutschland-Türkei.* Bonn: DAAD, 1995, 29–36.

Scholem, Gershom. *Sabbatai Sevi: The Mystical Messiah, 1626–1676.* Princeton, NJ: Princeton University Press, 1973.

Schwartz, Philipp. *Notgemeinschaft: Zur Emigration deutscher Wissenschaftler nach 1933 in die Türkei.* Marburg: Metropolis-Verlag, 1995.

Schwarzenbach, Annemarie. "Die Reorganisation der Universität von Stambul." *Neue Zürcher Zeitung*, 03. Dezember 1933, Blatt 8 (Sonntagsbeilage).

———. *Winter in Vorderasien*. Basel: Lenos Verlag, 2002.

"Şehrimizdeki Alman Musevileri Almanlıktan Çıkardılar." *Yeni Sabah*, 12 Ağustos 1939.

Senemoğlu, Osman. "1933 Üniversite Reformunda Batı Dilleri ve Prof. Dr. Süheyla Bayrav." *Alman Dili ve Edebiyatı Dergisi* 11 (1998): 59–64.

Seyhan, Azade. "German Academic Exiles in Istanbul: Translation as the Bildung of the Other." In *Nation, Language and the Ethics of Translation*, ed. Sandra L. Bermann and Michael Wood. Princeton, NJ: Princeton University Press, 2005, 274–288.

Sezen, Yümni. *Hümanizm ve Atatürk Devrimleri*. Istanbul: Ayışığıkitapları, 1997.

Shaw, Stanford J. *Turkey and the Holocaust: Turkey's Role in Rescuing Turkish and European Jewry from Nazi Persecution, 1933–1945*. Hampshire, UK: Macmillan Press, 1993.

Silverstein, Theodore. "Dante and the Legend of the Mi'raj: The Problem of Islamic Influence on the Christian Literature of the Otherworld." *Journal of Near Eastern Studies* 11, no. 2 (1952): 89–110.

Sinanoğlu, Nüshet Haşim. *Dante ve Divina Commedia: Dante ile İlk Temas*. Istanbul: Devlet Matbaası, 1934.

Sinanoğlu, Suat. *Türk Hümanizmi*. Ankara: Türk Tarih Kurumu Basımevi, 1980.

Sitzler, Kim. "Humanismus und Islam." In *Humanismus in Geschichte und Gegenwart*, ed. Richard Faber and Enno Rudolph. Tübingen: Mohr Siebeck, 2002, 187–212.

Spanos, William V. "Humanism and the Studia Humanitatis after 9/11/01: Rethinking the Anthropologos." *symploke* 7, no. 1–2 (2005): 219–262.

Spector, Scott. "Forget Assimilation: Introducing Subjectivity to German-Jewish History." *Jewish History* 20, no. 3–4 (2006): 349–361.

———. *Prague Territories: National Conflict and Cultural Innovation in Franz Kafka's Fin de Siècle*. Berkeley: University of California Press, 2002.

Spies, Otto. *Die türkische Prosaliteratur der Gegenwart*. Leipzig: Otto Harrasowitz, 1943.

Spitzer, Leo. "The Addresses to the Reader in the *Commedia*." *Italica* 32, no. 3 (1955): 143–165.

———. "Bocaccio." In *Üniversite Konferansları 1935–1936*. Istanbul: Ülkü Basımevi, 1937, 165–176.

———. "Cervantes." In *Üniversite Konferansları 1935–1936*. Istanbul: Ülkü Basımevi, 1937, 177–188.

———. Letter to Karl Jaspers, December 5, 1935. Literaturarchiv Marbach, A: Jaspers 75.14541.

———. Letter to Karl Löwith, April 21, 1933. Literaturarchiv Marbach, A: Löwith 99.17.113/1.

———. Letter to Vice Consul Saucken, December 10, 1935. Politisches Archiv des Auswärtigen Amts, Berlin, Akten des Generalkonsulats Istanbul, GK Istanbul 164, Band III 1935–1936.

———. Letter to Vice Consul Saucken, December 12, 1935. Politisches Archiv des Auswärtigen Amts, Berlin, Akten des Generalkonsulats Istanbul, GK Istanbul 164, Band III 1935–1936.

————. "Rabelais yahut Rönesans'ın Dehası." In *Üniversite Konferansları 1935–1936*. Istanbul: Ülkü Basımevi, 1937, 209–224.

Stephan, Alexander, ed. *Exile and Otherness: New Approaches to the Experience of Nazi Refugees*. Oxford: Peter Lang, 2005.

Stilla, Gabriele. "Gerhard Fricke: Literaturwissenschaft als Anweisung zur Unterordnung." In *Deutsche Klassiker im Nationalsozialismus: Schiller-Kleist-Hölderlin*, ed. Claudia Albert. Stuttgart: Metzler, 1994, 18–47.

Strauss, Herbert A., Klaus Fischer, Christhard Hoffmann, and Alfons Söllner. *Die Emigration der Wissenschaften nach 1933: Disziplingeschichtliche Studien*. München: Saur, 1991.

Sunar, Şebnem. "Türkiye Cumhuriyeti'nin Batılılaşma Sürecinde Filolojinin Örgütlenmesi (İstanbul Üniversitesi Alman Filolojisi Örneğinde)." Unpublished dissertation, Istanbul University, 2003.

Tanpınar, Ahmet Hamdi. *Beş Şehir*. Istanbul: Dergâh Yayınları, 2008.

————. *Edebiyat Üzerine Makaleler*. Istanbul: Milli Eğitim Basımevi, 1969.

————. *Yahya Kemal*. Istanbul: Dergah Yayınları, 1982.

————. *Yaşadığım Gibi*. 2nd ed. Istanbul: Dergah Yayınları, 1996.

Taussig, Michael. *Mimesis and Alterity: A Particular History of the Senses*. New York: Routledge, 1993.

Tepe, Sultan. *Beyond the Sacred and the Secular: Politics of Religion in Israel and Turkey*. Stanford, CA: Stanford University Press, 2008.

Timms, Edward. *The Wandering Jew: A Leitmotif in German Literature and Politics*. Brighton, UK: University of Sussex, 1994.

Todorova, Maria. *Imagining the Balkans*. New York: Oxford University Press, 1997.

————. "Spacing Europe: What Is a Historical Region?" *East Central Europe/L'Europe du Centre-Est* 32, no. 1–2 (2005): 59–78.

Toktas, Sule. "Citizenship and Minorities: A Historical Overview of Turkey's Jewish Minority." *Journal of Historical Sociology* 18, no. 4 (2005): 394–429.

Toynbee, Paget Jackson. *Dante Studies*. London: Clarendon Press, 1921.

Treml, Martin. "Auerbachs imaginäre jüdische Orte." In *Erich Auerbach: Geschichte und Aktualität eines europäischen Philologen*, ed. Karlheinz Barck and Martin Treml. Berlin: Kulturverlag Kadmos, 2007, 230–251.

Trumpener, Ulrich. *Germany and the Ottoman Empire, 1914–1918*. Princeton, NJ: Princeton University Press, 1968.

Tunaya, Tarık Z. *Türkiyenin Siyasi Hayatında Batılılaşma Hareketleri*. Istanbul: Yedigün Matbaası, 1960.

"Türkiyede Nazi Propagandası." *Haber*, January 1, 1938.

Turner, Bryan S. *Weber and Islam*. London: Routledge, 1998.

Uzun, Mehmed. "The Dialogue and Liberties of Civilizations." Paper presented at the Second International Conference in the European Union Parliament on the European Union, Turkey, and the Kurds, September 19–21, 2005. http://www.eutcc.org/articles/8/20/document217.ehtml (accessed February 10, 2009).

————. *Ruhun Gökkuşağı*. 2nd ed. Istanbul: İthaki, 2007.

Varoğlu, Hamdi. *Dante Alighieri: Hayatı, Eserleri ve İlahi Komedi.* Istanbul: Cumhuriyet Matbaası, 1938.

Vialon, Martin. "Ein Exil-Brief Erich Auerbachs aus Istanbul an Freya Hobohm in Marburg—versehen mit einer Nachschrift von Marie Auerbach (1938). Transkribiert und kommentiert von Martin Vialon." *Trajekte* 9 (2004): 8–17.

———, ed. "Erich Auerbach: Gesammelte Briefe 1922–1957." Forthcoming.

———, ed. *Erich Auerbachs Briefe an Martin Hellweg (1939–1950): Edition und historisch-philologischer Kommentar.* Tübingen: A. Francke Verlag, 1997.

———. "The Scars of Exile: Paralipomena concerning the Relationship between History, Literature, and Politics—Demonstrated in the Examples of Erich Auerbach, Traugott Fuchs, and Their Circle in Istanbul." *Yeditepe University Philosophy Department: A Refereed Year-book* 1, no. 2 (2003): 191–246.

———. "Wie das Brot der Fremde so salzig schmeckt: Hellsichtiges über die Widersprüche der Türkei: Erich Auerbachs Istanbuler Humanismusbrief." *Süddeutsche Zeitung,* October 14, 2008, 16.

Vico, Giambattista. *Die neue Wissenschaft über die gemeinschaftliche Natur der Völker.* Trans. Erich Auerbach. 2nd ed. Berlin: Walter de Gruyter, 2000.

———. *New Science.* London: Penguin Classics, 1999.

Vossler, Karl. *Die Göttliche Komödie,* vol. 2. Heidelberg: Carl Winters Universitätsbuchhandlung, 1925.

Watenpaugh, Keith David. *Being Modern in the Middle East: Revolution, Nationalism, Colonialism, and the Arab Middle Class.* Princeton, NJ: Princeton University Press, 2006.

Wellek, René. "Leo Spitzer (1887–1960)." *Comparative Literature* 12, no. 4 (1960): 310–334.

Werfel, Franz. *Die vierzig Tage des Musa Dagh.* Frankfurt am Main: Fischer, 2006.

White, Hayden. *Figural Realism: Studies in Mimesis Effect.* Baltimore: Johns Hopkins University Press, 1999.

Widmann, Horst. *Exil und Bildungshilfe: Die deutschsprachige akademische Emigration in die Türkei nach 1933.* Bern: Herbert Lang, 1973.

Yahudi Fıkraları. Istanbul: Akbaba Yayını, 1943.

Yelda. *Istanbul'da, Diyarbakır'da Azalırken.* Istanbul: Belge, 1996.

Yücel, Faruk. "Türkiye'nin Aydınlanma Sürecinde Çevirinin Rolü." *Hacettepe Üniversitesi Edebiyat Fakültesi Dergisi* 23, no. 2 (2006): 207–220.

Yücel, Hasan Ali. "Önsöz." *Tercüme* 1, no. 1–2 (1940).

Yunus Emre. *The Wandering Fool: Sufi Poems of a Thirteenth-Century Turkish Dervish.* Trans. Edouard Roditi. San Francisco: Cadmus, 1987.

Zaborowska, Magdalena J. *James Baldwin's Turkish Decade: Erotics of Exile.* Durham, NC: Duke University Press, 2008.

Zorlu, Ilgaz. *Evet, Ben Selanikliyim: Türkiye Sabetaycılığı.* Istanbul: Belge Yayınları, 1998.

Zürcher, Erik J. *Turkey: A Modern History.* London: I. B. Tauris & Co., 1998.

Index